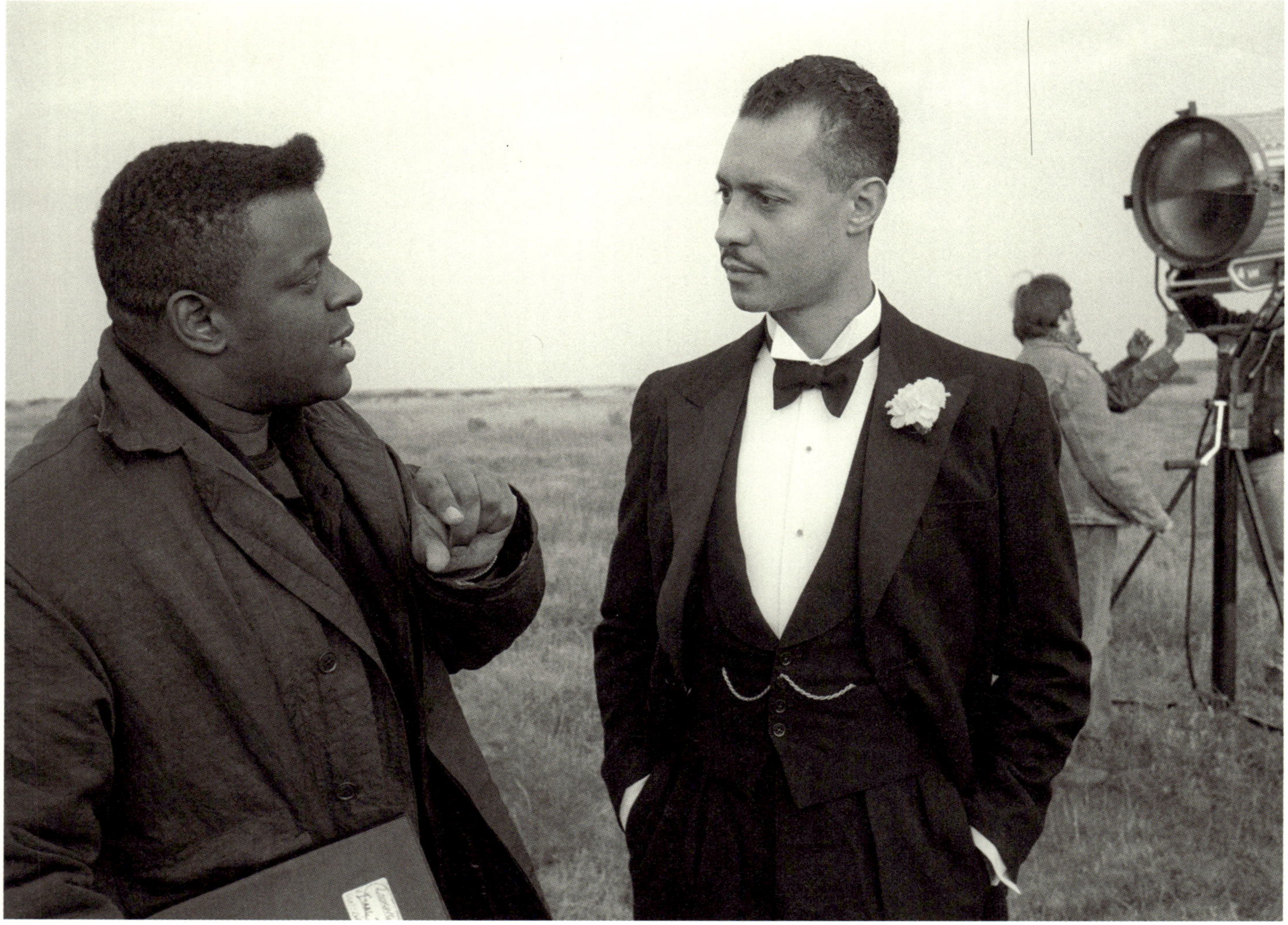

*Mise-en-scene No.2 (Looking for Langston Vintage Series)* 1989/2016

Isaac Julien

# What Freedom Is To Me

Edited by Isabella Maidment

Consultant Editor Vladimir Seput

With contributions by

Caleb Azumah Nelson
Maria Balshaw
Celeste-Marie Bernier
Adam Finch
Jack Halberstam
Isaac Julien
Nina Kellgren
Nathan Ladd
Luigia Lonardelli
Isabella Maidment
Mark Nash
Irit Rogoff
Wole Soyinka
Bradford Young

TATE

First published 2023 by order of the Tate Trustees
by Tate Publishing, a division of Tate Enterprises Ltd,
Millbank, London SW1P 4RG
www.tate.org.uk/publishing

On the occasion of the exhibition
*Isaac Julien: What Freedom Is To Me*

Tate Britain, London
26 April – 20 August 2023

Kunstsammlung Nordrhein-Westfalen, Düsseldorf
23 September 2023 – 14 January 2024

Bonnefanten Museum, Maastricht
4 February – 9 June 2024

*Isaac Julien: What Freedom Is To Me*
is in partnership with

LOCKTON

Also supported by

FORD FOUNDATION

With additional support from the Isaac Julien Exhibition
Supporters Circle:
Cockayne – Grants for the Arts
The London Community Foundation

Tate Americas Foundation, Tate International Council
and Tate Patrons



A catalogue record for this book is available from the British Library

ISBN 978 1 84976 872 6 (hbk)
ISBN 978 1 84976 839 9 (pbk)
ISBN 978 1 84976 840 5 (special edition)

Distributed in the United States and Canada by ABRAMS, New York
Library of Congress Control Number applied for

Designed by Duncan Whyte
Colour reproduction by DL Imaging, London
Printed and bound in Italy by SIZ

Front cover: Isaac Julien, *What Freedom is to me (Homage)* 2022
Back cover: Isaac Julien, *Who Killed Colin Roach?* 1983 photographic installation, (detail)

FSC www.fsc.org MIX Paper from responsible sources FSC™ C130819

## Augmented Reality App

The Isaac Julien App is an extension of this publication, which brings the video stills in this book to life.

1.
Search for *Isaac Julien App* in the App Store or Play Store and install the app on your smartphone or tablet.

2.
Open the app and hold your smartphone over the images on pp.17, 41, 57, 89, 103, 115, 137, 153, 157, 169 where the ▶ symbol appears.

# Contents

As the world's largest independent insurance brokerage firm, Lockton's philosophies embody innovation, creativity and an entrepreneurial spirit. Servicing over 65,000 clients across six continents, Lockton is committed to promoting greater cultural awareness and supporting communities of all types.

We believe in the power of the arts to enrich societies through improved access, inclusion and education. That's why Lockton is extremely proud to support the *Isaac Julien: What Freedom Is To Me* exhibition at Tate Britain.

A pioneer in his field, Isaac Julien investigates the movement of peoples across different continents, times and spaces in his work. This exhibition highlights his critical thinking and the way he breaks down barriers between different artistic disciplines, while drawing on critical themes of history and culture.

We are excited about our support of this exhibition which marks the first in our multi-year partnership with Tate, encompassing our shared values of independence, excellence and an unwavering commitment to social and civic responsibility.

*EJ Hentenaar*
*CEO of Lockton Europe*

LOCKTON®

Celebrated for his compelling lyrical films and his video art installations, Isaac Julien is one of the leading artists working with film and video today. This ambitious solo exhibition marks the first time that his work across forty years has been presented in the UK.

It highlights Julien's critical thinking and the way in which his work breaks down barriers between different artistic disciplines, drawing from film, dance, photography, music, theatre, painting and sculpture, by utilising the themes of desire, history and culture. It reveals the scope of Julien's pioneering work in film and installation from the early 1980s through to the present day, spanning early films made as part of Sankofa Film and Video Collective to the large-scale, multi-screen installations investigating the movement of peoples across different continents, spaces and times for which he is justly celebrated today.

After graduating from Saint Martin's School of Art in London in 1984, Julien came to prominence with his 1989 documentary-drama *Looking for Langston*, which earned him a cult following, while his debut feature *Young Soul Rebels* (1991) won the Semaine de la Critique prize at the Cannes Film Festival. Julien has since participated in many leading international exhibitions: the Venice Biennale; the Gwangju Biennial, South Korea; Prospect 1, New Orleans; and Documenta 11, Kassel. Reflecting the importance of research to each of his film projects, Julien has taught extensively, holding posts such as Chair of Global Art at University of the Arts London (2014–16) and Professor of Media Art at Staatliche Hochschule für Gestaltung Karlsruhe, Germany (2008–16). In 2018, Julien joined the faculty at the University of California Santa Cruz, where he is Distinguished Professor of the Arts leading the Moving Image Lab together with Arts Professor Mark Nash, and at present divides his time between London and Santa Cruz.

Julien's film projects are the outcome of research that combines insights from many intellectual disciplines. Some orbit around a single extraordinary cultural and historical figure whose significance (as Julien's films reveal) extends to our own time, such as Frederick Douglass, the Black American abolitionist and statesman; Langston Hughes, poet of the Harlem Renaissance; or Lina Bo Bardi, the Afro-Brazilian-inspired modernist architect. Beginning with Julien's lived experience of the political, cultural and existential struggles of both Black and LGBTQ+ communities in London in the 1980s, the geography and temporality of his work have since extended across continents and centuries, reflecting the global movements of people, culture and capital.

Within this, there is a recurring focus on the transatlantic, intercontinental vectors of the African diaspora, and a corresponding conception of identity as liminal, hybrid, mutable and expansive. Reality, during the course of Julien's films, gives way to dreams, history to fantasy, the normative to the queer, with music, choreography and montage ushering viewers into immersive states of sensual, psychic and imaginary exodus and transcendence. The museum itself, whose historic roots lie in the European Enlightenment, is not immune to these forces of dreamlike, cross-cultural dissolution and appropriation: in *Vagabondia*, Sir John Soane's Museum – that most idiosyncratic and paradoxical classical interior – becomes 'creolised' by the voice and reveries of the female guard, the French Creole she speaks echoing Julien's parents' Windrush-era migration from Saint Lucia to London.

The exhibition at Tate Britain is curated by Isabella Maidment, formerly Curator, Contemporary British Art at Tate Britain and now Senior Curator at The Hepworth Wakefield, and Nathan Ladd, Curator, Contemporary British Art, in close dialogue with the artist. The making of an exhibition is a collective endeavour and we would like to warmly thank colleagues from across Tate for their essential contributions. Particular thanks are due to colleagues in the Time-Based Media Conservation team: Francesca Colussi, Marco Testa-Ryan and Jake van Dugteren, and to Andy Shiel and Liam Tebbs in the Installation and Art Handling team.

*Isaac Julien: What Freedom Is To Me* travels to K21 Kunstsammlung Nordrhein-Westfalen, Düsseldorf, in September 2023 and to Bonnefanten Museum, Maastricht, in February 2024. Our sincere thanks to Susanne Gaensheimer, Director, Kunstsammlung Nordrhein-Westfalen, Doris Krystof, Curator, Kunstsammlung Nordrhein-Westfalen and to Stijn Huijts, General and Artistic Director, Bonnefanten, for their essential collaboration and commitment to the project.

This publication has been edited by Isabella Maidment: we are indebted to her and to Caleb Azumah Nelson, Maria Balshaw, Celeste-Marie Bernier, Adam Finch, Jack Halberstam, Nina Kellgren, Nathan Ladd, Luigia Lonardelli, Mark Nash, Irit Rogoff, Wole Soyinka and Bradford Young for the insightful writing and reflections they have so generously contributed to these pages.

Our thanks are due to the Tate Publishing team: Publishing Director Tom Avery, Senior Editor Nicola Bion, Picture Researcher Roz Hill and Production Controller Roanne Marner; to the book's designer, Duncan Whyte; as well as to Vladimir Seput, Juanita Boxill, James Keith and Paul Smith from the Isaac Julien Studio.

For their vital support throughout the making of this exhibition, we would like to warmly thank Isaac Julien's galleries Victoria Miro, Jessica Silverman, and Ron Mandos. Special thanks are due to Victoria Miro, Glenn Scott Wright, Erin Manns, Jessica Silverman, Ron Mandos, Roslyn Oxley9 Gallery, Helga de Alvear Gallery, Nara Roesler Gallery, and Metro Pictures for their unwavering support throughout the project.

*Isaac Julien: What Freedom Is To Me* is in partnership with Lockton. It is supported by Ford Foundation, with additional support from the Isaac Julien Exhibition Supporters Circle: Cockayne – Grants for the Arts, and the London Community Foundation; Tate Americas Foundation, Tate International Council and Tate Patrons. On behalf of Tate, I would like to express our gratitude to Lockton and to Ford Foundation for their generous support of the exhibition, as well as to the other donors who have been so essential to the show.

The exhibition at Tate Britain has been made possible by the provision of insurance through the UK Government Indemnity Scheme, and we thank HM Government for providing this, and in particular the Department of Culture, Media and Sport, and Arts Council England for arranging the indemnity.

Finally, our deepest thanks go to Isaac Julien for the vision, dedication, energy, and restless ambition he has brought to the making of this exhibition, which we are proud to share with audiences in his home city and beyond.

*Alex Farquharson*
*Director, Tate Britain*

# Acknowledgements

An exhibition of this ambition would not be possible without the tireless work of a host of colleagues behind the scenes. We would like to thank Maria Balshaw, Director, Tate, and Alex Farquharson, Director, Tate Britain; Andrea Schlieker, Director, Exhibitions and Displays; Carolyn Kerr, Head of Programme Management for her invaluable guidance and expertise; Wendy Lothian, Senior Programme Manager, International Collaborations; and Sionaigh Durrant, Senior Registrar.

We could not have achieved an exhibition of such technical complexity without our colleagues in Time-Based Media Conservation: thank you to Francesca Colussi, Marco Testa-Ryan and Jake van Dugteren, as well as to Sophie Sardokie, Paper Conservator, for their diligence and expertise. For overseeing the exhibition build and installation with such professionalism our thanks to Andy Shiel, Caroline Smith and Liam Tebbs. The installation was made possible by the invaluable support of Isaac Julien's long-time collaborators Tom Cullen and Jorma Saarikko and Eric Brun at ProAV Art: thank you for sharing your knowledge with us. We also extend our sincere thanks to David Adjaye for the exhibition design.

In Development we owe our wholehearted gratitude to Claire Gylphe, Charlotte Reeves and Heidi Luedecke. We are grateful to our colleagues in Visitor Experience: Emma Garrett, Marcus Dickey-Horley, Sabrina Kaïci and Toyin Omirin. Thanks are due to Zoe Bromberg-McCarthy and Hannah Geddes for their thoughtful work on the exhibition interpretation; to Annie Bicknel, Mark Miller, Rachel Noel and Tram Nguyen for the Learning programme; to Marketing Manager Georgina Ramkoleea, Marketing and Communications Designer Margot Lombaert, Senior Press and Communications Manager Rachael Young; to Susan Doyon, Lucy Noakes and Bill Ward in Tate Digital; to Figgy Guyver and Enrico Tassi at Tate Etc.; and to Irena Cater and Tylar Napolitano in Advocacy and Events.

For this exquisite publication we are indebted to designer Duncan Whyte, Vladimir Seput at Isaac Julien Studio and to Senior Editor Nicola Bion in Tate Publishing, to all of whom we are eternally grateful for their meticulous work, good humour and camaraderie. Thanks are also due to Tom Avery, Roz Hill and Roanne Marner in Tate Publishing for their essential support.

A heartfelt thank-you to those who generously contributed to these pages: Caleb Azumah Nelson, Maria Balshaw, Celeste-Marie Bernier, Adam Finch, Jack Halberstam, Nina Kellgren, Luigia Lonardelli, Mark Nash, Irit Rogoff, Wole Soyinka and Bradford Young.

Special thanks are due to Juanita Boxill, Paul Smith, Vladimir Seput and James Keith at the Isaac Julien Studio for their tireless work, commitment and care; and also to curator Christine van Assche, and Mark Nash, curator, film historian and filmmaker, for their inspirational insights and thoughtful guidance.

Last but by no means least, it has been our great honour – and enormous pleasure – to work in close dialogue with Isaac Julien, to whom we offer our deepest gratitude and heartfelt appreciation. This exhibition is testament to his restless energy, fearless ambition and generosity of spirit.

*Isabella Maidment*
*Senior Curator, The Hepworth Wakefield*

*Nathan Ladd*
*Curator, Contemporary British Art, Tate Britain*

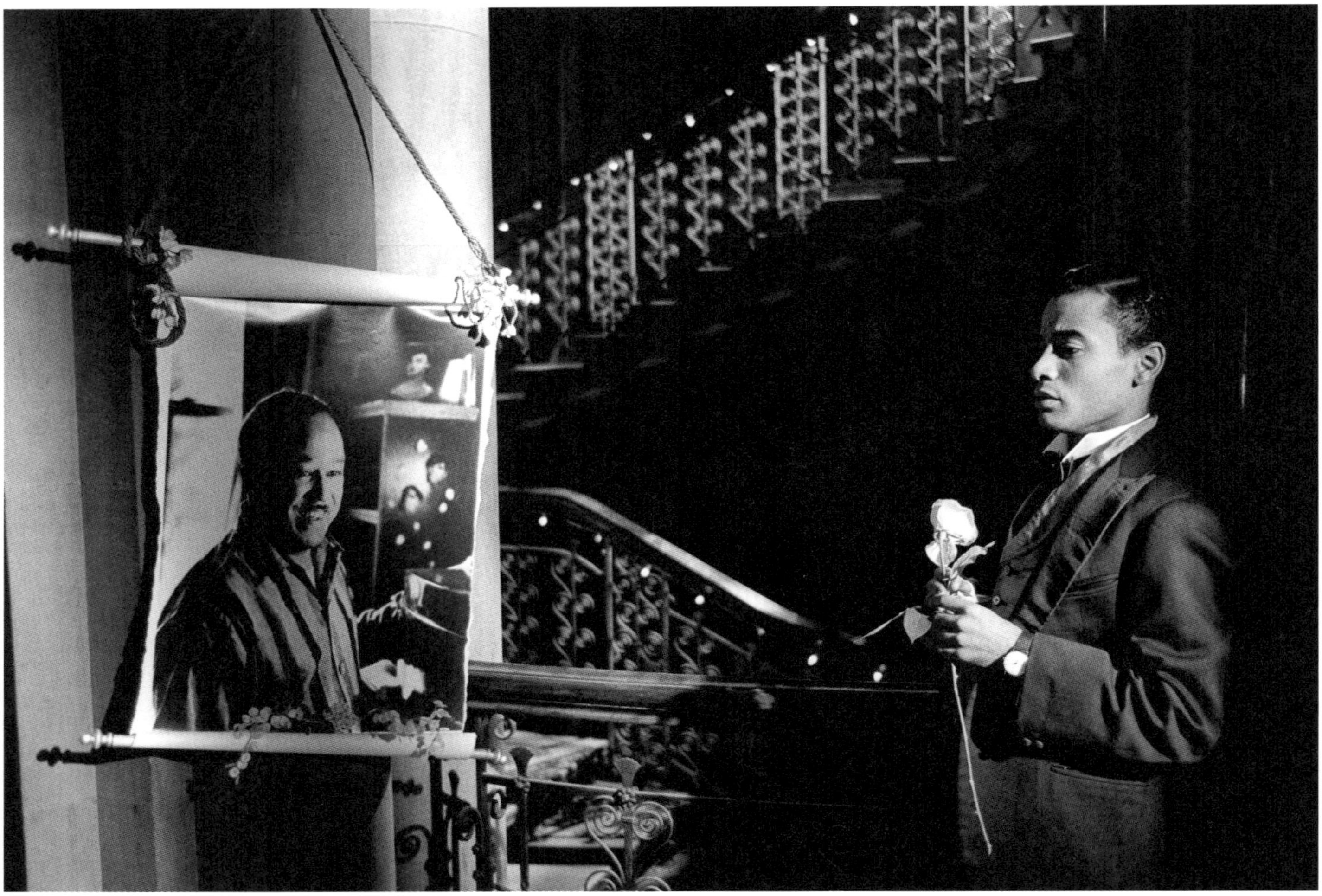

*Hommage Noir (Looking for Langston Vintage Series)* 1989/2016

Isabella Maidment

In late August 1984, Isaac Julien set up a Super 8 mm camera in the window of the home of the legendary performer, club promoter and fashion designer Leigh Bowery, overlooking London's Portobello Road. There he captured Notting Hill Carnival, the city's annual affirmation of Caribbean music and pan-African unity.[1] The footage forms the basis of the experimental short *Territories*, Julien's ground-breaking portrait of Black British culture and critical interrogation of national identity; of the connecting and disconnecting territories of race, class, labour and sex – the contradictory, shifting spaces and geographic expressions and the city they cohabit. 'We are struggling to begin a story, a history, a herstory, of cultural forms specific to Black peoples', the opening voiceover states and repeats. 'A history, a herstory, of its creation and recreation in a diaspora.' With *Territories*, Julien defied the orderly narrative linearity of documentary convention, choosing instead a montage approach to both image and sound that has come to define his practice over the past four decades. After shooting on film, Julien transferred the footage to video, experimented with the images and then re-filmed the whole, determined to 'disband all the categories'.[2] The resulting spatio-temporal mashup of fractured image and sound, original cinematography and found footage has the effect of collapsing territorial boundaries in a poetic challenge to the presumed homogeny of the nation state.

It feels appropriate to begin a survey of the pioneering work of Isaac Julien in this context, overlooking that London street, on the boundary between the public and the private, surveying multiple territories: the racial, the sexual, the psychic, the social, the political. Born of an environment of cross-pollination between art, club culture and fashion against a tumultuous backdrop of rising nationalism, racial tension and social unrest, Julien's forty-year-long practice as an artist and filmmaker is inherently pluralistic. By trespassing between disciplines he creates films and installations that exist as structures of feeling for political remembering.[3]

From the outset, as a young student studying Painting and Fine Art Film at London's Saint Martin's School of Art, Julien was resistant to being categorised as a Black, queer filmmaker. He preferred instead to position himself as 'a broader cultural activist', one dealing with the semiotics and politics of image-making in an expansive sense that foregrounds – but is not exclusively limited to – his own lived experience.[4] As he presciently asserted, 'There exist multiple identities which should challenge with passion and beauty the previously static order'.[5] The exhibition which this book accompanies is the first to survey and celebrate the passion and beauty with which Julien has challenged that static order over the past four decades. It charts the development from the early works he directed as part of Sankofa Film and Video Collective (1983–92), through his pioneering three-screen video installations made for the gallery setting to the kaleidoscopic, sculptural multi-screen installations for which he is internationally acclaimed today. Far from being fully comprehensive – for Julien's artistic output is too prolific to survey in its entirety – this exhibition takes the form of a concise edit of a career that remains as fiercely experimental and politically charged as it was forty years ago. The presentation is conceived a-chronologically, echoing Julien's own spatio-temporal approach to history, offering multiple pathways through a practice which revisits the past to create spaces of cultural memory that invite us to reframe our representational priorities in the present.

1. Notting Hill Carnival was founded by the Trinidadian activist Claudia Jones in 1959. It has taken place on the streets of Notting Hill since 1966.

2. Isaac Julien, 'Riot', in *Isaac Julien: Riot*, exh. cat., The Museum of Modern Art, New York 2013, p.31.

3. 'It was through the fusion of club culture, fashion, and music ... that I started to figure out some basic artistic correlations.' Isaac Julien, 'Fire', in Julien 2013, p.18. Here I borrow Raymond Williams's concept of a structure of feeling, first articulated by Williams in 1954; see Raymond Williams and Michael Orrom, *Preface to Film*, London 1954, p.33. A structure of feeling was used initially as a means of theorising the problem of historical changes in dramatic convention in film. Williams's central claim was that 'it is in art, primarily, that the effect of the totality, the dominant structure of feeling is expressed and embodied'. Importantly, structures of feeling allow for art to become a primary and constitutive force in social cohesion and social change.

4. 'I rejected the role of "black gay filmmaker"; I wanted to see myself as a broader cultural activist, someone who was engaged in making films about the black and gay experience but who equally dealt with the semiotics and the politics of the image ... I was much more interested in making interventions of different kinds than in being seen as representing any community.' Isaac Julien, 'Mirror' in *Isaac Julien: Looking for Langston*, exh. cat., Victoria Miro Gallery, London 2017, p.12.

5. Isaac Julien quoted in 'Aesthetics and Politics: Working on Two Fronts?', *Undercut*, no.17, Spring 1988, p.36.

Since the early 1980s, Isaac Julien has championed the potential of thinking through filmmaking as a shared process of making. This exhibition and publication are testament to the extent to which he deeply values collaboration. Julien's early experiments with the moving image were produced in the context of the Sankofa Film and Video Collective he founded in the summer of 1983, together with Martina Attille, Maureen Blackwood, Robert Crusz and Nadine Marsh-Edwards, a group of London art students from across the African, Asian and Caribbean diaspora committed to articulating a multitude of Black experiences through filmmaking.[6] The name Sankofa, an Akan word meaning 'to retrieve', was chosen as a metaphor for the act of reaching back to past knowledge to effect positive change in the present order. The collective played a vital role in the establishment of Black independent cinema: 'Sankofa was trying to break apart the master discourse of race relations – something that was always a binary discourse, a discourse between black and white', Julien has explained.[7] Four works he directed in this context appear here: *Who Killed Colin Roach?* 1983; *Territories* 1984; *This Is Not an AIDS Advertisement* 1987; and *Looking for Langston* 1989.

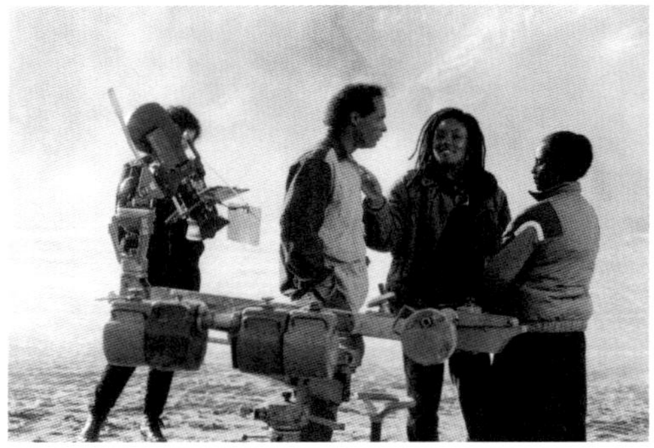

Filming *The Passion of Remembrance*, 1985
From left to right: a continuity supervisor, unknown; Joseph Charles; Maureen Blackwood; Anni Domingo

Filmed in East London where Julien was born and raised, *Who Killed Colin Roach?* – acknowledged by the artist as his very first film – addresses the death of Colin Roach, a twenty-one-year-old Black man shot dead at the entrance to Stoke Newington police station in the London Borough of Hackney.[8] The resulting video and the accompanying set of photographic prints with which it is displayed document the protests that followed Roach's death in police custody. Julien portrays the local community's grief, anger and urgent calls for justice, intersplicing protest footage with interviews with the Roach family, local campaigners and the writer and poet Benjamin Zephaniah. Through its direct questioning of police tactics, the justice system and the agency of mainstream media, the video served as a work of activism demanding an independent inquiry into Roach's death. With this work Julien explored the idea of the camera as a street weapon: 'I wanted to utilize this camera taken out of an art school context and repurpose its technology for the street', he said. 'I wanted to redirect the gaze of the ruling media. My real aim was to turn that gaze on the police, because, in *Colin Roach*, *they* are the people rioting.'[9] In *Who Killed Colin Roach?* we see the beginnings of the Black political consciousness and deep commitment to social justice that has defined and motivated Julien's approach to filmmaking for the past four decades.

The art of memory as a means to move beyond the ethnographic coding dominant in documentary filmmaking in the 1980s – conventions he actively resisted from the start – was a strategy Julien adopted from Sankofa onwards, beautifully articulated in his landmark film *Looking for Langston*. Released in 1989, at the height of the AIDS crisis, *Looking for Langston* is an exquisite visual and philosophical meditation on the life and desires of the African American poet Langston Hughes. Shot in black and white on 16 mm film, the work was conceived as an experimental portrait of Hughes and the Harlem Renaissance, a 'querying', as Kobena Mercer put it, 'of the archival relations of the High Modernist moment of the 1920s in which the first generation of Black American artists had been buried as merely a passing vogue'.[10] Its groundbreaking exploration of the complexity of the queer gaze led to the film gaining cult status, becoming a hallmark of what critic B. Ruby Rich termed the New Queer Cinema.[11] The impetus to make the film came when Julien and his partner Mark Nash attended the funeral of the American writer James Baldwin (1924–87) in New York in 1987: 'That event was one of the main reasons I made the piece', Julien said.[12]

*Looking for Langston* launched a crucial element of Julien's practice, one which has remained a defining feature both of his work and his activism to this day: the instrumentalisation and rearticulation of the archive as a space of critique – a means through which to reimagine important historical figures from the African diaspora and to push against the ways in which those characters

6. Sankofa was founded in 1983 amid the advent of the Workshop Declaration, an active call-out by significant stakeholders to support the diversification of the independent film scene in the UK. Julien received a BA in Fine Art Film from Saint Martin's School of Art, London, in 1984 and completed his postdoctoral studies at Les entrepreneurs de l'audiovisuel européen, Brussels, in 1989.

7. Julien, 'Mirror', 2017, p.11.

8. Isaac Julien was born in London in 1960 and raised in Bow in the East End.

9. Julien, 'Riot', 2013, p.29. At the time of writing, the tragedy of racist police brutality remains headline news in the UK as a Metropolitan Police Officer has been suspended for the fatal shooting of Chris Kaba, an unarmed twenty-four-year-old Black man, in south London in September 2022.

10. Kobena Mercer, 'Avid Iconographies', in Kobena Mercer and Chris Darke, *Isaac Julien*, London 2001, p.15.

11. *Looking for Langston* was commissioned by Channel 4 for its first gay and lesbian series, *Out on Tuesday* (later retitled *Out*), which ran from 1989 to 1994. The term 'New Queer Cinema' was coined by B. Ruby Rich in a number of publications, including the film journal *Sight & Sound* and the New York weekly *The Village Voice*, to describe the appearance of certain films at Sundance Film Festivals in the early 1990s that evinced a politicised stance towards queer culture. See B. Ruby Rich, *New Queer Cinema: The Director's Cut*, Durham, NC 2013.

12. Julien, 'Mirror', 2017, p.54. The script developed out of fragments of research from the archives of the Schomburg Center Library, The Museum of Modern Art, the Library of Congress, the New Brunswick Archives and the John E. Allen archives where, Mark Nash undertook research.

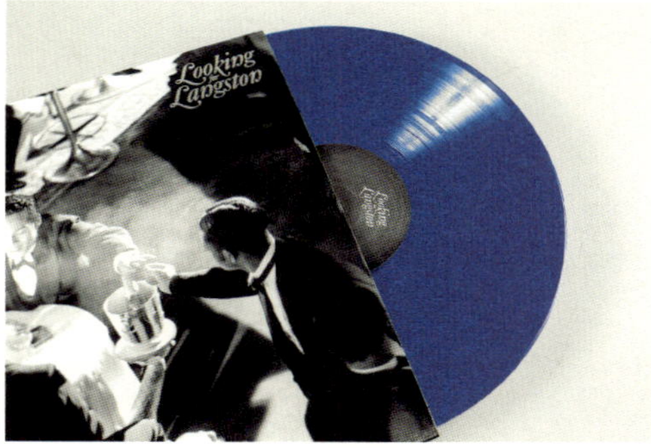


The soundtrack to *Looking for Langston*, released by The Vinyl Factory, 2017

were previously constructed. Music played a vital role in shaping this space of cultural memory: 'I had a soundtrack eighteen months before I shot anything, so the first mode of research for the whole project was sonic', Julien recalled. 'In addition to the actual poems of Langston Hughes, the input of jazz and blues was extremely critical, especially when it came to ideas of pacing and structure. Long before I attempted to visualise I was *listening*.'[13]

Since 2018 Julien has divided his time between London and Santa Cruz, where he is Distinguished Professor of the Arts at the University of California. Inherently transnational, his life echoes something essential to the conceptual thinking that drives his work: the 'rhizormorphic, fractural structure' of the Black Atlantic.[14] Migration, the movement of peoples and displacement are subjects to which Julien has returned repeatedly, as evidenced in two major works conceived as a diptych: *Western Union: Small Boats* 2007 and *Ten Thousand Waves* 2010. In these works, temporal and geographic displacement is articulated across multiple screens in a spatial development of Julien's ongoing interest in the conceptual potential of montage.[15]

Precisely executed and impeccably installed, Julien's works are characterised by meticulous attention to detail at every stage: the depth of research and scholarship he undertakes; the script, cinematography, location, art direction and costume; and the work's specific installation, sound mixing and situation of display. Every decision has meaning and poetic intentionality. It is through a deep understanding of, and commitment to, the poetic power of aesthetic experience – to painting, photography, sculpture and choreography; to visual art in all its forms – that Julien's work in the moving image achieves its extraordinary depth of feeling and, with it, political potency, that unique state of critical reverie.[16] His long-time collaborator cinematographer Nina Kellgren notes, 'Isaac is a poet, he is a painter, he's many things. The work is not documentary, it's not fiction, it's not feature. It makes you see and make connections in an entirely different way. It trades on the fact that we can all speak images, and then it takes you somewhere that you didn't expect to go. That is the real extraordinary power of the work.'[17]

There is a subversive beauty to Isaac Julien's prolific output. As Chris Darke has commented: 'Pleasure is at the heart of the politics of this work, beauty a quality of critique.'[18] That beauty is palpably present in the sculptural multi-screen video installations which have been the focus of Julien's work since the turn of the millennium, in which acts of transgression into multiple counter-histories invite new modes of encounter with the moving image. This book showcases three such works made in the past five years – the ultra high definition 4K video installations *Lina Bo Bardi – A Marvellous Entanglement* 2019, *Lessons of the Hour* 2019, and *Once Again ... (Statues Never Die)* 2022 – in which the relationship between the edit, montage, soundscape and the situation of the viewer's encounter with the work are inextricably intertwined. In these works, sound – which has played a prominent role in Julien's work from the outset, aiding narrative, scoring and underscoring the moving image – is given equal agency in the making of meaning, in sonic tapestries of music, text, tone and texture as rich and layered as the image sequences they accompany. Dance and choreography have also played an important role: on the streets of *Territories*, in the heady warehouse scene of *Looking for Langston* and in the solo performances that feature in *Vagabondia* and *Lina Bo Bardi – A Marvellous Entanglement*, but crucially also in the logic that informs the decisions of cinematography and the conception of the multiple-screen installations as a form of scenography – one that invites a mobile spectatorship, sculpting attention through space and through time.[19]

Julien's long-term interest in the sculptural properties and possibilities of the moving image is made manifest in his latest video installation, *Once Again ... (Statues Never Die)*, a prismatic portrait of Alain Locke (1885–1954), the philosopher, educator, cultural theorist and leading figure in the Harlem Renaissance.[20]

13. Ibid.

14. See Paul Gilroy, *The Black Atlantic: Modernity and Double Consciousness*, London and New York 1993. p.4.

15. In its original version, *Ten Thousand Waves* was conceived as a nine-screen installation in which Julien choreographed the multiple screens as a scenography. The work premiered at the 17th Biennale of Sydney in 2010.

16. See Mercer 2001, p.8.

17. Nina Kellgren in conversation with the author, 26 July 2022.

18. Chris Darke, 'Territories: The tell-tale trajectory of Isaac Julien', in Mercer and Darke 2001, p.81.

19. For *Vagabondia*, Julien collaborated with the Venezuelan choreographer Javier de Frutos to create the dance featured in the film, performed by the British contemporary dancer Ben Ash. The work's title is a reference to the dancer, who is based on the Black vagabond who appears in Hogarth's *A Rake's Progress* 1734. For *Lino Bo Bardi: A Marvellous Entanglement*, Julien made imaginative use of the spiral staircase at Museu de Arte Moderna da Bahia, Brazil and invited the local choreographer Zebrinha and the Balé Folclórico da Bahia to create a site-specific piece.

The film explores the relationship between Locke and the American art collector Albert C. Barnes (1872–1951), founder of the Barnes Foundation in Philadelphia and one of the most significant collectors of African material culture in the first half of the twentieth century. Making use of the inherently sculptural properties of black and white 16 mm film, *Once Again* meditates on Locke's 'lifelong mission to reorient the aesthetic compass of the African diaspora in the direction of its rightful artistic heritage'.[21] The camera follows Locke's gaze as he returns to Oxford University, where he was the first Black Rhodes Scholar, and to the Pitt Rivers Museum. Julien's footage is interwoven with historical footage taken from the Ghanaian filmmaker Nii Kwate Owoo's *You Hide Me*, a recently rediscovered film shot in the stores of the British Museum, which argued for the repatriation of the Benin Bronzes back in 1970. Julien's film plays out across an installation comprised of five back-projected screens suspended from the ceiling to rest lightly on the floor with sculptural gravity. They are reflected and refracted in the surrounding walls, on which panels of mylar mirror of the same dimensions are installed. Through the illusion of a hall of mirrors, they have the effect of doubling, sometimes trebling the image, while troubling our gaze, reflecting it back on ourselves. The work can never be seen in its entirety in a single field of vision, nor can any one screen be seen in isolation. Once again, Julien invites new ways of seeing, new depths of feeling. A haunting performance by the singer Alice Smith recurs throughout the work. Heavy with pathos, it punctuates the film like a chorus: 'Once again, I begin ...', she sings.

As we look back over Isaac Julien's prolific career to date, so too we celebrate his legacy: the path that he forged for the next generation of LGBTQ+ and Black artistic communities, and the space he has helped shape for those yet to come. A line in the final moments of *Once Again ... (Statues Never Die)* resonates powerfully with what is at stake in Isaac Julien's interdisciplinary imaginary: 'As we mature as artists in the mythical diasporic dream space, a culture of infinite possibility is ready to receive us. This is artistic freedom as pure and unsullied as falling snow.'

20. Alain Locke is largely known for assembling *The New Negro*, the 1925 anthology that immortalised a group of young writers – among them Langston Hughes, Claude McKay, Zora Neale Hurston and Jessie Fauset – as America's first Black literary movement.

21. Gwendolyn DuBois Shaw in *Isaac Julien: Once Again ... (Statues Never Die)*, exh. booklet, Barnes Foundation, Philadelphia 2022, p.7.

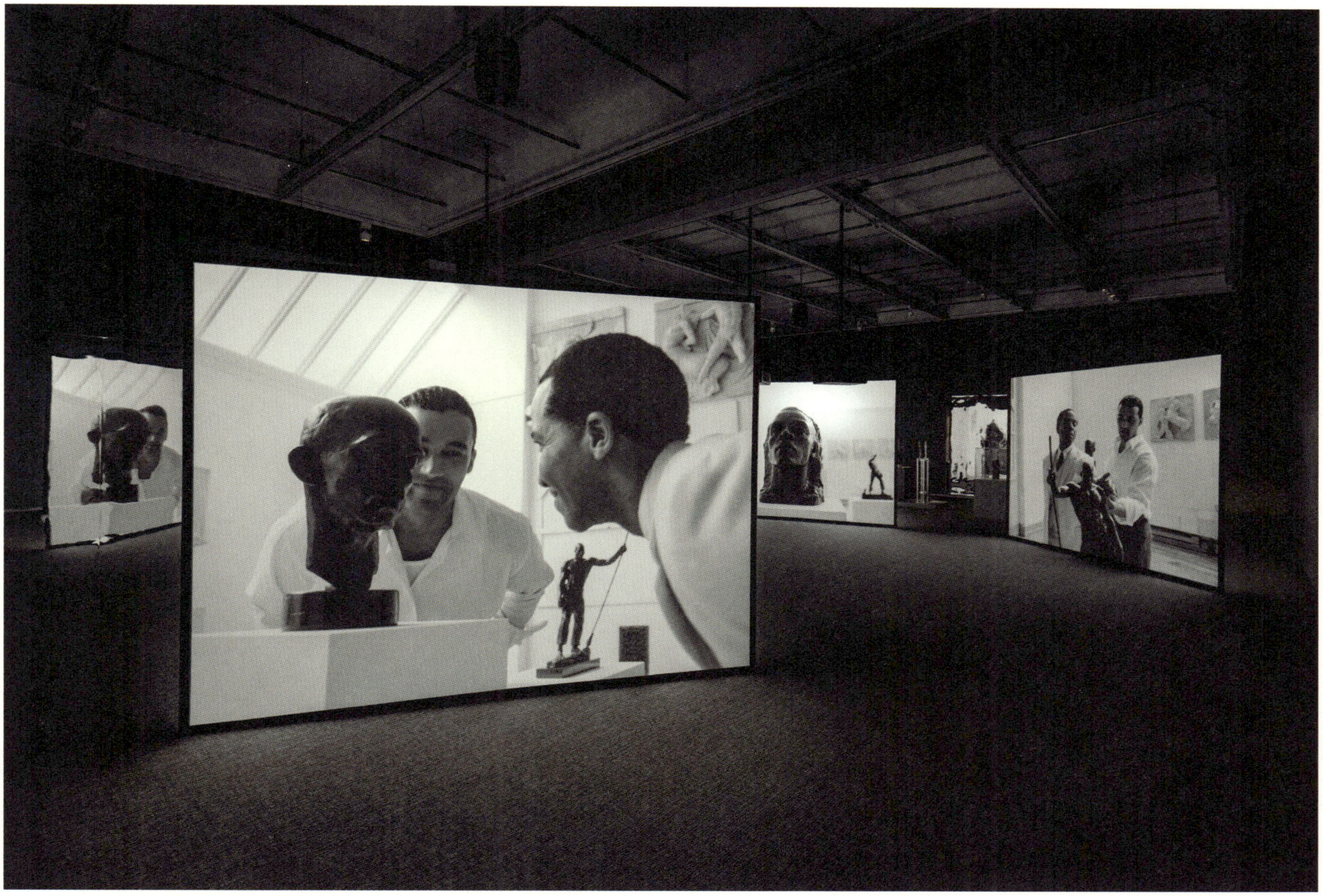

*Once Again ... (Statues Never Die)*, installation view, Barnes Foundation, 2022

# ONCE AGAIN ... (STATUES NEVER DIE)

## 2022

▶ 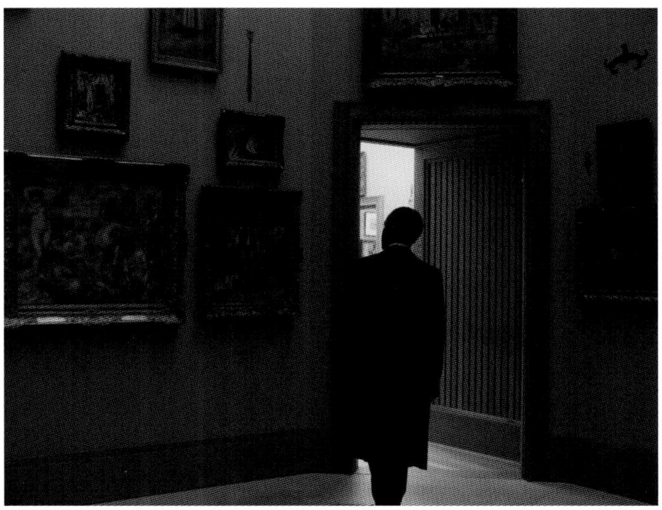

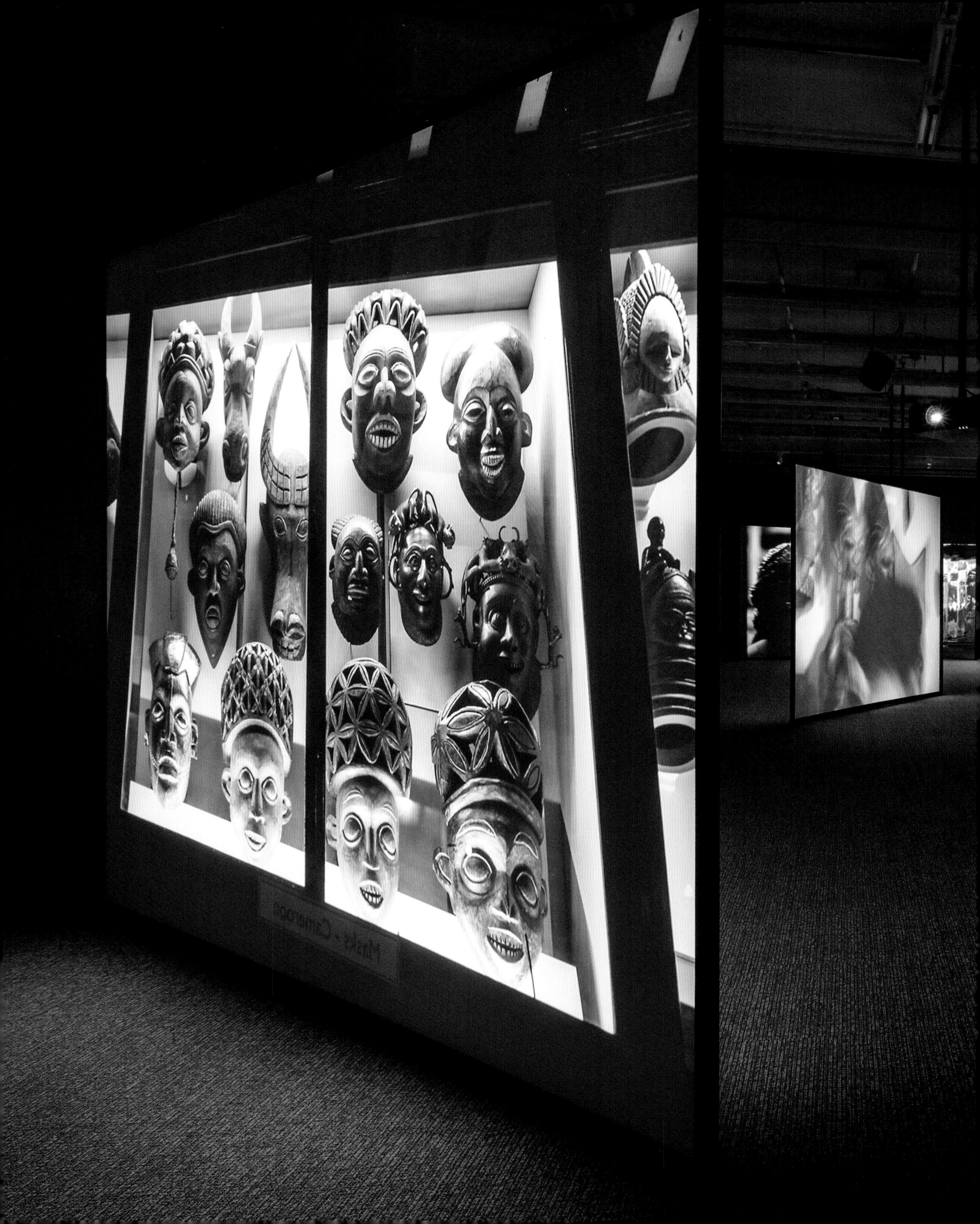

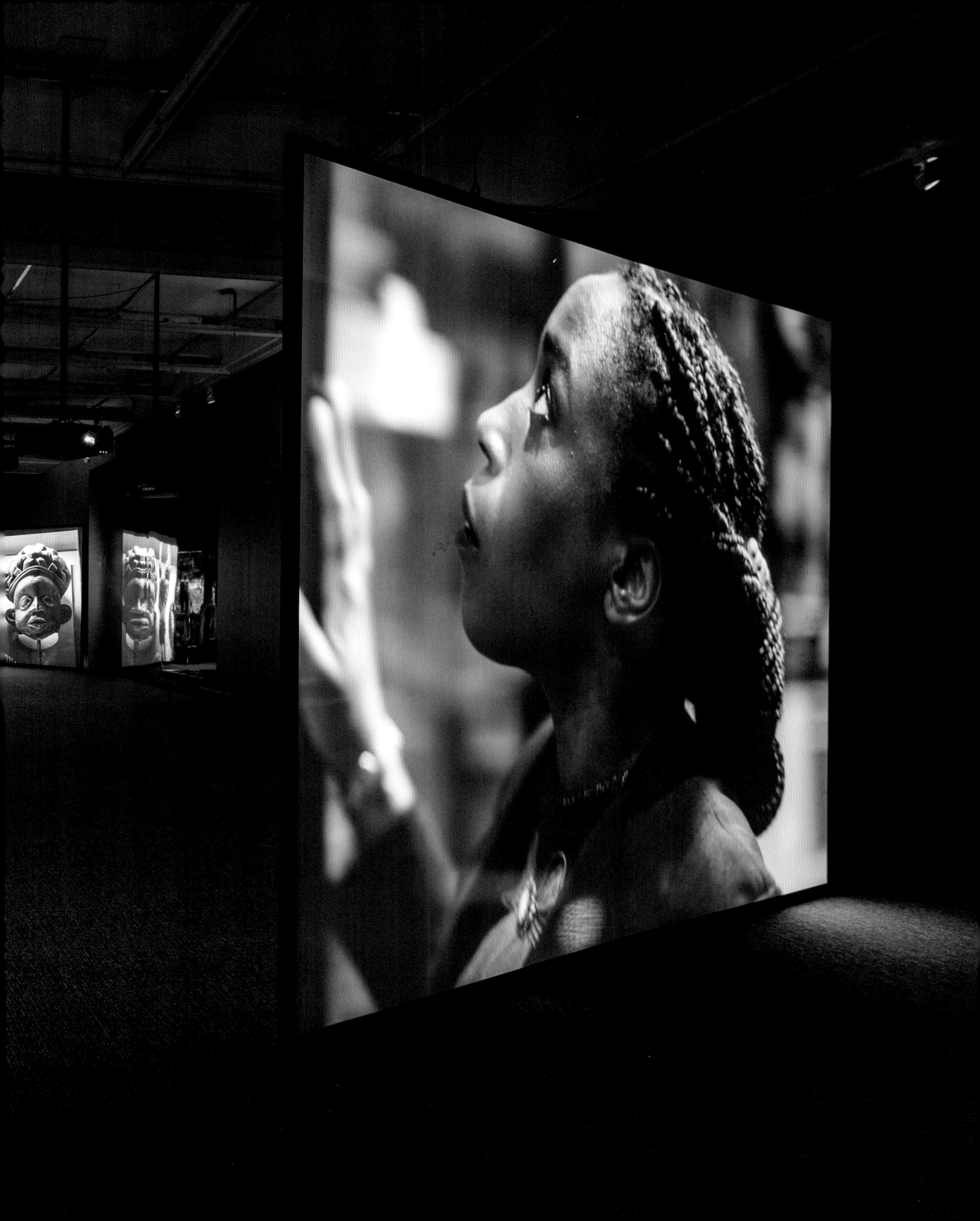

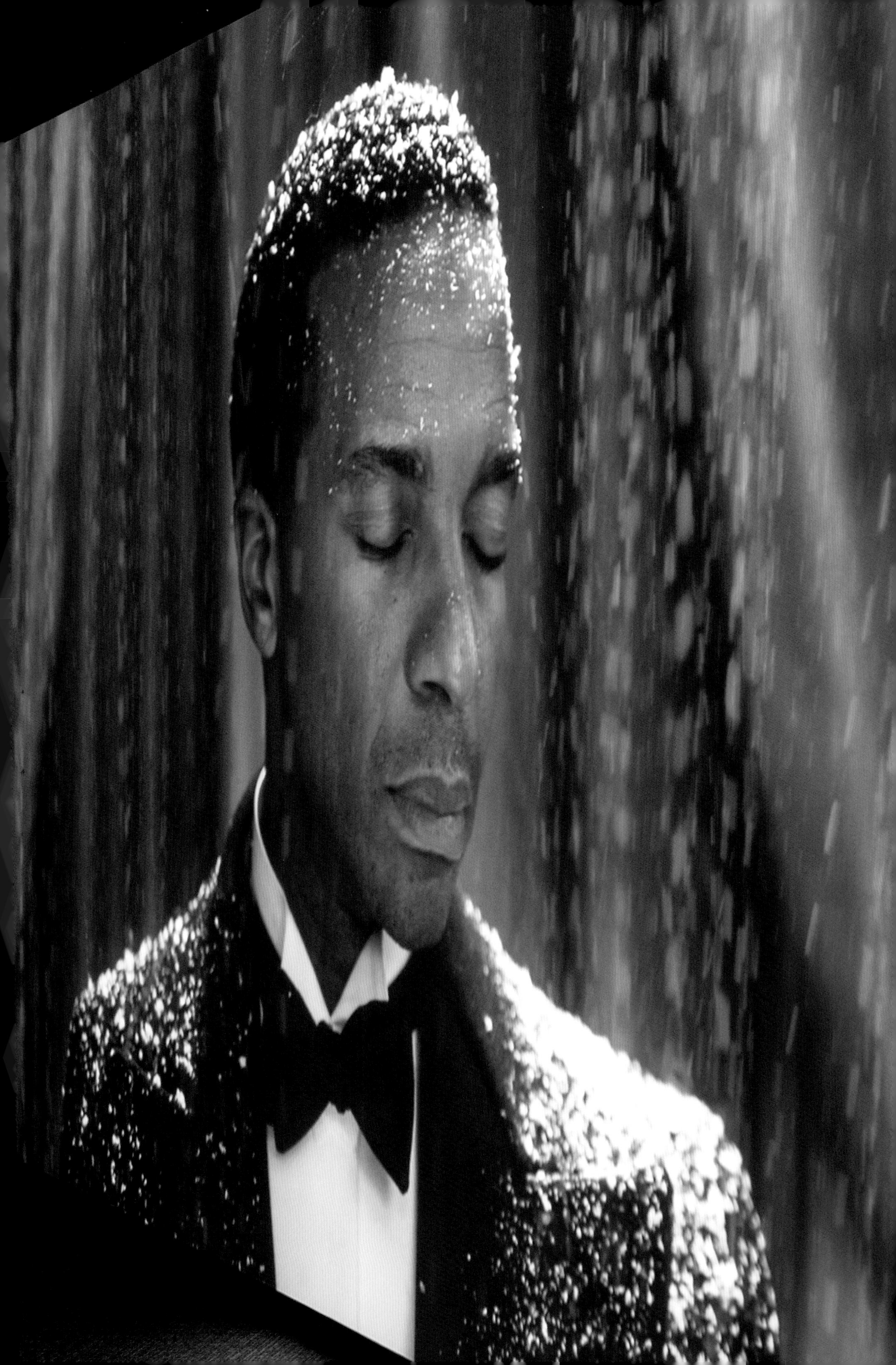

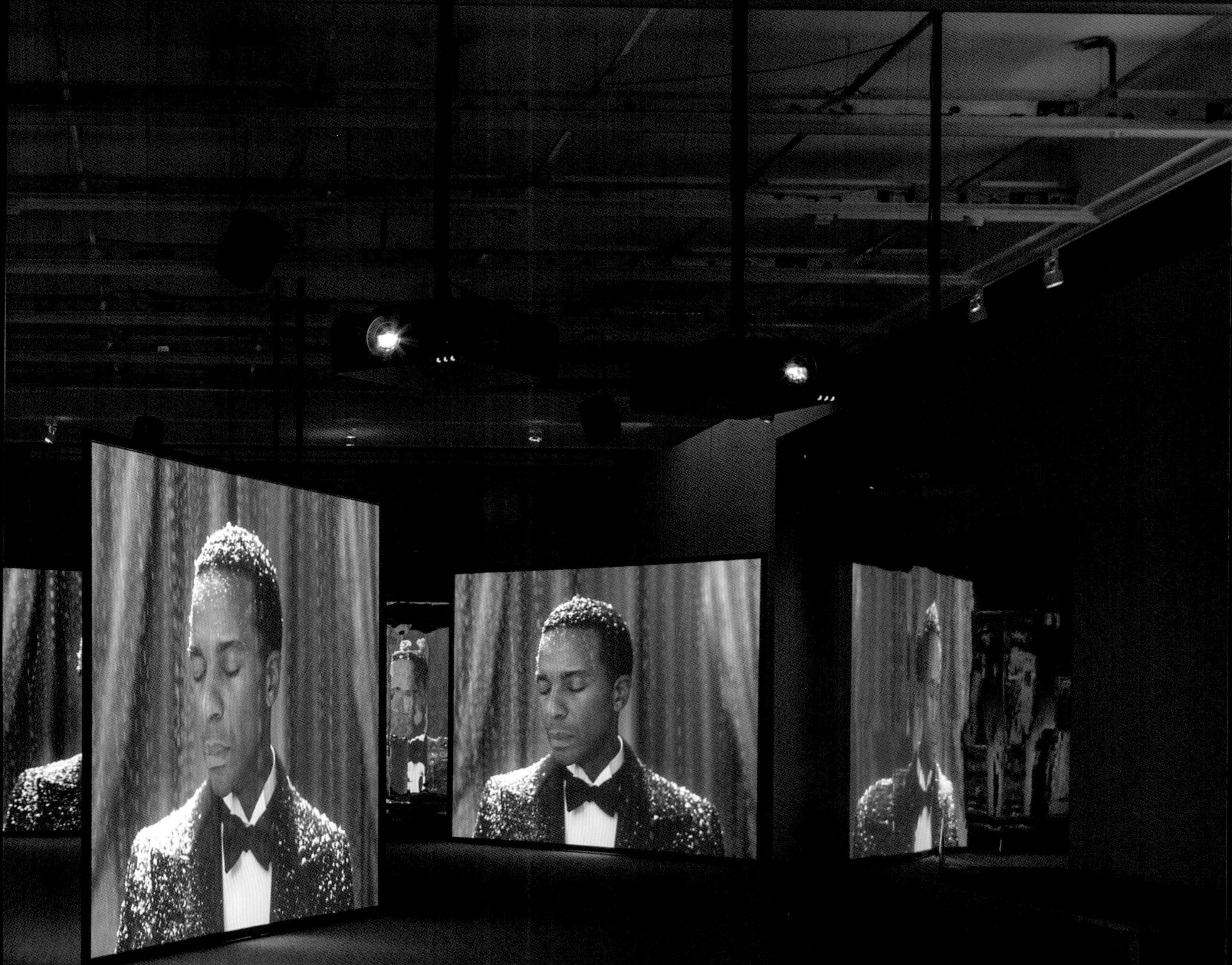

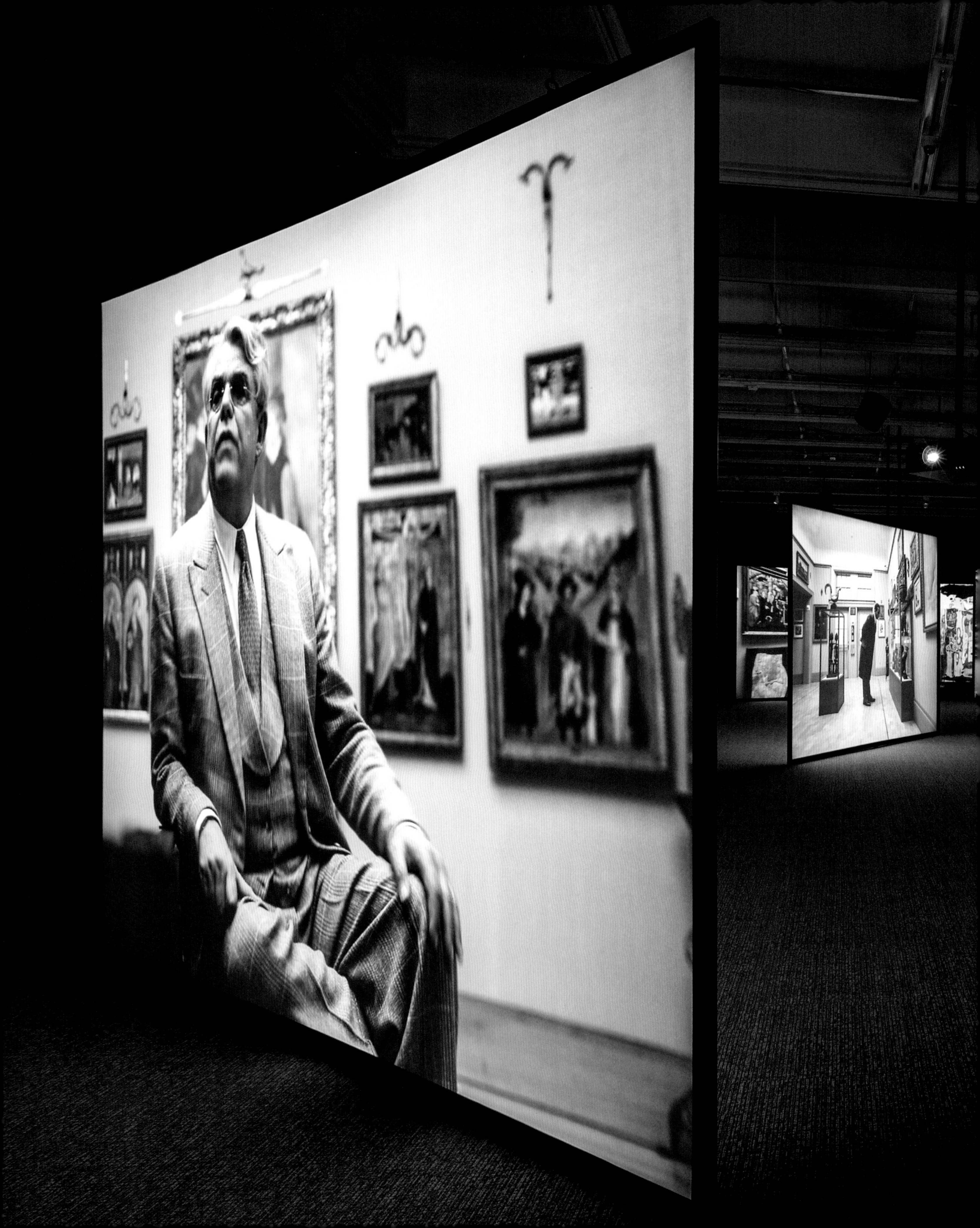

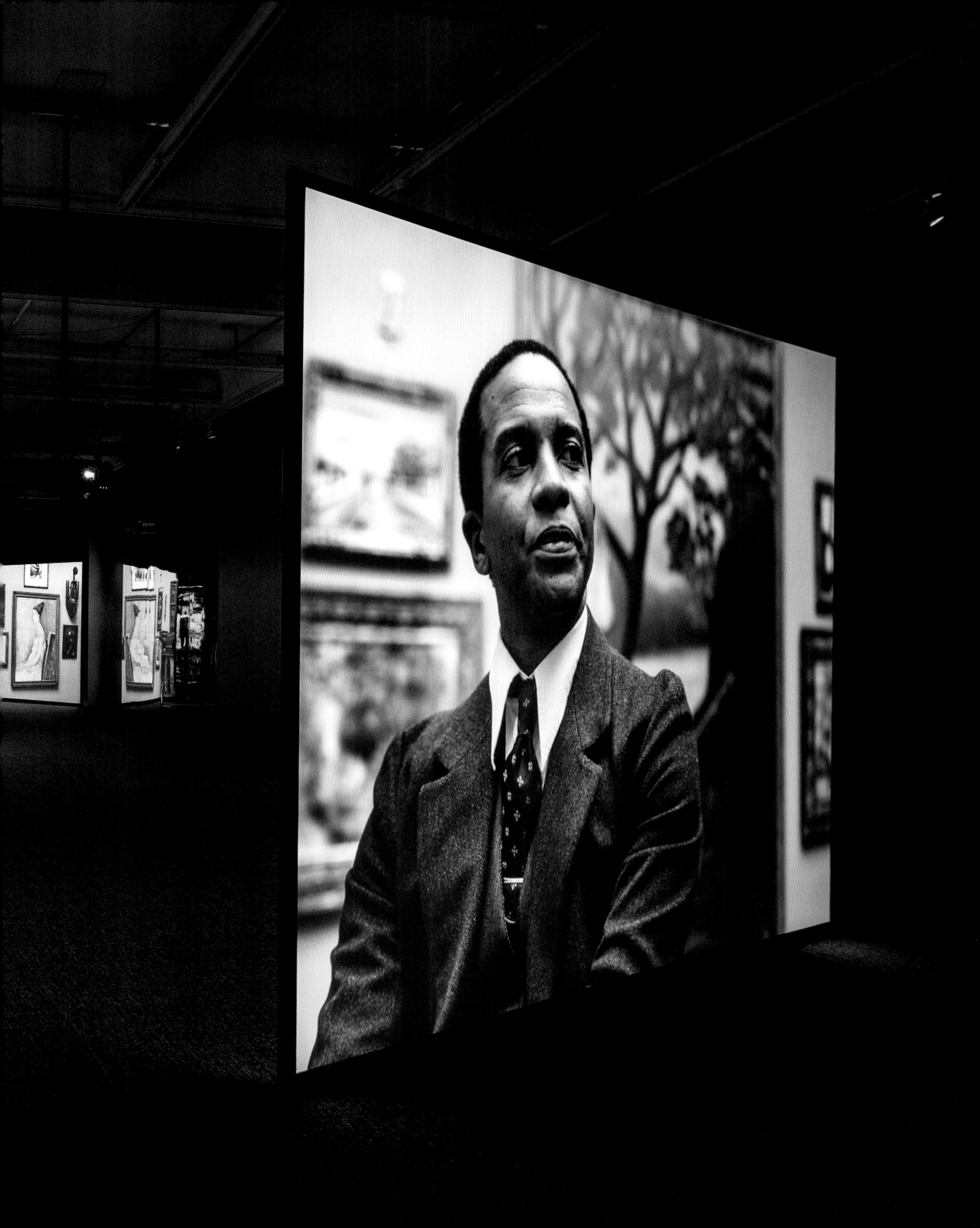

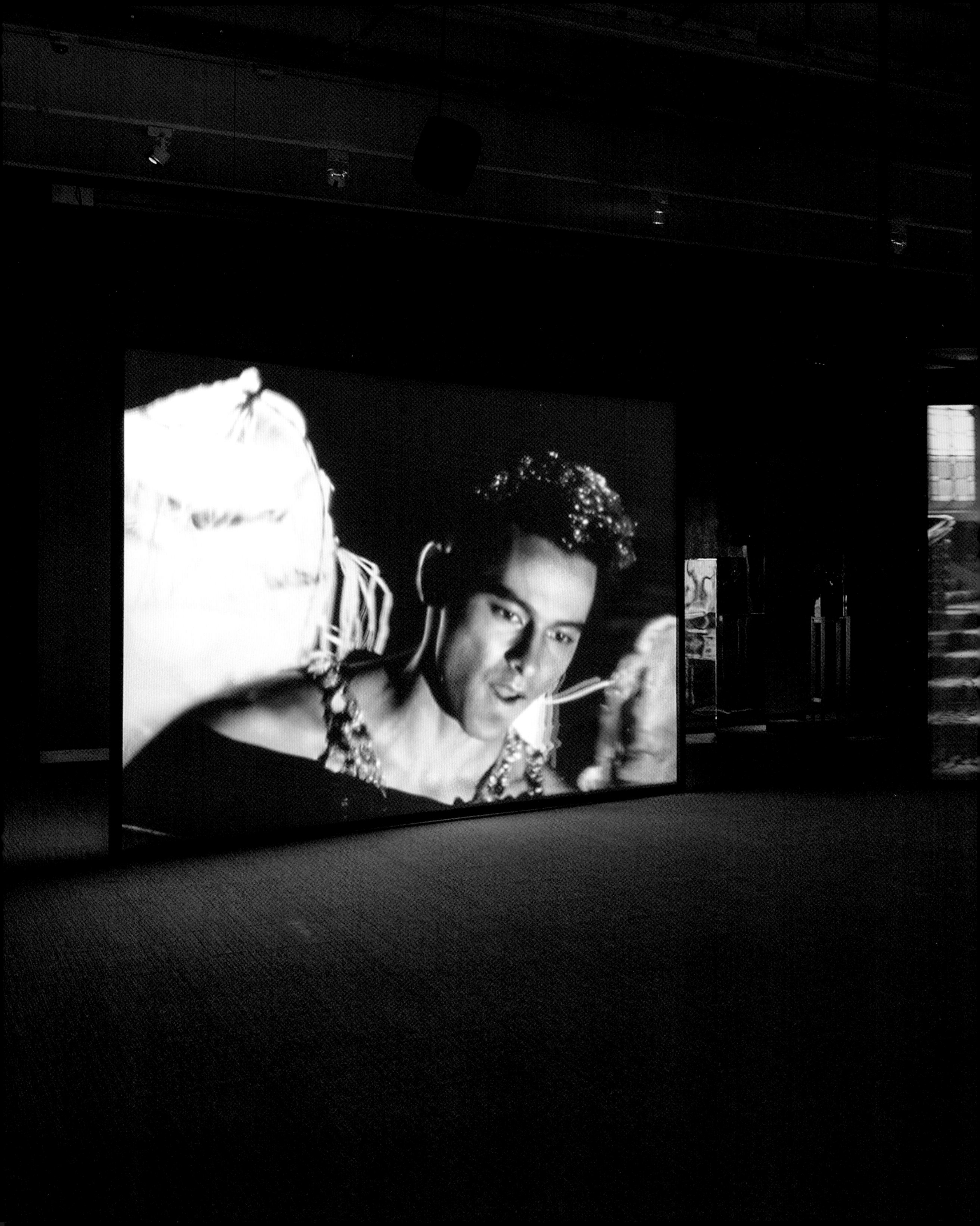

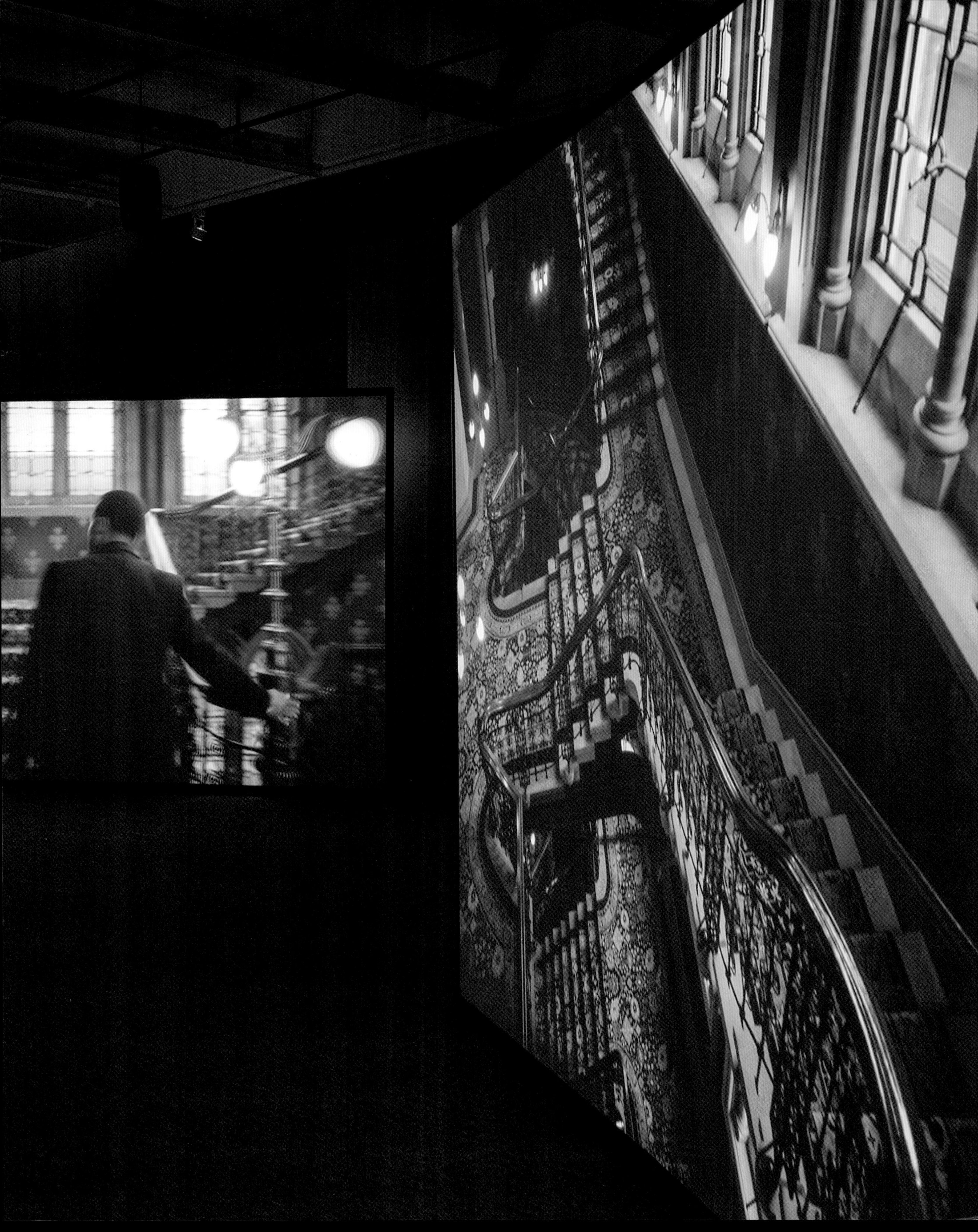

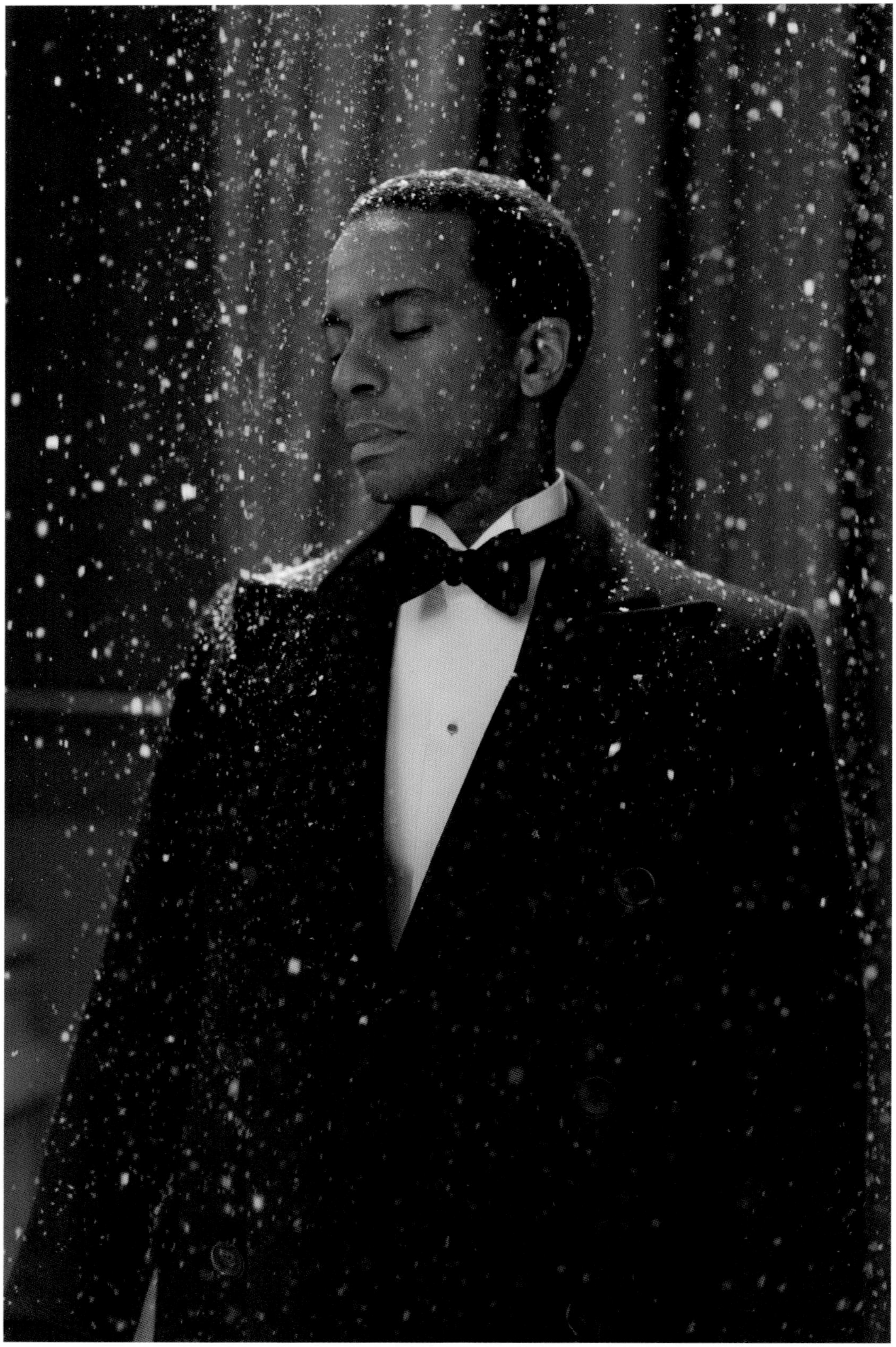

*What Freedom is to me (Homage)* 2022

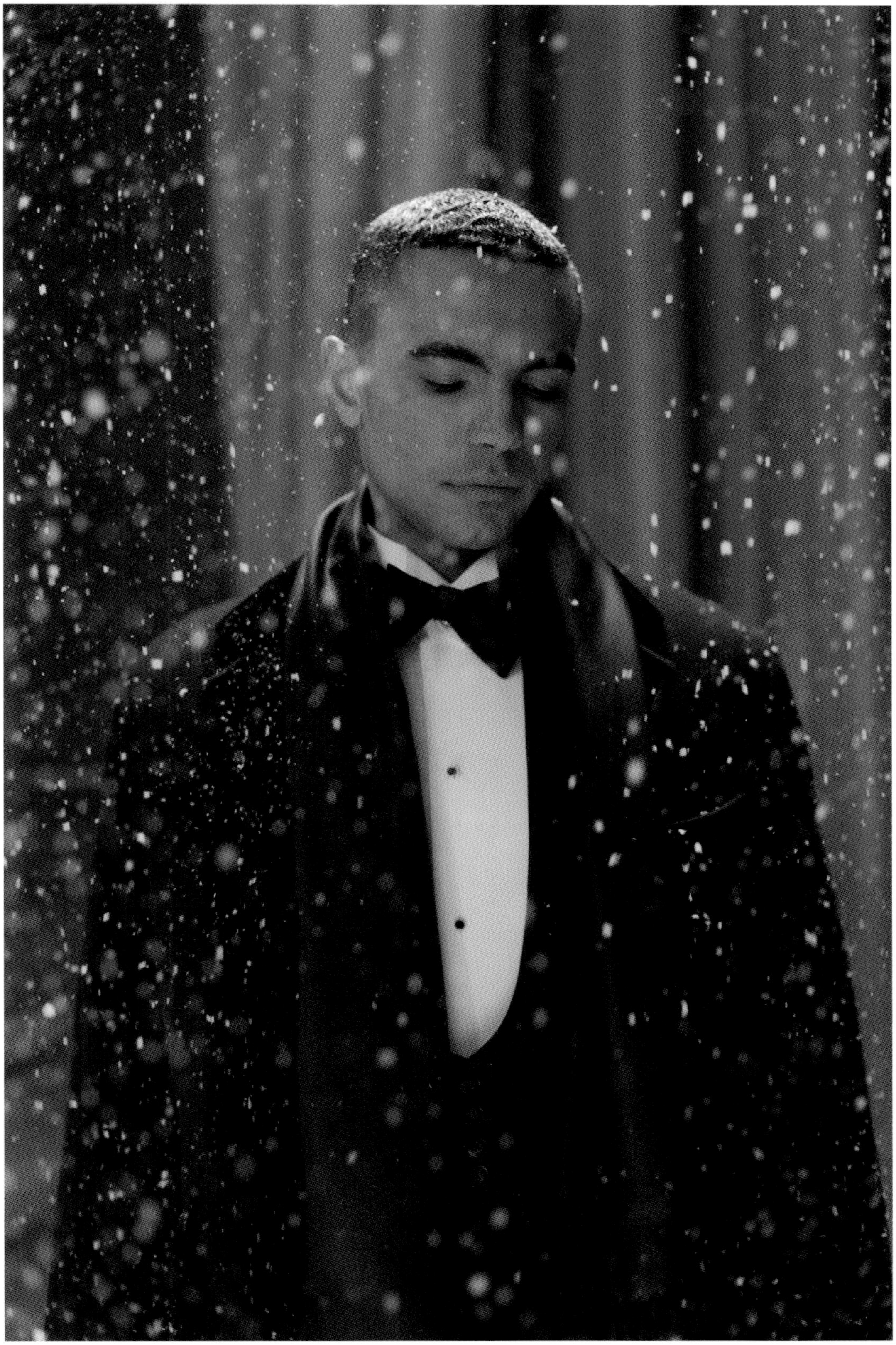

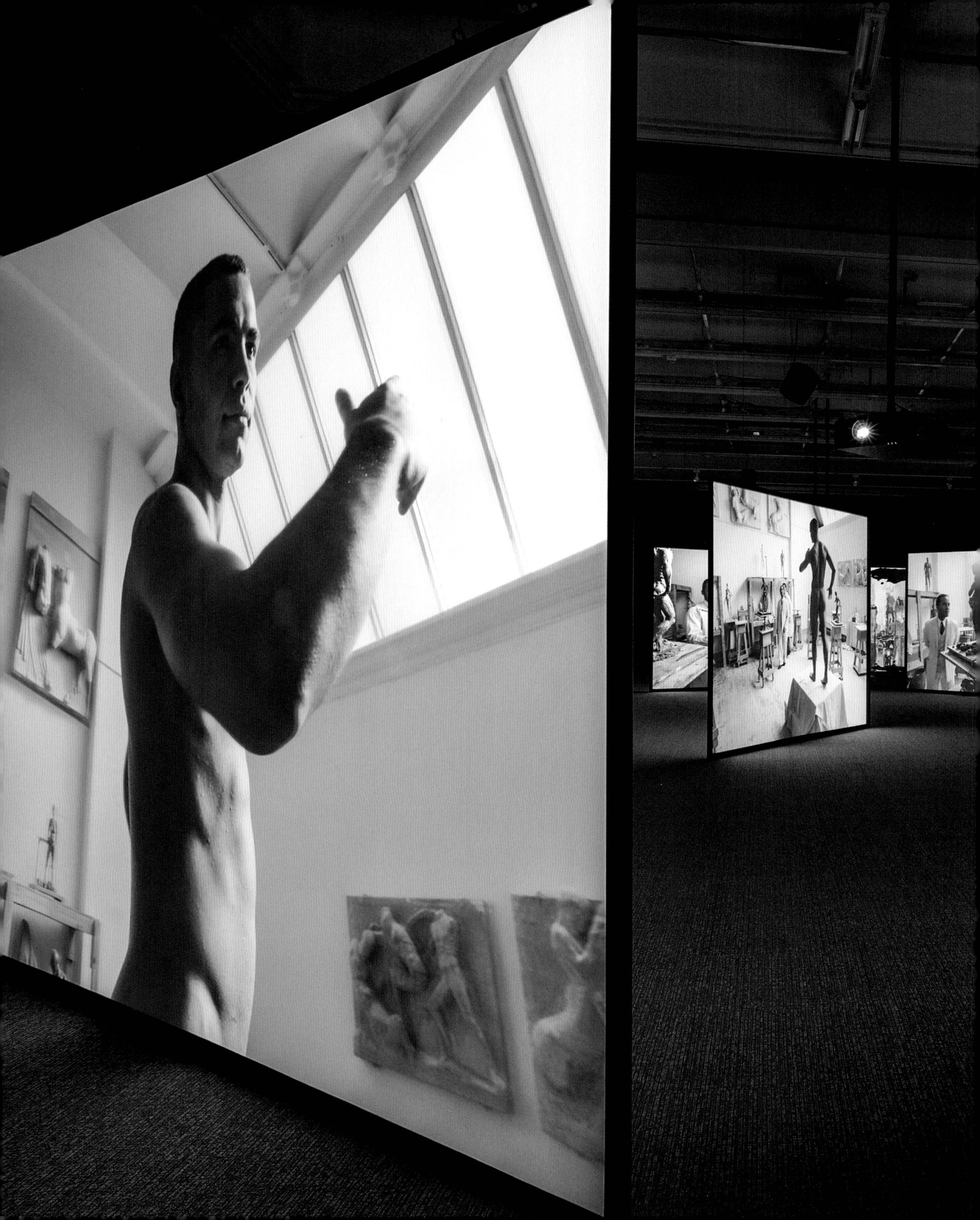

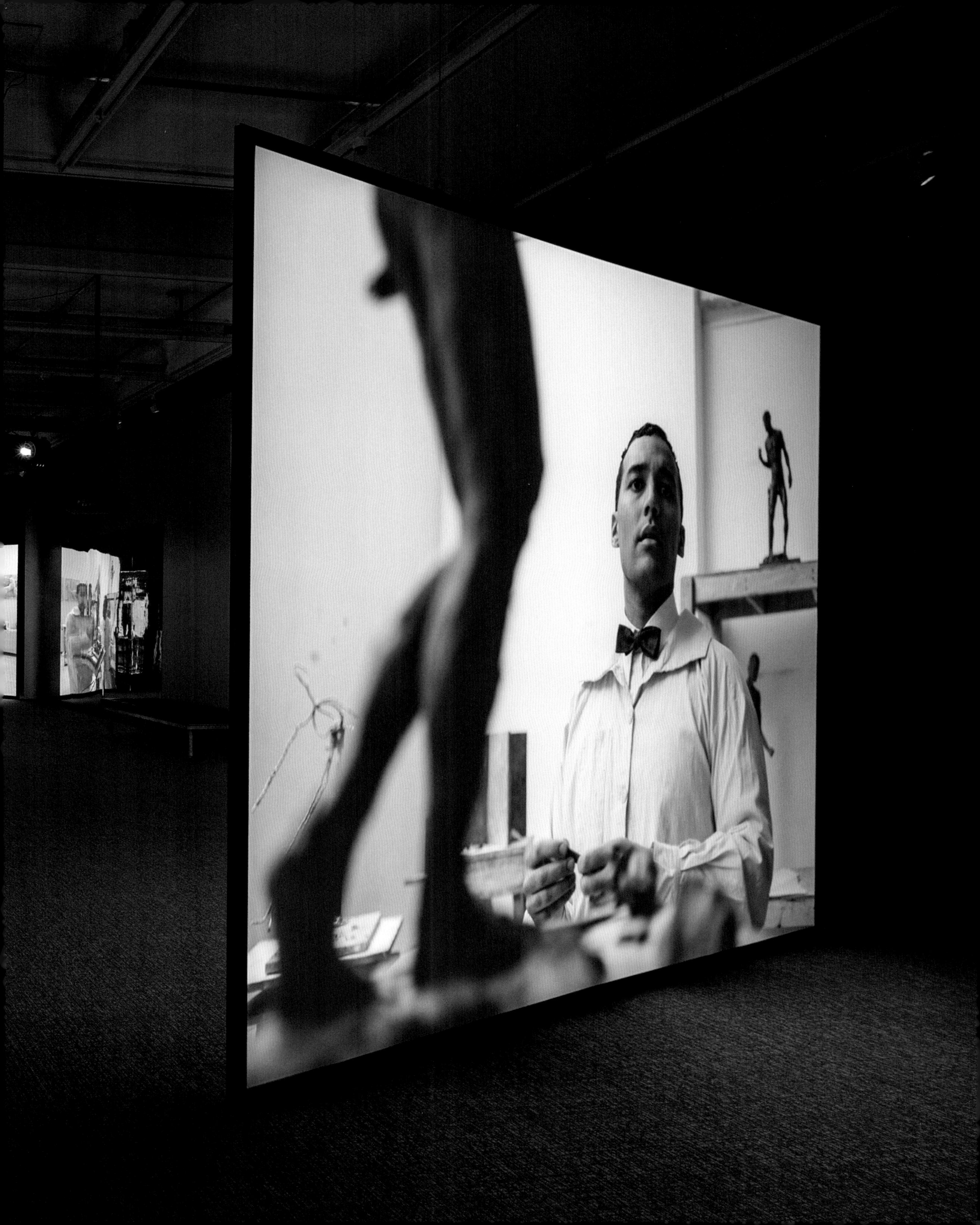

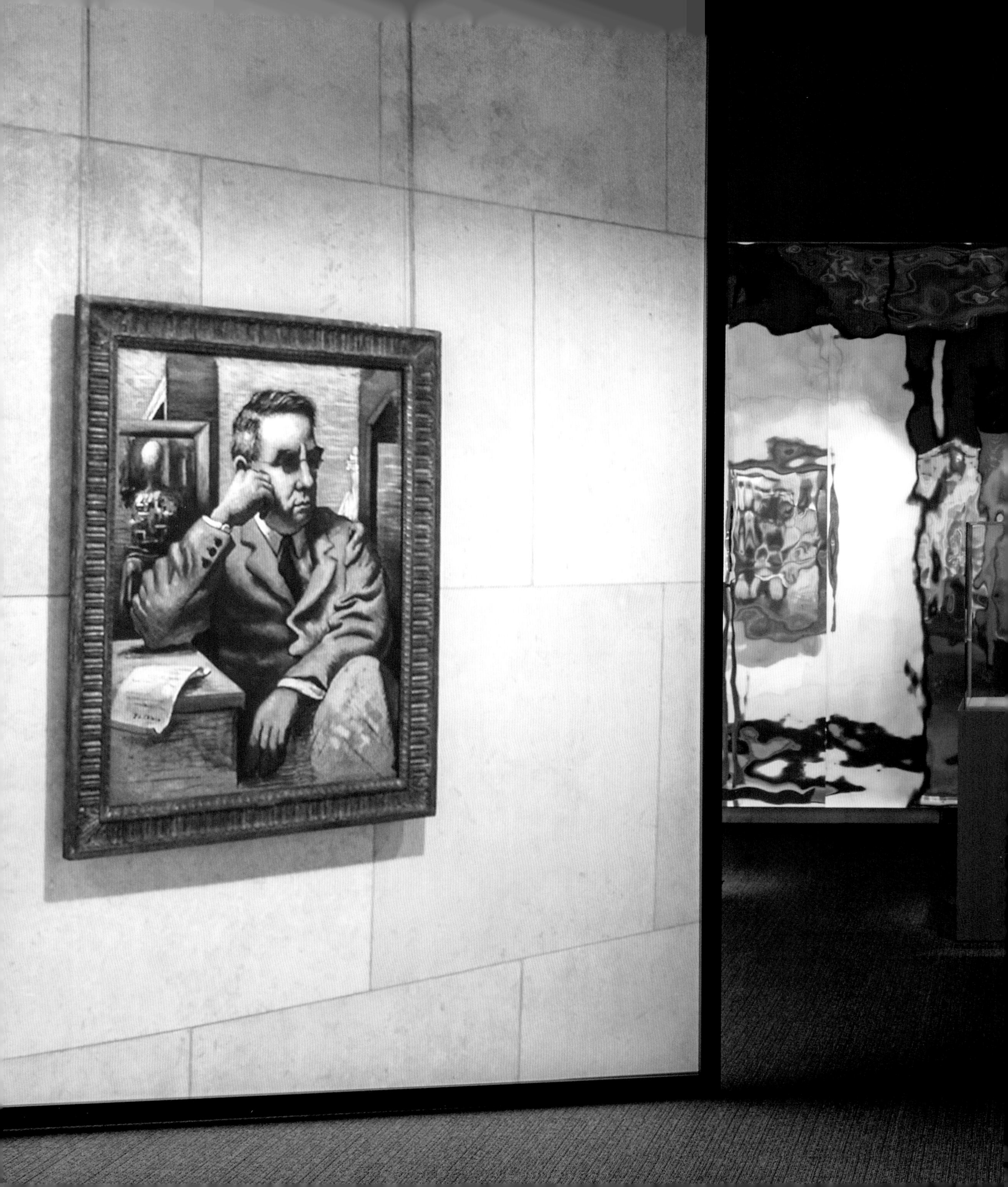

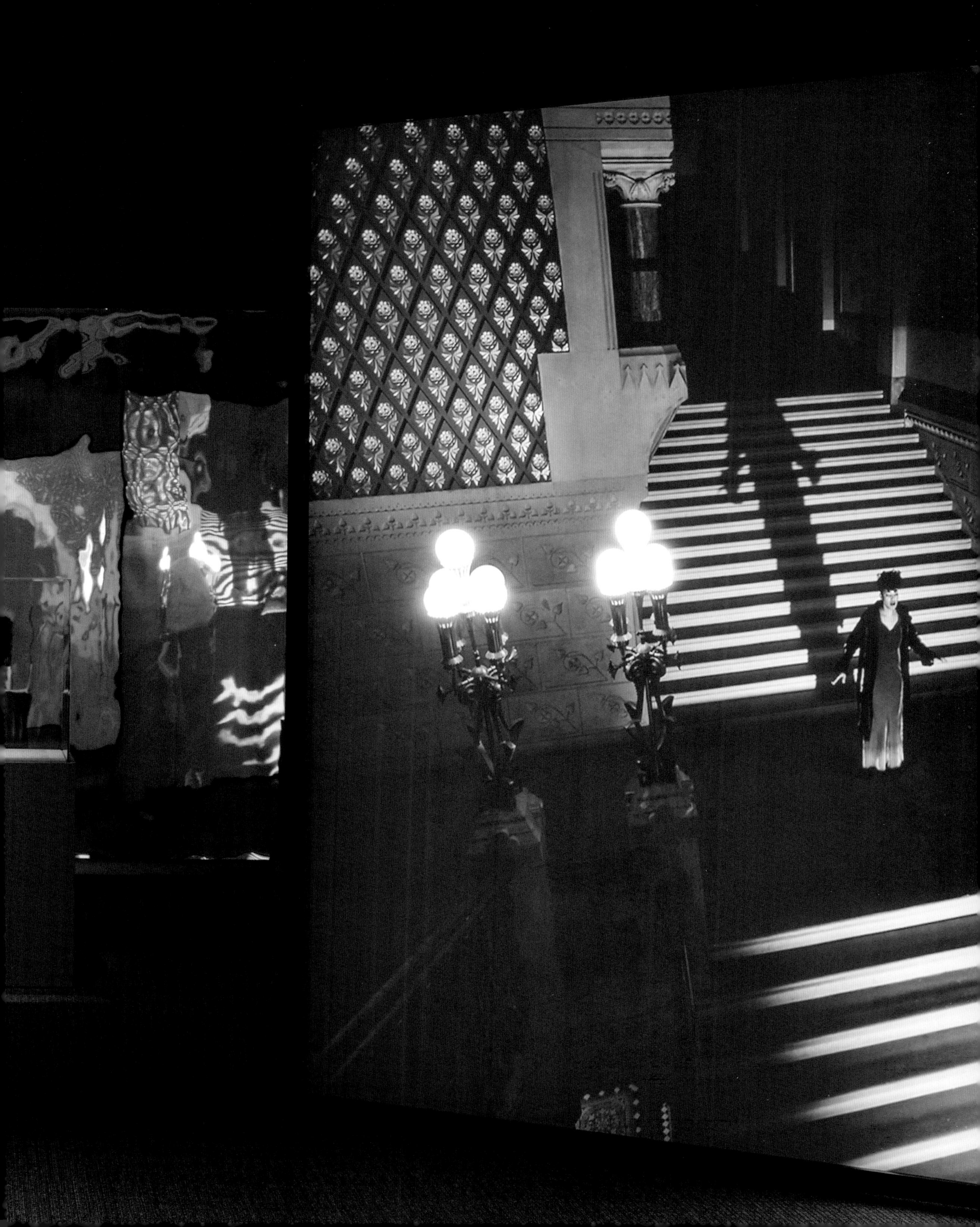

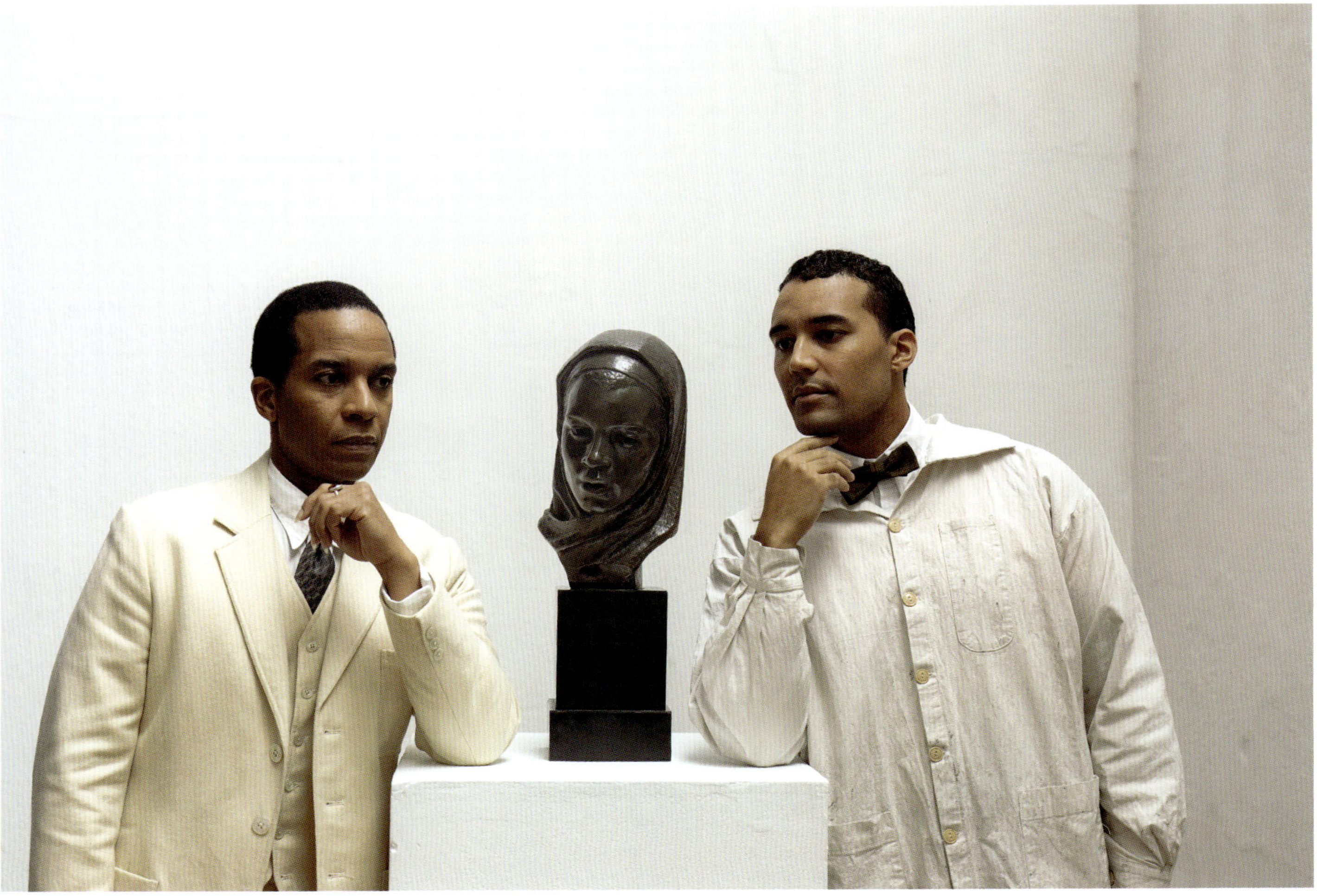

*In the Life (Iolaus), Once Again … (Statues Never Die)* 2022

No, not for the people of Mbari, whose relationship with the creative process is manifested in the paradox of creativity and dissolution. For a routine exemplar of that principle, we need seek no further than the Mbari statuary 'installation' of the Igbo, where clusters of sculptures are created to honour the earth-goddess, Ala. We encounter what is left of these religious sculptures either singly or in group formations on the Eastern Nigeria landscape, mostly hidden in bushes, left to collapse and decay from weather and neglect, and lately, suffer even a worse fate at the hands of latter-day Christian and Islamic fundamentalists. Such outsiders, especially the extremist brainwashed among the so-called world religions, maintain that Mbari - among other cultures of human figuration - are nothing but pandering to superstition and diabolism, and deserve no less than instant demolition. We shall waste no more words on these falsifiers of human spirituality. They are enemies of the world of intuition, imagination and originality, and deserve only one's pity.

However, we should not totally dismiss the religious season of unprecedented anti-humanism that is convulsing countries like Nigeria, Somalia, Mali, Kenya, of which many warnings have been pronounced, and such voices proved prescient. The lethal eruption of extreme intolerance by off-shoots of the Islamic faith, such as Boko Haram, Al Shabaab, Isis, Da'esh and others from that spore, currently exacts from the world - including from mainstream Islam - severe forfeit for our failure to confront, right from the start, the loudly proclaimed agenda of divinely mandated intolerance and eradication as the only language possible in relating to other vectors of spirituality. Even till today, in this second decade of the twenty-first century, the iconoclastic desperation, if anything, is constantly fuelled by religion-inspired mayhem all over the globe. Each eruption leads others to emulate, even exceed the destructive frenzy routinely unleashed by those who claim to be divine guardians of the purity, and singularity of faith. However, the missionaries of artistic renewal, wherever they are, are opening new horizons with works of innovative artists such as Isaac Julien - *Once Again* reads Beyond Time in these works! - and reassure us that the philistine temper cannot prevail over the creative spirit of humanity.

Destruction does however wear multiple faces, and not all emerge from the anti-creative desperation of the atavistic minority. There does exist a natural order of destruction whose essence is, paradoxically, renewal. Our spiritual equilibrium is restored by this knowledge which, in any case, is the natural order of human consciousness - this is where the ethos of the Mbari instructs, and consoles. Mbari statuary is conceived and moulded to succumb to the principle of death and re-birth. Made principally of mud, adorned in a free-wheeling mixture of sombre and flamboyant hues, the figures are displayed, then left to disintegrate. Even the 'houses' in which the figures are sometimes sheltered form part of the total sculptural composition, no different from friezes on houseposts, plaques, caryatids, and other offertory in wood or bronze. The same principle of disintegration applies to animal figures and objects that adorn what might be a domestic situation, a royal or religious procession or the depiction of a special event in the calendar of the people.

The process that precedes the creation and emergence of the finished product is perhaps even more more significant - a mechanism of community cohering for which the artist becomes the identified medium of a people's communal awareness, albeit basically a token of adoration of the earth-goddess, Ala. The artists are selected by revelation from the priest, although there are also cases where the individual artist claims inspiration directly from the godhead. The collective response results in the isolation of the chosen artist or artists in a special compound built by the entire community. In early times, the artists would be led into this space in a celebratory procession by the entire village, after which they are sealed off from the world. They undergo a process of purification and communion, and then commence work, remaining within the compound for weeks, sometimes months. Depending on the productive level of artistic inspiration, they might remain within for almost a year, fed and attended by the community. To summarise: during this period of artistic seclusion, all mundane preoccupations are banished; the artist devotes himself or herself entirely to the creative mission in homage to earth and its goddess, Ala, through a replication of her own mission of creativity.

When they indicate their readiness, the outer walls of the compound are ceremonially taken down, the statues revealed for the first time. They are purified, consecrated and, for a while, the environment of these artworks is carefully tended. Sometimes, the statues themselves are renovated as needed - a new coat of paint here and there, restoration to some cracks in the figures, and so on. This continues until the priest receives yet another vision for a new act of homage and communion, the earlier sculptures are then left to fend for themselves. They are overgrown by foliage, collapse or survive out of human sight, obeying the rhythms of birth and decay as an integrated process of Nature. It is necessary to remark also that individually inspired artists, working in their own secluded spaces, also undergo the same process of purification, seclusion, communal care and outing. Process and product constitute one seamless community-cohering phenomenon in which the entire people are involved. The latter goes on display, is then abandoned, eventually disintegrates, only to resurface, again through the spiritual and creative impulses of the people.

No, for the begetters of Mbari, the statues never die ...

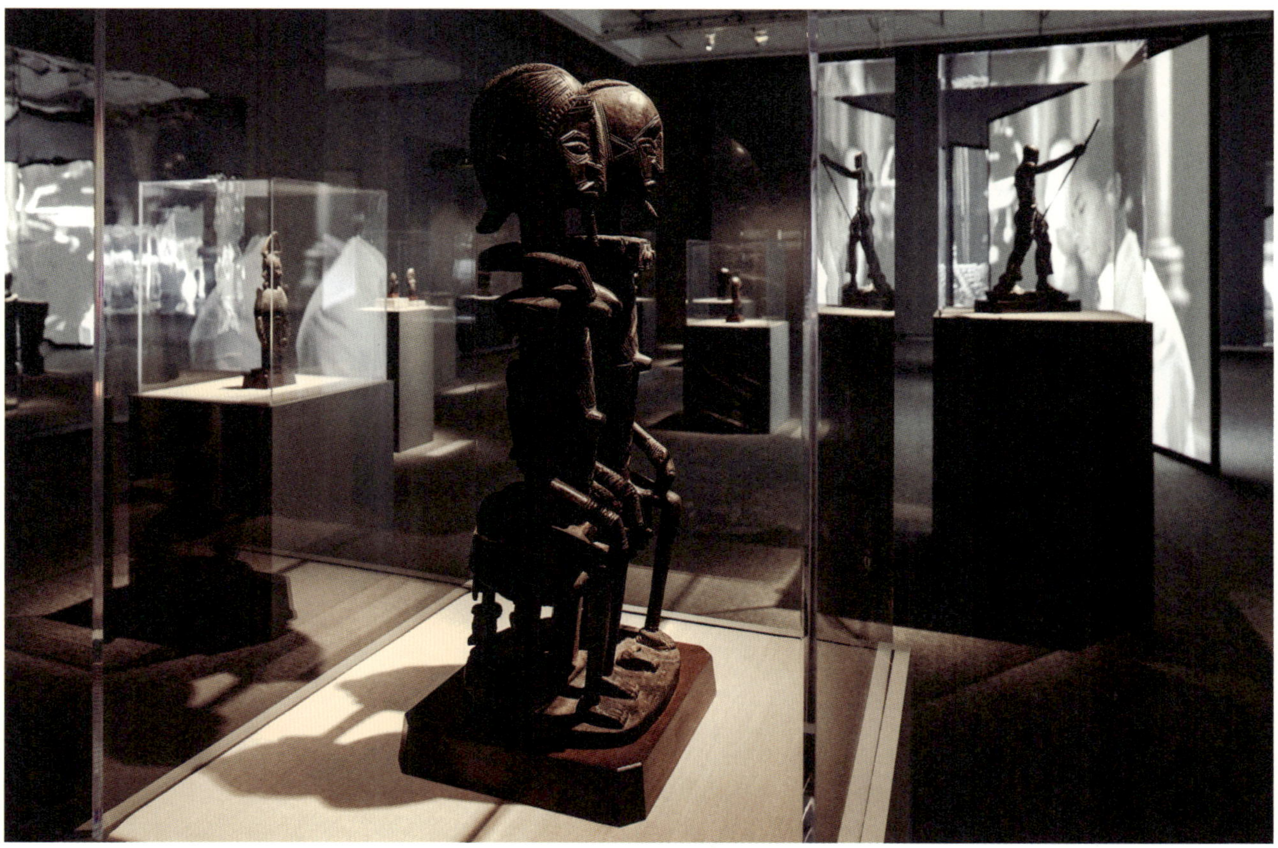

*Once Again ... (Statues Never Die)*, installation view, Barnes Foundation, 2022
Foreground: Barnes Foundation Master, *Seated Couple*, late 19th–early 20th century

Celeste-Marie Bernier: Frederick Douglass was a world-leading liberator, human rights author, activist, freedom-fighter, philosopher and orator. He delivered thousands of speeches during his lifetime and repeatedly transformed public spaces in the USA and the UK into radical platforms for human rights activism. The Music Hall, where we are here in Edinburgh on 6 August 2021, was one of those spaces: he made repeated visits to Scotland and gave hundreds of revolutionary lectures here. Every time he spoke here, there were over two thousand people inside the building, while the windows were thrown wide open so thousands more would be listening on the streets outside.

Here in Scotland Douglass educated his transatlantic audiences on Black liberation histories and movements across the African diaspora, and inspired his listeners to really think about what these meant and continue to mean as activist tools necessary for understanding Black revolutionary and radical heroism: past, present, and future. And an understanding of the history of Black heroism is very important, Isaac, when watching *Lessons of the Hour*, your poetic meditation on the fight for liberation and the united struggle against historical and contemporary global systems of enslavement today. We see that especially in the intercutting in your film between historical and political injustices in the past and political atrocities in the present, and in the powerful way in which you end the film around the Baltimore that Douglass knew and the Baltimore we know today.

Isaac Julien: Celeste, your scholarship was really at the forefront of our minds when we were undertaking our initial research for this film. In some ways, the journey begins with going to Rochester and walking around with the amazing curator John Hanhardt, who lives there, and who commissioned me, alongside Jonathan Binstock. We came across the statue of Douglass in Highland Park and in a way it was just done. I thought, 'Okay, Frederick Douglass – this is a project that I have to do.' Later, I was going through that wonderful pictorial book on Douglass which you co-edited and I began to realise, yes, I had read Frederick Douglass and come across him before, initially through the writings of Henry Louis Gates Jr. But it was really when I read your work that I became properly activated in relation to Douglass – these amazing documents with which you had been involved, so many publications and journals. And then when I found out that you lived in Edinburgh, too, I just couldn't believe it! [laughs]

CMB: And in the thirty years I've been dedicating my life to Douglass, you've single-handedly brought Douglass and the Douglass family – and the power of the ancestral force of radicalism, resistance and fighting injustice by any means necessary – back to us in the twenty-first century.

Douglass's mission in the nineteenth century, as he repeatedly spoke of it to audiences here, was to galvanise the power of the African diaspora freedom struggle in the face of white supremacist acts of atrocity, of violence, of annihilation, of persecution, of torture and death. In Scotland his mission was to teach his audiences that they should understand their nation was built on blood. In *Lessons of the Hour*, you speak to the lessons he taught then, as well as to those we need now and in the future. At the same time, your film brings to life and honours the intergenerational Black liberation movement that was the entire Douglass family – not just Frederick Douglass, but Anna Murray Douglass, his wife and partner of over forty-four years, and their children, Rosetta, Lewis Henry, Frederick Jr, Charles Remond and Annie Douglass. His mother, Harriet Bailey, was a trailblazing liberator, educator and human rights revolutionary in her own right. Today, we know Frederick Douglass's name, if we're lucky – as he knew we would if he was lucky – while he knew that the untold millions who died would be 'nameless, faceless and bodiless'. But who knows Anna Murray Douglass's name? One of the greatest compliments Douglass could ever pay an image was to say it could 'speak', and in your beautiful reimagining of Anna Murray Douglass, she speaks. She herself was a brilliant human rights philosopher and phenomenal orator, and although we have very few words that she spoke, even the very few we do have – 'Why not I enjoy hardship that my race may be free?' – speak to the power of her revolutionary life as a world-leading activist and trailblazing liberator.

IJ: Anna Murray Douglass's role in the piece was really important for me – the way in which she too had this incredible kind of persona and resonance. One aspect that came out of a lot of the scholarship with which you have been involved, Celeste, is how Frederick Douglass is writing about photography, developing his own aesthetic theories about the medium, and is also actually the most photographed man in the nineteenth century – more so than figures like Abraham Lincoln, even. Yet at the same time there are so few representations of Anna Murray Douglass. So I see it as fairly progressive to recentre her,

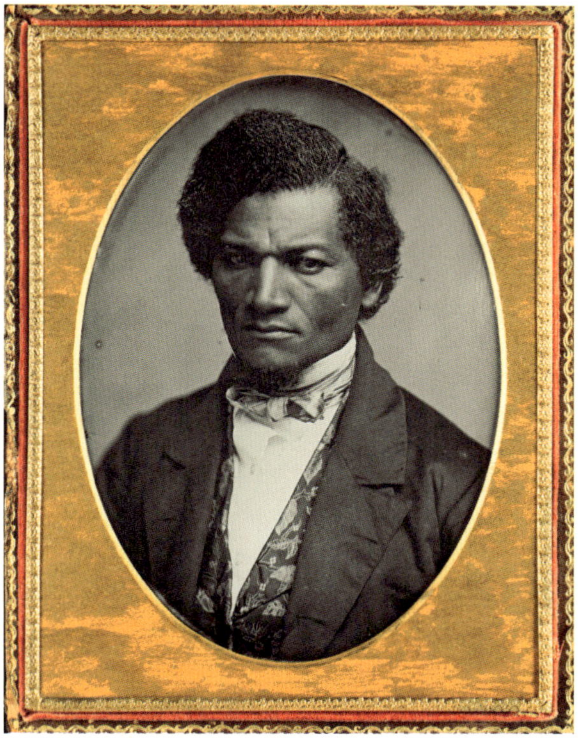

Samuel J. Miller, *Portrait of Frederick Douglass (1847/52)* Daguerreotype, Art Institute Chicago

and the portrait *Lady of the Lake* is part of that. It really foregrounds her role in the Douglass family and how they worked as a team. Anna Murray Douglass is a person who *made* Frederick Douglass and the Douglass family. She was a free slave, an incredible organiser ...

CMB: And a freedom-fighter, a liberator, a philosopher, an orator, a financial manager, a singer, a chef, a human rights activist, a fashion designer, a seamstress ...

IJ: An incredible seamstress. In a way, she is literally making Douglass's reimagined South, at least in a sartorial sense. In the work she is played by the brilliant Sharlene Whyte, and I tried to reference some of these aspects, as in the scene where she's making Douglass's fabulous blue coat. Our costume designer Annie Symons really did an incredible interpretation! Again, you get the different modernities - Douglass on the train, and the way in which that as a kind of technology is enabling him to move, while Anna's sewing is, as a technology, enabling her to refashion Douglass's Images. That combination in this moment - the suturing of different images, and the connections I'm trying to make across space and time and geography - is connected to this question of the desire for liberation and how that looks and feels. And so I really focused on the aspect of sewing as a technology and an apparatus, versus the technology of the train, which is another apparatus of modernity. These two modernities are at work, and they are edited together, making Anna Murray Douglass and her role in them really pertinent for me.

CMB: All five children were social justice campaigners, radical activists and human rights liberators; as Kenneth B. Morris, Jr. inspirationally describes his legendary family, they were a 'freedom-fighting liberation collective'. And so your film is an act of reclamatory and revelatory justice in the way in which you are speaking back to white racism and white supremacy today, and to the ways in which we only remember Frederick Douglass ('there can be only one') when the entire Douglass family was an intergenerational movement of liberation in their own right, one that reflects and memorialises the revolutionary collectives of untold millions of people across the African diaspora. In the twenty-first century white supremacy trades in monuments, in icons, in the idea that 'there can be only one', while Douglass's Black liberation manifesto was 'There is all of us - there are millions.' What's so powerful in your poetic meditation is that memorialisation of the struggle in the past, in the present and what we need to do in the future.

For Douglass, photography was a social justice tool and human rights weapon, a way to represent and reimagine Black subjectivities as a stimulus to revolution. Through the power of portraiture, he resisted, defied and fought against the dehumanising objectification of the white racist world of enslavement. By becoming a 'work of art' he revolutionised vision, changed practices of seeing, altered modes of perception and recreated and re-envisioned the world from an 'enslaved person's point of view'. Douglass really understood that 'pictures are a power', and he believed - as you do in your film - in the visual mode itself as a weapon of revolution, that art was the way out. 'This is how we move from chattel records, to be bought and sold in white racist imaginaries, to become our own revolution through works of art', he said, and, 'When you see a child looking at a work of art, tell me they are not entitled to human rights.' His was a philosophy in which art wasn't in any way an afterthought: 'Art is agitation' was the artery of his manifesto, of his life existence. He understood that European art was rooted and made possible in white supremacist and racist atrocities committed against untold millions of people living in enslavement across the world. He absolutely understood that the blood money of the Western art world was made possible by the suffering, sacrifice and subjugation of 'my people'. And in his photographs, he's memorialising not just himself and his struggle but the struggle of millions. He survived, and his struggle was to remember the suffering of those who didn't, and those who continued to survive and to fight for survival, whether in the nineteenth century or today.

IJ: As a technology, photography does that even to this day - it's the apparatus that has created, for example, the whole Black Lives Matter movement, documenting the horrible murder of George Floyd. In my own practice I'm thinking about the ways in which new technologies and the moving image and photography can become means of progressing particular causes. At the same time, I'm thinking about the aesthetics of those, as giving subjectivity to subjects who have not always had access to them. My work is about looking at the ways in which photography and film can enlighten subjects and people, and create a certain autonomy and agency. The power of that technology can also have very damaging effects, which I think Douglass was aware of. But we don't appreciate enough the ways in which his philosophy enables one to really grapple with these questions in a way that remains relevant for today. If you are making works of art, films in this case, or images, you need a certain aliveness to make that connection to these questions. Of course, reading a book is important, but if you want to create a certain form of activism – which Douglass was doing – then to realise there's this line of activism connecting Douglass to what's happening today with Black Lives Matter gives lineage, respect, to struggles which have been going on for so long.

Thus, *Lessons of the Hour* is a ten-screen work whose installation mirrors that of a nineteenth-century Salon-hang, but it is at the same time a work with a certain radicality to it. It's a way of trying to utilise the new technologies and the effects of bricolage, of montage, to propel a new and different way of looking – a way that I think connects to the critical looking that is also very much part of the way in which Douglass examined and viewed the nineteenth-century world. The film tries to build into the pictures this sense of rupture and also sublimity, and at the same time to use those to look back into a history of slavery that I would say, in the West in the twenty-first century, we've been resisting, but which nonetheless haunts the spectre of all our actions in everything that we do. That feeling of simultaneous rupture and sublimity was beautifully transposed through Nina Kellgren's cinematography and Derek Brown's production design; without their work it would be impossible to create such an alluring yet anguished atmosphere.

CMB: That's a beautiful and powerful way of doing justice to what Douglass was doing then and to what his revolutionary life and human rights legacy means now. Certainly, throughout his life Douglass carried what he felt was a burden of representation and to bear witness. That burden was one of the key aspects I discussed with Ray Fearon, who plays Douglass in the film – the public Frederick Douglass and the private Frederick Douglass: the monument, the memorial, but also Douglass as a human being in the struggle.

IJ: I think Ray completely understood Douglass after your conversation and his brilliant and powerful performance shows it.

CMB: He inspirationally memorialises Douglass's persona as the unrivalled orator, the unrivalled speaker, and the unrivalled testifier to the atrocities he experienced in enslavement, which he transformed into a platform for liberation. When he pauses and holds back in one of those final moments of the film, he powerfully remembers and does justice to the members of Douglass's family who died in enslavement. And the power of your film, in the way in which you have that black canvas come behind Douglass to replace that Arcadian natural scene, does incredible and transformative justice to Douglass the individual and mortal human being.

IJ: It's extraordinary the way in which Douglass also mastered language, if we're thinking about this dialectically. That really became another important way in which Douglass was able to create this resonance. And with his interest in Shakespeare which propelled, Ray Fearon's performance: Ray is a Royal Shakespeare Company actor himself, and he said, 'I can see the Shakespearean influences in the text and the work'. There's that sense of oratory, of course, but there's also the way in which Douglass was able to utilise language and, in a way, transcend these boundaries to enable a certain identification with the audience.

CMB: Frederick Douglass's spirit lives again in Ray Fearon, and he beautifully memorialises the power of language in Douglass's life. Douglass was an inspirational author as well as an unprecedented orator: he wrote over seven thousand speeches, letters, essays and narratives. He was a virtuoso of the spoken and written word. You interpret and imagine and recreate that for us, Isaac, by doing justice both to 'Frederick Douglass the freeman', as he described himself in speeches he gave in this nation, and also, as he remembered himself, 'a very different man', 'Frederick Bailey, the slave'. Certainly, Douglass felt all his life that white supporters, even the most well intentioned, carried prejudice, paternalism and racism to such a mind-, body-, and soul-destroying degree that they only understood 'Frederick Douglass, the freeman' while they showed no interest in even attempting to understand the life of 'Frederick Bailey, the slave'. What's so powerful in Ray Fearon's performance – and in the 'lexicon of liberation', as Donald Rodney stated decades earlier, memorialised in your film – is exactly the way in which 'Frederick Bailey, the slave' lives in 'Frederick Douglass, the freeman'.

IJ: It's incredible that what you found through your research into Douglass still resonates today. Because we're still in this particular moment, aren't we? We're still struggling in relation to these questions around humanity. Can Black subjects be seen in this particular manner? Questions of indigeneity, too. All these things are part of a whole discourse and policies and practices that resonate deeply in our culture today.

CMB: Douglass's revolutionary interest in photography was in the act and art of reclaiming, revealing and recognising the equal human subject as a visual manifesto of human rights. In one of his speeches here on the eve of the US Civil War, for instance, he spoke not about himself, but about a revolutionary act of Black heroism that took place on a white enslavers' ship going across the Atlantic. He honours a liberator called Madison Washington, a self-liberated man born into enslavement who became one of the most renowned Black liberators in US history. Before an audience of thousands here in this Music Hall, Douglass jubilantly informs his listeners, 'in ten minutes Madison Washington was master of that ship and all the crew lay at his feet'. His deliberate use of that word 'master' reveals his lifelong commitment to eradicating any and all trace of white supremacist power, and instead replacing it with an African diasporic definition of Black power based in an egalitarian philosophy of equal human rights. All his life, the fight for such a philosophy was Douglass's lifeblood, and was in all the speeches he gave across the world.

A hundred and fifty years ago, he said, 'My life's mission is to wake Scotland up to the atrocities of slavery'. In every speech, in every hall, he would tell audiences, 'You can be better, you can live a new life of liberty', and that, I think, was something he didn't see in England. In Edinburgh he's the leading figure in a campaign against white Scottish ministers taking 'blood-stained money' from white enslavers in the US South. He's fighting against the injustices of the Free Church of Scotland – 'Never', as he says, 'was a church more ironically named' – and he made sure the streets of Edinburgh had these words written on them: 'Send back the blood-stained money'. At one point he says, 'I saw that slogan everywhere – I saw it in Arbroath at the train station. I saw it in the city of Edinburgh'. The hills and mountains of Scotland were alive with that slogan, and you memorialise this reality in your film, too, in the scene when Douglass and the white female campaigners climb Arthur's Seat and carve those words into the land of Scotland.

IJ: And then there are the amazing Scottish folk songs we came across, like 'Send Back the Money'. When I first heard them, I couldn't really believe that there were actual ballads where Douglass is the protagonist. It's fantastic to be able to have those songs in the film.

CMB: All his life, Douglass was committed to an egalitarian human rights philosophy for all people of all nations, a philosophy of social justice that extended to the natural world and to animal rights. He lived as he spoke, and dedicated his life to his egalitarian humanitarianism. He was renowned for his compassion and kindness, and found suffering of any kind intolerable. Here in Scotland, his love and compassion was for people living destitute on the streets across the nation. It was children who were living penniless and starving at the foot of Arthur's Seat who helped him carve out his slogans, so when I hear 'Send Back the Money', I hear those human rights activist children who followed Douglass, and who sang his words back to him. What you beautifully bring to life, too, is Douglass as a person sitting by the fire in the York Hotel, Edinburgh, just back from Glasgow, and victoriously writing to a friend, 'Scotland is all ablaze with anti-slavery excitement'. So you memorialise the lifelong struggles he experienced as he dedicated his life and work to the undying fight to transform pain into power on all of 'freedom's battlegrounds'.

IJ: This is where Scotland becomes very important in sharing that as a kind of legacy, because of course Douglass chose Scotland, not England, to reside in, and today we can say that Scotland leads the way in thinking about certain questions in a way that England doesn't. Which makes me very happy to be here too! And it feels very right to have *Lessons of the Hour* making not just its UK but its European premiere in Scotland. I think Douglass would have approved of that.

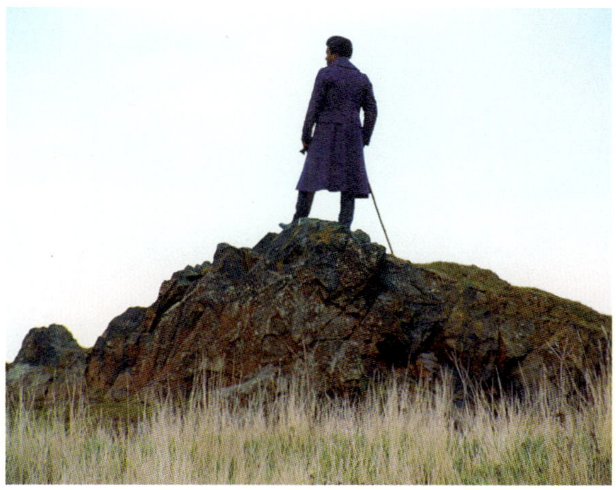

Film still from *Lessons of the Hour* 2019, featuring Ray Fearon as Frederick Douglass

1. Nina Simone speaking in the documentary *Nina: An Historical Perspective* by Peter Rodis, 1970

# LESSONS OF THE HOUR

2019

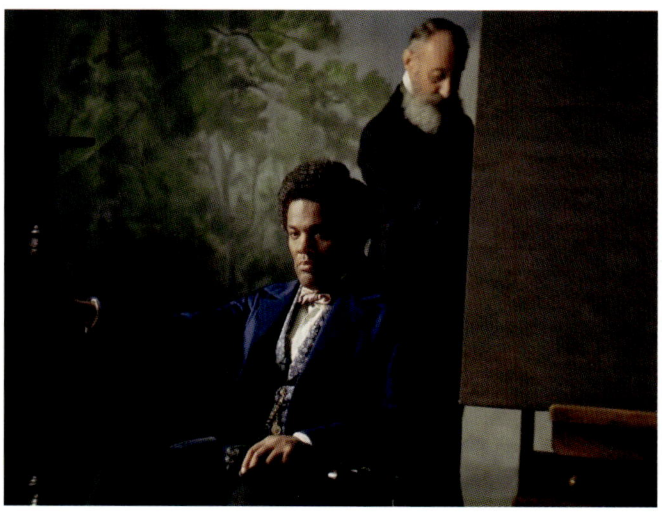

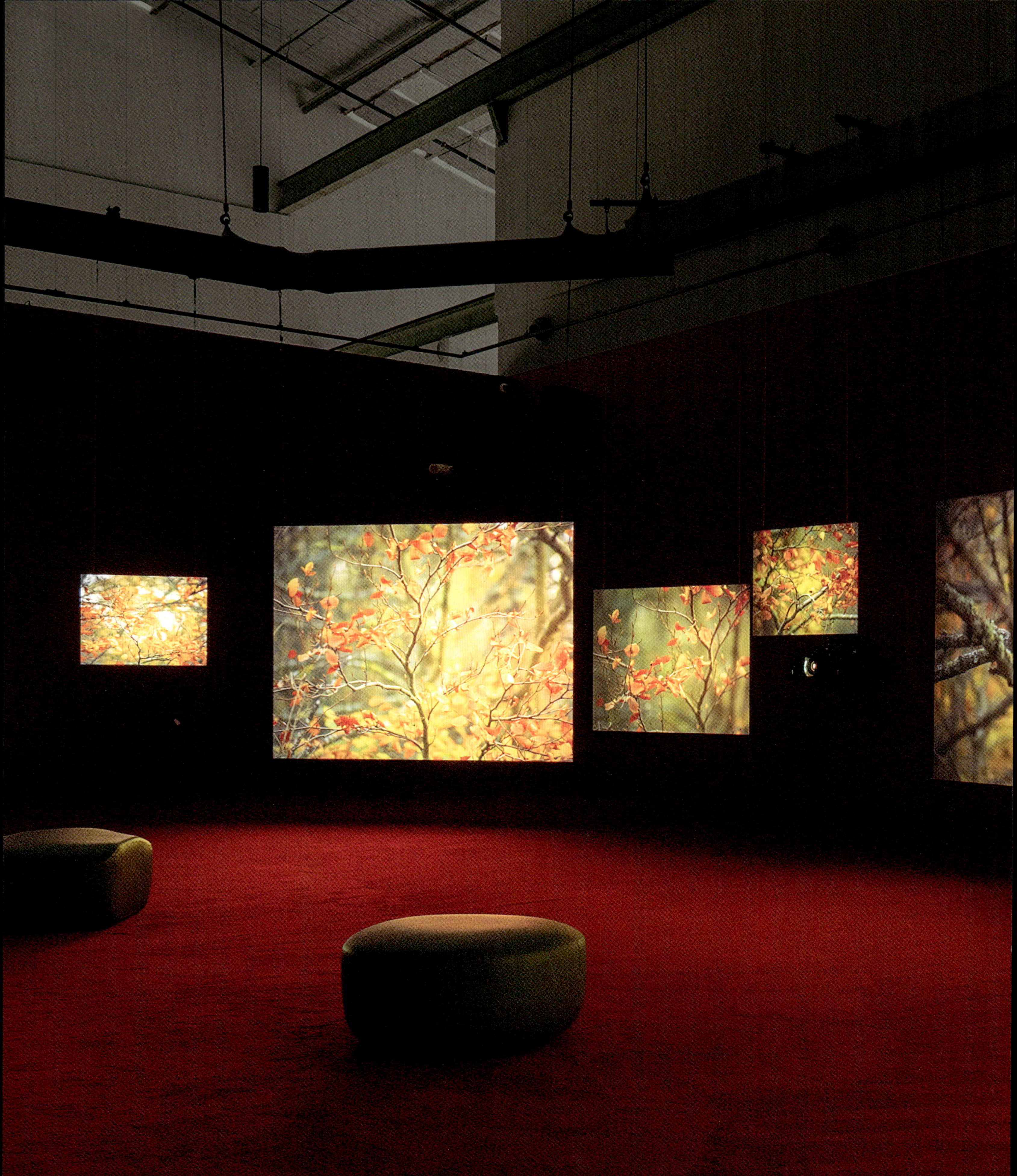

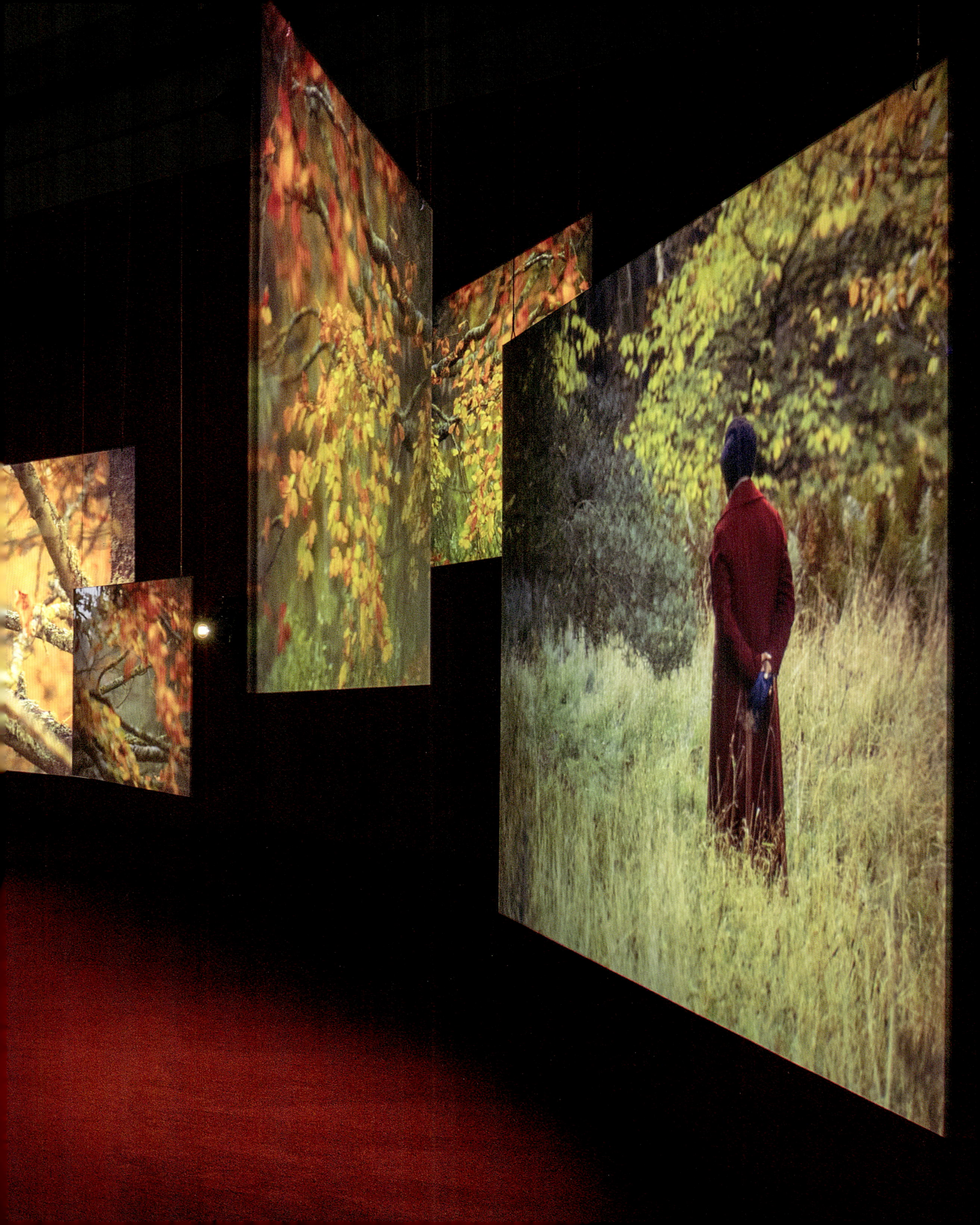

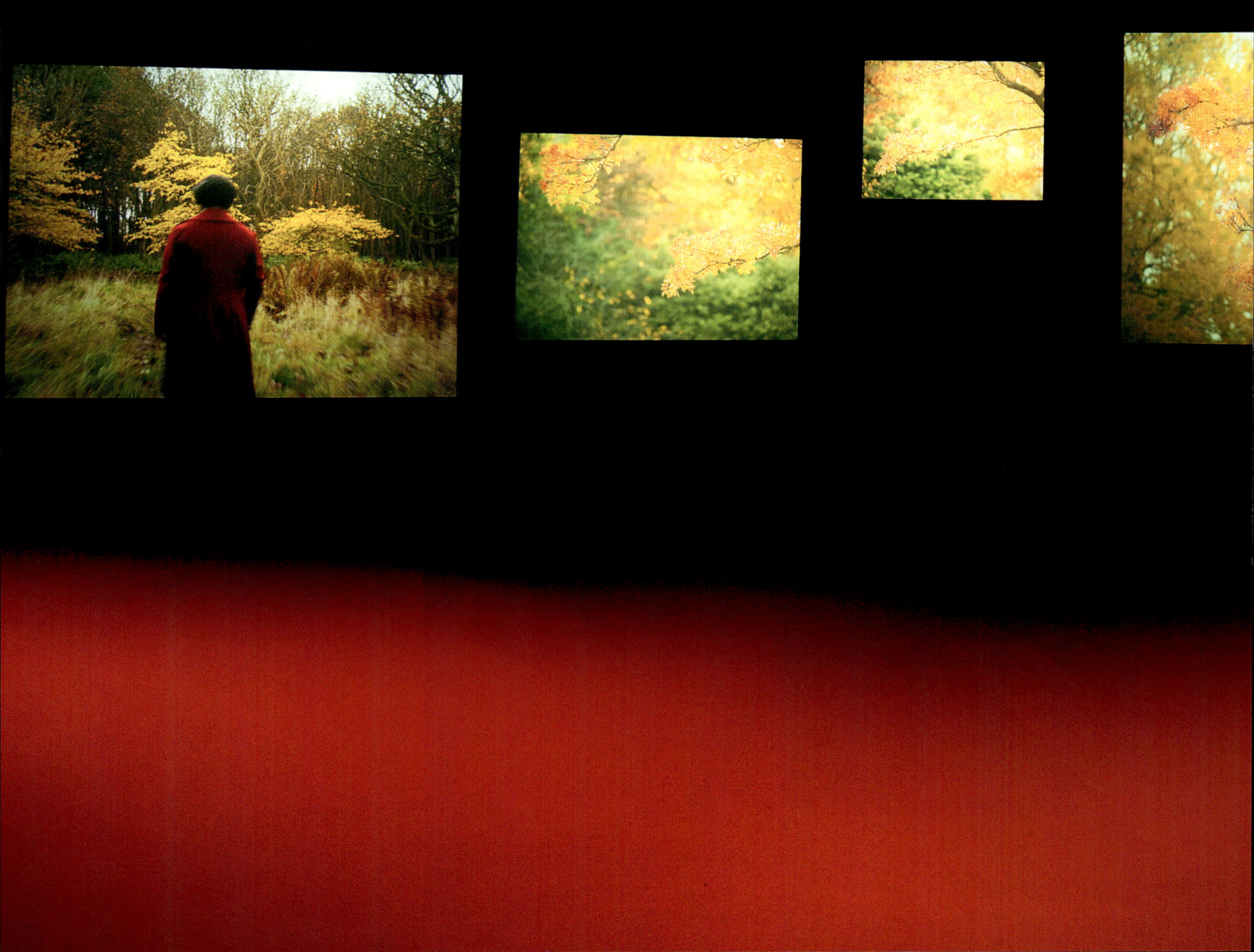

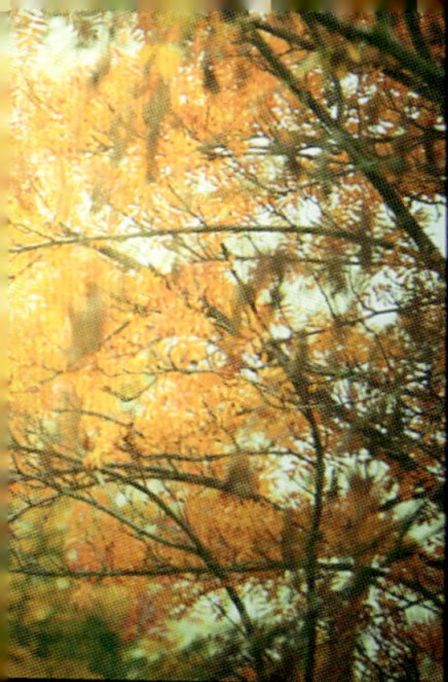
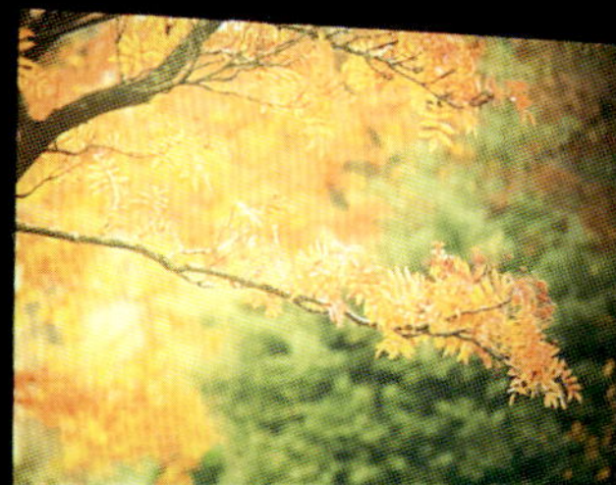
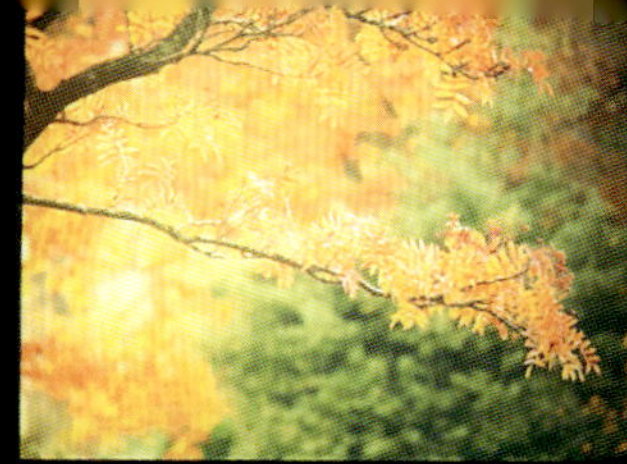
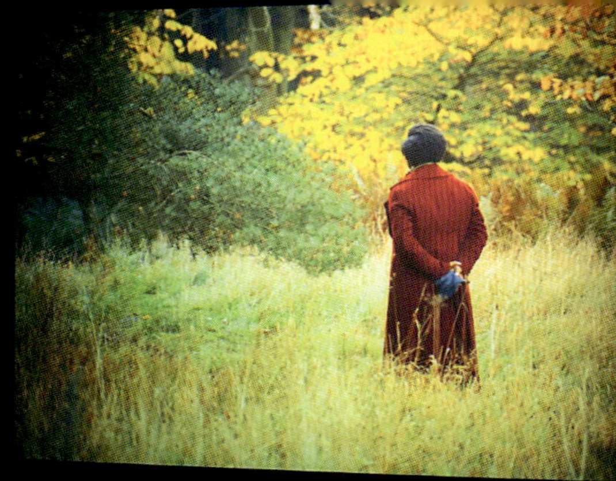

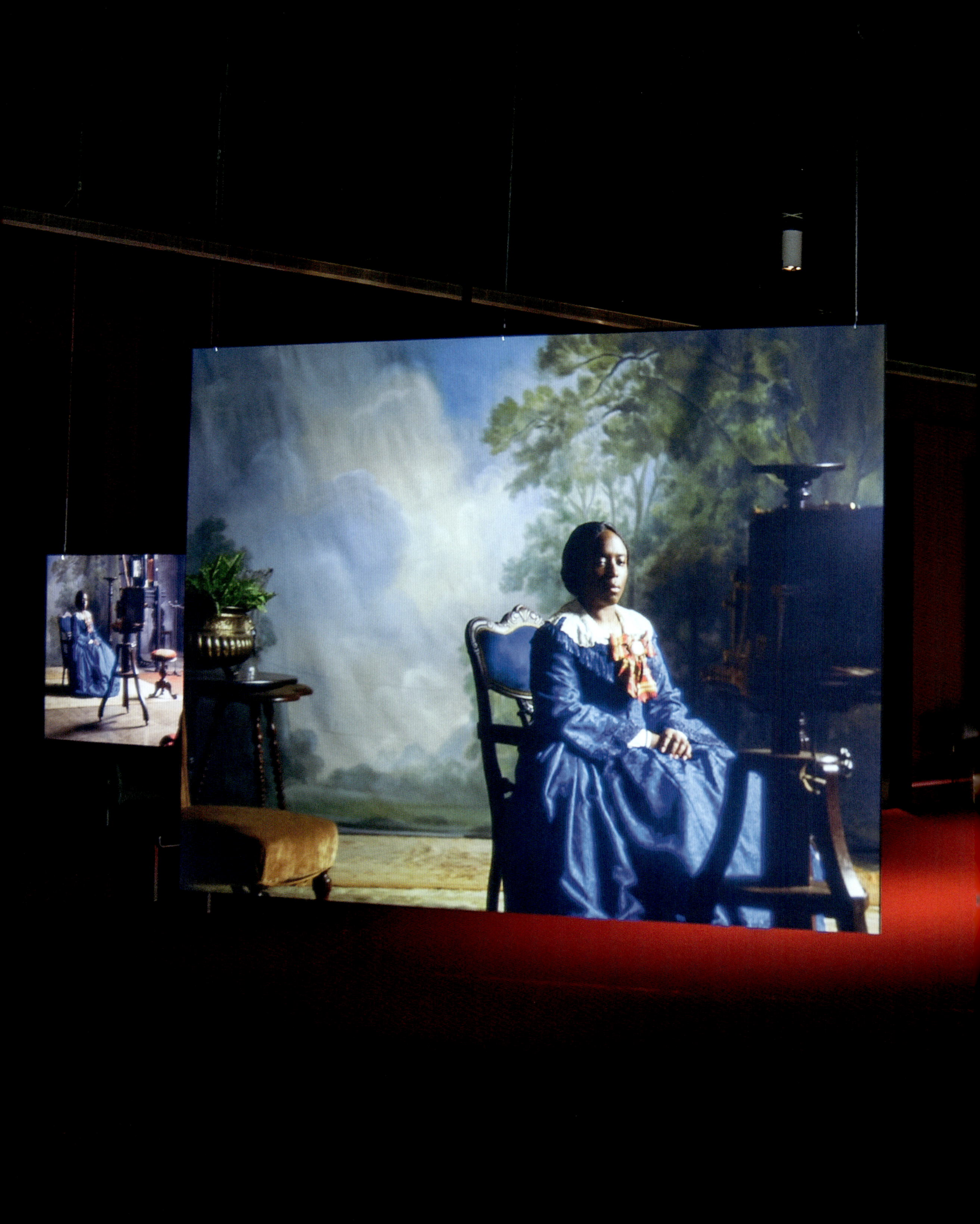

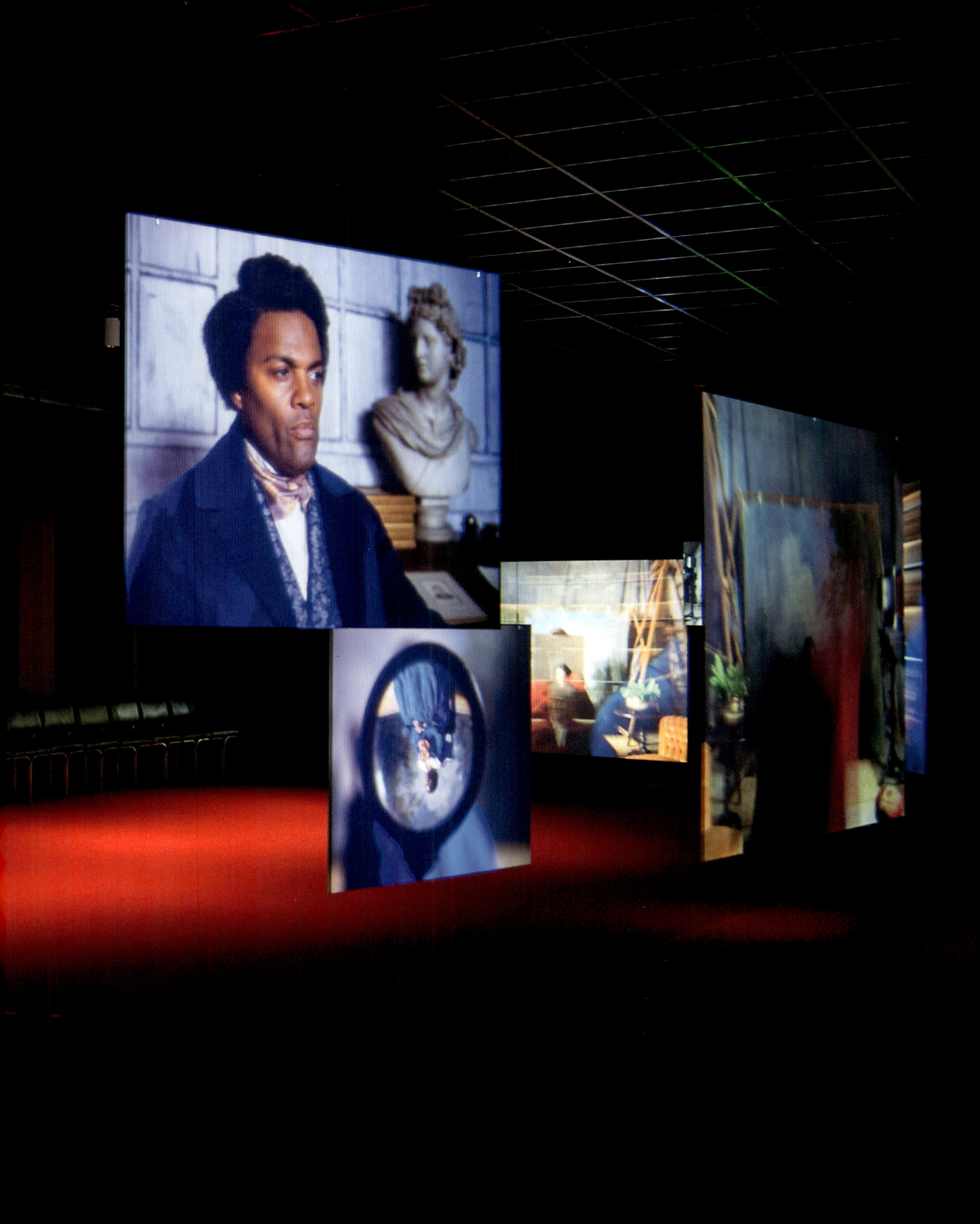

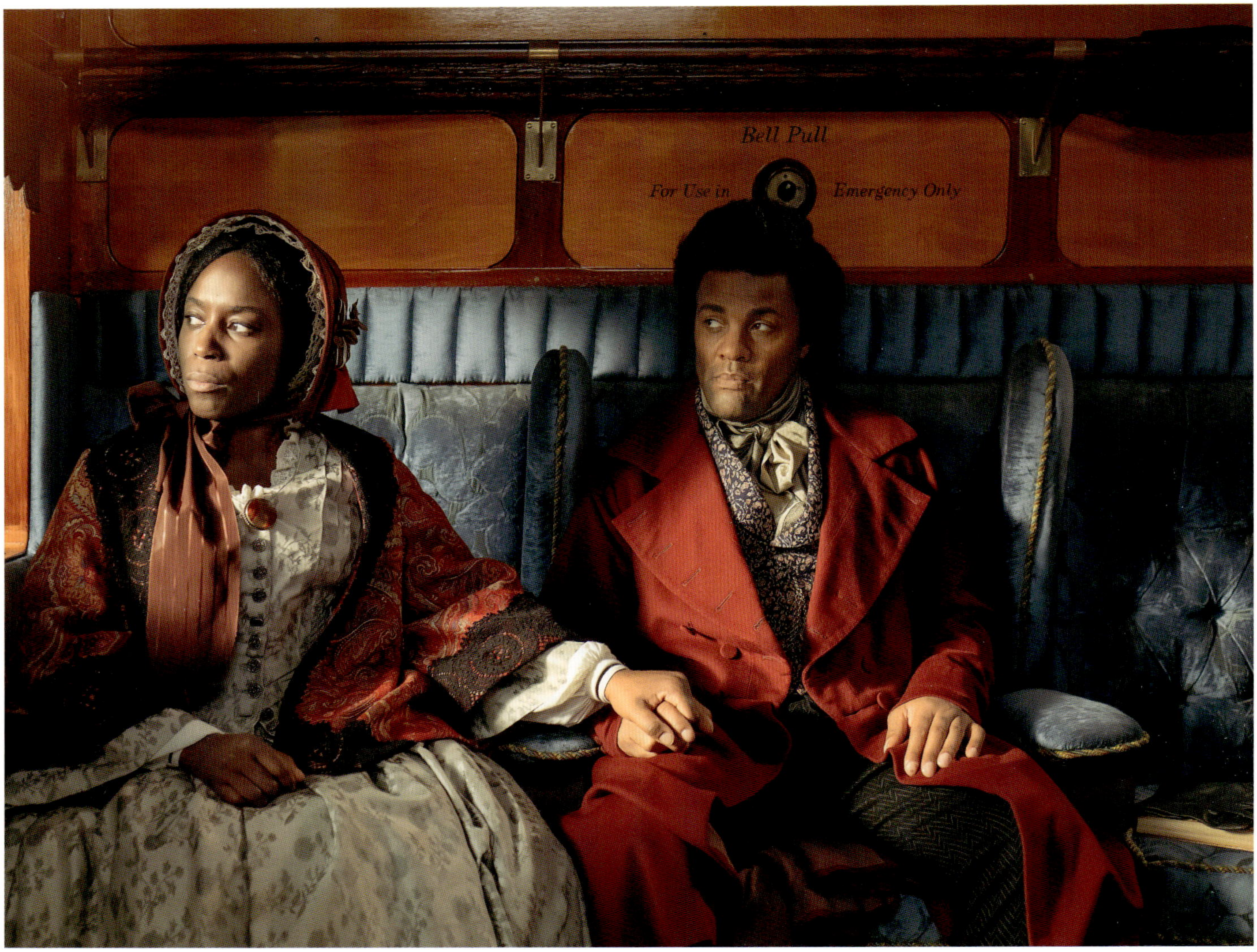


*The North Star (Lessons of the Hour)* 2019

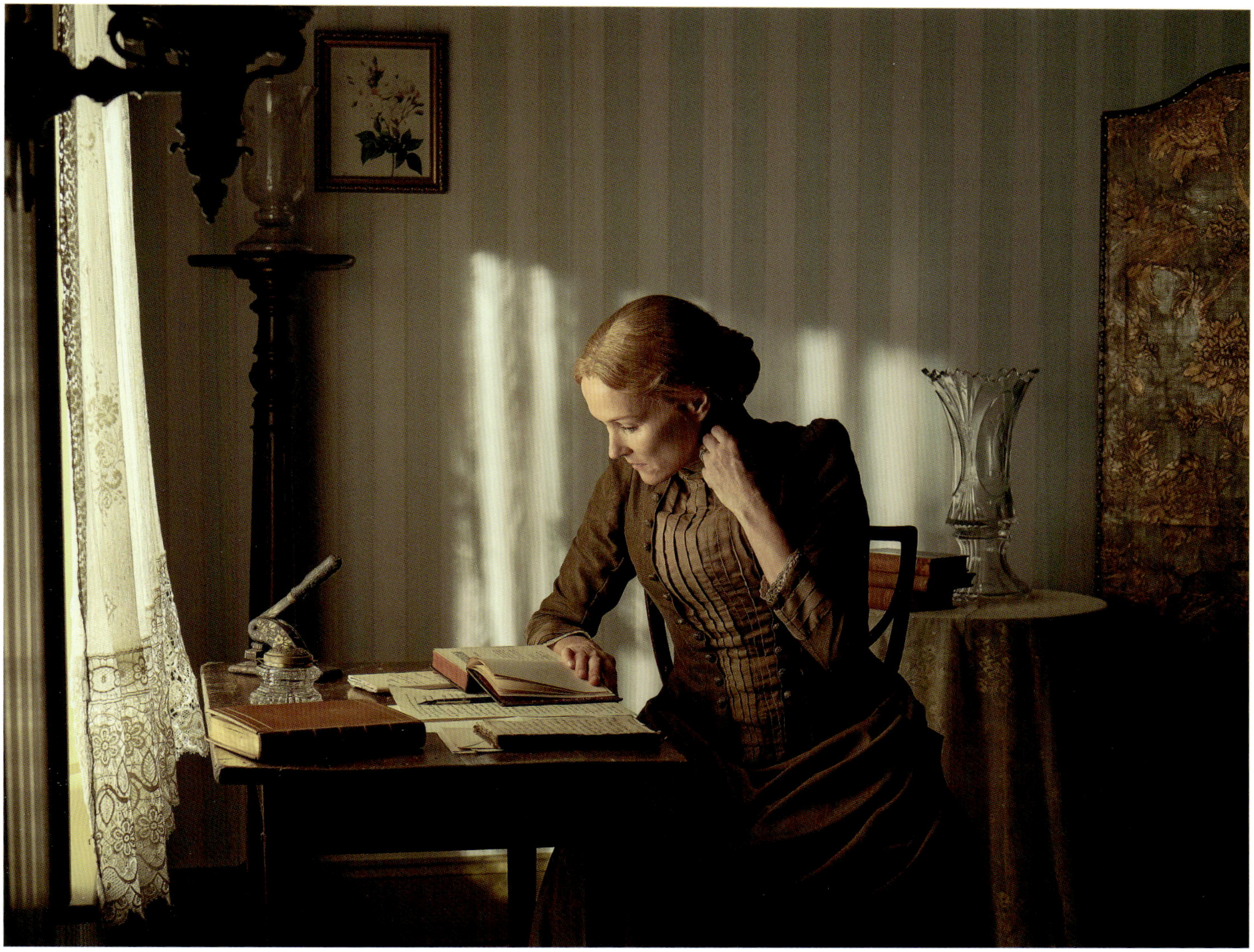

 *Helen Pitts, Class of 1859 (Lessons of the Hour)* 2019

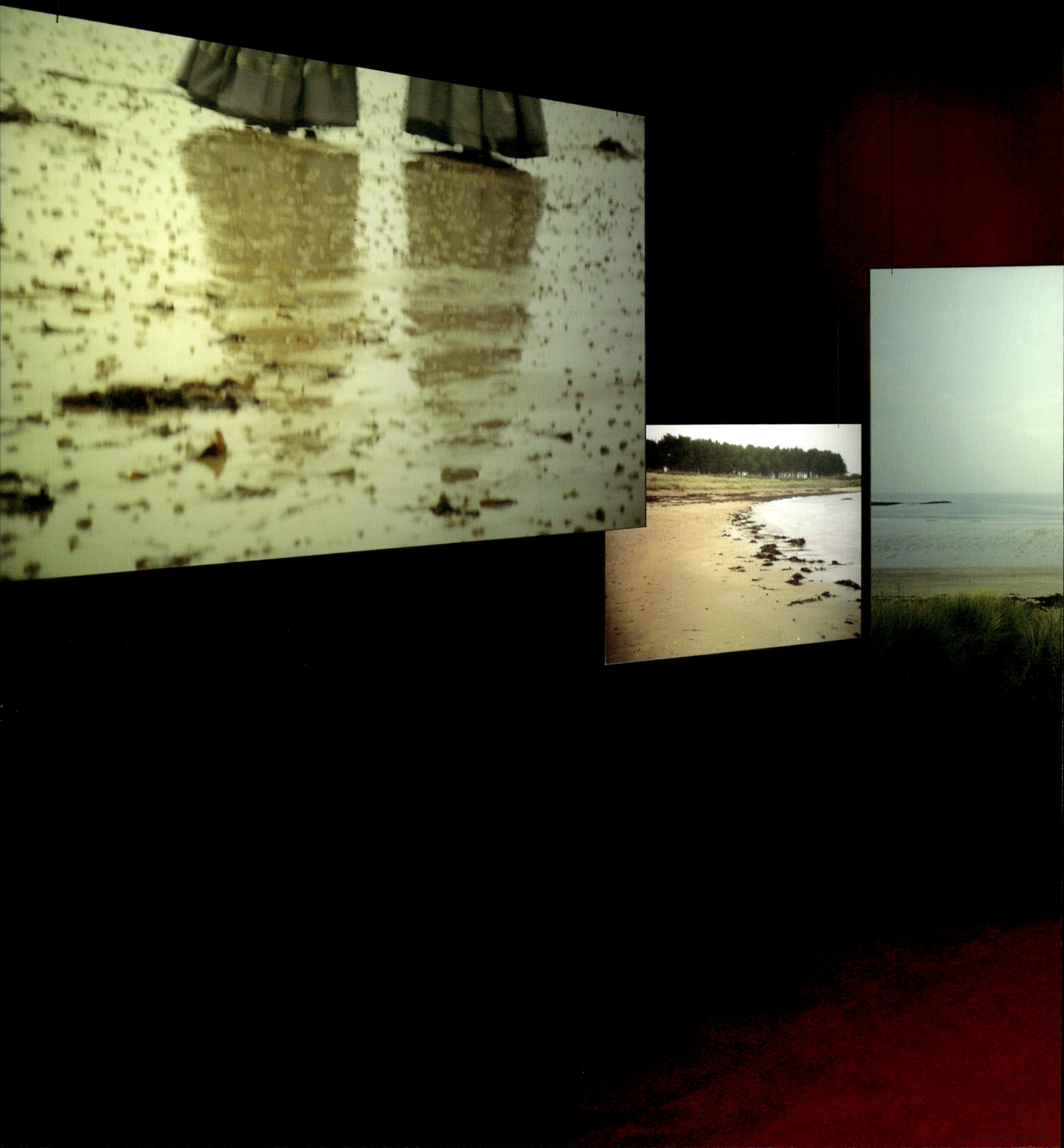

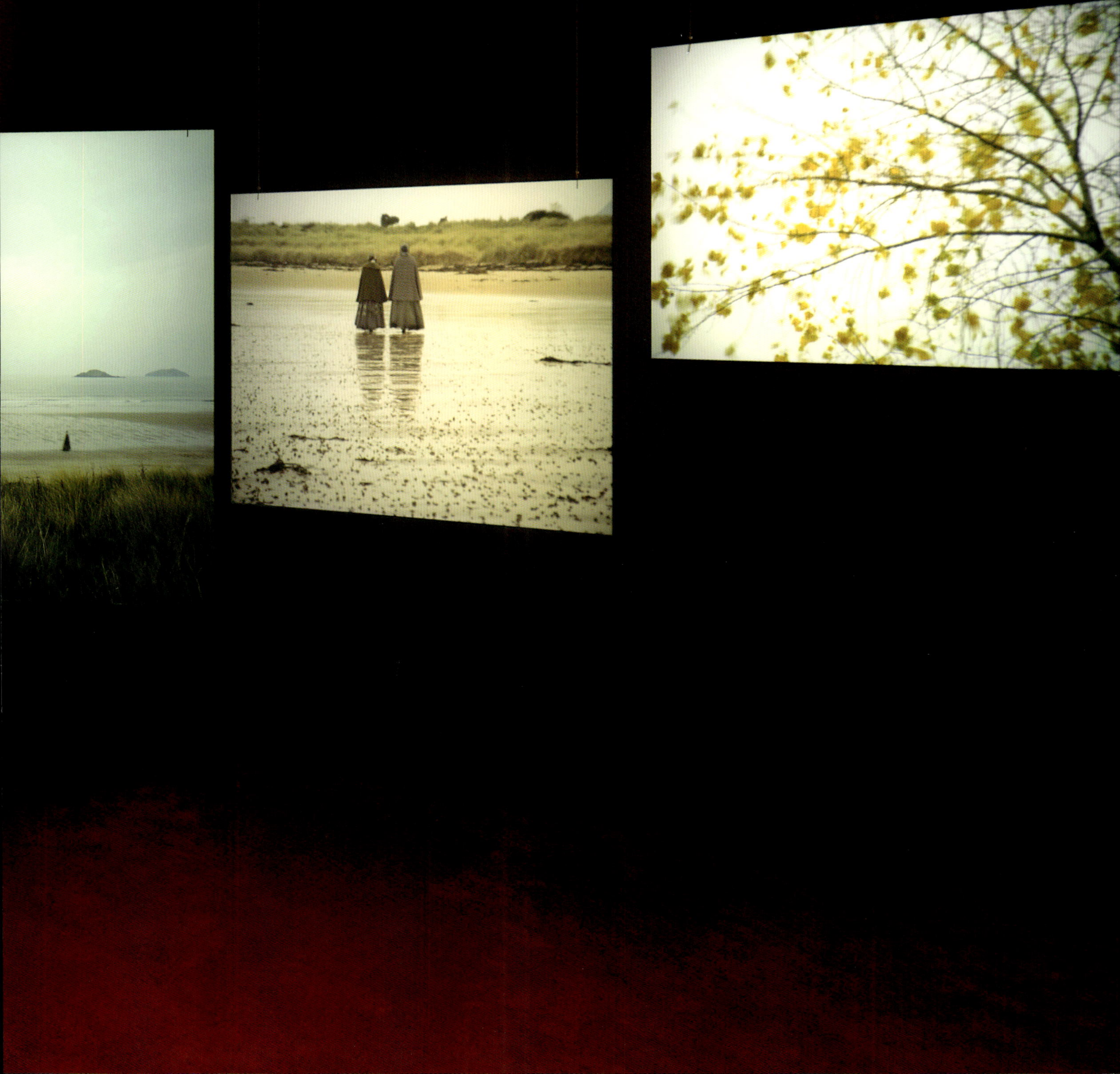

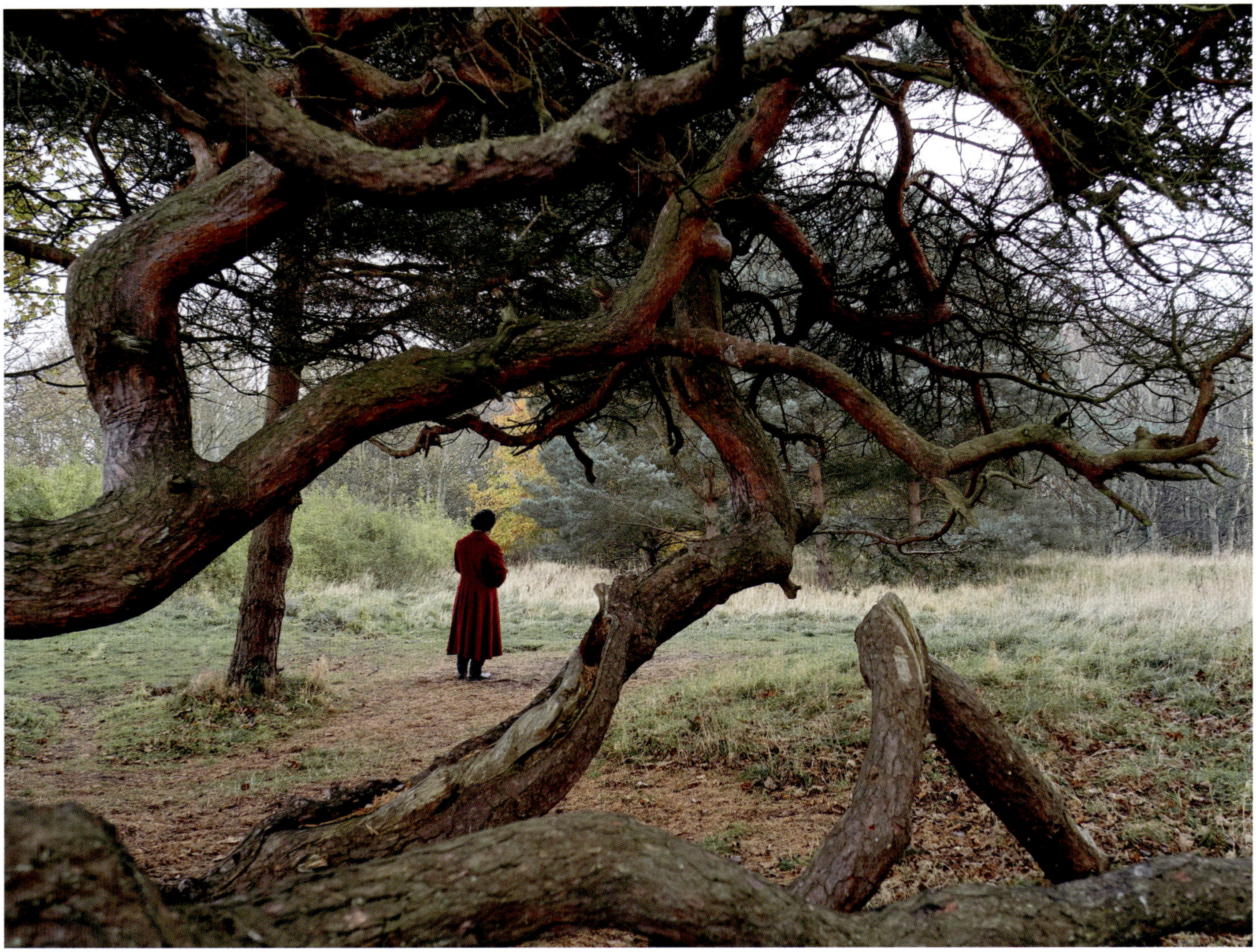

*Rapture 1846 (Lessons of the Hour)* 2019

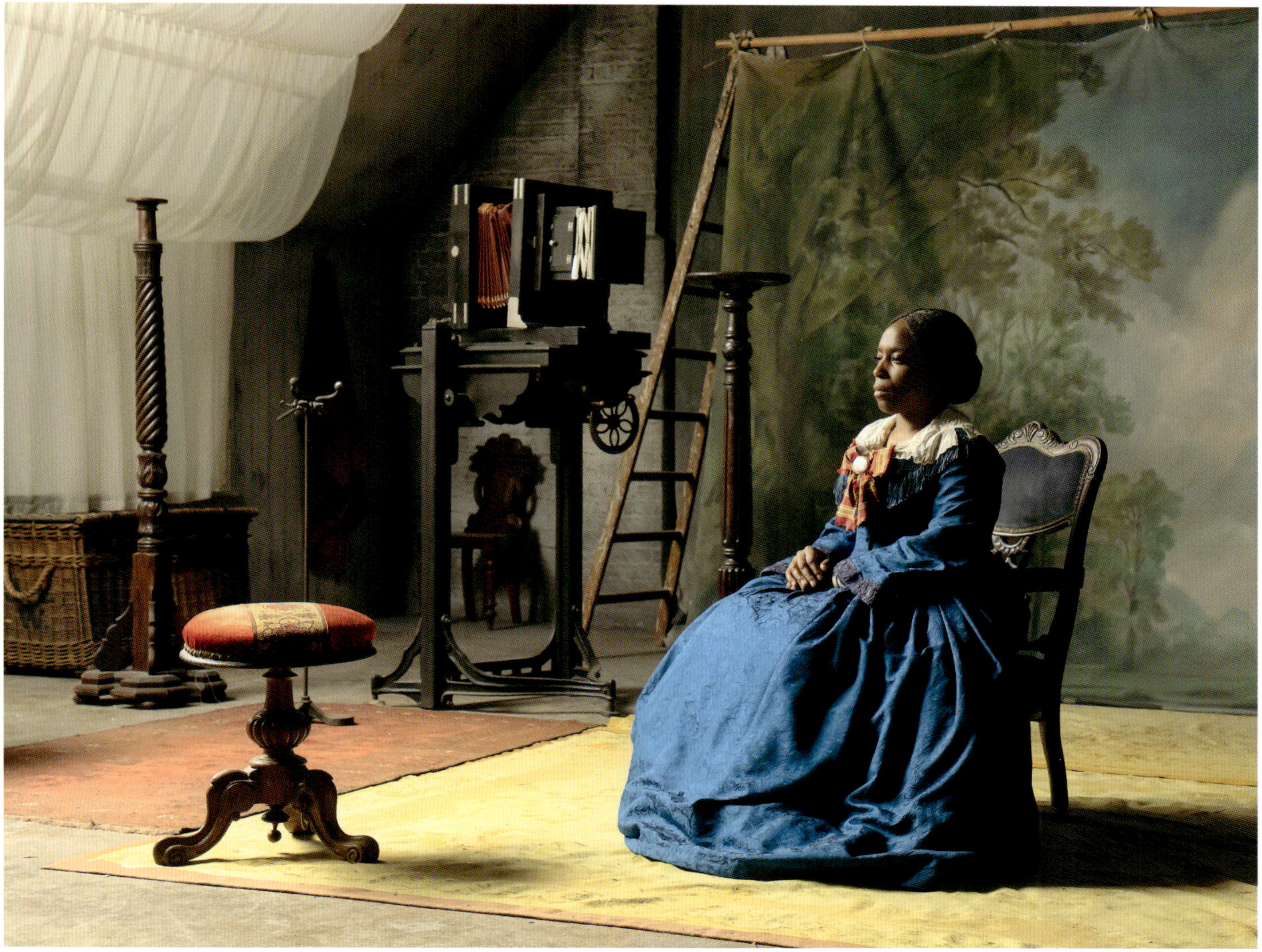

 *The Lady of the Lake (Lessons of the Hour)* 2019

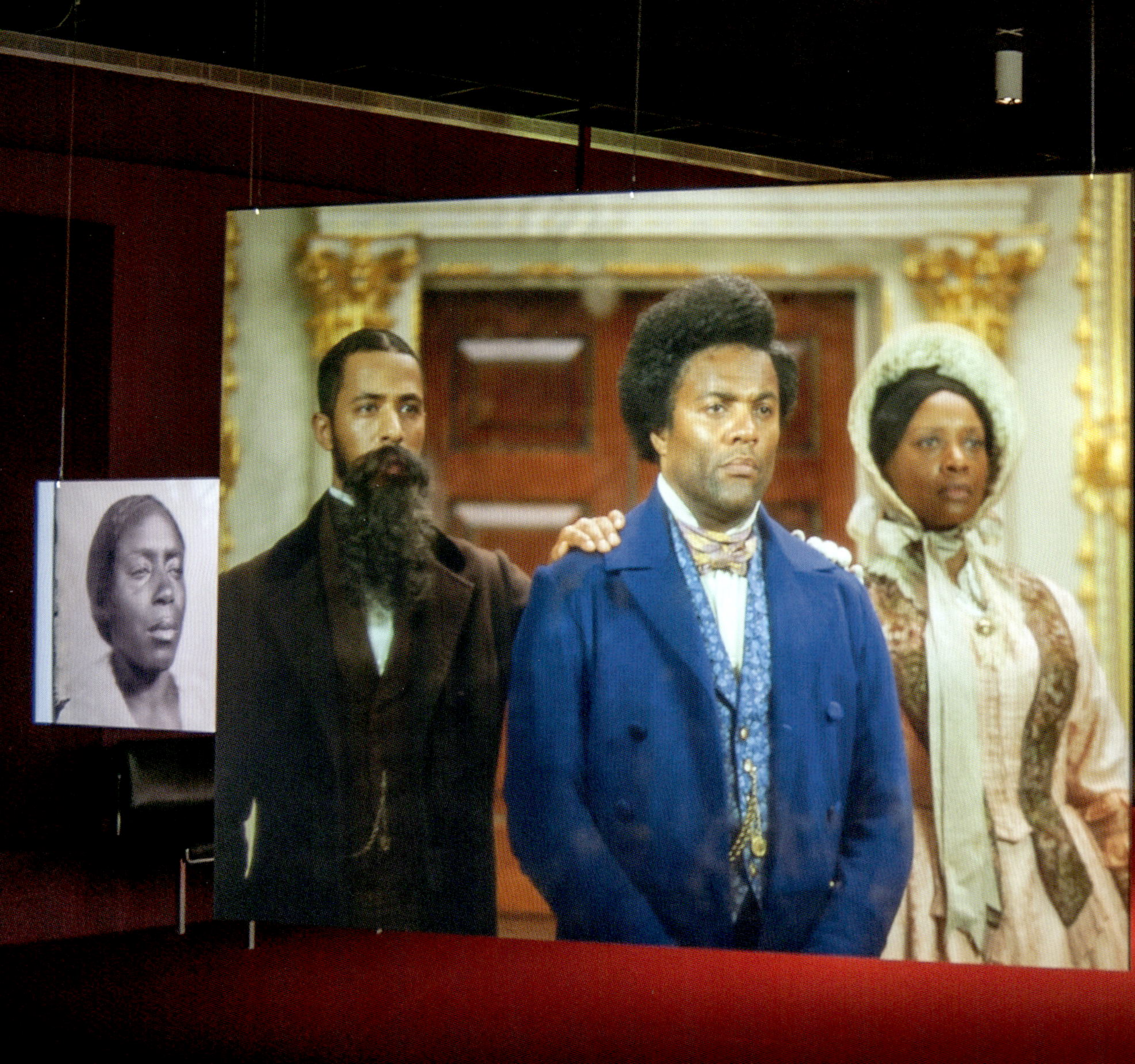

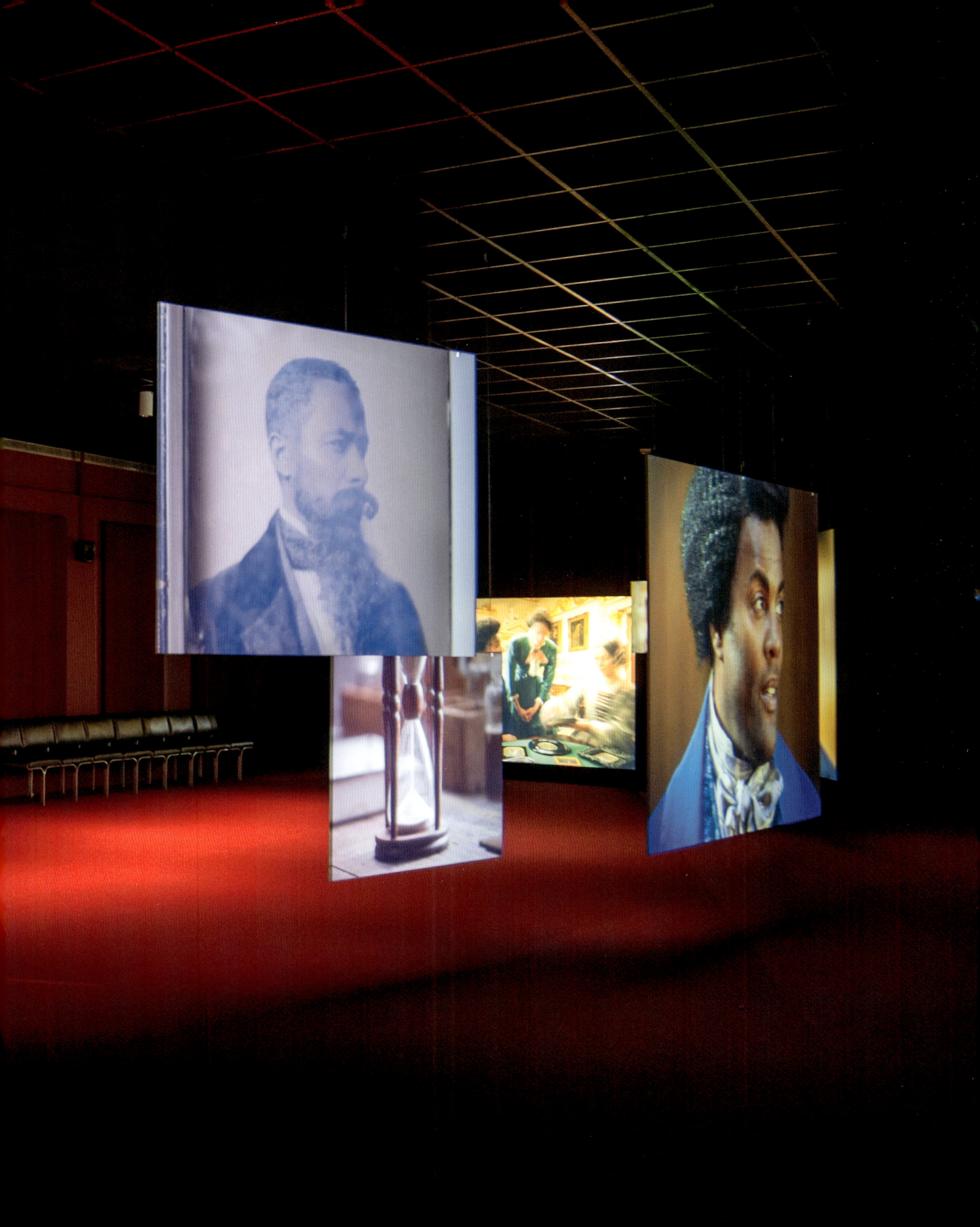

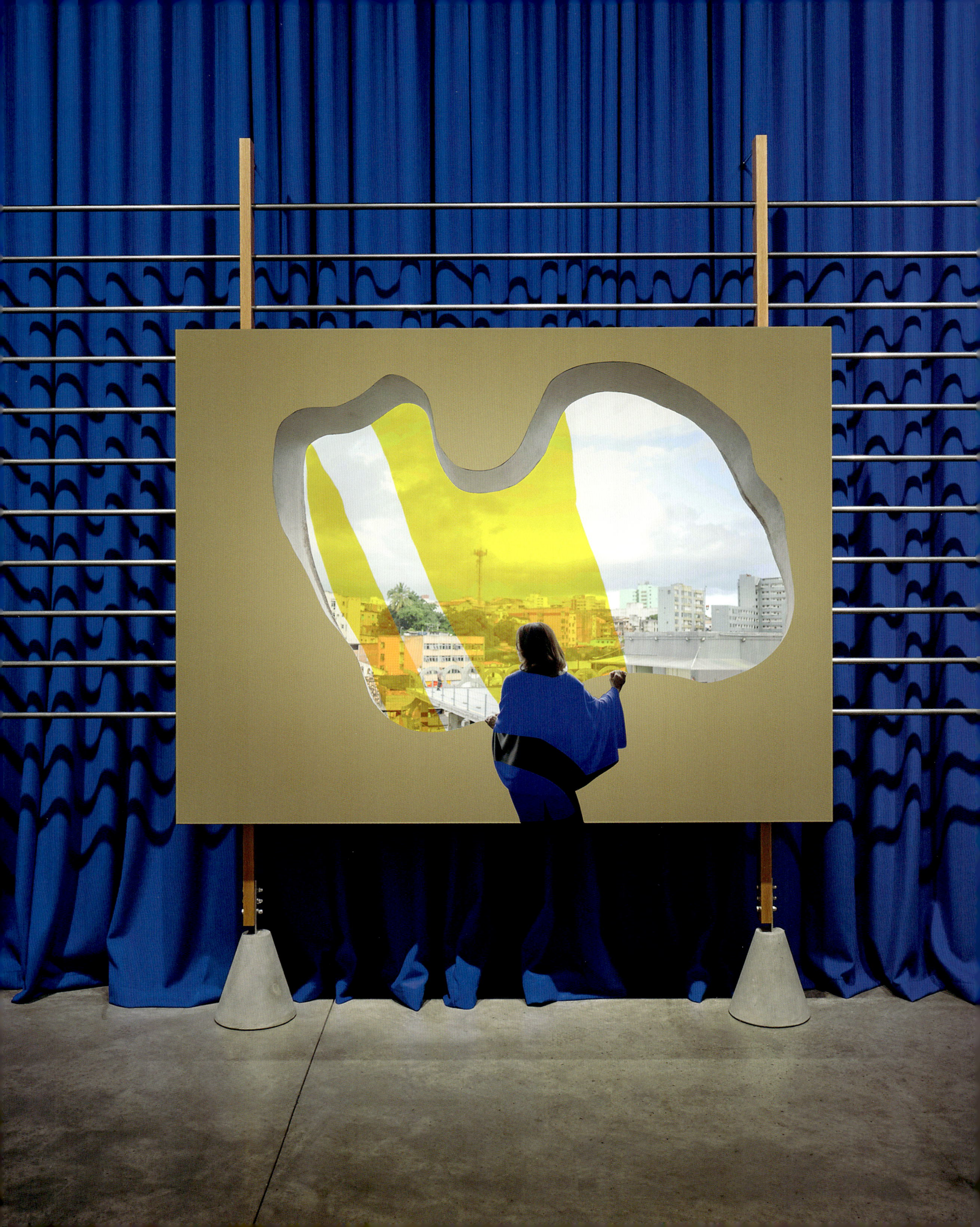

# LINA BO BARDI - A MARVELLOUS ENTANGLEMENT

2019

▶ 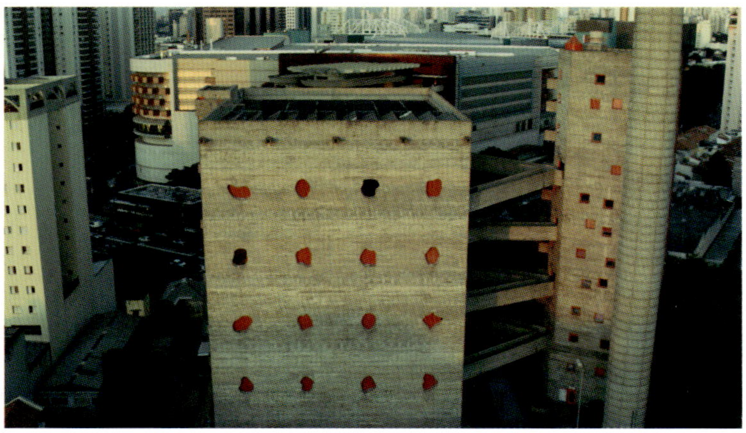

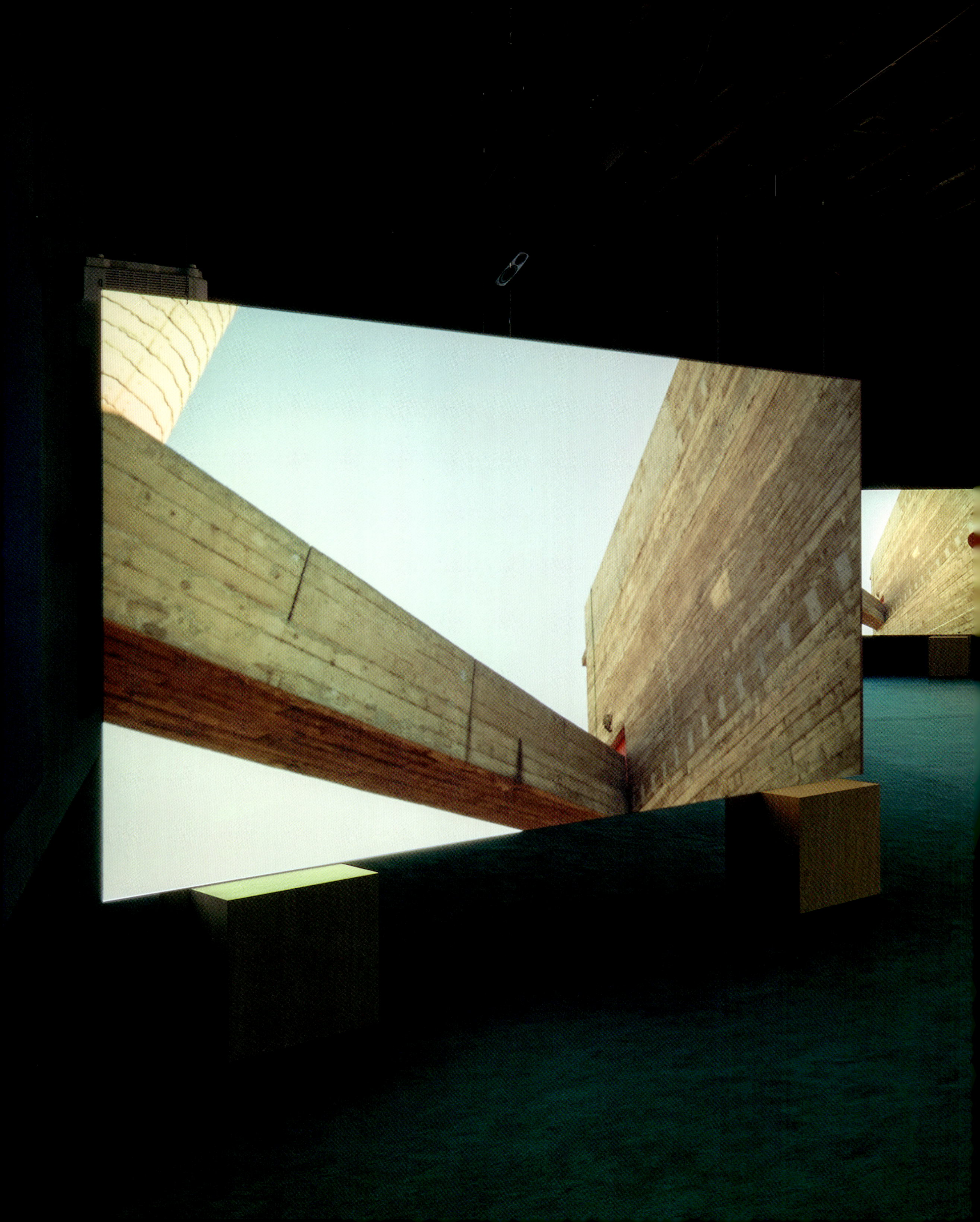

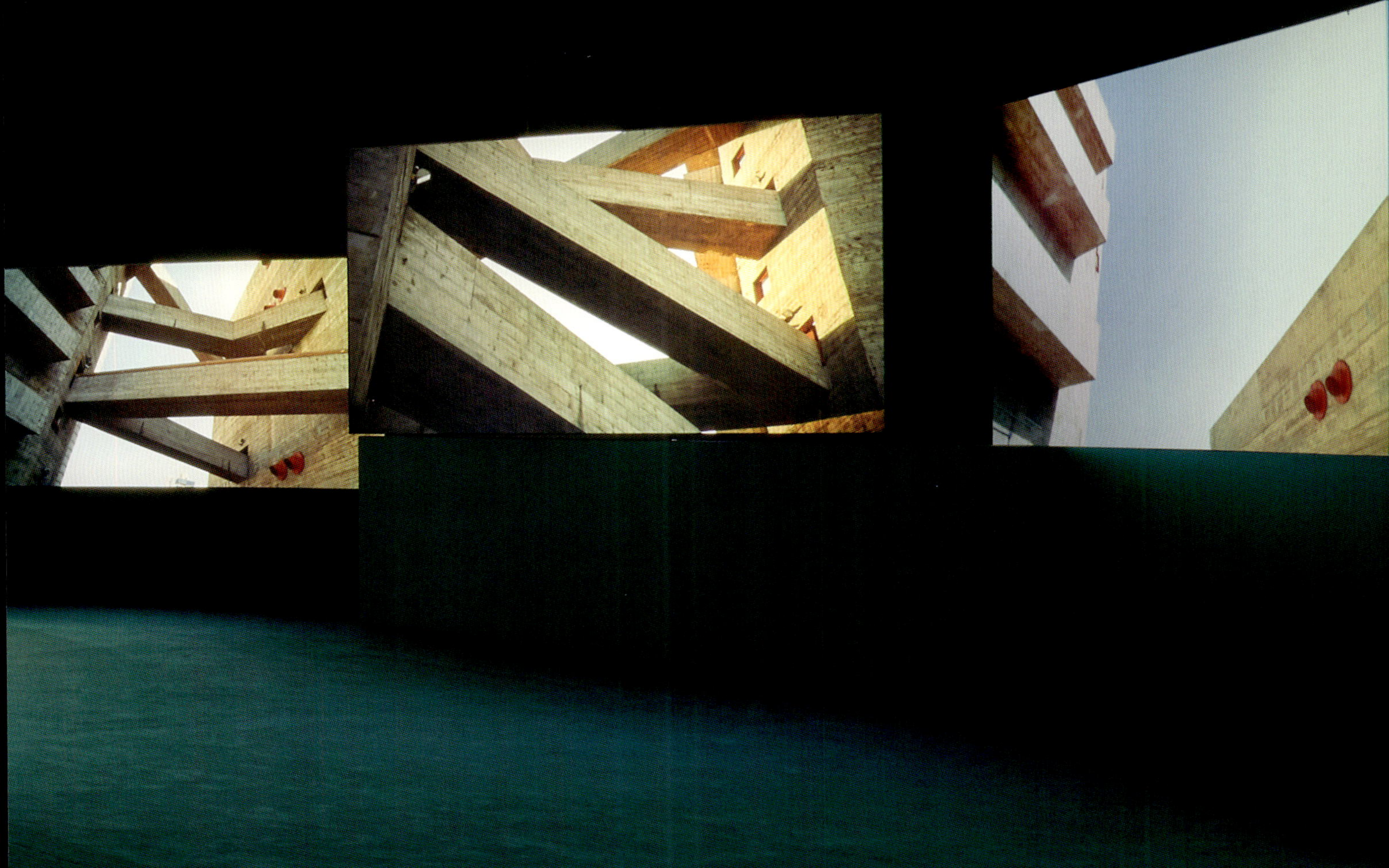

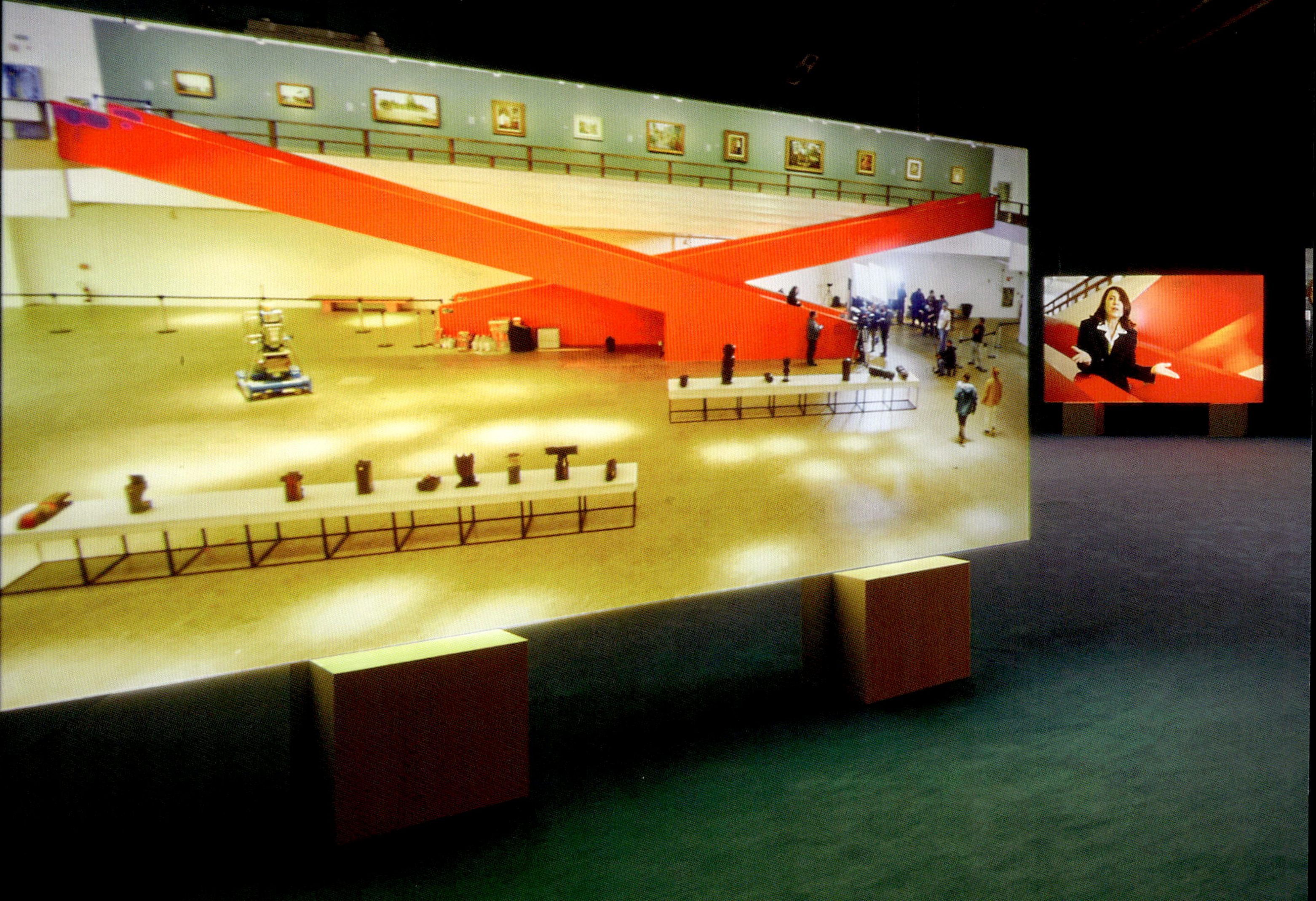

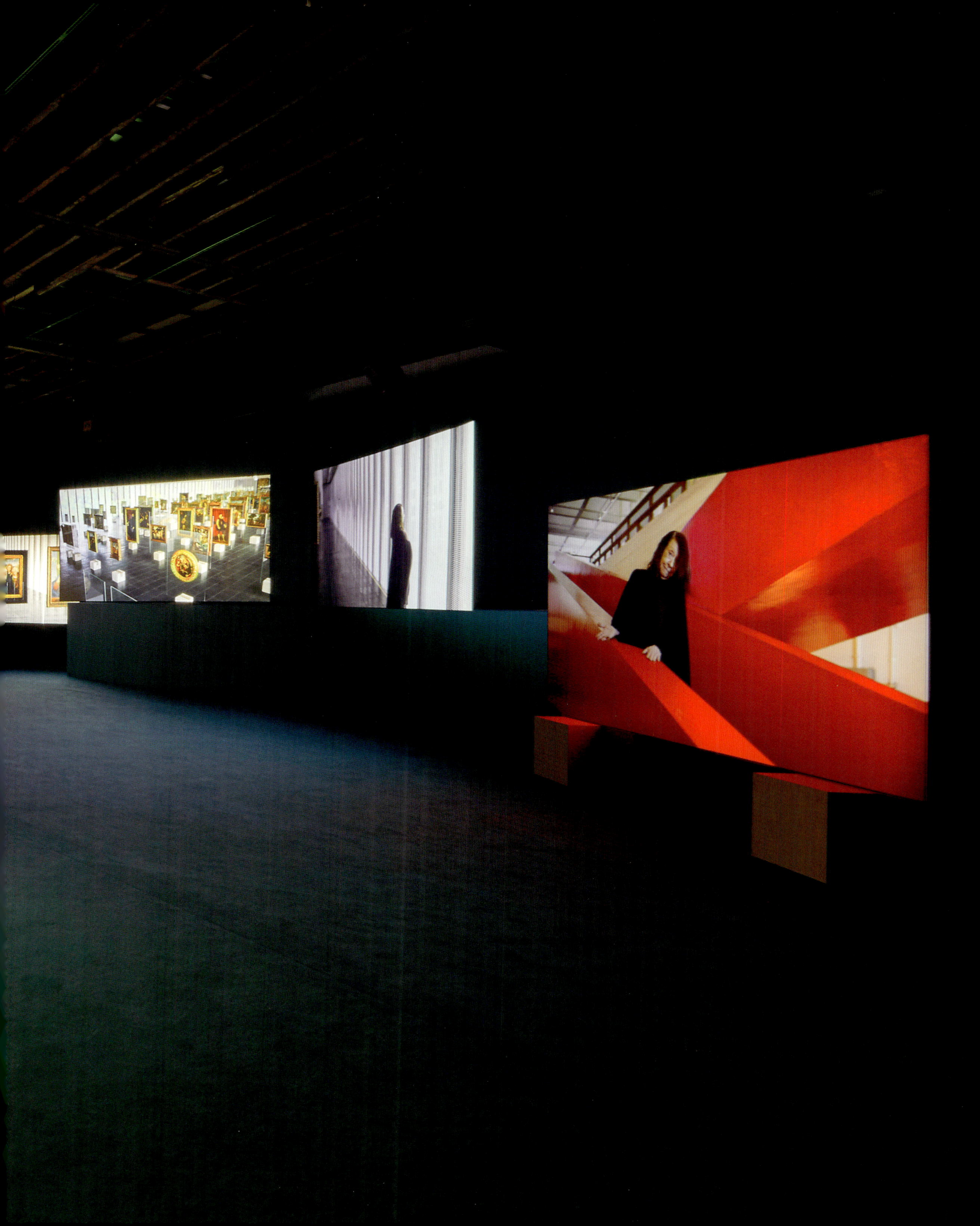

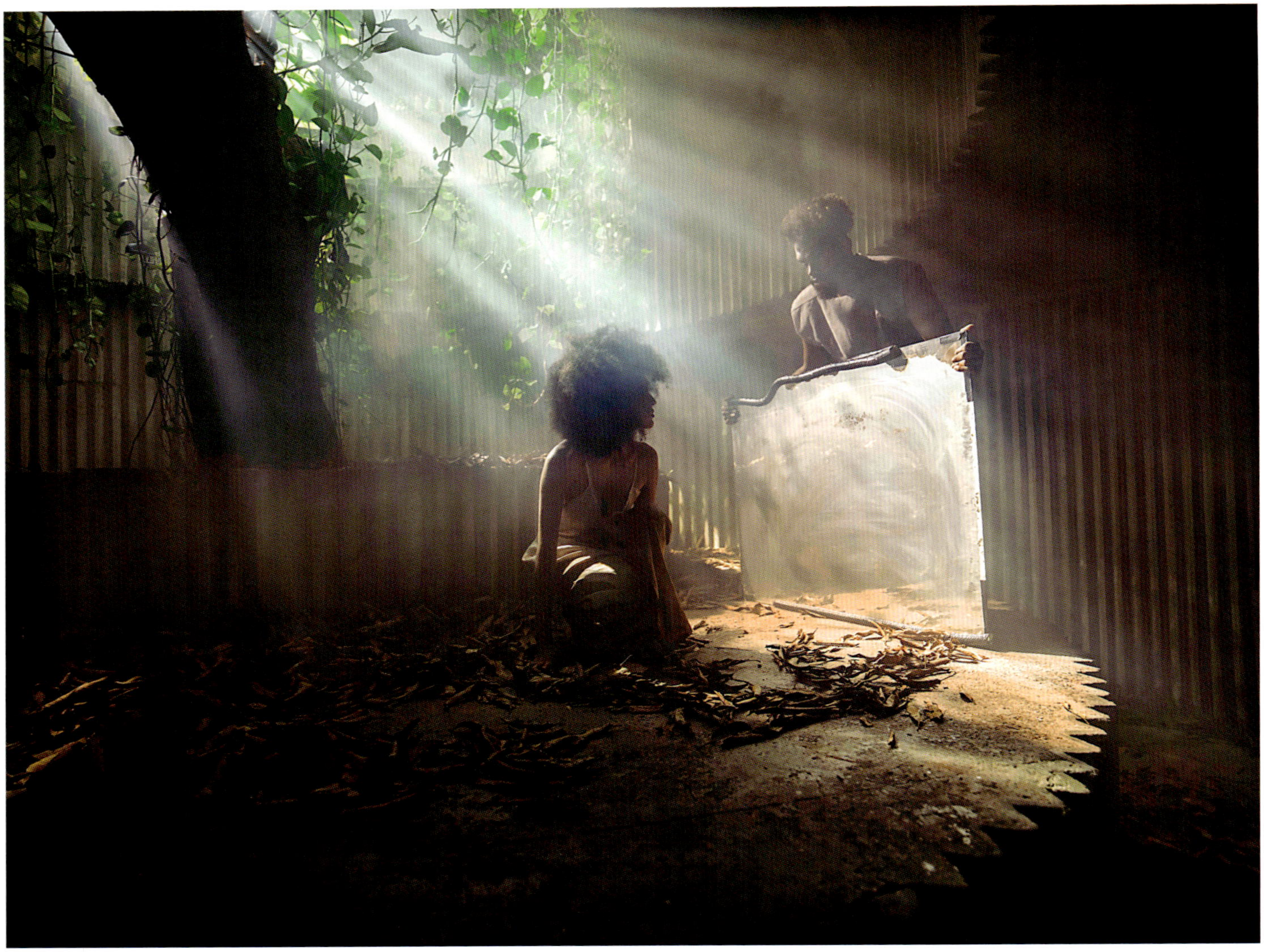

*Almas belas, almas menos belas / Beautiful Souls, Less Beautiful Souls (Lina Bo Bardi – A Marvellous Entanglement)* 2019

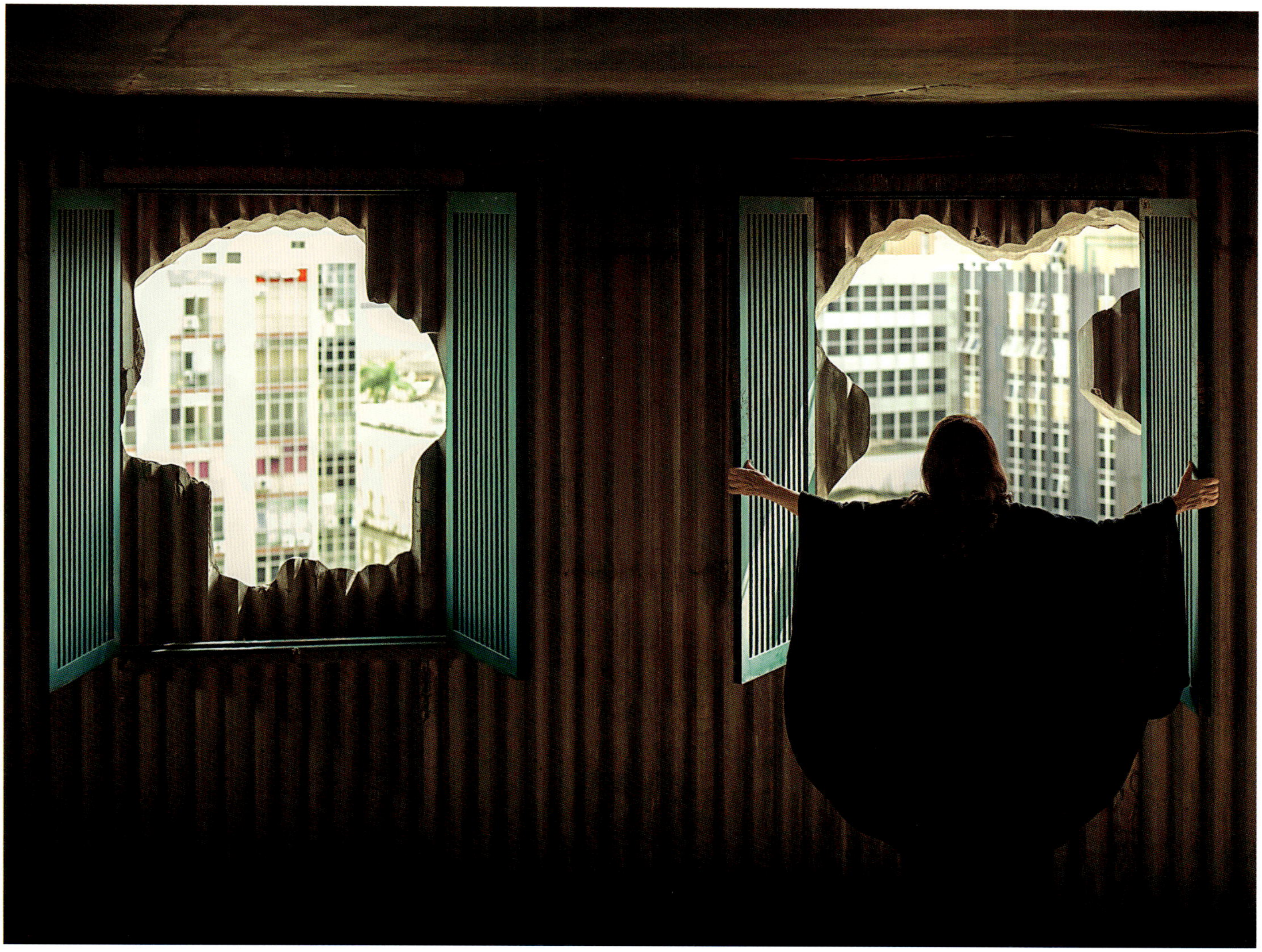

63 *Tecnologia pré-histórica / Prehistoric Technology* (*Lina Bo Bardi – A Marvellous Entanglement*) 2019

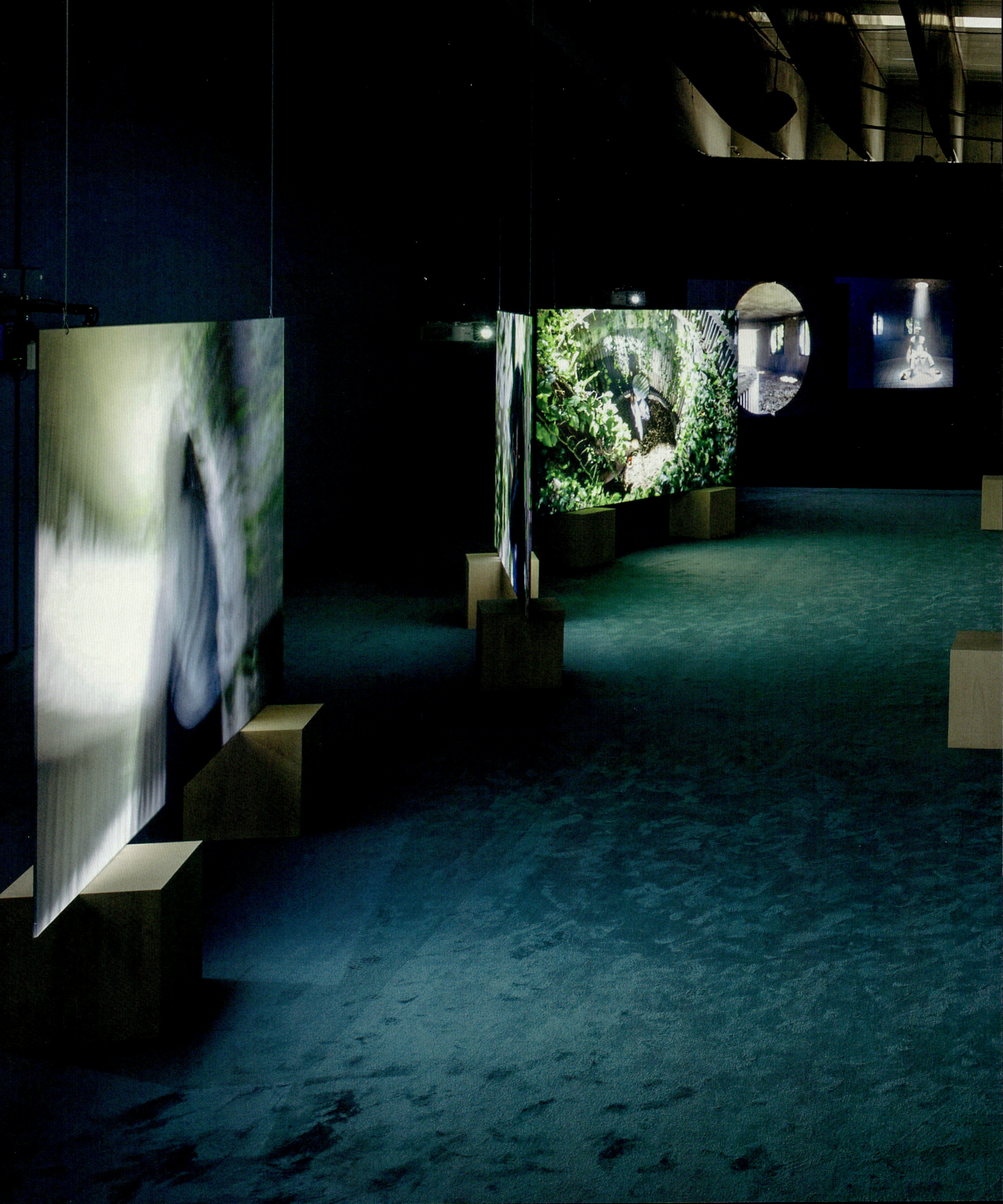

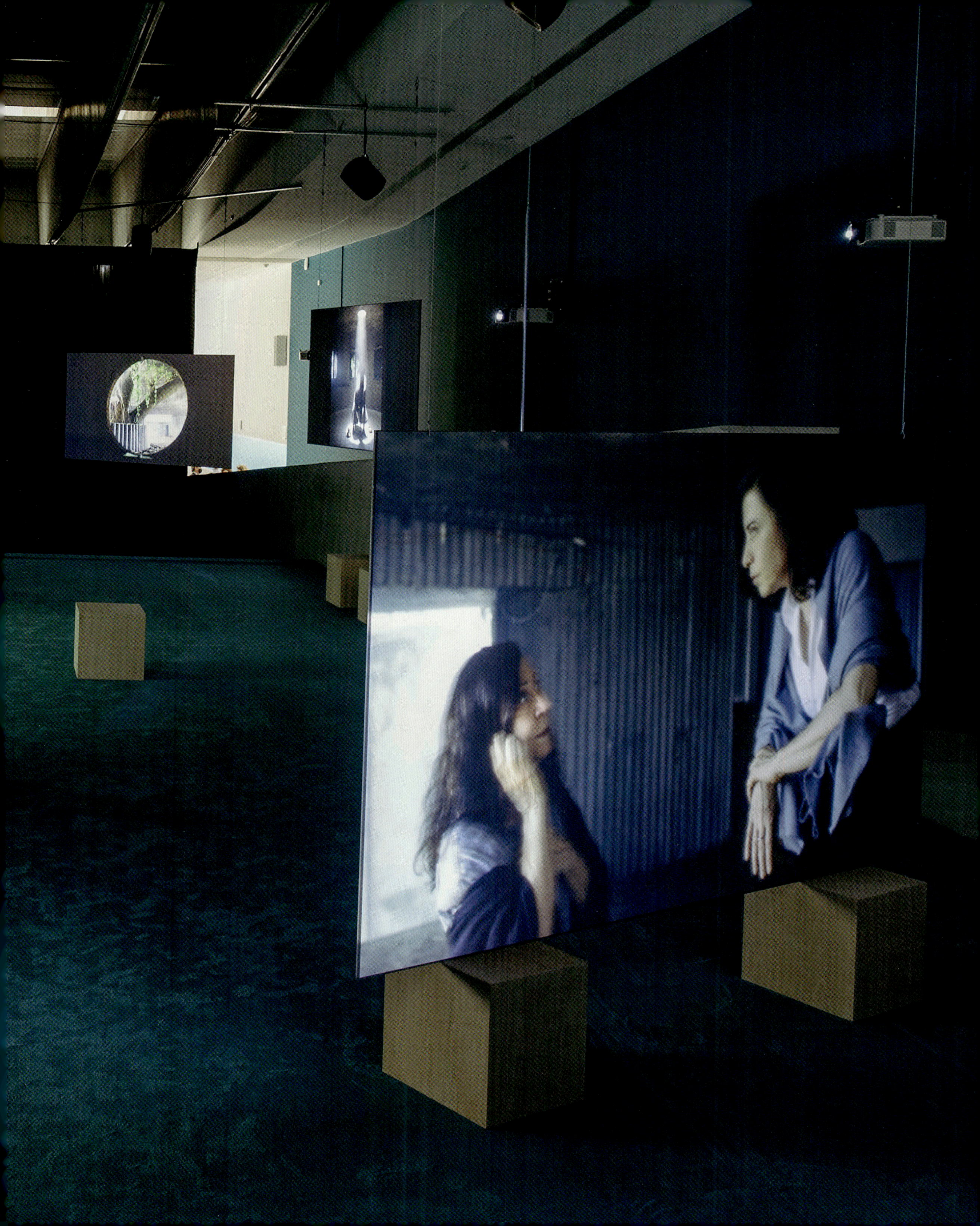

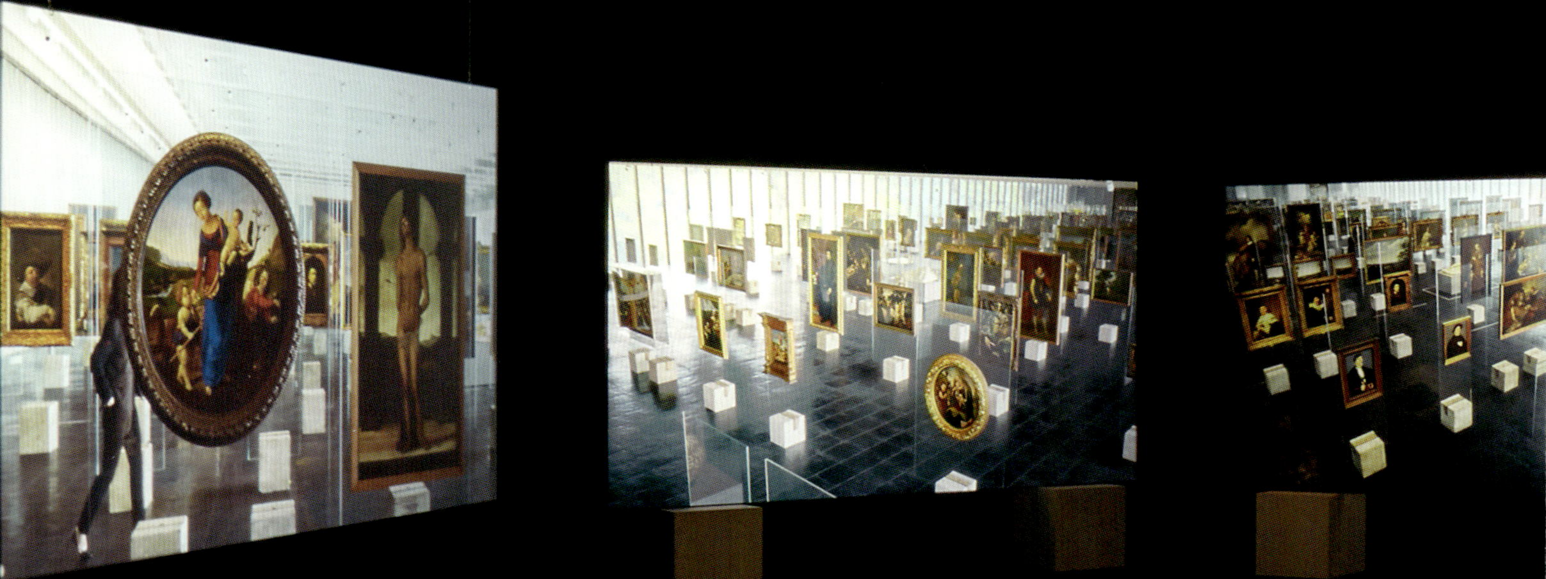

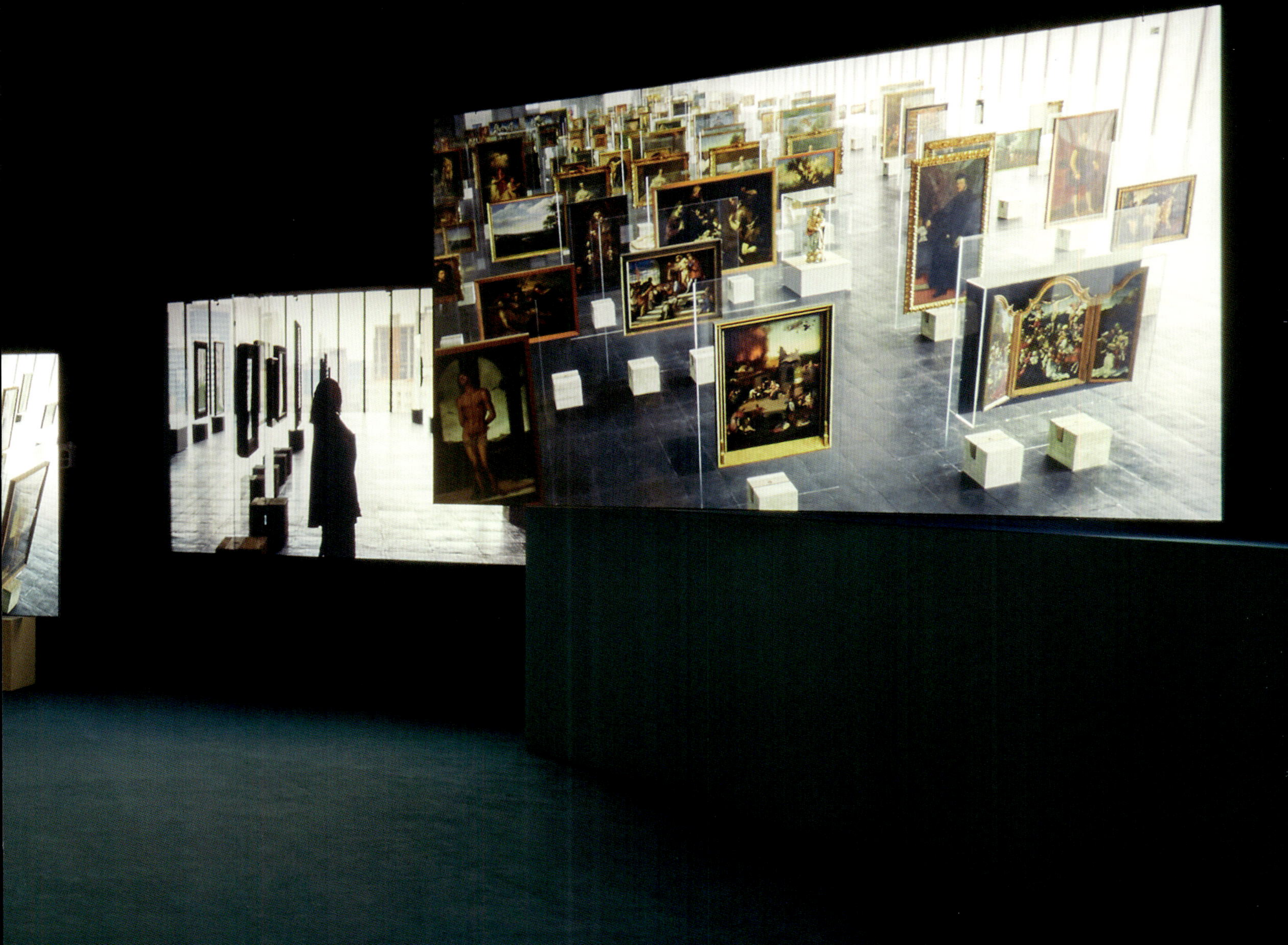

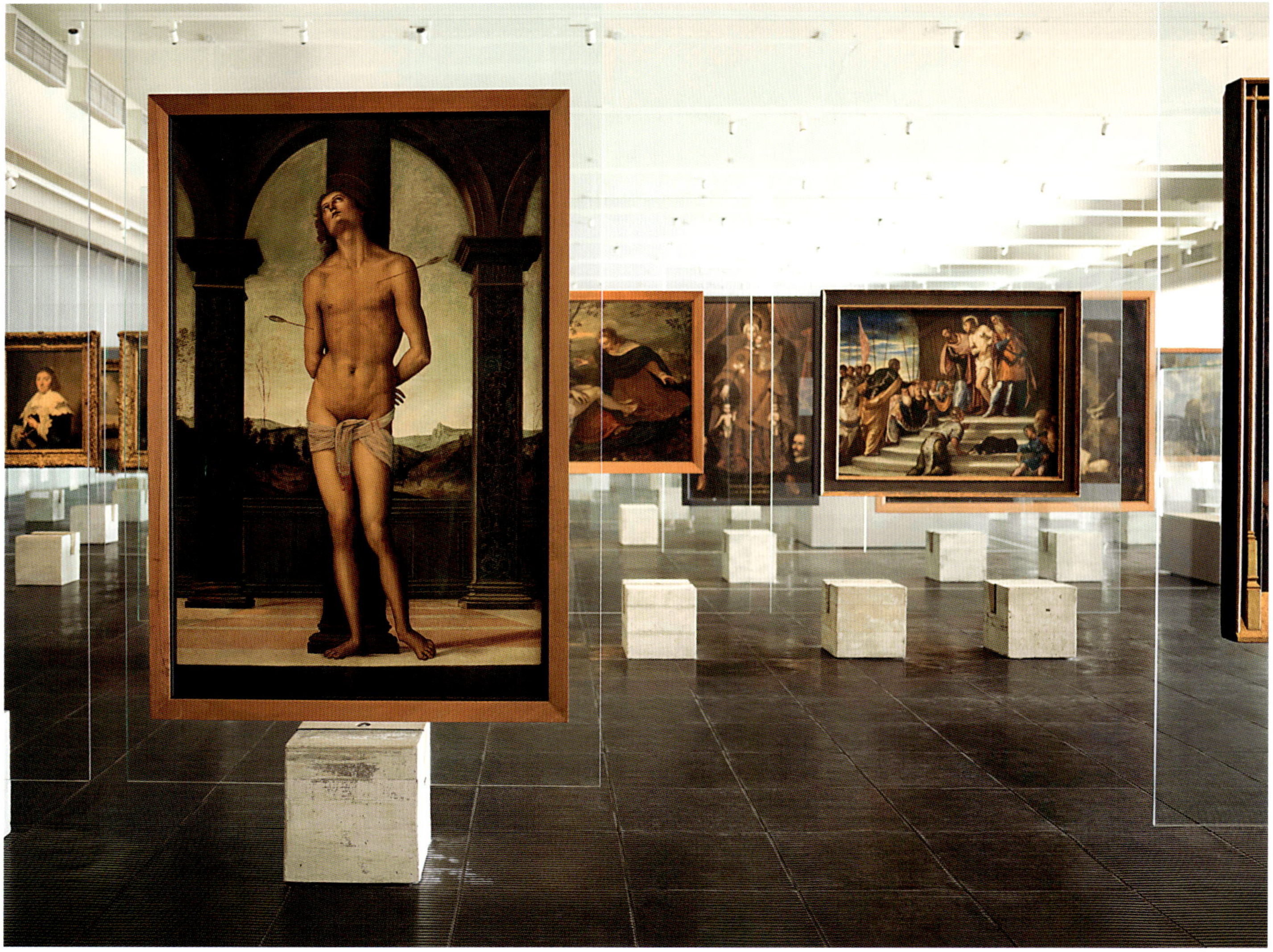

*Sem começo nem fim / Without Beginning or End (Lina Bo Bardi – A Marvellous Entanglement)* 2019

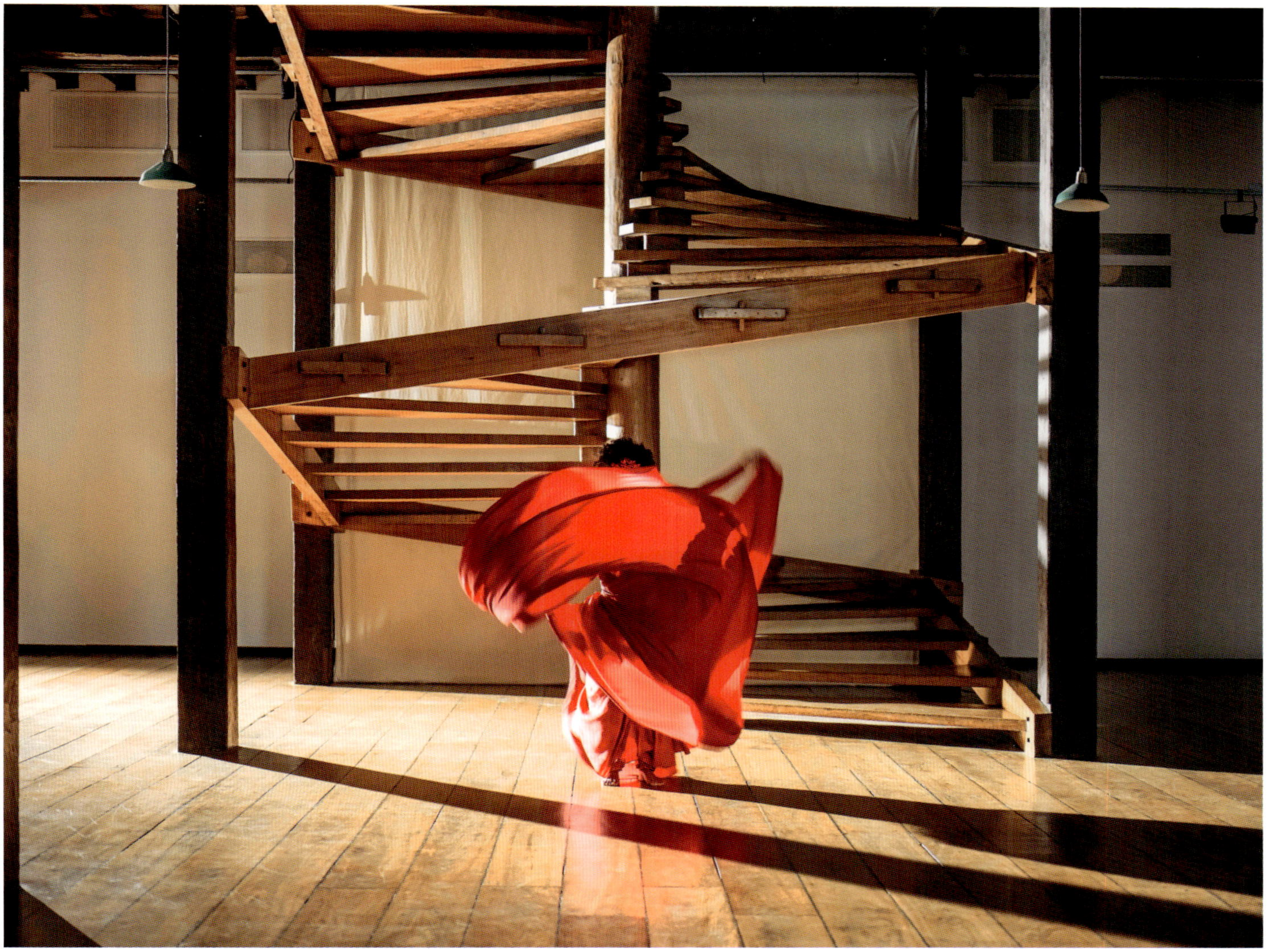

 *O que é um museu? / What is a Museum? (Lina Bo Bardi – A Marvellous Entanglement)* 2019

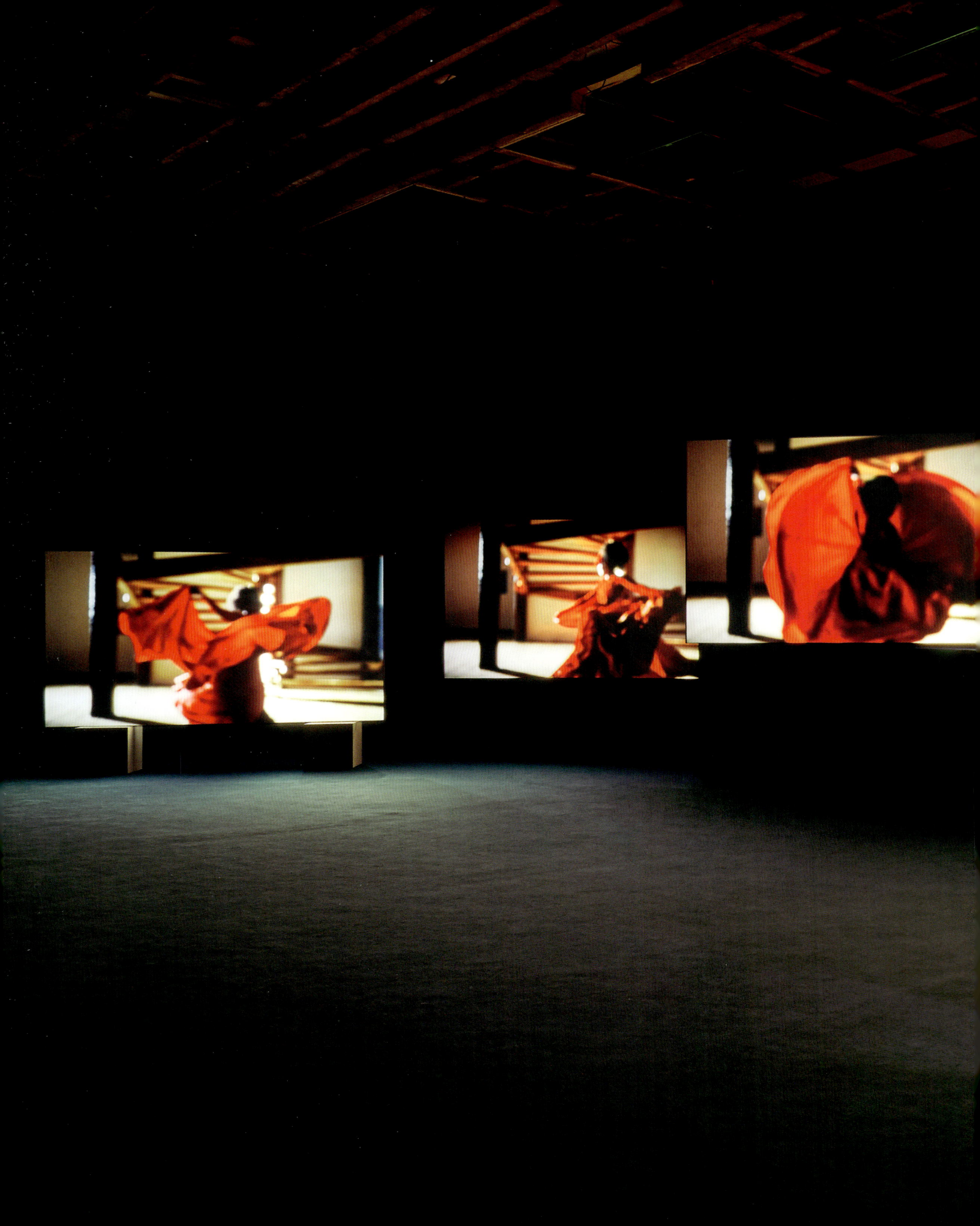

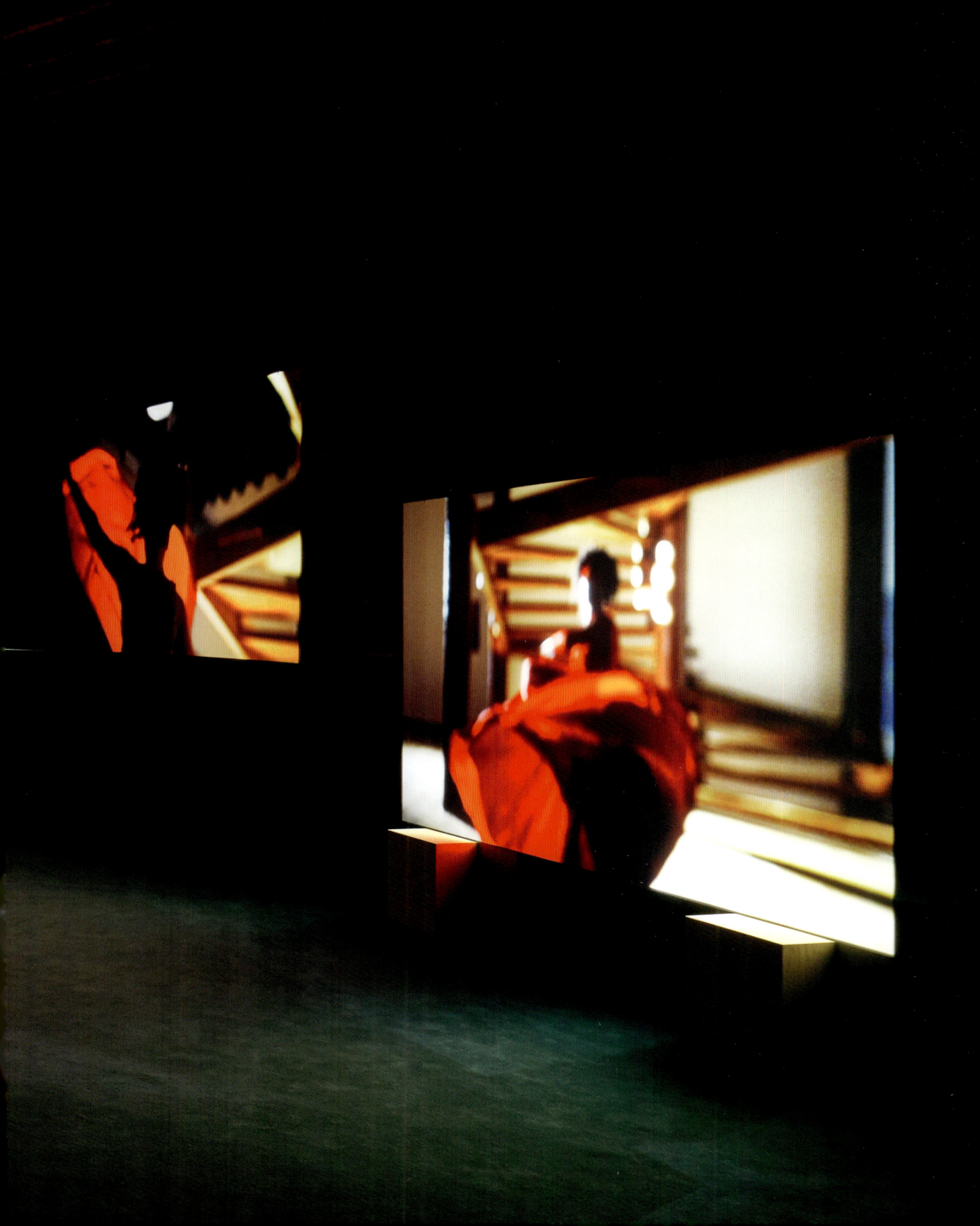

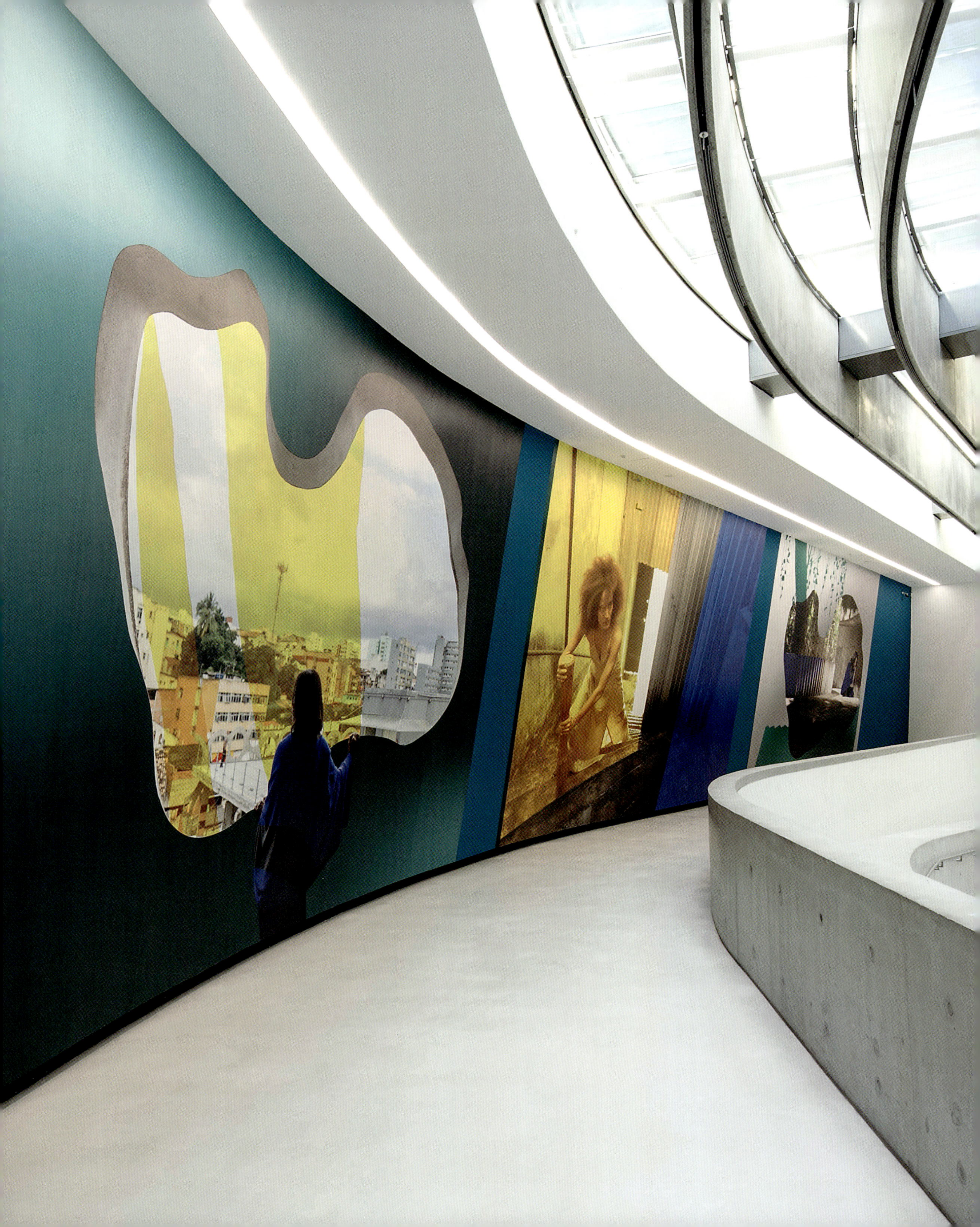

It is a fascinating and complex dialogue which we encounter in Isaac Julien's installation *Lina Bo Bardi - A Marvellous Entanglement*. At face value, it would appear to be no more than a perfect homage to one of the most important architects of the twentieth century - but what is revealed on closer inspection is a conversation about how time solidifies history, how constructed space can open up to the outside world, and how the presence of people and community can modify the space itself. Ultimately, it is about the complex relationships that bind representation and self-representation in human society, and about the capacity of culture to modify progress. In this vision, we traverse urban landscapes and distant biographies perfectly captured by Julien's expert eye in the story of an extraordinarily innovative and unconventional woman.

Through Julien's eyes, Bo Bardi's biography is transformed into the perfect mirror of how Western society journeyed through the twentieth century, finding in other lands unexpected and improved means of expression. After emigrating from Italy to Brazil at the end of the Second World War, Bo Bardi developed an innovative and experimental form of expression by connecting her background - until that point decidedly modernist - with the local language to create her own particular Esperanto free from any influence of colonialism or the exoticism common in European art. In this way, her work clearly anticipated the contemporary age that was to come, but without ever being limited by the Western vision. Rather, Bo Bardi placed her work in multiple contexts and left it open to modification and to other external influences.

At the same time, Julien's video installation provides a complete and thorough tour of the architect's Brazilian projects from the 1960s to the 1980s. As the narrator, almost godlike and prophetic, we hear Bo Bardi herself in two distinct personalities, played by Fernanda Montenegro and Fernanda Torres, mother and daughter in real life, who in the film become the architect in her old age and her youth. Their views and their words guide us through her life's journey and her research, establishing clearly the multifarious aspects which combine to make a single individual. In addition, they provide a learned reflection on the vital part that creativity plays in society.

Anyone who enters the semicircle of screens will be completely transfixed by a space which is itself conceived as a complete work of art: from the curtains to the seats, everything has been meticulously curated and designed by Julien. Visitors are fully immersed in the scenes on the nine screens, which portray episodes from Lina Bo Bardi's life, filmed inside her own buildings. The simultaneous presence of both Montenegro and Torres in some scenes serves to disorient the viewer, putting into sharp relief the concepts of fiction and reality beyond the simple linearity of the biography of a life: in the story of a person who dedicated herself to creativity, the various phases of research form the tiles of a mosaic often wrongly read by the critics as a linear progression of events in which that which comes later is a natural progression from, or a revision of, that which preceded it. In their conversations with one another, the two actresses playing the younger and older Bo Bardi give the lie to any such vision, providing instead an almost dreamlike record of a story which oscillates continually between fiction and documentary.

Since the late 1980s, Julien has been interested in how different languages can influence each other, in particular those of the visual arts, cinema and museums. It is not difficult to imagine how, arriving at SESC Pompéia in São Paulo for his

Production documentation of *Lina Bo Bardi - A Marvellous Entanglement* 2019, featuring Fernanda Montenegro as Lina Bo Bardi

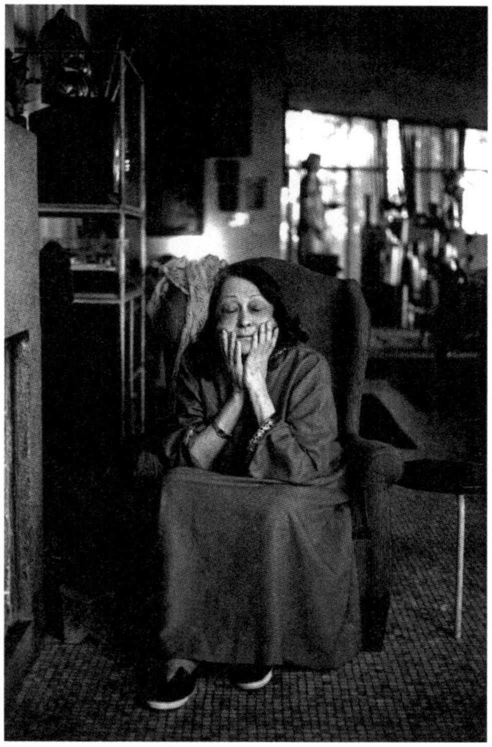

Juan Esteves, *Portrait of Lina Bo Bardi* 1991

2012 exhibition *Geopoetics*, Julien was struck by the personality of the architect who designed the layout of the museum and that he started an inner dialogue with her. Indeed, in 2015, during his residency at the American Academy in Rome, he visited the exhibition *Lina Bo Bardi in Italia* at the MAXXI modern art museum, saying, 'What I wanted was to have the story'. The intellectual conversation started immediately. The perseverance required to overcome all the difficulties Julien faced in the various phases of the film's production, from casting to the selection of locations, demonstrates that this work is more an act of love rather than a simple homage. It seems to be none other than the crystallisation of that long conversation that began many years before, and the words pronounced by the actresses unify Julien's thoughts with various quotes taken from Bo Bardi's writings.

The many steps required to bring the film to fruition were accompanied by diligent research into Bo Bardi's practice, into the context that existed in Brazil at the time she lived and worked there, and into the identity of the architect who found safe harbour in this new home country. Bo Bardi endured not only the feelings common to all exiles of being far from her country of birth but also an internal exile as a result of being a woman, an architect and a foreigner in a completely male-dominated world. Brazil welcomed her with all her contradictions, and the country became for her a testing ground for experimenting with a new language free from other existing languages. Although Julien does not like the interpretation of his research as a reflection on his own biography, it is an inevitable suggestion given that the lives of these two artists, separated in time and distance, are so similar in how they constructed an identity which always remains open to the world. By perfectly capturing this affinity, however, Julien transforms his work into a sort of act of devotion to the architect.

The versatility and topicality of Bo Bardi's architectural projects seem to spill out in an interrupted sequence of powerful, visionary images where the architect is both Julien's subject and his muse. This coincidence of views and perspectives between two individuals who seem at first so dissimilar is not affected by chronological distance because, as Bo Bardi wrote, 'time is not linear, it is a marvellous entanglement in which, at any moment, it is possible to select points and invent solutions, without a beginning or an end'.

The multifaceted character of time is recalled in the installation's continually overlapping narratives. Fernanda Montenegro and Fernanda Torres, portraying the architect in old age and youth, discuss and interact in the same space as if, for an instant, two different moments from the same life coincide. In this game of continual back and forth there are also two distinct registers of speech, reflecting the actors' backgrounds in theatre and television respectively. Their words bring to mind a universe of fiction and staging which results in sudden glitches in the rhetorical plane of the work. It thus becomes difficult to classify the film according to any predefined genre: it is not a documentary but, at the same time, nor is it fiction; as so often in Julien's work, the film is suspended in a no man's land that refuses definition. In the speeches of the two Fernandas – the shared name underlining their common identity despite the disparities between them – can be found all the experiences and traditions of the inhabitants of Salvador and São Paulo. The actors' words, often solitary, echo in the space, interspersed with long pauses, while sound and music punctuate the human event and thereby create a dialogue between individual experience and that of the community as a whole regarding the space in which they live. Therefore, while the words remain the prerogative of individual expression, the value of both individual and collective experience is amplified. The same mechanism of overlapping in the temporal plane is employed in the film's review of the architecture: some buildings, such as the complex of Solar do Unhão – which currently hosts MAM-BA, the Museu de Arte Moderna da Bahia – have changed function through time, but at the same time preserve the memory of past events in their history.

In Julien's film, the spaces designed by the architect are shown in the present day while the past is represented by films and documents collected by Julien from the archive of the French photographer and ethnographer Pierre Verger (1902–96), who was interested in the phenomenon of the Black African diaspora. Julien's work features images by Verger, projected onto white sheets, of men arriving in Brazil after having completed a long ocean crossing in ships - a forced migration that recalls, despite the clear difference in historical and geographical context, the journey that Lina Bo Bardi herself made in 1946 when, with her husband Pietro Maria Bardi, she left Italy for South America. In this way, present and past continually intersect. The presence of voyages is fundamental to all of Julien's work: although it remains unsaid and silent, the voyage stands as a metaphor for the definitive change needed to be able to construct a new identity. For Bo Bardi, her voyage meant that she could enjoy new opportunities as a designer in a country that was completely open to the new.

The concept of time is thus fundamental in the works of both Julien and Bo Bardi. In Julien's work, time encapsulates the movement in the film while, for the architect, time is evident in all her projects: re-use and reconditioning often feature in the structures, both conserving the memory of their previous use and acting as a reminder of the stratification of the community in which she found herself living. Similarly, both artists developed their own identity within a biographical course which takes the form of successive layers of identity, each configured always as a choice and never as a preconceived membership of a particular group. Julien finds in Bo Bardi's work an opportunity to describe a multicultural society which is formed in the overlap of time and space. The film recounts parallel yet distant lives in which can be found, apparently inexplicably, various points of intersection.

One of the most evident elements inside Julien's installation is movement. This becomes explicit in the constant relation between the space and those who inhabit it. The continual movement of people inside the constructions emphasises a choice of composition common to Lina Bo Bardi and Isaac Julien: both follow a principle of research into visual and dynamic equilibrium that can reinstate the complexity of language and expression.

Movement speaks of the opportunity for their spaces to reach fulfilment, be it the immersive spaces of the video installation or the spaces in architecture. Ultimately, movement represents the opportunity to understand the space in which we find ourselves: as a result of this movement the ego becomes related to the interior of the place. Thus, the architecture can be understood only when we are moving in its interior. Just as Julien's installation has no preferential viewpoints - the scenes continually move between one screen and another - so too the very architecture of Bo Bardi demonstrates the attention she paid to establishing a relationship with the community which would inhabit those spaces. None of Bo Bardi's projects is out of scale; each one is bedded in the community that is going to make use of it and in which it will have to exist. Perhaps it is for this reason that, after so many years, her spaces continue to feel so alive.

These works also inform us of our own potential, as visitors and users of the buildings, to give purpose to the spaces in which we live: it is we who allow them to fulfil their purpose. In the film, Bo Bardi's buildings are in motion. They perform, proving that they have a poetic rhythm, as when the spiral staircase of Solar do Unhão becomes the backdrop for the choreography of a group of dancers. The performers move their bodies, reproducing perfectly the swirling form of the staircase's steps, and we the viewers are transfixed by the red dress of the lead dancer. The choreography makes plain that the staircase is a movement in and of itself. Indeed, it was born from movement, its design inspired by the structure of the wheel of a traditional cart.

The architect's spaces are designed according to the collective events and rituals each will host, such as dance or processions expressing human nature.

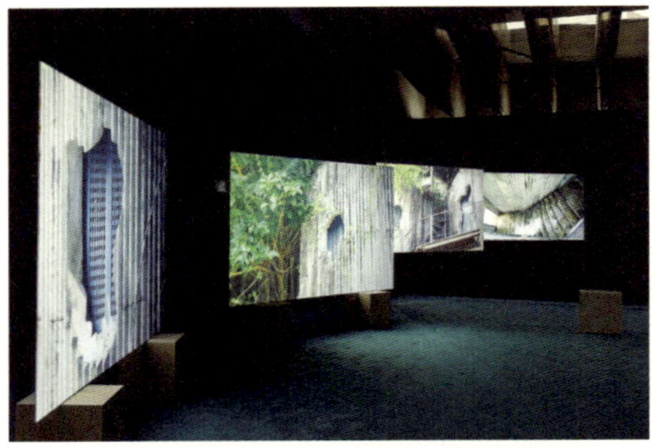

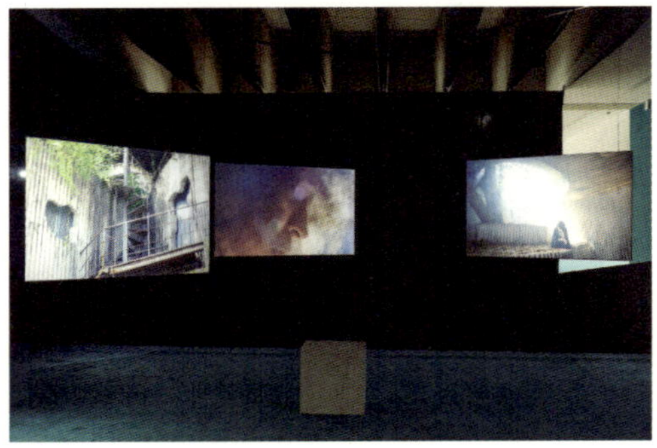

*Lina Bo Bardi - A Marvellous Entanglement*
2019, installation views, MAXXI, Italy, 2020

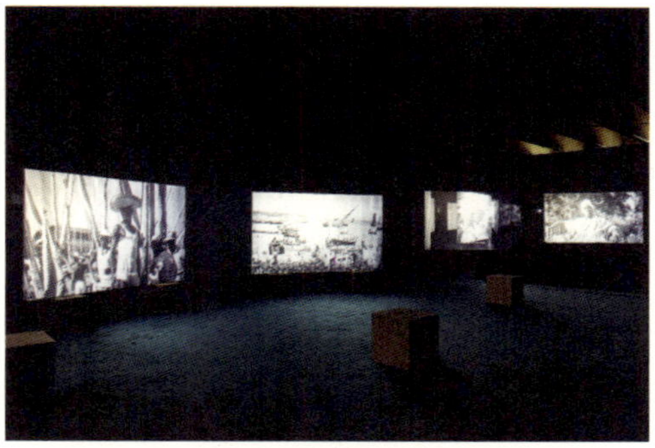

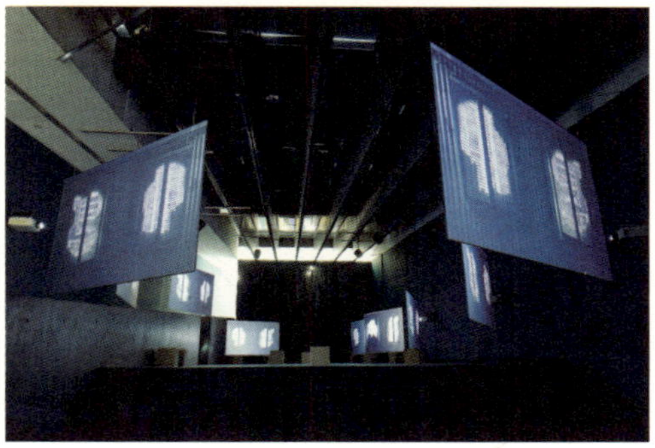

On the screens appear people who process, sing and clap their hands, moving in time to the musical rhythm. The architect, believing the theatre to be a place for meeting and interacting with other people, rethinks the arrangement of the seats and the stage using essential forms and simple materials. The visitors who enter the video installation have the same experience. We too are invited to take possession of the space with our bodies while we walk between Julien's screens or among Bo Bardi's works displayed in the Museu de Arte de São Paulo (MASP). This vision of a public experience coming to fruition through their movement in space is common to both Lina Bo Bardi and Isaac Julien. The seats distributed by Julien in the exhibition space quote, in their turn, elements of the displays of Bo Bardi's work: this has the effect of making even more dynamic the dialogue established between the screens, which appear to mirror each other in a continuous game of cross-references and temporal and narrative overlapping. In walking and stopping between screens arranged, like time as Bo Bardi sees it, in a non-linear fashion, the viewer's eye creates its own flow of frames, as if every frame were its own single screen and the eye searching for a continuity in the images jumping from one screen to the next.

The openings employed in the work of both artists are full of significance. Those in the architecture of Bo Bardi are real, physical openings rather than metaphorical ones: windows, gratings and mirrors appear on the video installation's screens and characterise the environments in which these scenes were filmed. But naturally, beyond their physical form, openings also have a metaphorical value: they symbolise the relation between ourselves and the world beyond our own space, whether a private one or a public one such as a museum or a theatre. Such places, though assuredly public, are clearly defined within a system, and tackling the planning of these places in a society like Brazil's was for Bo Bardi a very important testing ground – although that is not to say that her research was especially dominated by developments of this type.

In his work, Julien lingers on the openings designed by Bo Bardi. It seems as if they are holes in the film and that the film itself wants to face the external world. We as viewers are inside looking out, in an intense dialogue between individual identity and the community of the outside world. The windows and glass walls create contrasting light, accentuating the formal lines of the design elements and the seats of SESC Pompéia, the new home of the Serviço Social do Comércio – the result of the conversion of a former metal barrel factory into a centre for sport and cultural activities accessible to all. Having carried out intensive research into the relationship between cultures and how these cultures can be superimposed on each other, Julien understood that in the dynamic between the interior and exterior of these buildings there was the opportunity for reflection on how the individual planes relate to an outside world containing the hubbub of forms and colours of the everyday society which Bo Bardi saw and in which she lived. The openings establish a deep connection between the nature and the vibrant reality of a metropolis, a subject that is at the heart of the project.

Bo Bardi's own research included how to create new modes of expression, how to find different models of theorisation and how to look out of the window of one's own identity. Her affinity for creating a free flow of ventilation is a key feature of her practice, and was the result of her research into primitive authenticity as well as her natural aversion to air conditioning. She wrote that ancient cave dwellings didn't have the benefit of air conditioning or windows: it was left to a flow of air to regulate their temperature. In Julien's film, Bo Bardi tells us that in these caves the first 'glassless holes' permitted a 'permanent lateral ventilation' – this is what happens in her buildings, where the continual flow of people crosses the border between the inside and the outside, establishing a dialogue between different cultures and generations. In an absolutely innovative way, her buildings often do not have conventional windows but rather openings which make them permeable and link interior and exterior. This is not only a technical solution, but also allows a real connection to be made between our internal being and that which is around us.

Isaac Julien invites us to explore physical and metaphorical spaces through openings that connect individuals and contexts. Humans don't always manage to achieve such a connection. In scenes filmed in São Paulo's Teatro Oficina (designed by Lina Bo Bardi in partnership with Edson Elito), the two actresses portraying the architect find themselves one in front of the other, but do not communicate because they are separated by the surface of a mirror in which each sees only her own image. Here the mirror represents a breach in the relationship. Neither actress can see herself reflected in the other person: they see instead only their own reflection with their two diverse identities and ages.

With this profound work full of intuition, Isaac Julien constructs a complex overlaying of meanings which speak to us about the world in which we live today. In this sense, Brazil is once more a testing ground: not just a film set but also a stage on which to place the architecture of Bo Bardi, which proves the endurance of light in the turmoil of recent decades. The marvellous entanglement that gives Julien's work its title deconstructs and weakens every discourse which tries to relate history and culture in a normative way, refuting any notion of a linear narrative. The experience at the heart of the video installation is a total loss of control in respect of the linearity and the impartiality of the human gaze: it is not possible to understand the beginning and the end, nor the storyboard, nor the historic progress which marks the life of Bo Bardi. We are captivated by the entirety of a work where every scene is superimposed on another and the latter seems to be the cause of the former. In the images in the film, Bo Bardi's later constructions seem to be a foreword to those realised in her youth, and not the contrary. The marvellous entanglement that punctuates her own life is fully depicted in the knowing compositional capacity with which Julien plays using the screens. The viewer is left mesmerised at the centre of this ellipse like an orchestra conductor without a score, enthralled by the perfection of the images and liberated from any linear narration.

*Translated by Jim Smart*

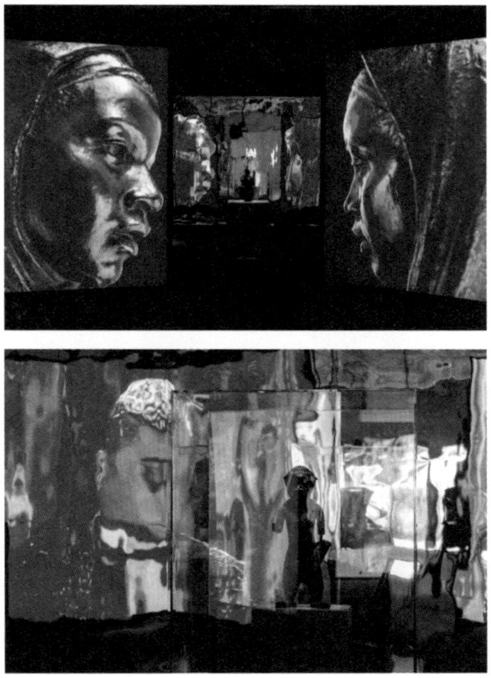

*Once Again ... (Statues Never Die)* 2022, installation views, Barnes Foundation, 2022

Striding into the lecture room at the Centre Pompidou in Paris, Theaster Gates puts on Mahalia Jackson's 'It's Gonna Rain' at full volume until the glass panes of the building vibrate. 'If you grew up as I did', says Gates, 'you arrive with no history, no memory, no narrative, no archive and you look around for the residues of what you came from, but they are not there. What was there were the stirring sounds of Mahalia Jackson, James Brown, Bobby Byrd. And although all the institutions who were supposed to be the custodians of some fragmentary history did nothing but erase them, they were not quite able to, for even rhythm leaves behind some traces, and from those traces we can begin to invoke a lineage.'[1]

At this riveting moment of resounding music rattling the window panes of an august European art institution, the imperative of interruption becomes clear: the interruption that effects a breach and allows for another entry point, an interruption that doesn't merely protest but conjures up a genealogy of the 'Unarchivable' – that which has always been uncomfortably there, stirring and quivering, but uncapturable in its alienation from the historical categories which might contain it, pin it down and make it join the general choir.

There is a line of works in Isaac Julien's oeuvre that performs this work of quivering, diaphanous genealogies. It is not historical correctives that these works establish but a Foucauldian notion of genealogy – an investigation into those elements we tend to feel are without History with a capital 'H', without history because they have been positioned as an exception, an anomaly, not indicating a legitimate part in some lineage of great groundswells of thinking, of writing or of creating. Being 'without history' does not call forth a simple demand for restitution, for recognition. The forces that police, hollow out and make invisible are always at work to establish lineages that celebrate the narrowest locations and parameters of achievement. For subjects of colour and artists of colour, these have historically been either a marginal participation in valorised forms of cultural innovation – various avant-gardes in which they might play a subsidiary role – or have been under the banner of declaring a collective identity and producing a linguistic or visual idiom for it, imposing a politics of identity onto a seam of imaginative invention. Either a separateness or a communing of exceptionality have dominated these perceptions and discourses of the arts. It is only quite recently that we have had the chance to recognise independent conjunctions of cultural and artistic positions, deeply anchored in alternative archives and having ambitions to do far more than represent or docu-dramatise. The works and exhibitions we have been fortunate to encounter lately don't take on affiliate roles in celebrated narratives but stand for their vision as unique within a historical interruption. These interruptions read a specific moment through completely different terms and values than a conventional norm – a reading that re-evaluates rather than makes restitution.[2]

The critical history that we so badly need is about the 'revaluing of values' (after Foucault) in the present day. Brian Massumi has recently issued a rally cry, stating: 'It is time to take back value. For many, value has long been dismissed as a concept so thoroughly compromised, so soaked in normative strictures and stained by complicity with capitalist power, as to be unredeemable. This has only abandoned value to purveyors of normativity and apologists of economic oppression. *Value is too valuable to be left in those hands.*'[3] Interruption is one of the tools we have for the dismissive power of refusing normative value and the narratives that sustain it.

1. Theaster Gates, 'Cosmopolis I', at the Centre Pompidou, Paris, December 2017. I have loosely paraphrased the words of Gates's lecture performance.

2. We have been fortunate of late that a number of prominent exhibitions have done this work, notably *Life Between Islands* (Tate Britain, London, 2021), *Lubaina Himid* (Tate Modern, London, 2021), and *Isamu Noguchi* (Barbican, London, 2021). All of these have worked to rewrite a historical period: from the perspective of those who had historically not been perceived as full members of a national creative scene, as in *Life Between Islands*; of those who had been claimed by a bland 'modernism' that erased their exciting and contradictory cultural multivalences, as in the case of Noguchi; or of those whose inventive power allows for a fluid mobility between styles, iconographies and subjectivities, as in Himid's work, or for the cross-cutting of multiple archives and fictions, as in the recent films of John Akomfrah.

3. Brian Massumi, in *99 Theses on the Revaluation of Value: A Postcapitalist Manifesto*, Minneapolis, MN 2018, T1;https://manifold.umn.edu/read/99-theses-on-the-revaluation-of-value/section/7a105a04-8cb5-4b6f-8818-2ca4cd070862, accessed 13 October 2022.

Historical interruptions are not about making visible the hidden or the unacknowledged, nor about setting the record straight or shining light on facts that have been disavowed or erased. Historical interruptions are always from the present and always *about* the present, deploying our most recent insights to rethink what connects us to earlier radical moments with some form of 'ephemeral glue' that eludes materialisation. If this revised understanding of their significant contribution to us can extract historical figures from representing just one thing – one crucial and militant thing – to being an arena of unexpected fissures (after Foucault), then they assume completely different historical roles. The dancing vagabond of Isaac Julien's *Vagabondia* 2000 surreptitiously interrupts the narrative of empire in London's Sir John Soane's Museum, and the winged poet graces the queer ballrooms of Harlem suspended between desire and fierce, hot, angry words in *Looking for Langston* 1989. Frantz Fanon, in *Frantz Fanon: Black Skin, White Masks* 1996, strides between a militant anti-colonialism enacted in Martinique, France and Algeria and attending to the psychic intricacies of wounded souls, and *Lessons of the Hour* 2019 transforms the life of Frederick Douglass from a slave history into grand narratives and a set of lofty and superior perspectives on some of Western culture's most admired institutions. And the subject of *Lina Bo Bardi – A Marvellous Entanglement* 2019 turns her back on the dirtiest of European politics to scrape vestiges of modernism from them and fuse these with the deep mythicality she encounters in Brazil.

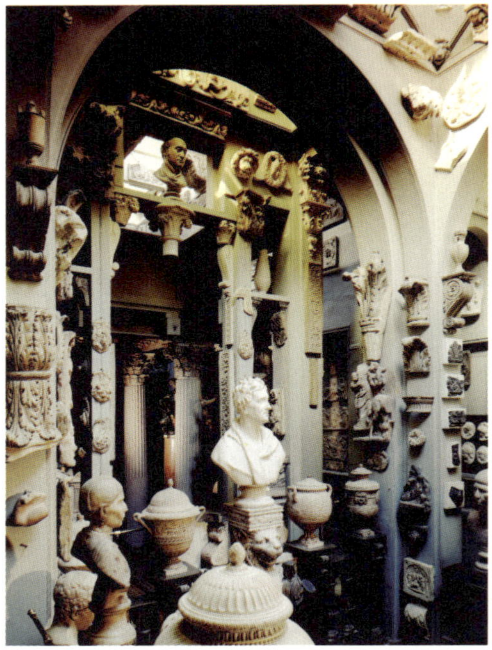

Sir John Soane's Museum, London

None of these protagonists is heroic: all are flawed, all are suspended between contradictions and all inhabit a non-linear history. I remember my excitement on first reading Foucault's 'Nietzsche, Genealogy, History', in which he positioned himself as the bad son of a bad son[4] – Nietzsche, the bad son of philosophy, who had interrupted the seamless progress of European philosophy, and Foucault, who mercilessly refused the harrumphing histories of great men and great moments and led us to the attenuated details of history as moments of chaos theory. Aside from all the other things I learned from that text, perhaps the most important was the understanding of how to rethink 'lineage' away from grandiose achievements and towards stealthy interruptions.

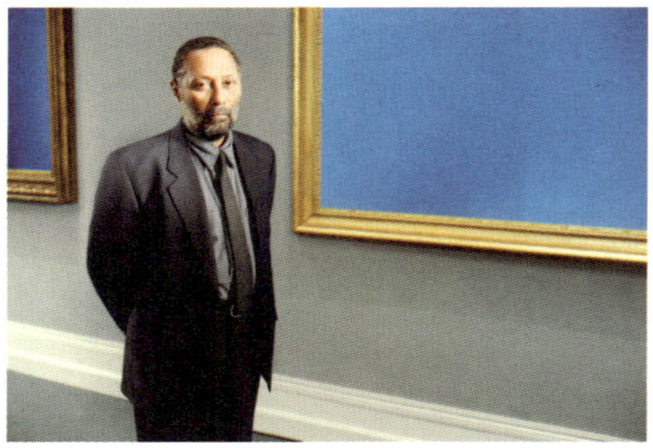

*Encoding _ Decoding in Blue (In Memoriam Stuart Hall)* 2014

Julien performs historical interruptions. The protagonists in these films are never singly inscribed, but forever suspended between worlds, simultaneously heralding future radicality and rehearsing the deep, oppressive contradictions of their present state. In *Vagabondia*, a contemporary Black female conservator walks the halls of the Soane Museum. Here there is an inherent kinkiness to the sumptuous setting and everything is suffused with dissonant contradiction:[5] eccentric as the collection might be, it is nevertheless a hegemonic fusion of Grand Tour aesthetics with brutal colonial heritages – classical nudes, panels of Hogarth paintings, metal shackles viewed against classical architraves. Historical figures of young Black women in gorgeous gowns of vivid colours sit studiously looking at albums of architectural designs; the black leather sleeves of the conservator brush against the nude torsos of the sculptures; there are glimpses of Sir John himself in the hallways; and then comes the interruption – in sneaks the interloper Vagabond, who dances jerkily around the spaces, another stealth ghost in a neoclassical pantheon.

The soundtrack plays with the legacies of those ghostly presences come to reinhabit a space which has both looted and hijacked them. The language is Creole, musical and tripping, but incomprehensible to the museum's historical founders or visitors. As Stuart Hall argued so persuasively, 'originally the term "*creole*" in the Caribbean had both a black and a white referent. It was applied to both native-born white and black populations ... It was never historically, and is not today, fully fixed *racially*.'[6] The Soane Museum, so iconic of imperial aristocratic appropriation and hoarding, reverberates with this racial *unfixity*: none of the protagonists represents any expected notion of where they should be, and Soane, founder and guiding spirit, conducts himself as the true interloper.

4. Michel Foucault, 'Nietzsche, Genealogy, History', in *Language, Counter-Memory, Practice: Selected Essays and Interviews*, Ithaca, NY 1977.

5. *Vagabondia* was made simultaneously with an AHRC research project I directed, 'Translating the Image' (Goldsmiths, 2001–6), in which Isaac Julien was senior research fellow. Its thematics came into our conversations as ours did into the work, an entanglement that set our thinking racing.

6. Stuart Hall, 'Créolité and the Process of Creolization', in Okwui Enwezor et al. (eds)., *Créolité and Creolization*, Ostfildern-Ruit 2002.

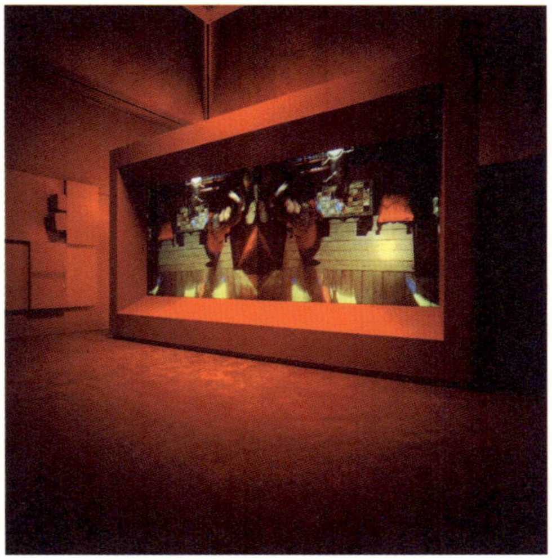

*Vagabondia* 2000, installation view, *The Turner Prize*, Tate Britain, 2001

The music, lush and seductive, situates the dancing figure (played by Ben Ash) – assumed interloper as he may well be – as the most grounded figure in the film. It is this figure who is infused with a sense of anticipation; he is the unknown factor, the one who points towards the surprises that might take place in future, the shifts in power that are potential. He is futurity in this case: the dissenting power of decolonising. 'Traces of zest, adventure, and wonder troubling its pure quality would keep beauty processually honest', says Brian Massumi. 'In the processual vitality they make felt, discord would be palpable. *Dissensus* – the unerasability of qualitative differentials and the incommensurability of co-motional tendencies – would be affirmed.'[7]

In contrast, the interruption affected by *Frantz Fanon: Black Skin, White Masks* could be claimed for an instance of 'world making' (as philosopher Jean-Luc Nancy perceives of the term). The figure of Fanon is a relational geography of the consequences of colonialism. Defying the very title of his most famous book, with its stark distinction between skins, Julien's Fanon (Colin Salmon) is an enmeshment in numerous layers of colonial struggle and occupation, bringing a far broader array of races and classes into the frame. Forced to leave a France ruled by Vichy's Marshal Pétain, Fanon returns to Martinique, ruled by another ally of Hitler's, Admiral Robert, and eventually goes to work as a psychiatrist in Algeria in the throes of its fight against colonial occupation by France. In the background of these linked and separate histories, there are side conversations with French Communist intellectuals and early moments of the Civil Rights movement in the United States. Set against this panoply of locations and struggles – European struggles with fascism, the struggles of the colonised against their oppressors – Fanon enters the arena of 'world making'. As described by Jean-Luc Nancy: 'To Create the World means: immediately, without delay, reopening each possible struggle for a world, for what must form the contrary of a global injustice against the background of a general equivalence.'[8] In doing the work of layering these struggles, Julien's film also makes it impossible to strictly divide between them: they are linked, and not by one ideological edict pertaining to race or class or ideology but through their entwining to create the 'social justice' that only 'world making' can take on. The heroic Fanon, involved in so many of the central political struggles of his world, opts not for a political position but that of a psychiatrist who links mental states to political prejudices, psychic oppression and enforced mimicry. Here again we find an echo of Nancy's closing words to his essay: 'to create as a struggle ... does not seek the exercise of power – nor property ... but seeks itself and its agitation, itself and its effervescence of thought in the act'.[9] The film serves us with an array of effervescent critiques: contemporary critics Stuart Hall, Homi K. Bhabha and Françoise Vergès; historic intellectuals Jean-Paul Sartre and Simone de Beauvoir; the writers from Martinique who were Fanon's early community and allies; and the impending distant shadows of the civil rights political activists in the far-off USA who represent the 'to come', the futurity of the work.

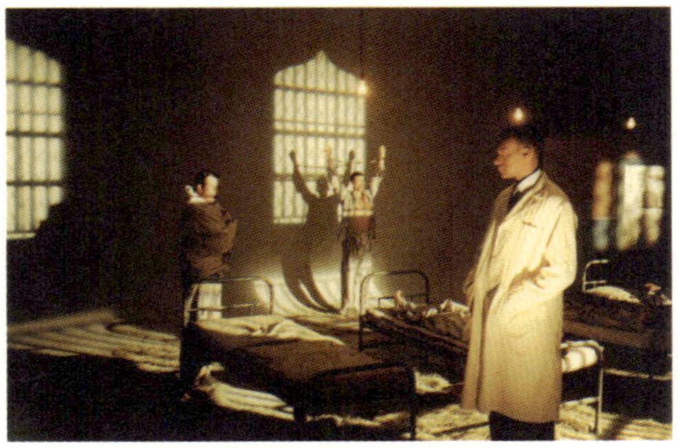

*Frantz Fanon: Black Skin White Masks* 1996

This multiple and simultaneous inhabitation across time and space, always at the heart of Julien's work, is uniquely suited to the medium of film, with its capacity to sustain multiple confluences. There is never a clear line of demarcation isolating this struggle from that: there is always a confluence of related and distant struggles, and attention is always paid both to the struggling protagonists and the theorists who distil their life's work into a political currency for the present.

Some of these struggles inhabit the terrain of revolutionary eruptions and some the slower burn of reflection and analysis. In *Once Again ... (Statues Never Die)* we encounter the struggle on a different terrain – that of the museums and art-historical narratives that established cultural hierarchies, and of the art that defied these – focused on the work of Alain Locke, philosopher, art historian and the first African American to hold a Rhodes Scholarship to Oxford University, who became

7. Massumi 2018, T98.

8. Jean-Luc Nancy, *The Creation of the World, or, Globalization*, Albany, NY 2007, p.54.

9. Ibid., p.55.

the main theoretical voice of the Harlem Renaissance with his most important book, *The New Negro* (1925).

Julien's work unfolds at several levels. We enter it via a conversation between Locke (André Holland) and Albert Barnes (Danny Huston), who founded the Barnes Foundation in Philadelphia in 1922 and was initially a collector of European modernism, much influenced by the avant-garde tastes of American expatriates in Paris such as the Steins. In their conversation, the two men reproduce the polar positions in the understanding of the relations between African art and European radical experimentation: Barnes, schooled in European art, saw arts from Africa as a catalyst for rejuvenating and shaking off the tired academicism of the turn of the century; Locke, in contrast, saw not only the inherent value of arts from Africa but also, importantly, that of their extension into African American modernist experiments within the loose frame of the Harlem Renaissance, and crucially as a wide diasporic terrain.[10] These positions were to harden over the coming years into those articulated by Locke, away from the essentialising of a 'black spirit' grounded on notions of race and emotion intertwined and towards a social and cultural self-consciousness.

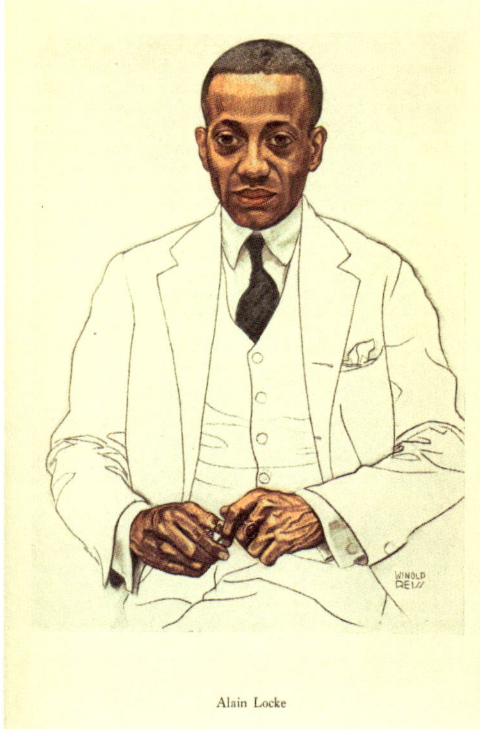


Winold Reiss, *Portrait of Alain Locke* (alternative title: *The New Negro*), National Portrait Gallery, Smithsonian Institution

Locke's words are full of elegant irony when he characterises the romantic, folklorising and exoticising Barnes as arguing 'European conventions' and positioning African art as having no other purpose than a 'vitalising influence'. Each man's rhetoric actually embodies his position, with Barnes's exemplifying all the sentiments of his age and Locke's articulating futurity, a far-sighted reflexiveness of understandings to come.

Essentially, the two poles of this debate were sustained by Locke's *The New Negro* on one hand and, on the other, Robert Goldwater's *Primitivism in Modern Art* (1938), which became the stalwart of art-historical studies on the subject of African influences on Western modern art well into the 1970s. Only then, buoyed by Marxist, feminist and postcolonial interventions into the field of art history, did revisions to the European narrative of the development of art begin re-establishing important figures from the African diaspora (incorporating very different writings on Harlem's 'Afro-Modernism', European avant-gardist 'Primitivism' and Caribbean 'Negritude') into the narrative of art history. In *Once Again ... (Statues Never Die)*, Locke and Barnes are historical figures portrayed by contemporary actors and standing for opposing notions of heritage; but, most significantly for this viewer, the film does the work of 'starting from elsewhere'. Julien is not simply arguing against art-historical hegemonies but shifting the ground sideways to show that there is another entry point, populated by figures and histories and intellectual excitements, pleasures and frissons and seductions – just as the celebrated bohemian lives of the European avant-garde have always been.

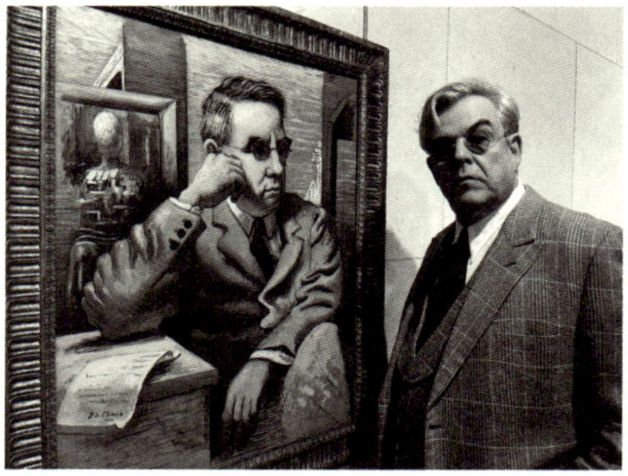

On the set of *Once Again ... (Statues Never Die)* 2022, with Danny Huston as Albert C. Barnes

The two figures respectively walk the halls of two collecting institutions. In the Barnes Collection in Philadelphia, the figure of Barnes is surrounded by iconic objects from Europe and elsewhere, bought, shipped and owned by his foundation. Walking the spaces of the Pitt Rivers Museum in Oxford, the mammoth ethnographic collection deeded by soldier and archaeologist Augustus Pitt Rivers and famously displayed by their use rather than their affiliation, Locke is surrounded by the huge and jumbled excess of looted objects, among them the Benin Bronzes. He intersects the spaces of the museum together with a pantheon of figures of the 'Harlem Renaissance' he coined and championed: artists Augusta Savage and Lois Mailou Jones are there haunting the corridors, and rare archival footage ushers in sculptor Richmond Barthé, artist Aaron Douglas, poet Countee Cullen, photographer Carl Van Vechten and educator and champion Harold Jackman.

Other figures such as Langston Hughes or James Baldwin enter courtesy of historical archives, quotes from earlier films by Julien, reconstruction of early ateliers for the study of live drawing and sculpting, and references from letters and essays. In this way Julien brings in not simply the documentary but the imaginary:

10. As Kobena Mercer writes: 'Conversely, when it is told in trans-national terms, as in *Rhapsodies in Black: Art of the Harlem Renaissance* (1997), we see that curatorial methods based on the wider concept of diaspora give us an inter-active rather than a separatist narrative and show how artists of different ethnicities were constantly entangled in cross-cultural dialogue.' Kobena Mercer, 'Cosmopolitan Contact Zones', https://www.liverpool.ac.uk/media/livacuk/csis-2/blackatlantic/research/Mercer_text_defined.pdf, accessed 13 October 2022. See also Mercer's recent book *Alain Locke and the Visual Arts*, New Haven and London 2022).

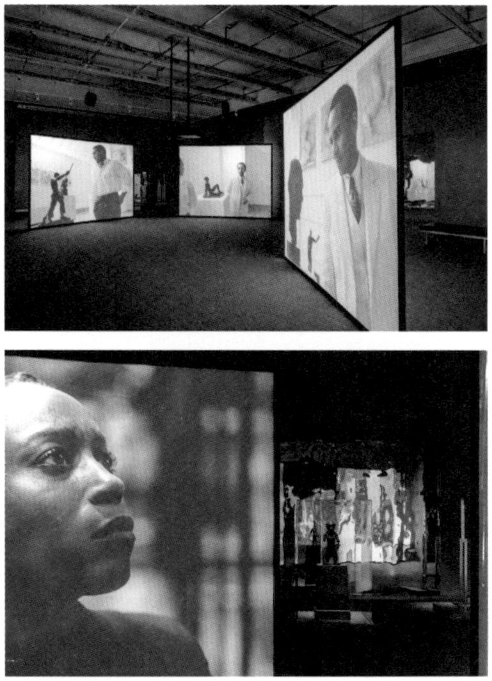

*Once Again ... (Statues Never Die)* 2022, installation views, Barnes Foundation, 2022

the necessary flights of fancy and trembling with desire that queer any history of art, and through which influence exerts itself as much as convincing ideas do.

Given their mutual imbrication as films depicting the exceptional and courageous talents of gay men at the heart of the Harlem Renaissance, it is tempting to compare *Looking for Langston* with *Once Again*, despite the nearly thirty-year gap between their making. Yet while they add to one another in fleshing out historical narratives, they are markedly different. In the intervening years, we have been through corruptions of our political systems, collapses of our economies, ever-escalating racist brutality, global pandemic and climate disasters. It is hard to re-establish the joyful innocence of that earlier moment, knowing what we know now. The magical exuberance of Langston Hughes, whose words trip from the tongue in musical whirlpools, is now balanced out by the measured philosophical utterances of Alain Locke, whose field of vision is so remarkably wide, who sees himself as a world maker, who takes on the task of 'reopening each struggle for a world' (Nancy) and who carries an enormous responsibility to both face the present and imagine a truly informed, rather than barbarically ignorant, future.

The pantheon of historical figures Julien depicts in his numerous films establish genealogies, long lines of connectedness that allow for – insist on – telling our histories differently, by centring marginalities and recognising invention, originality and daring in those places we may have not known to seek them. But here too is futurity, in Derrida's sense of always haunting the present. As Jean-Paul Martinon says: 'futurity has one overall meaning: it concerns the times ahead of us, the future times that we can sense coming ... In this way, futurity constitutes the present space of the future, what can be seen today as the future.'[11]

I'd like to conclude with an understanding of how different 'futurity' might be from correctives and from what Spivak calls 'Righting Wrongs'. Futurity is not a matter of redress but of eager anticipation that operates like a haunting. This anticipation is not a matter of drawing logical conclusions from known histories; it is a matter of spacing and temporising differently, creating the breaches and suspensions of belief that might allow something else in.

It is compelling to think of 'the interruption' I began with as the insertion of a haunting into a recognisable narrative. It's far from the notion of 'what if', of entertaining far-fetched possibilities that claim things could have gone otherwise, that history might have been different. It is a recognition that it has always been otherwise and we are there, standing in its presence, catching up with ourselves.



11. Jean-Paul Martinon, *On Futurity: Malabou, Nancy and Derrida*, Basingstoke 2007.

Mark Nash: One of the first multiple-screen film projection works that I saw was Robert Morris's double projection *Gas Station* 1969 at *Expanded Cinema*, the National Film Theatre's festival of independent avant-garde film in 1973. The film presented two synchronous views of an American gas station and ran for some twenty minutes without dialogue or voiceover, just ambient sound. There was a lot of moving-image artwork being produced around that time, as documented in Gene Youngblood's legendary 1970 book, also called *Expanded Cinema*. Multiple screens were an established genre in mainstream entertainment, but they weren't used in the way that Isaac, and subsequently others, then used them, as an extension of the cinema experience.

I'm interested in looking at the way screens function in Isaac's work – first the single-screen early works, then the two-screen works such as *Trussed* 1996. After that, there are multiple-screen works with projected images which are contiguous and can be read as a single image, as in *The Long Road to Mazatlán* 1999 and *Vagabondia* 2000, in which projected images were synchronised to create a widescreen image across three frames that occasionally morphed into a single image. And then his more recent works deploy screens in different sculptural configurations, most dramatically perhaps in the installation of *Ten Thousand Waves* 2010 in the Museum of Modern Art in New York.

Adam Finch: It's an interesting nexus between cinematic conventions and art-world principles, but I think you're right, there is still a lot of suspicion in art circles about the idea of entertainment. I came to multi-screen editing from a slightly different angle, from that cinematic side. In 1980, just before I met Isaac at Saint Martin's, there was a screening of Abel Gance's *Napoléon* (1927) at the London Film Festival. For the finale, the film suddenly expands into a triptych, three films projected using three projectors side by side – that was Gance's own experimental format, which he called Polyvision. Initially it presents a wide battlefield panorama across all three screens but then the individual screens take on a life of their own: in one we see Napoleon himself, in another his emotions and thoughts of Josephine, and in the third his conflicting strategic mind devising war stratagems. The sequence is a glitteringly cinematic montage of animations, superimpositions and mirrored images containing both dramatic development and an abstracting compositional treatment of the film frame.

Something seemed to happen to me when I saw those three separate images side by side, that exhilarating fracturing of time and space. It was like standing in front of a cubist painting. I could feel myself struggling to piece together the relationship between the disparate film images.

MN: I was at that screening as well. I think it demonstrates the maxim that there's nothing new under the sun in film history, that it's always already been done several times in the past.

AF: A lot of us went to that screening! And that idea of Polyvision, which lay dormant for so long, always stayed there in the back of our minds, so that many years later when Isaac said he wanted to make a three-screen Western in Texas, I immediately thought that I'd love to explore that method of storytelling across multiple screens.

With *The Long Road to Mazatlán*, we began experimenting with the possibilities of multi-screen drama and laying out a possible syntax for this kind of work. In format, it's quite a formal triptych reminiscent of altarpieces – one central image with supporting images on either side on a flat plane – and it is read very much in two dimensions, left to right. Digital editing was in its infancy, but for the first time we were able to edit three screens side by side and to choreograph their juxtaposition and the movement of images with precision. We could create a flow and synchronicity between and across the screens, but the real pleasure came when we started to disrupt that and confound expectation: when things move across the left but then don't appear on the right, or appear slightly later or with slightly different action. Suddenly there's a gap, in space and time, and the curious thing is that the gap is, in many ways, as interesting as the image.

MN: I'm interested in the gap, the spaces between screens, because these sort of chasms between the screens are actually where the viewer is located. The viewer has to reorient themselves to make sense of images that are being shown side by side, which are perhaps the same or perhaps slightly different, and create a relationship between them.

Traditional montage edits time, duration and space, contracting the time which the actions take. I was thinking of Pierre Huyghe's moving-image artwork, *L'Ellipse* 1998, which filled in the cuts in Wim Wenders's *The*

*American Friend* 1978. Wenders's film is an art cinema narrative, but there are ellipses in the story, and what Huyghe did was to try filling in those gaps between one scene and another. I see this as an anti-cinematic gesture – a form of trying to interrogate or destroy the montage principle which has been running in cinema for a long time.

AF: We're talking about two kinds of gaps here. There is the gap in time and action between shots, the bit that has been cut out, and in addition there's the physical space that exists between the images on the different screens in a multi-screen presentation, which can represent a gulf in space and time – or, conversely, simultaneity.

MN: Yes, you have a flow of narrative sequences of slow images, which is horizontal, like a sentence. Then you have the vertical axis from which, as a filmmaker, you make your choices of image. In single-screen film installations, as when you're editing a single-screen film, you have a series of choices but can choose just one image. However, with the multiple screens all the possible images are stacked, and then the viewer has the autonomy to choose one.

AF: Or they can choose all, viewing all three screens as one composite – though by 2005, after we had made a series of three-screen works, this was something that began to trouble Isaac. He wanted to make an ontological break with the triptych towards a more immersive form. That led to *Fantôme Créole* 2005, which was a combination of two three-screen works, *Fantôme Afrique* 2005 and *True North* 2004. The slightly disturbing thing for me was that *Fantôme Créole* was a four-screen work in a square formation, meaning that, for the first time, from any vantage point one of the screens would be invisible to the viewer. There would always be something that went unseen.

MN: I love that work, because of its formal experimentation. When it was shown at the Pompidou Centre, the seats were made mobile and the audience grew a bit desperate, moving their seats around to try and find a place where they could view all four screens simultaneously, even though that wasn't possible. One really had to make a choice. It was bringing in an element of an active spectator. I've observed this in subsequent works where audiences shift between getting the idea that they have to move around, or insist that they stay put, even if they're missing something. Those are two different regimes of looking.

AF: The piece that obviously deals with that head-on is *Ten Thousand Waves*. We showed that at the Hayward Gallery in 2010 as part of a group show called *Move: Choreographing You*, which explored ways that an artist can choreograph their audience. It's an epic, spacious nine-channel work edited so that the movement flows around the screens in a spiral formation. We also divided the film's scenes into smaller image clusters, left and right, which we alternated with blank screens, impelling the audience to shift position. Because the screens are so widely spaced, you need to calculate and allow for this in the editing – for example, there's a scene at the beginning of the work where we wanted to evoke being lost at sea, and when editing the sequence of waves I had to allow for a delay while the swell travelled across that imaginary space of the gallery before rising on the next screen. Only when the timing of this delay was correct did you get the kinetic effect of the wave moving around the space and creating an engulfing spiral vortex around the viewer. If you get it wrong, it doesn't work because the swells will be out of sync and the perceived fluidity broken.

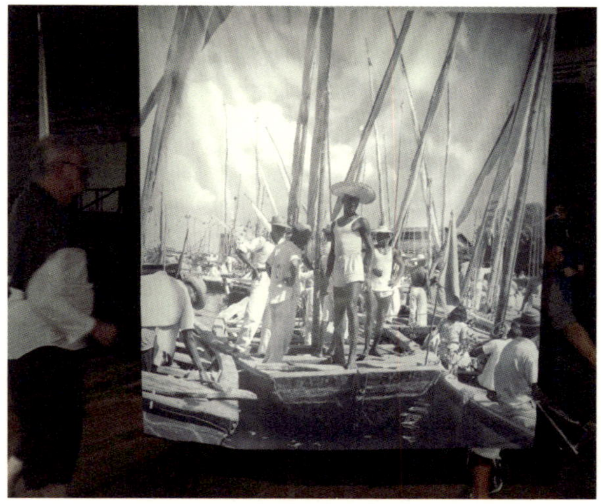
Production documentation of *Lina Bo Bardi – A Marvellous Entanglement* 2019, featuring Mark Nash

MN: Multiple screens also generate complex sounds, and the soundtrack for *Ten Thousand Waves* creates a sonic sense of immersion, submerging the viewer in the visceral experience of the Chinese cockle pickers who drowned in Morecambe Bay. Listening to the different tracks that you and Isaac have worked on over a twenty-five-year period, one is always conscious that there is a sort of sonata form structure in the music – there's always a repetition which is very important. Isaac's soundtracks are not predetermined, but there are phrases and elements which repeat and help create a sense of familiarity for the listener or viewer.

AF: Sound plays a large role in Isaac's work – I usually spend more time sound editing than I do on the picture montage. Although you can have a lot of things happening simultaneously visually, you can't do the same thing with the soundscape without it becoming cacophonous. So we've developed a form of sonic tapestry that weaves a lot of acoustic threads, found sounds and spoken texts with tones and textures created by sound designer Andy Cowton into an overarching composition.

For *Ten Thousand Waves*, we knew that we wanted nine speakers to match the screen array, but after a test install it became clear that Isaac wanted greater freedom to move the sounds around the space than was possible using a conventional cinema sound studio. In the end we rented a circular room at Peter Gabriel's Real World studios and the sound re-recordist Karl Mainzer built a bespoke system with a joystick which he could use to make sounds travel around the space.

MN: Gene Youngblood's *Expanded Cinema* was about the idea of expanding consciousness, whereas I think that Isaac's latest work is more about different kinds of attention – about a cinematic experience, but also about an emotional musical experience. All of that sutured together creates a unique intervention in the development of the aesthetics of the film installation works made today, and in the past forty years. The work that you and Isaac just finished, *Once Again ... (Statues Never Die)* 2022, uses a reflective mylar screen which echoes the kaleidoscopic effect in some of the early works.

AF: And the long tracking shots give the film a serpentine feel that immediately lends itself to being projected into a hall of mirrors, a Borgesian gallery that extends infinitely. In a way, that evokes the incomprehensible scale of the plunder which the film witnesses – that's the feeling and mood that I tried to accentuate in the edit, and it's reflected in that beautiful presentation with glass vitrines of sculpted figurines in the gallery extending the physical presence of the work.

MN: It becomes a real immersive installation. And even though the screens are positioned all around the exhibition space, there's not a radical break with experimental narrative. At first, *Once Again* is almost a traditional Hollywood version of montage, images and joins sutured together to create an illusion of space and narrative. But then, instead of images being joined together as in the early analogue and linear work, it's broken apart using the montage strategies of the multiple-screen works. All this other material invisible in the linear narrative comes through the gaps, and the multiple points of view emerge. One can't make too elaborate a psychoanalytic reading of the repressed images but there is something to that – the sense of freedom and possibility that you get when you turn from the linear, single-screen cinematic approach to other kinds of cinema of the moving image, which Abel Gance was exploring nearly a hundred years ago.

AF: Yes – if you delve a bit deeper, that's where the interest in these pieces comes from, though I don't think it's all that different in conventional cinema. The real film is the dream that the film evokes in the mind of the viewer. We all bring our own experiences and dreams, expectations, fears or hopes of where a scene is going to lead and we filter the experience through these. Fellini called film 'a dream we dream with our eyes open' and it is important to make space for that in the work.

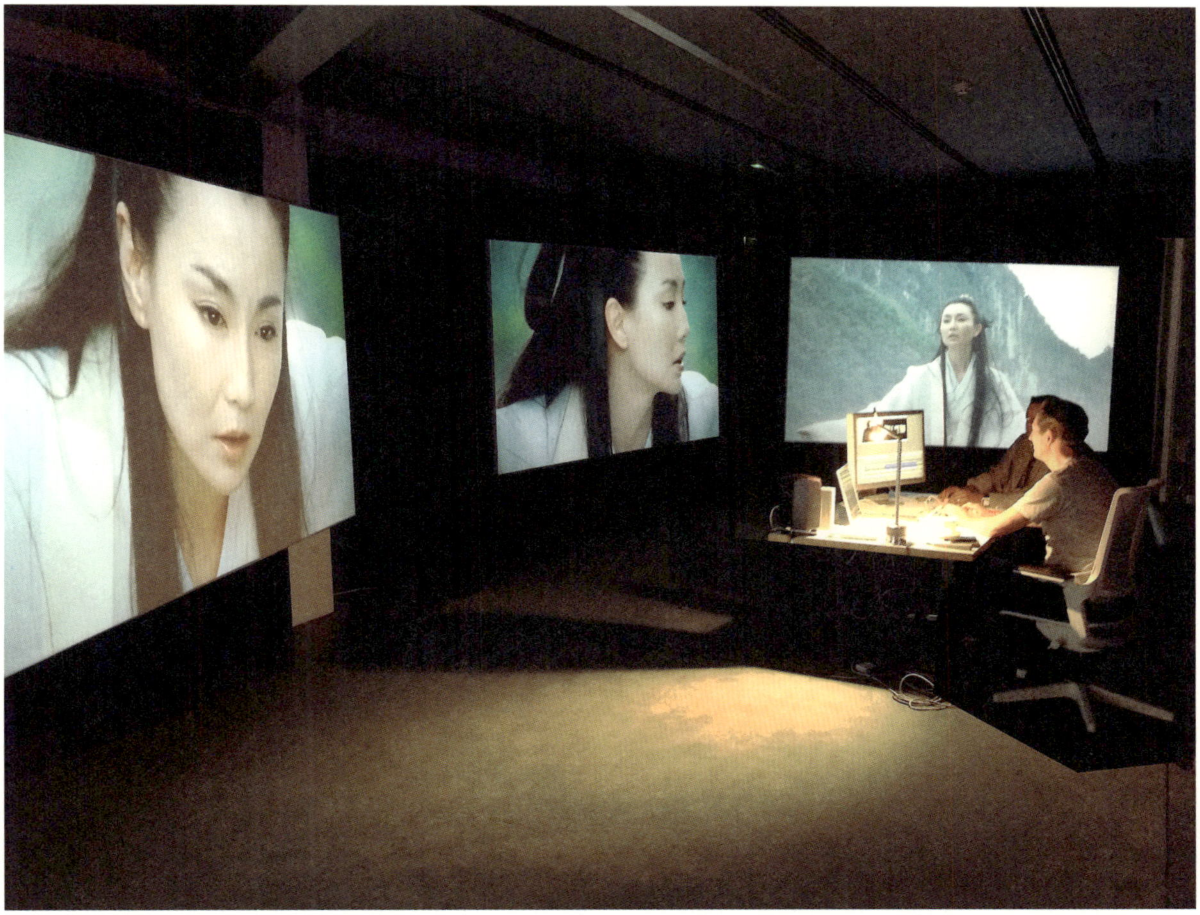

Adam Finch editing *Ten Thousand Waves* 2010

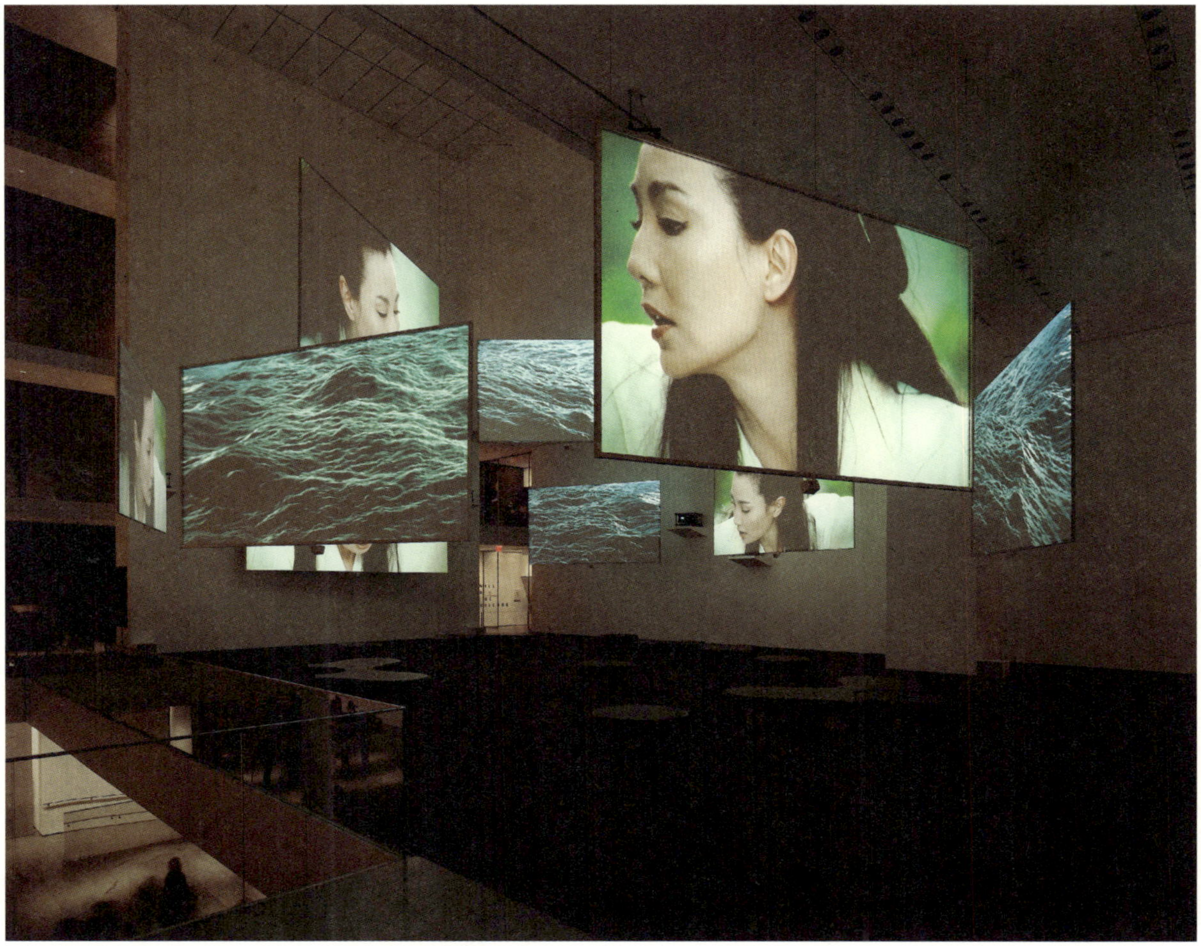

*Ten Thousand Waves* 2010, installation view, MoMA, New York, 2013

# TEN THOUSAND WAVES

2010

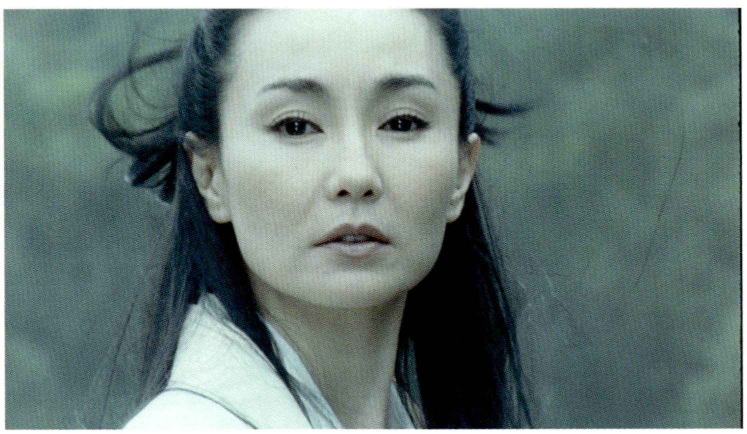

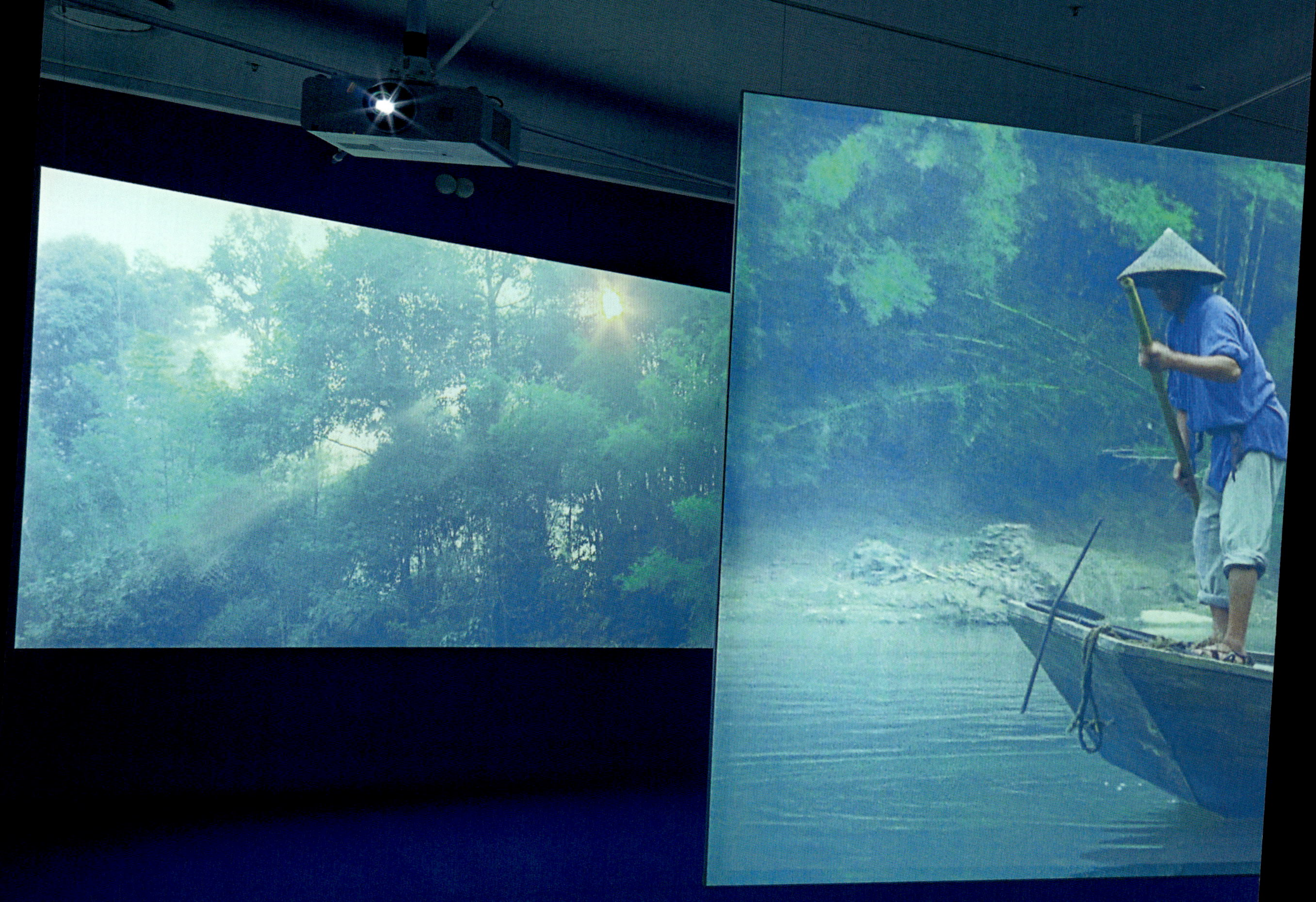

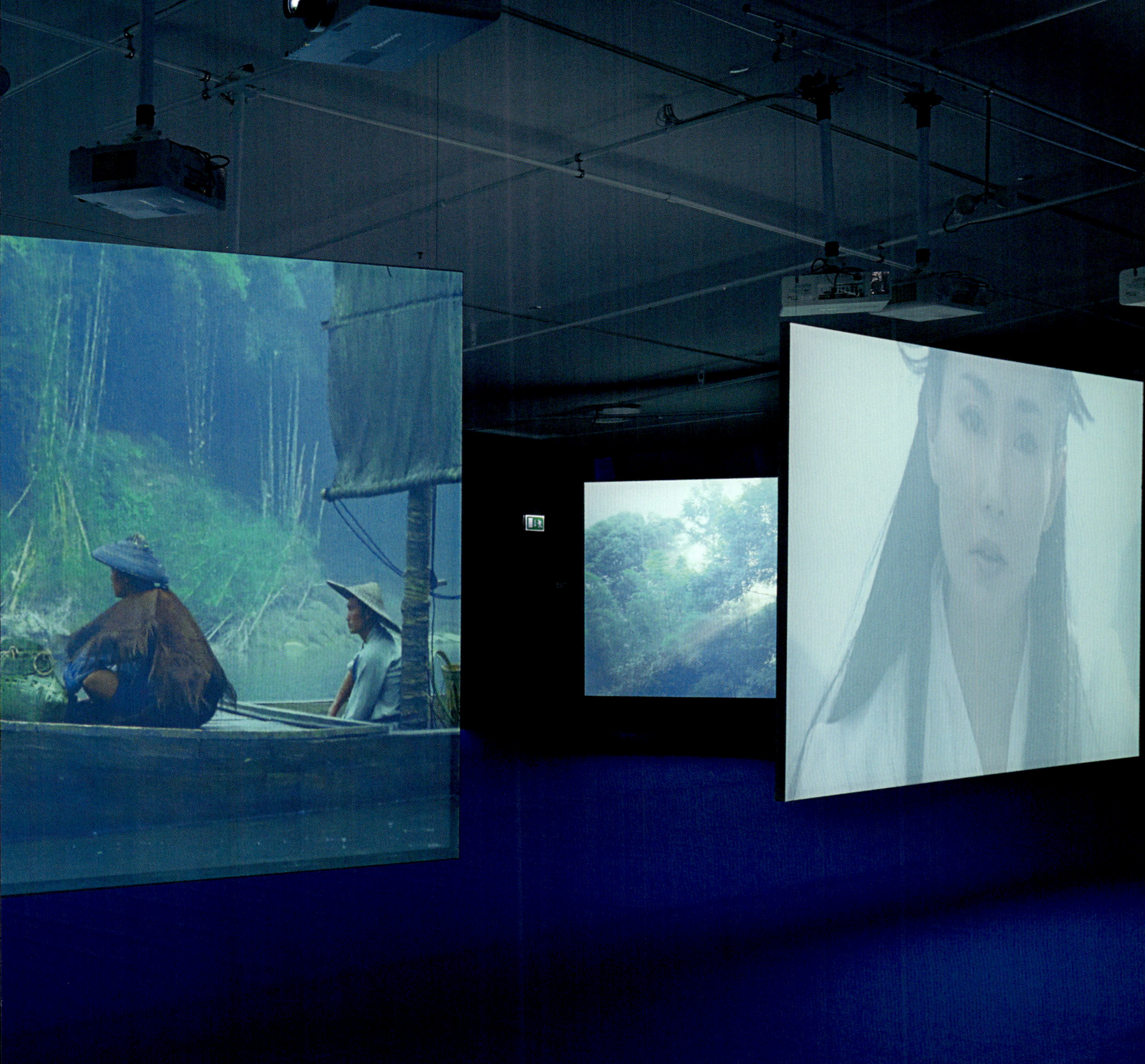

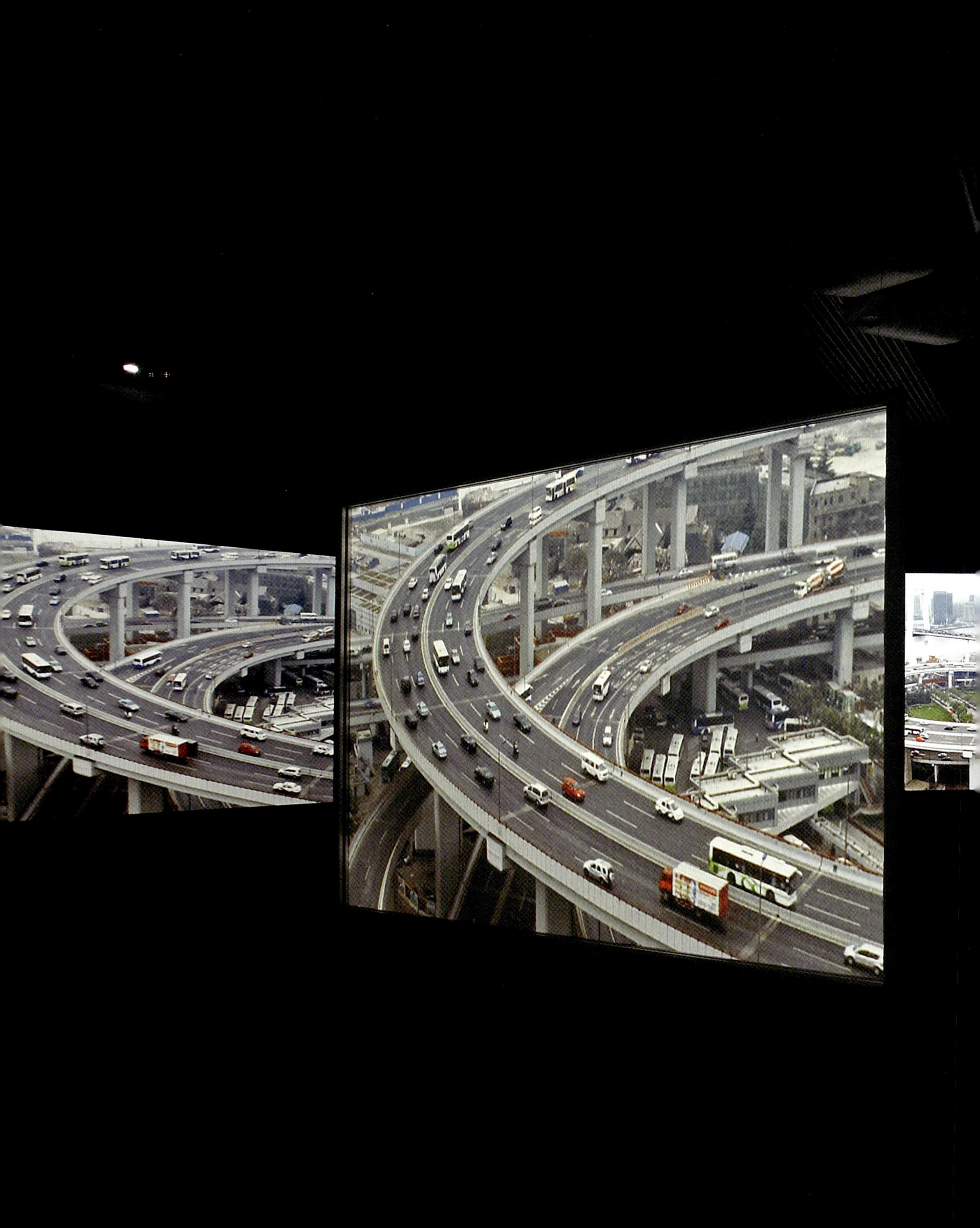

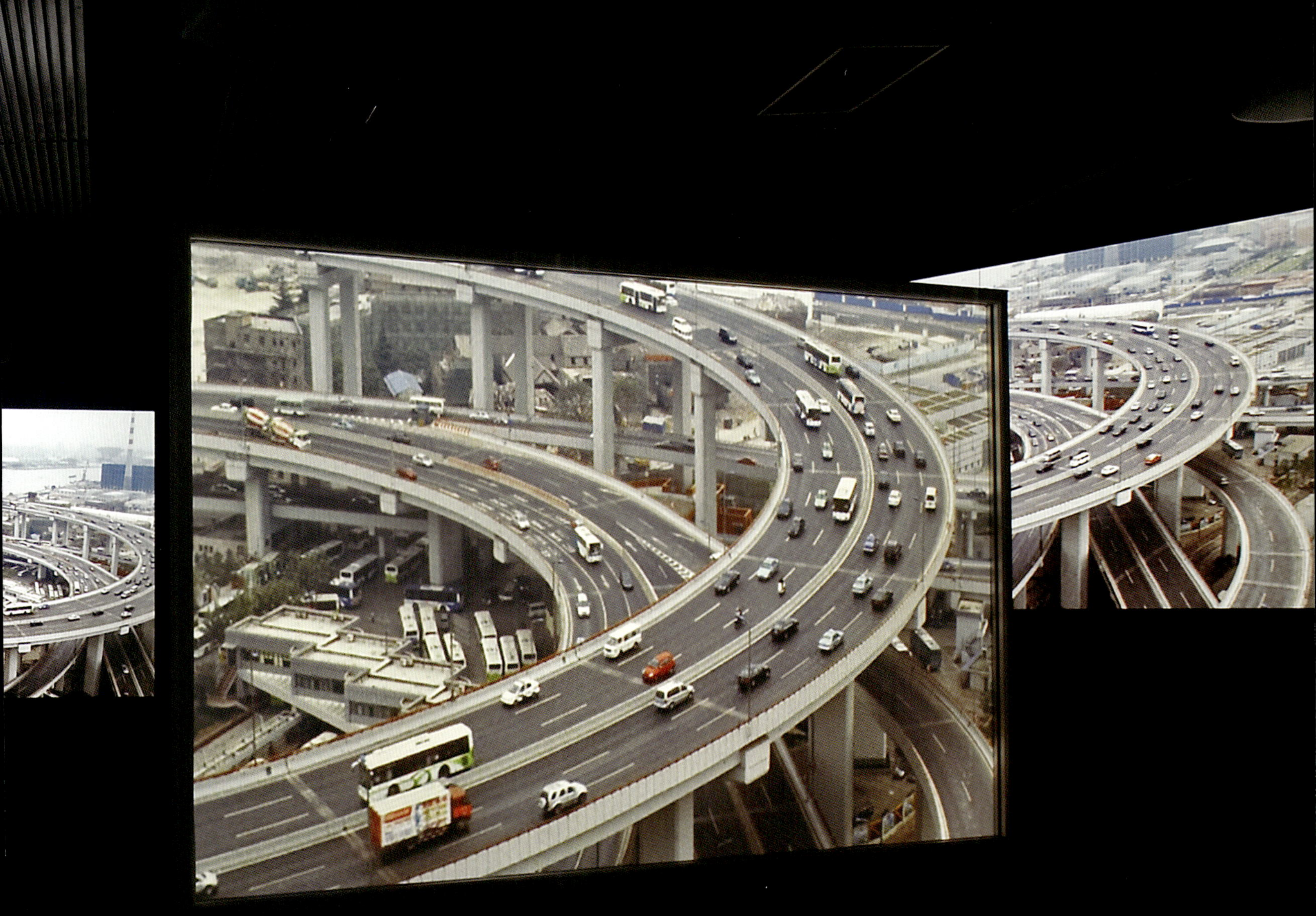

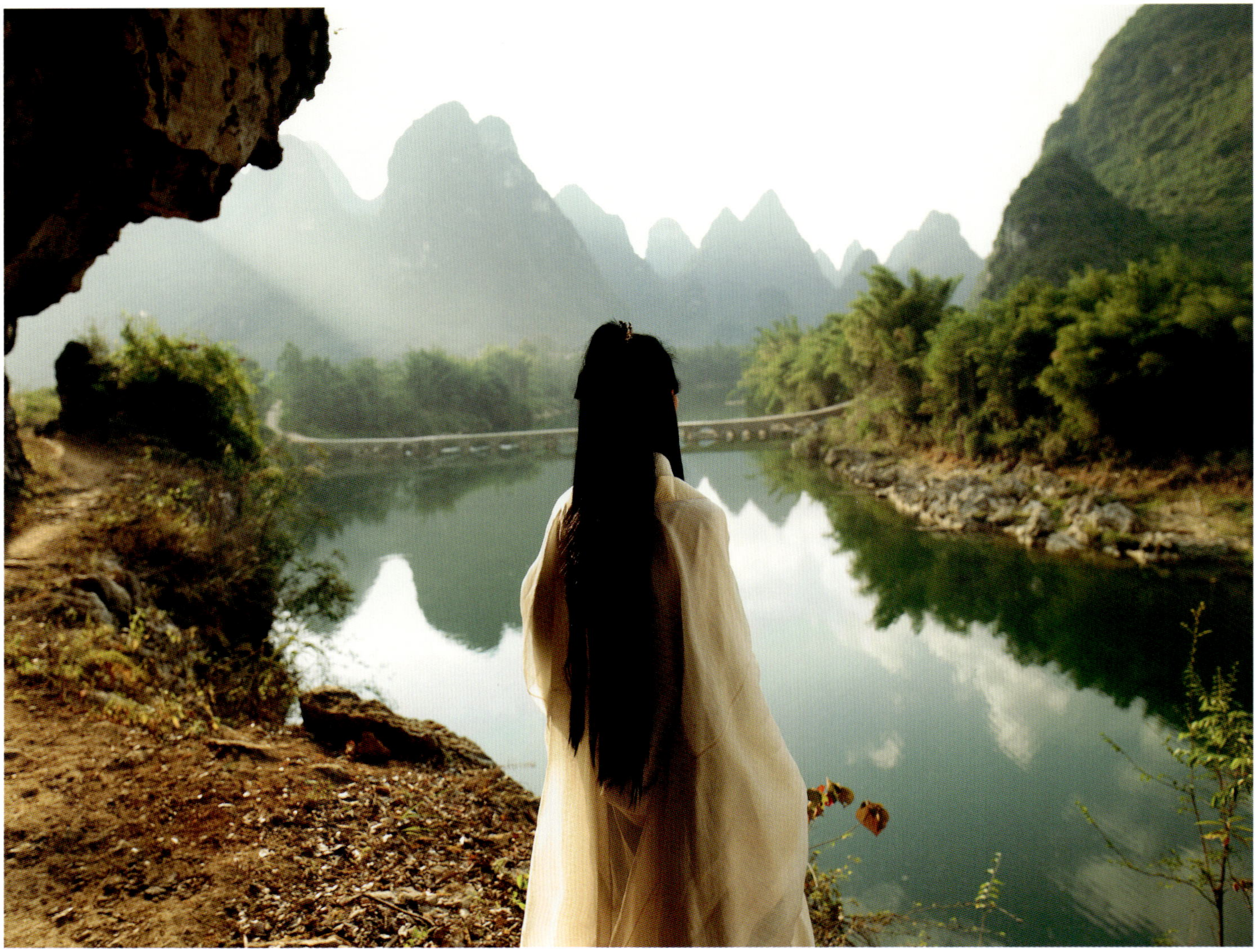

*Mazu, Silence (Ten Thousand Waves)* 2010

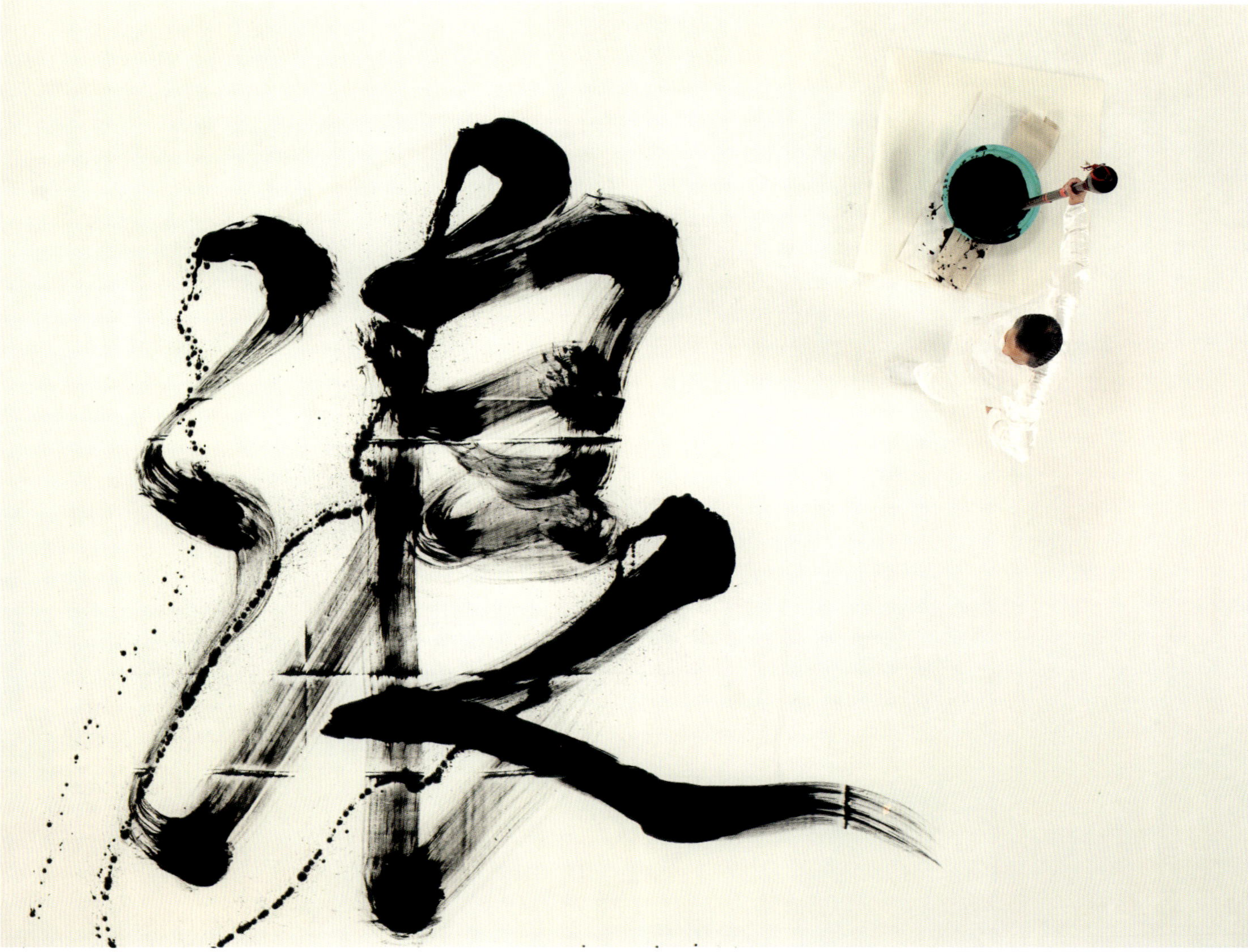

 *Waves (Ten Thousand Waves)* 2010

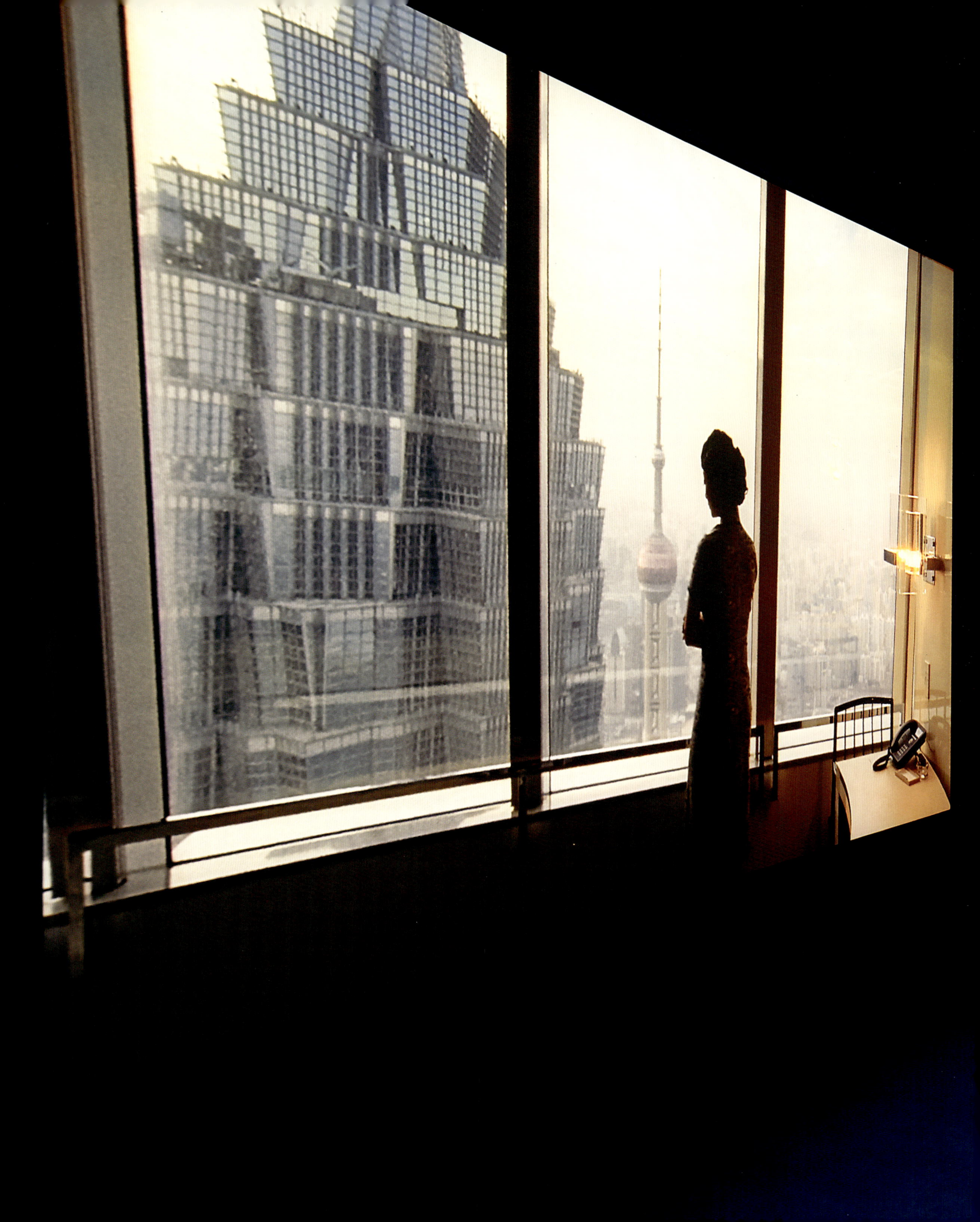

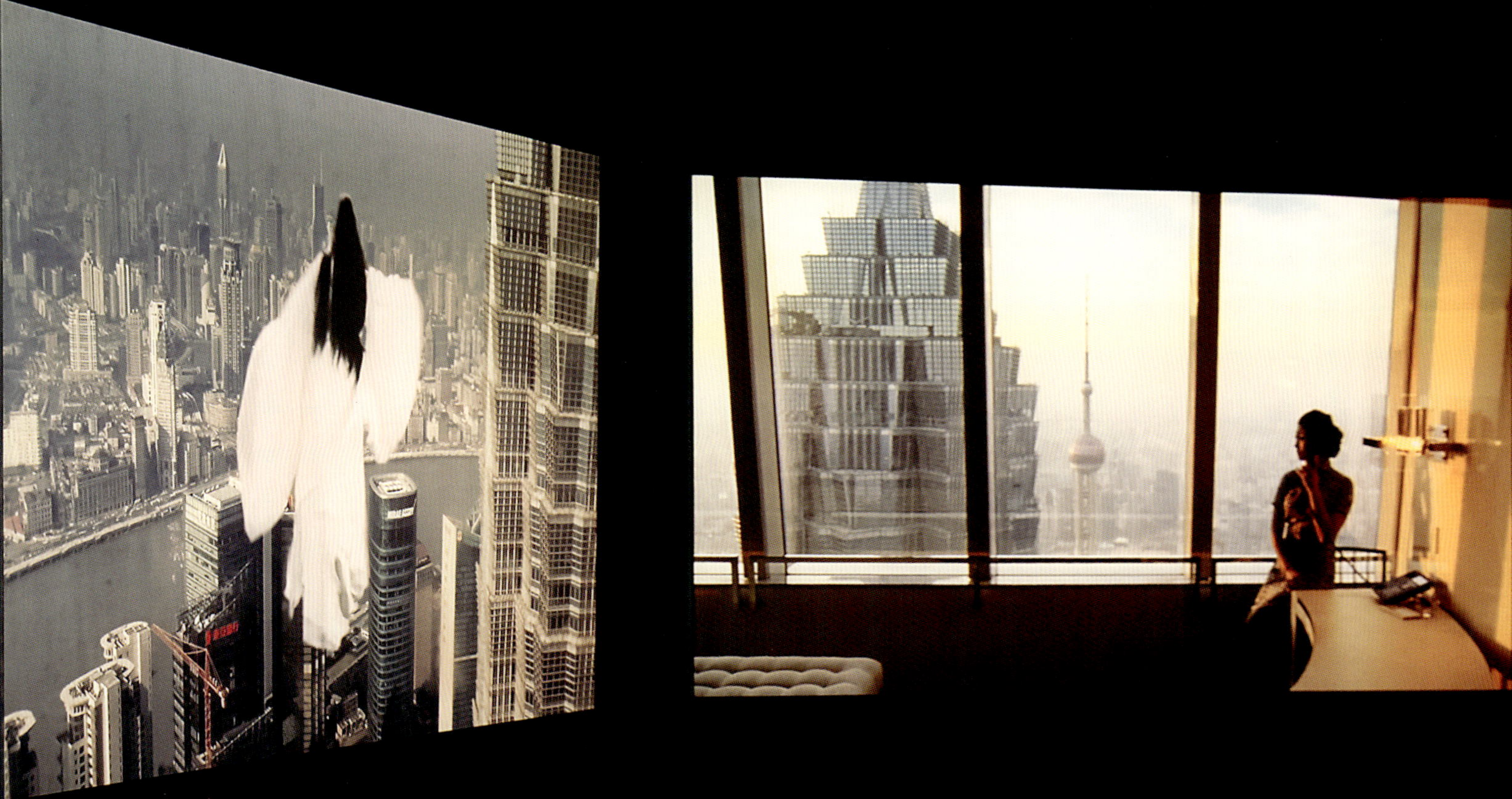

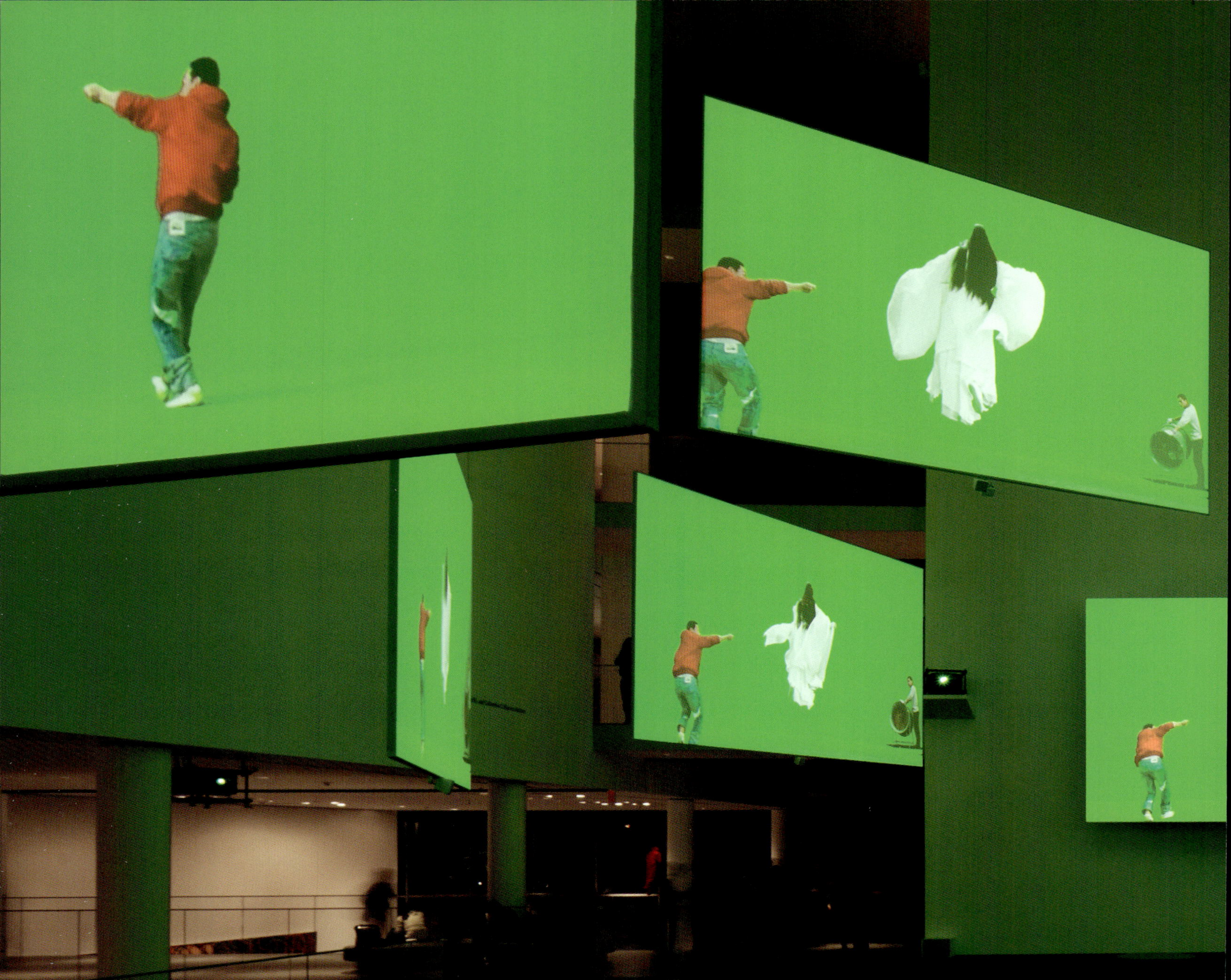

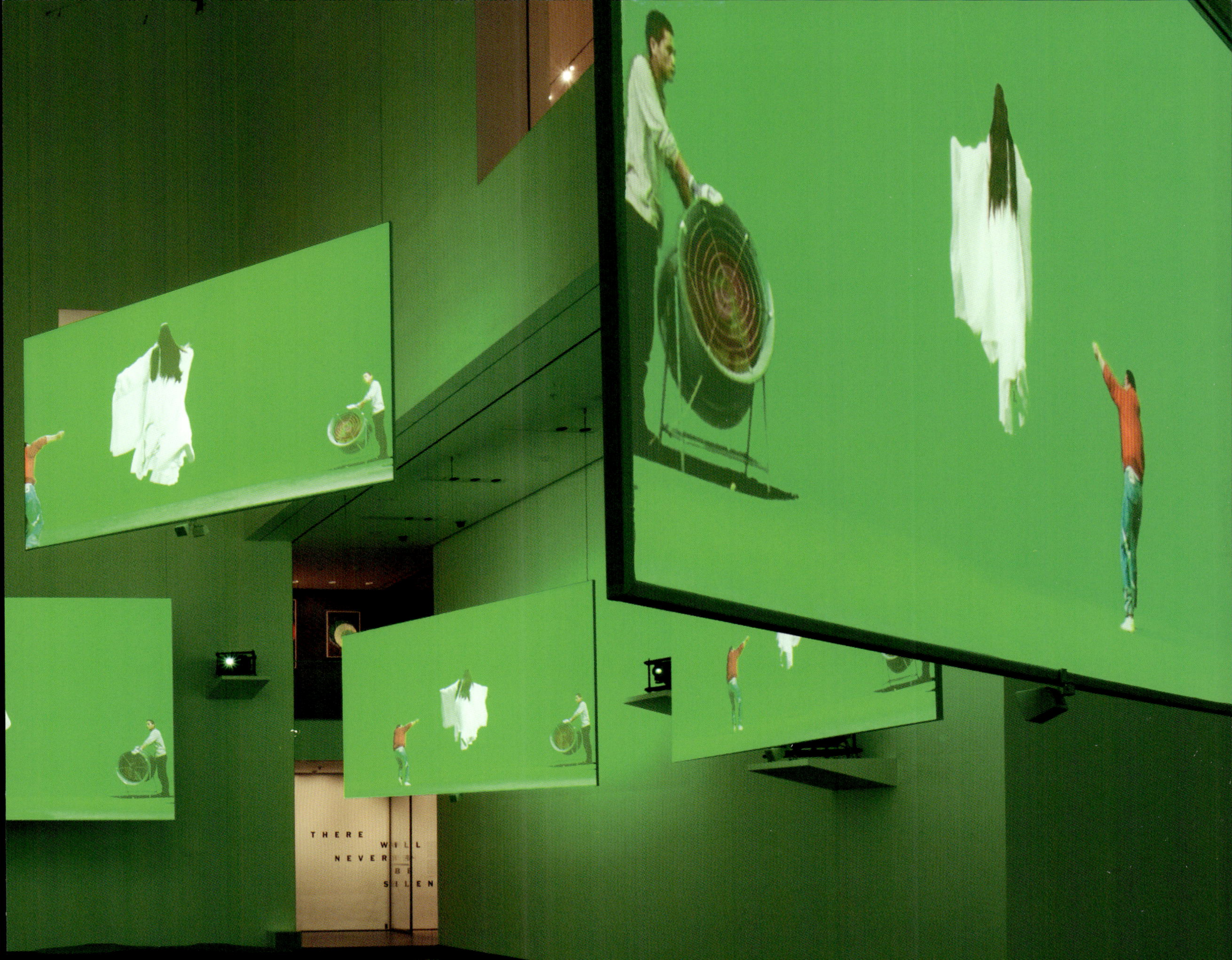
THERE
WILL
NEVER
BE
SILEN

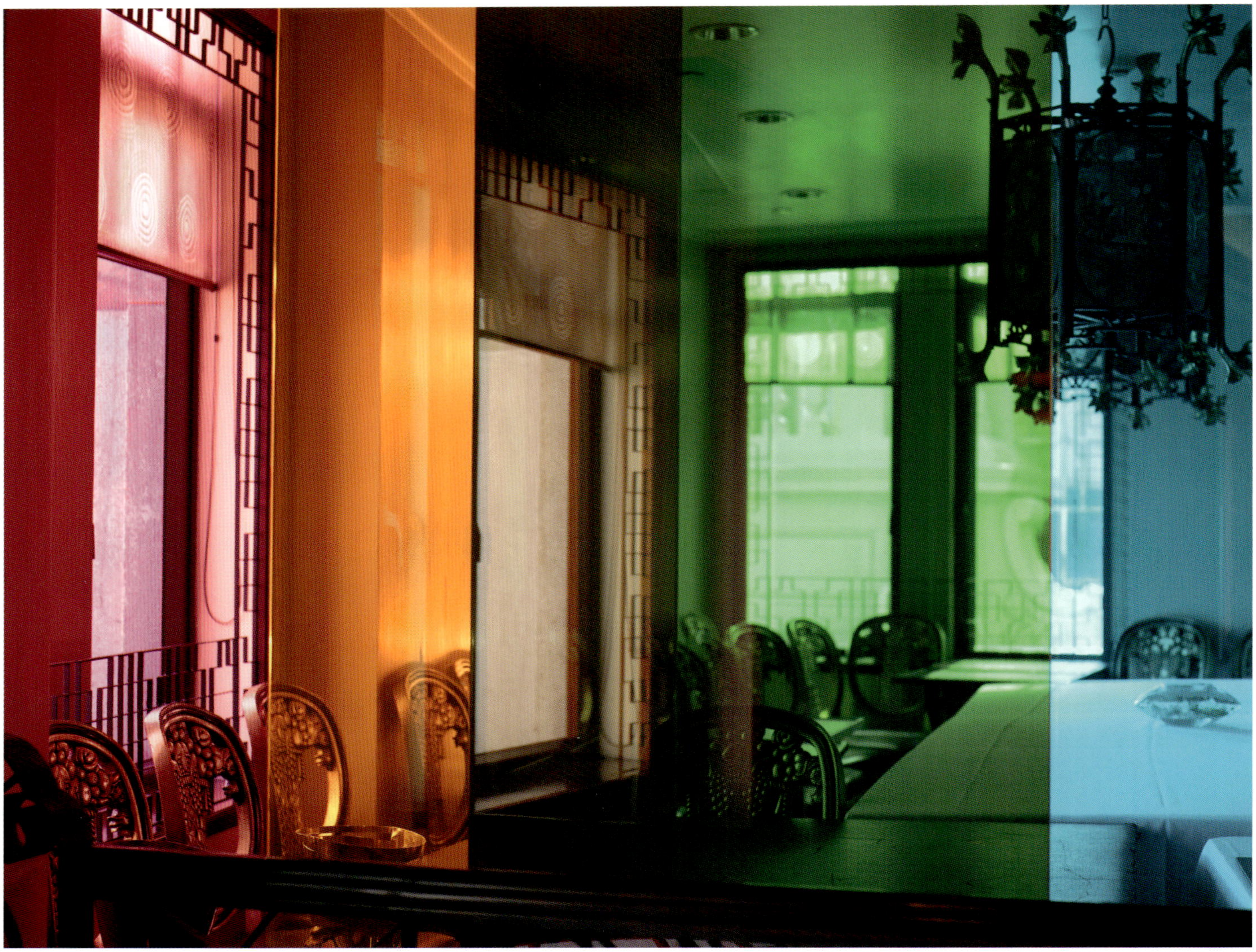

*Glass House, Prism (Ten Thousand Waves)* 2010, diptych

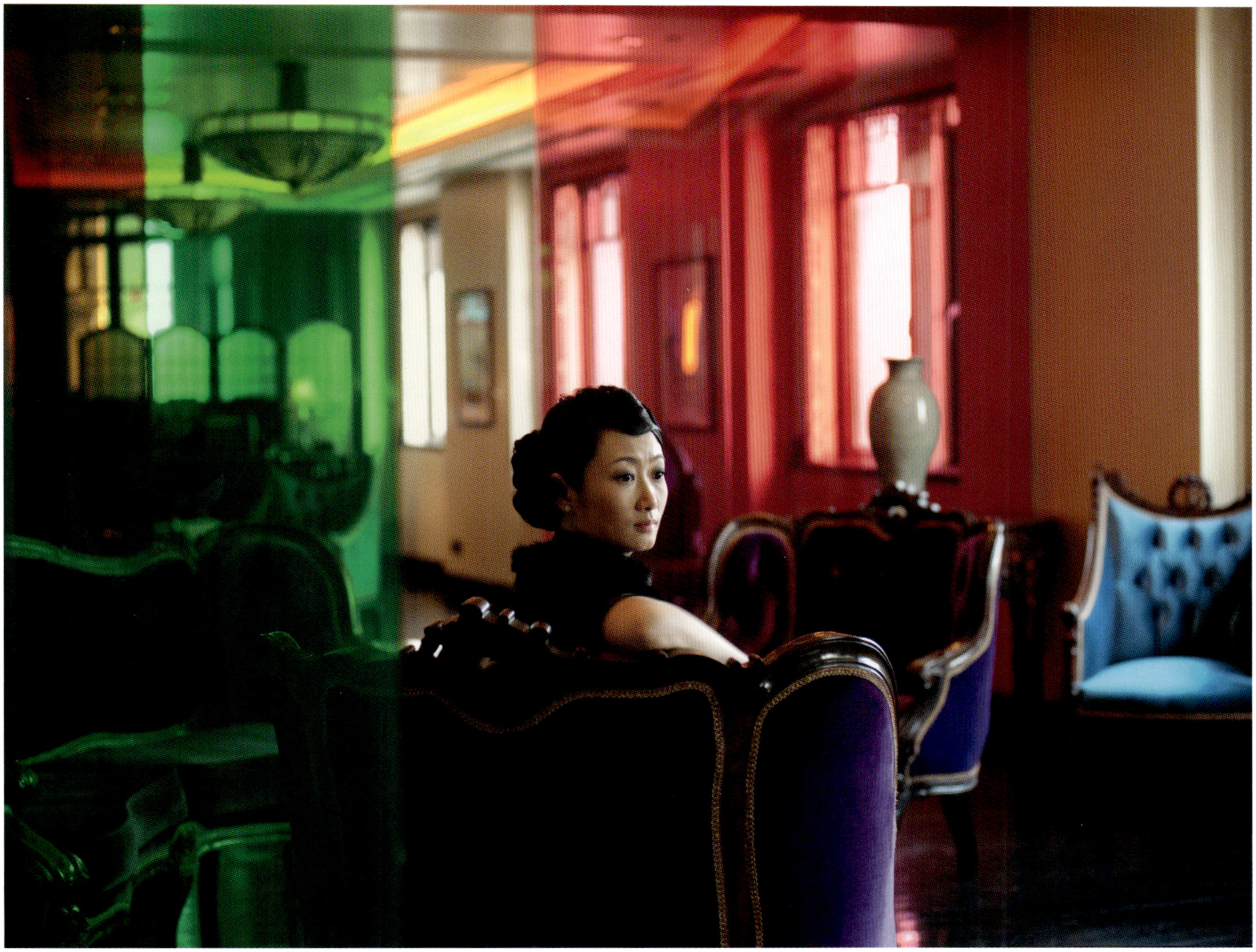

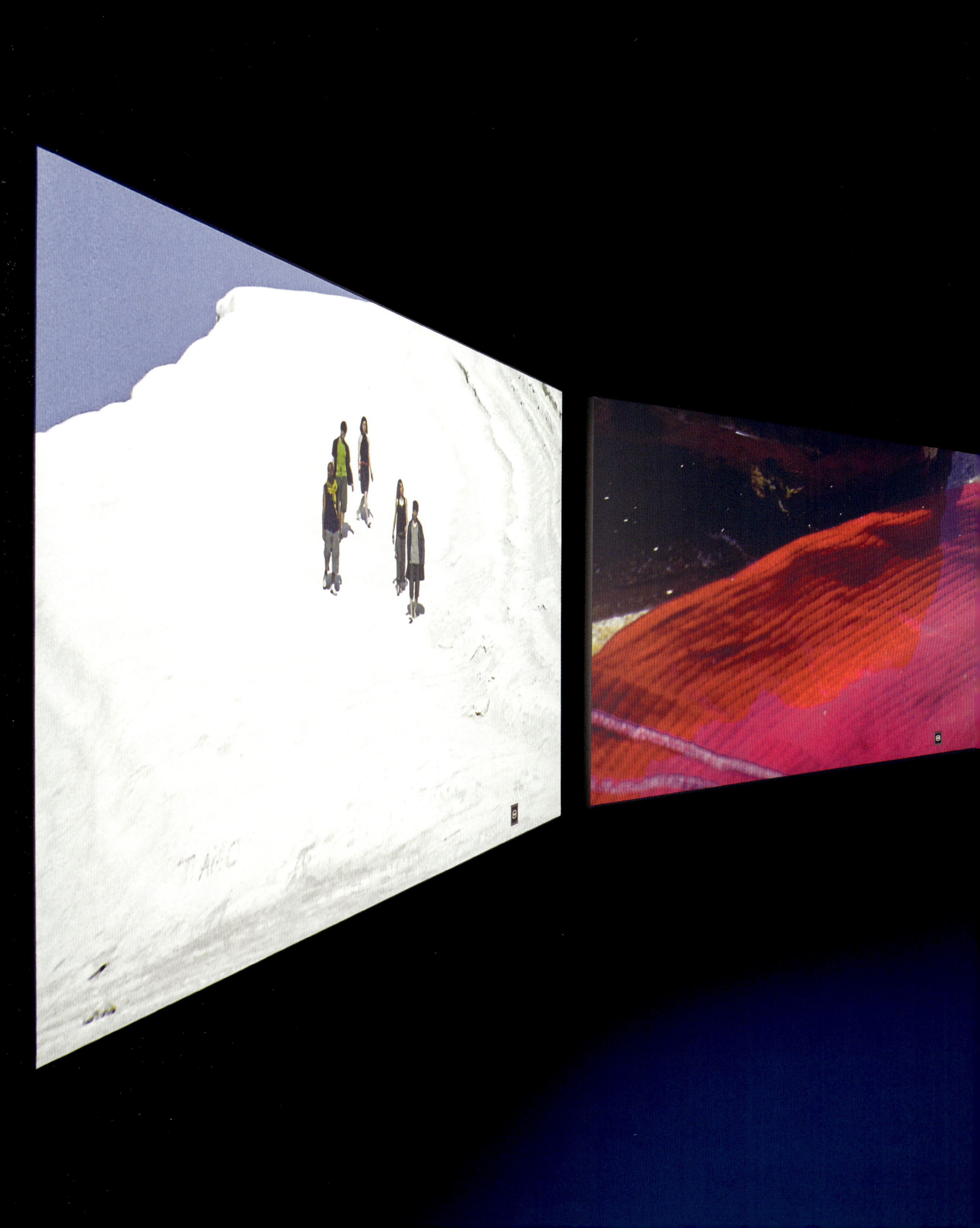

# WESTERN UNION : SMALL BOATS

2007

▶ 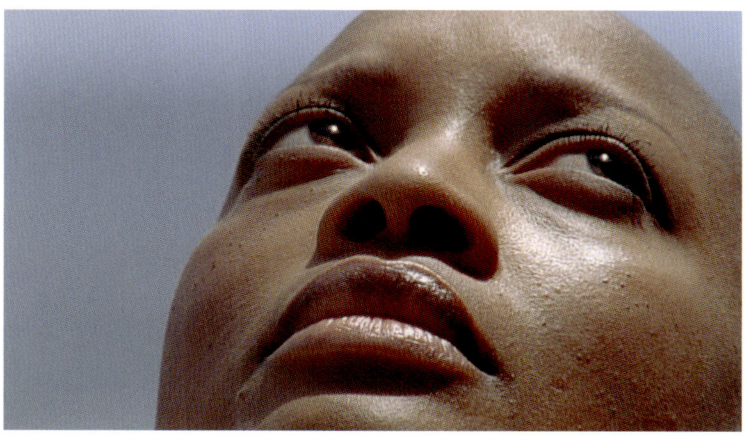

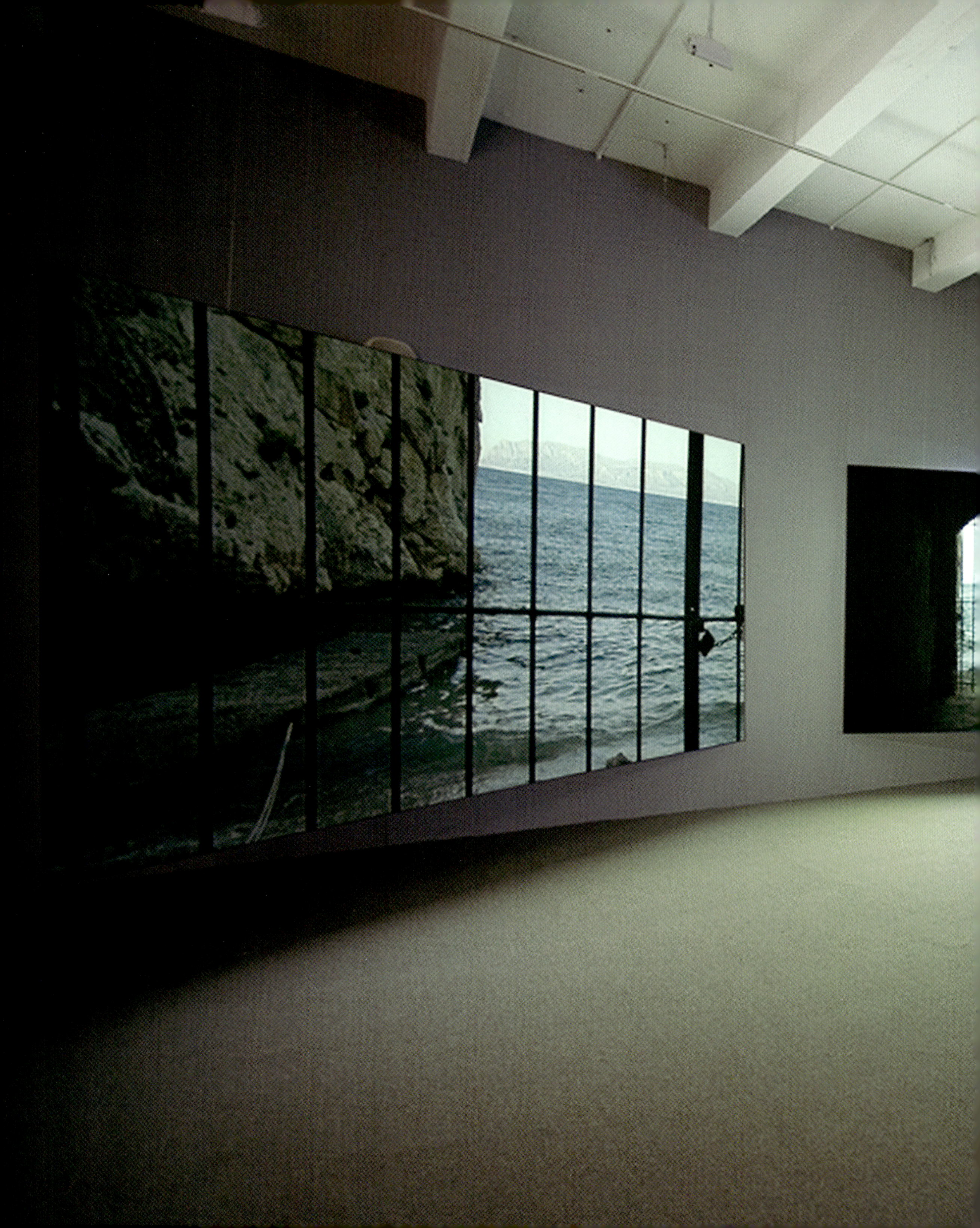

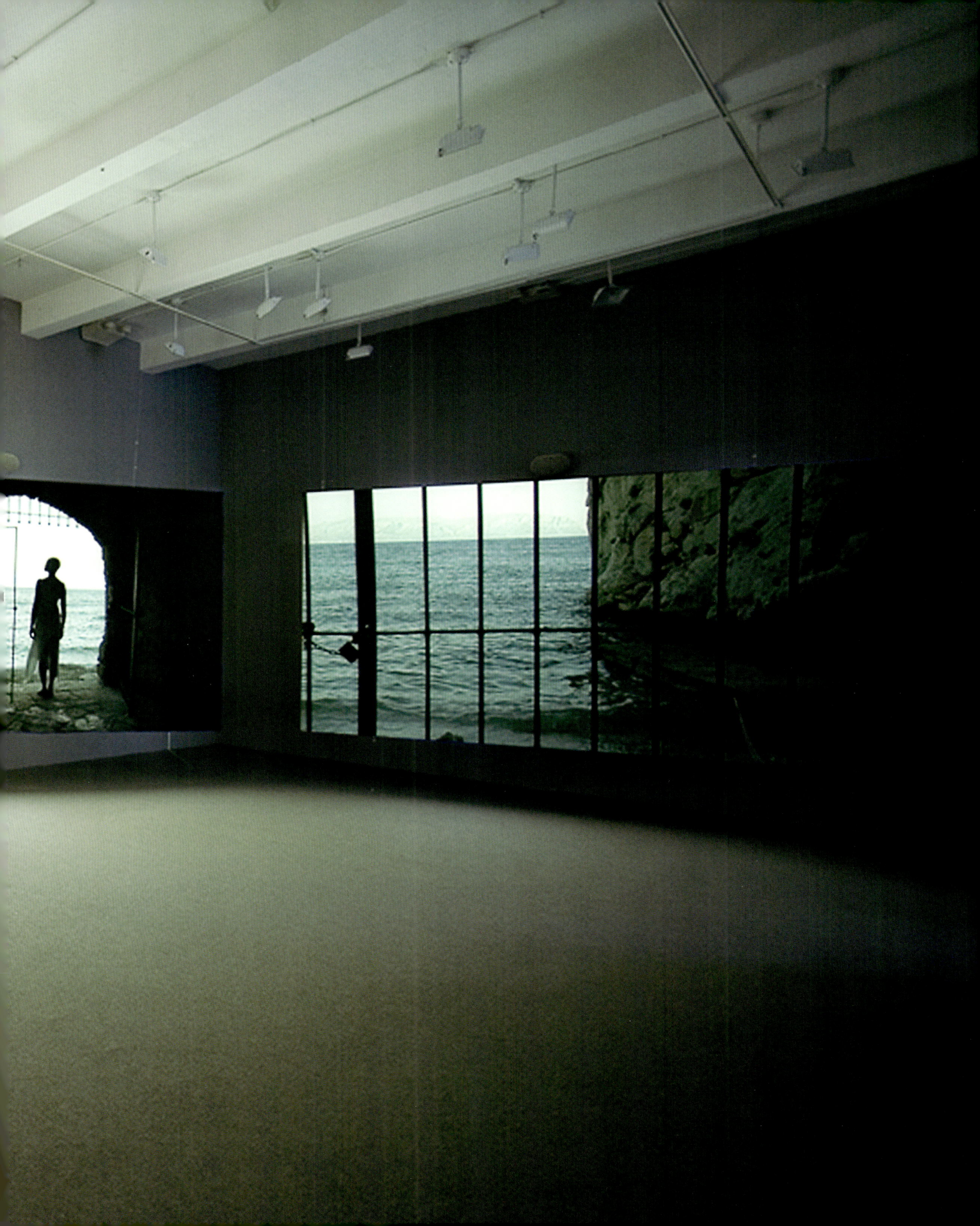

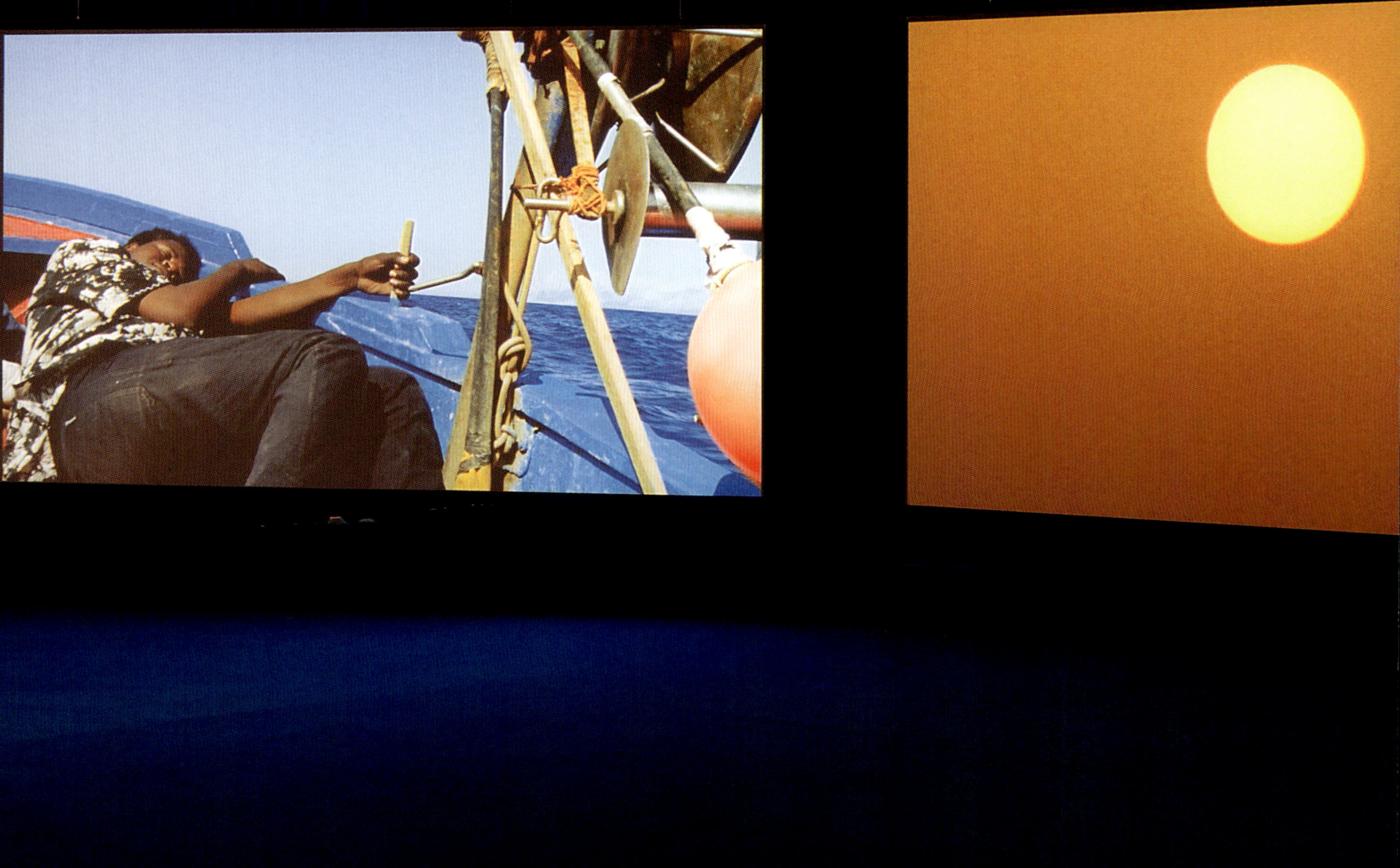

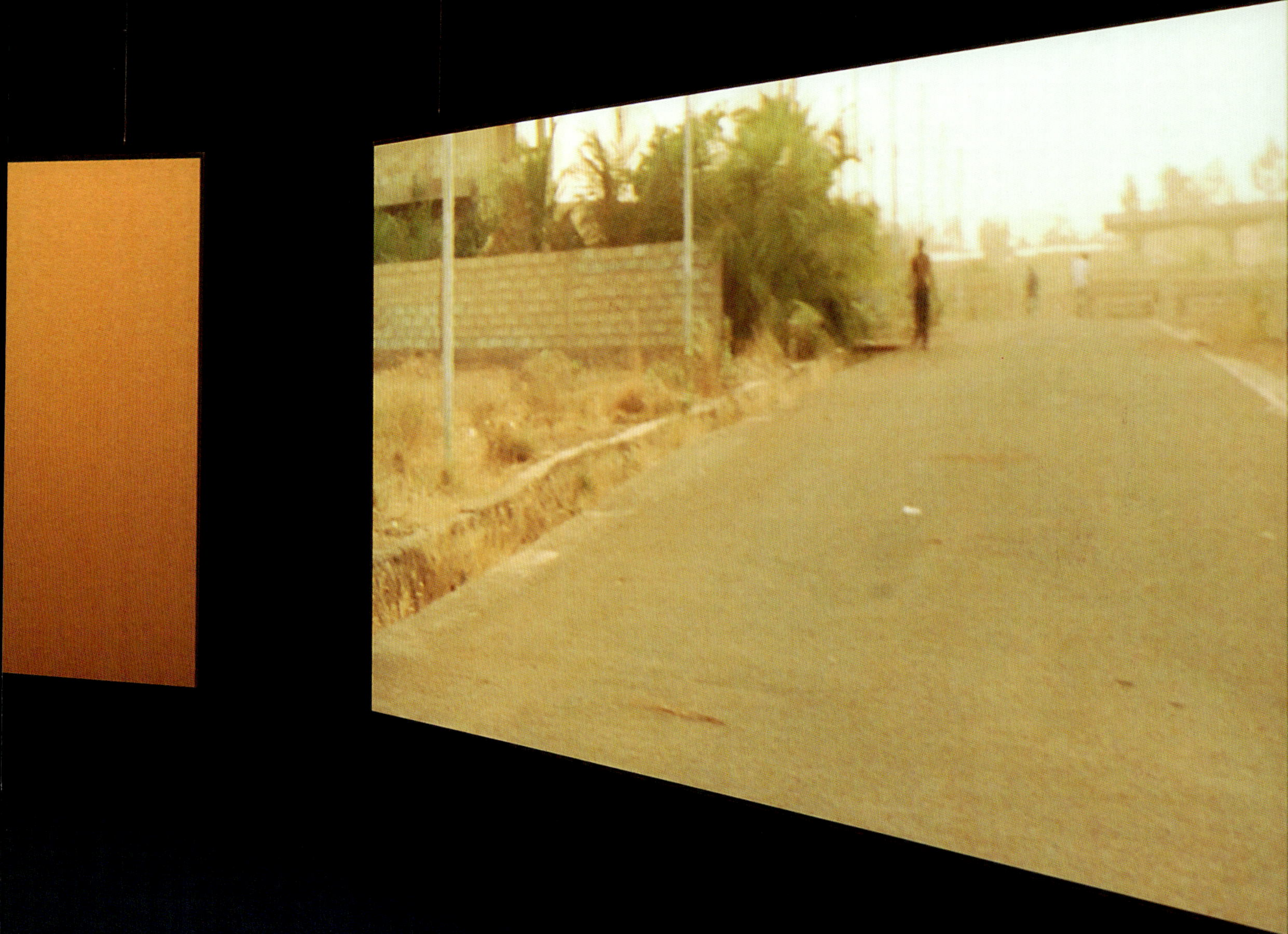

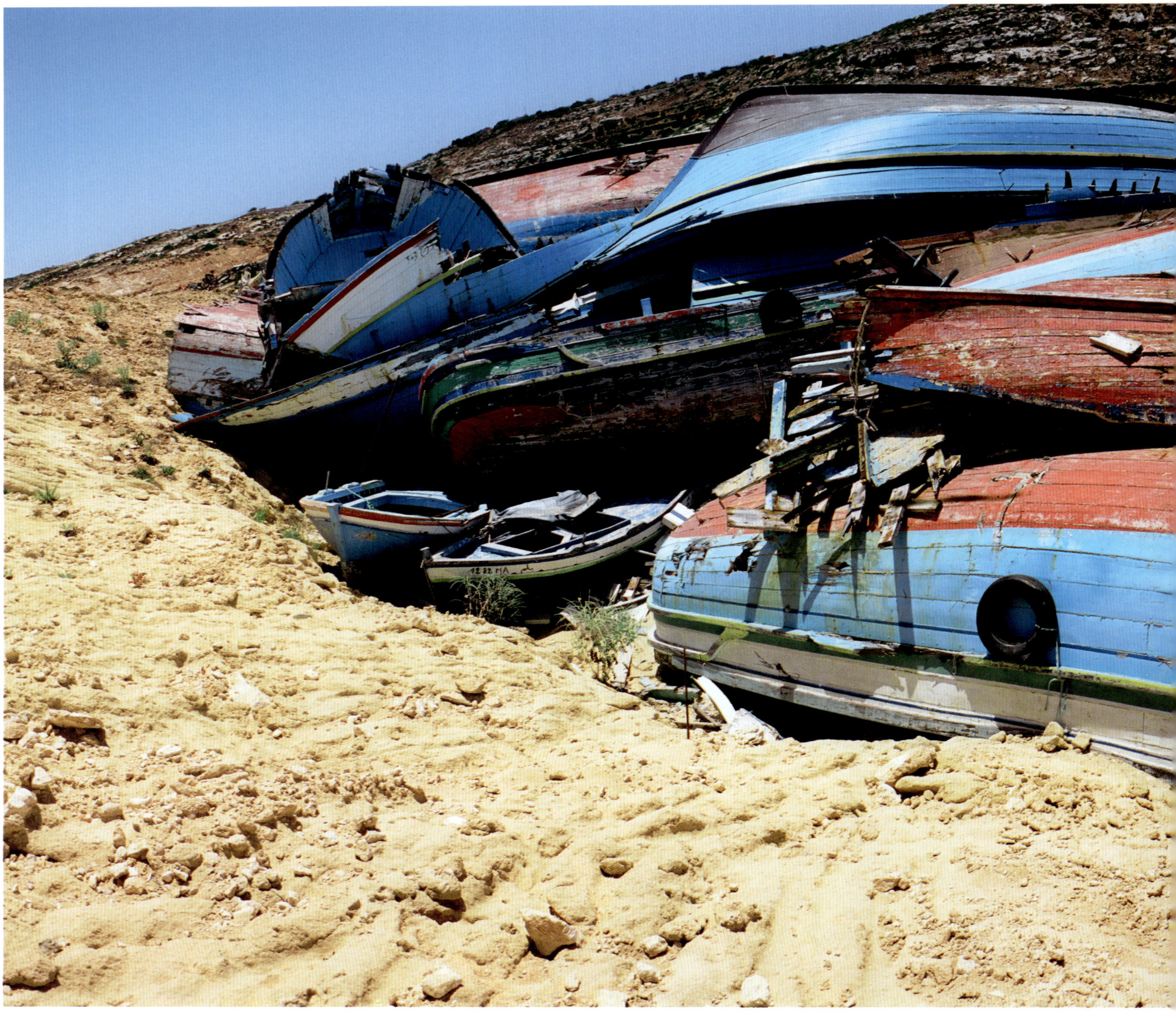

*Western Union Series No.8 (Sculpture for the New Millennium* 2007

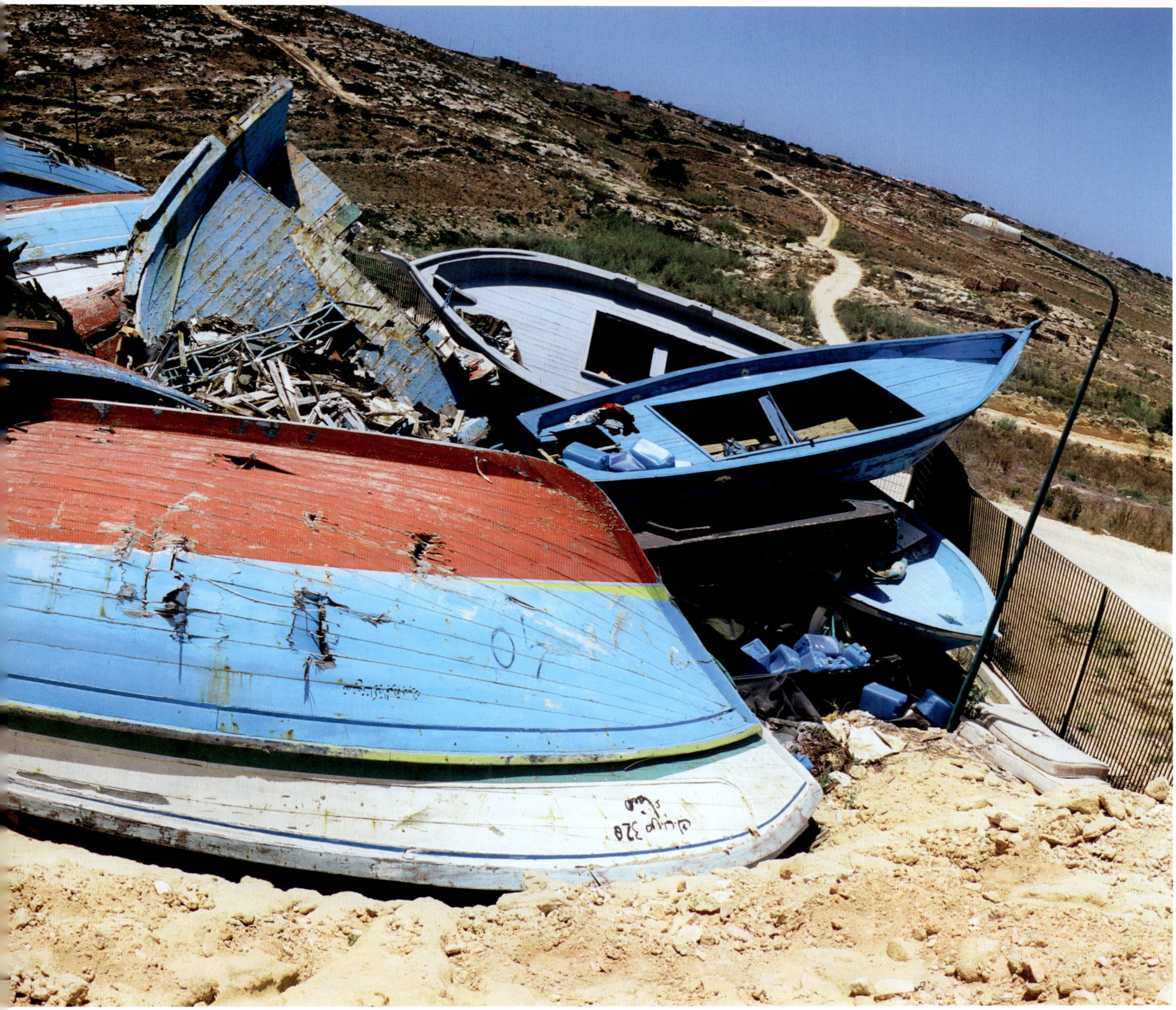

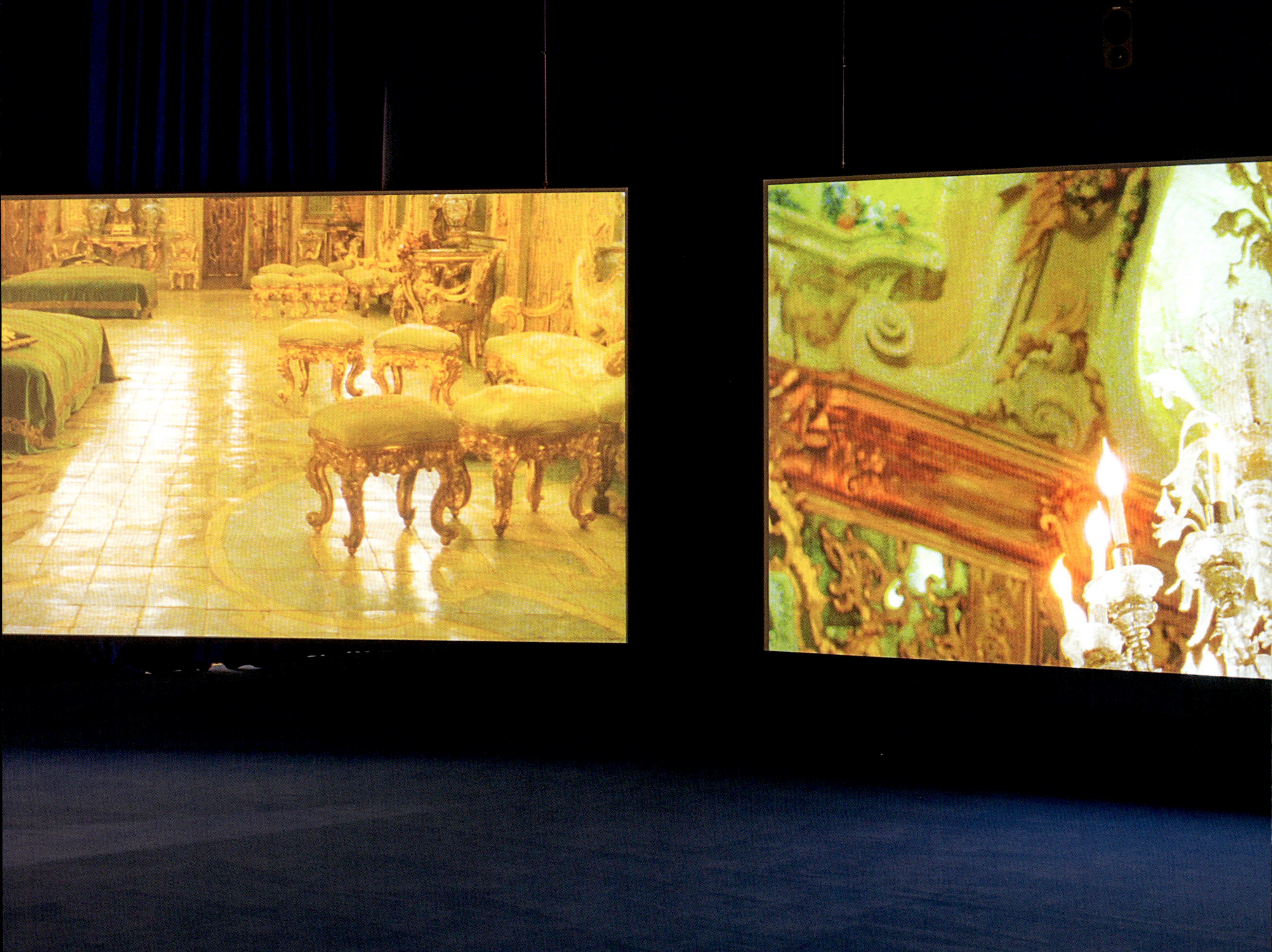

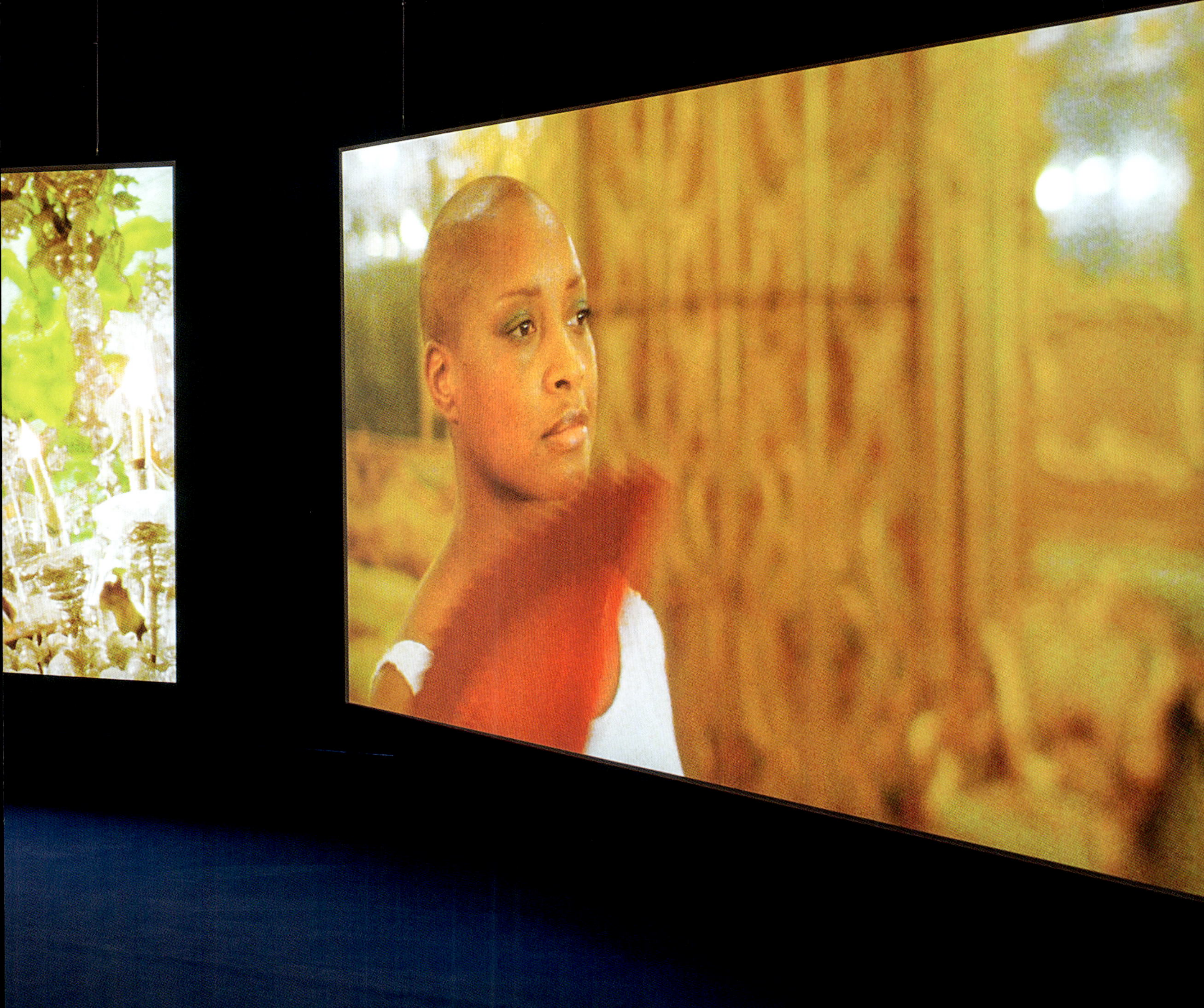

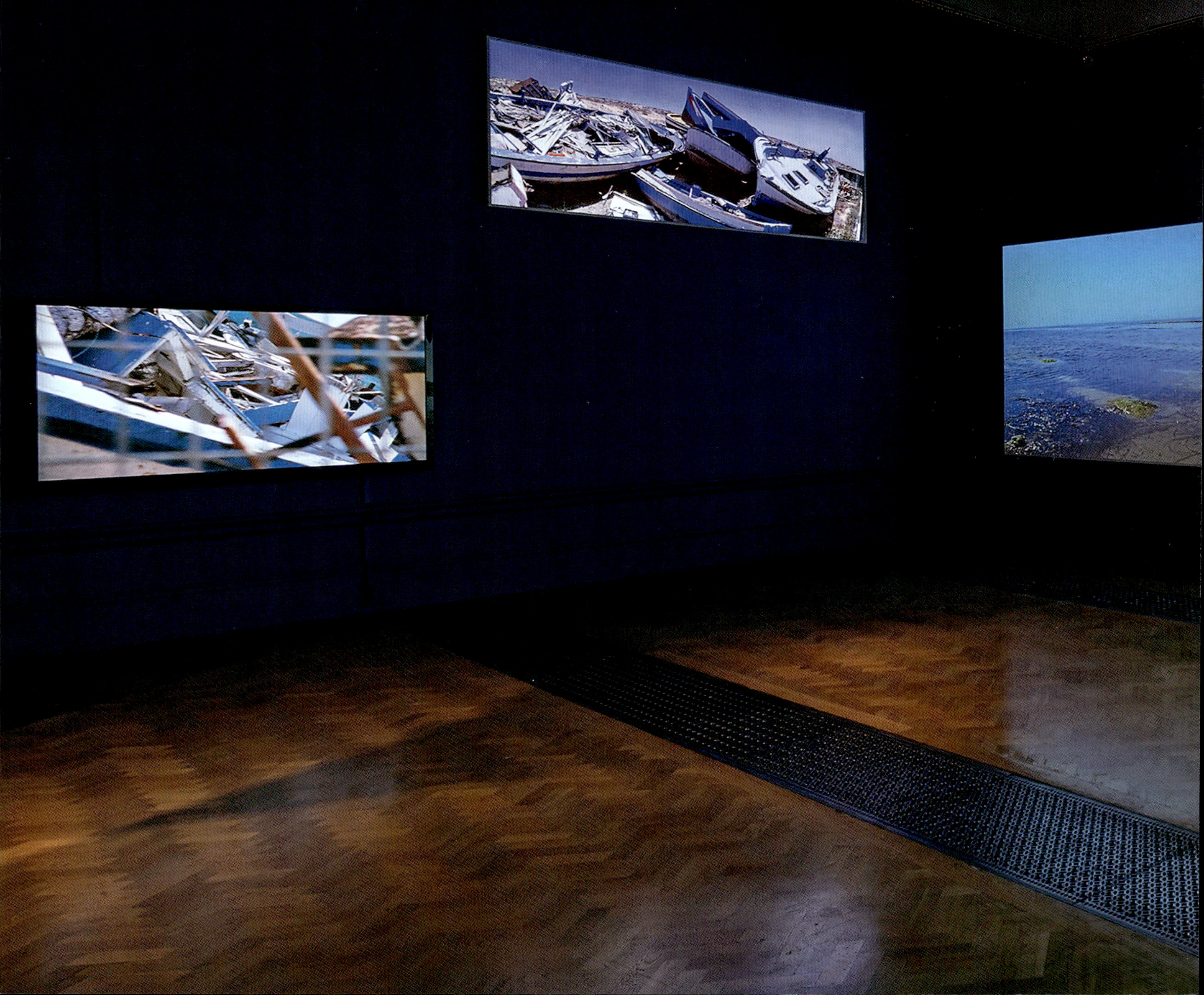

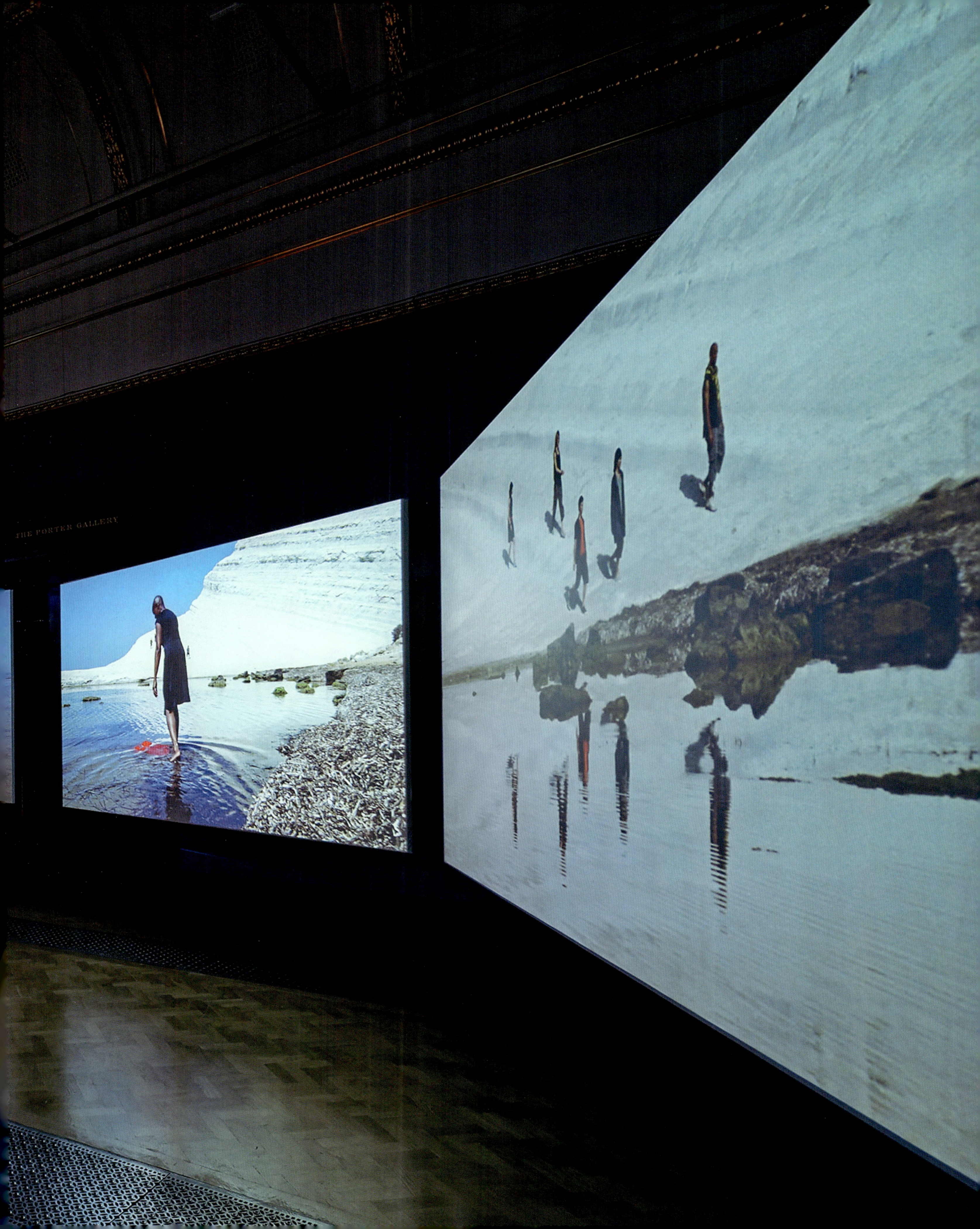
THE PORTER GALLERY

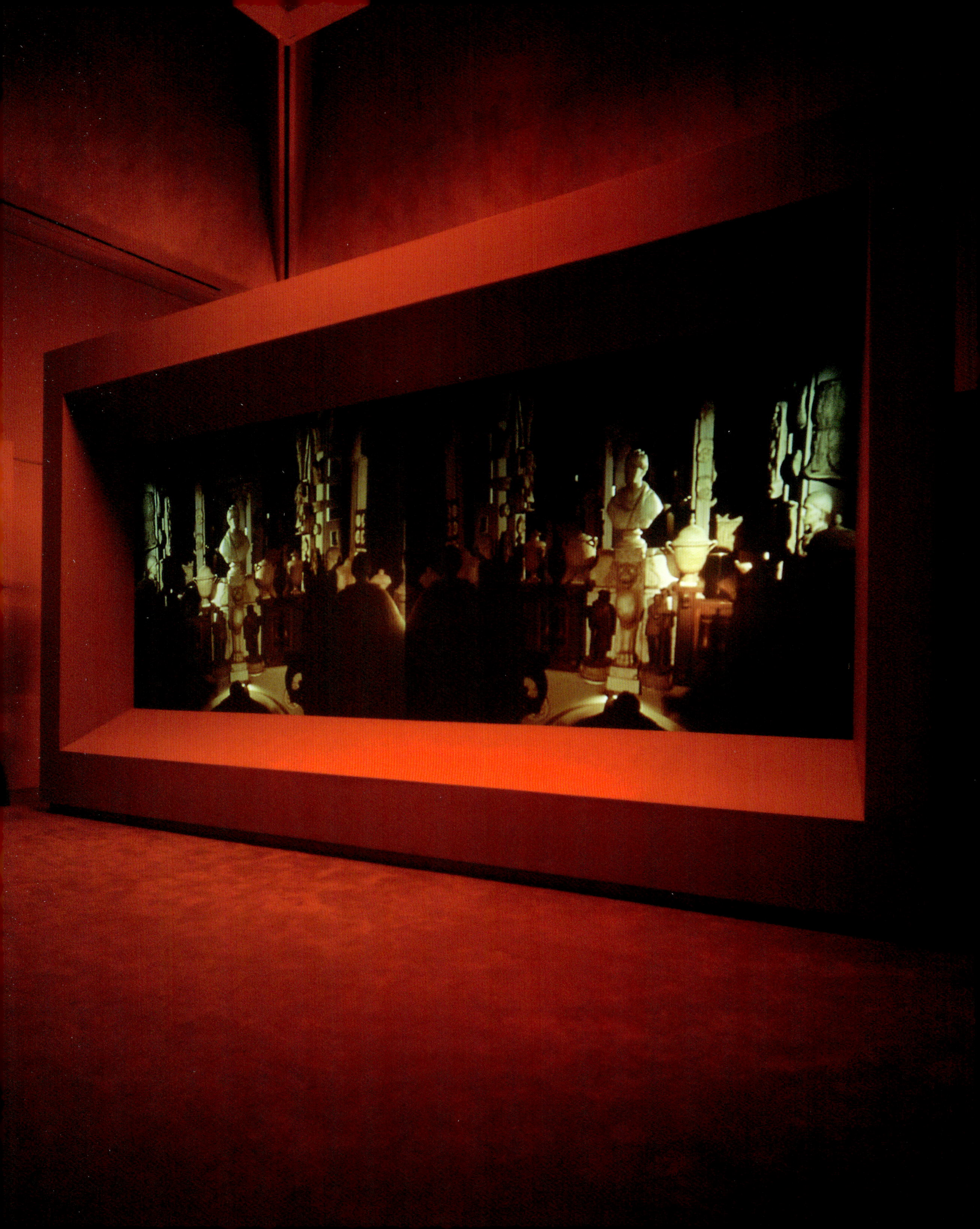

# VAGABONDIA

# 2000

▶ 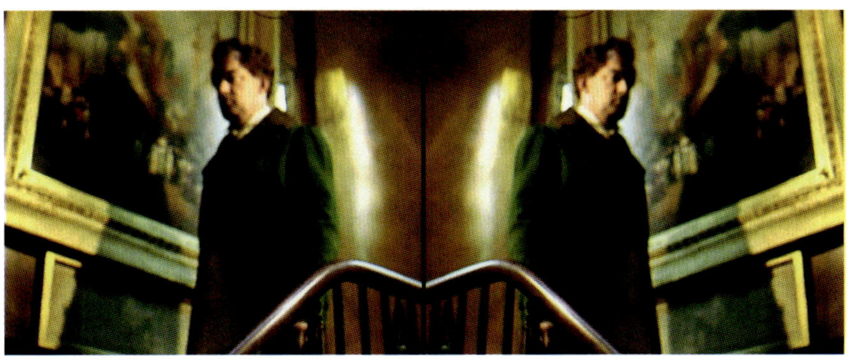

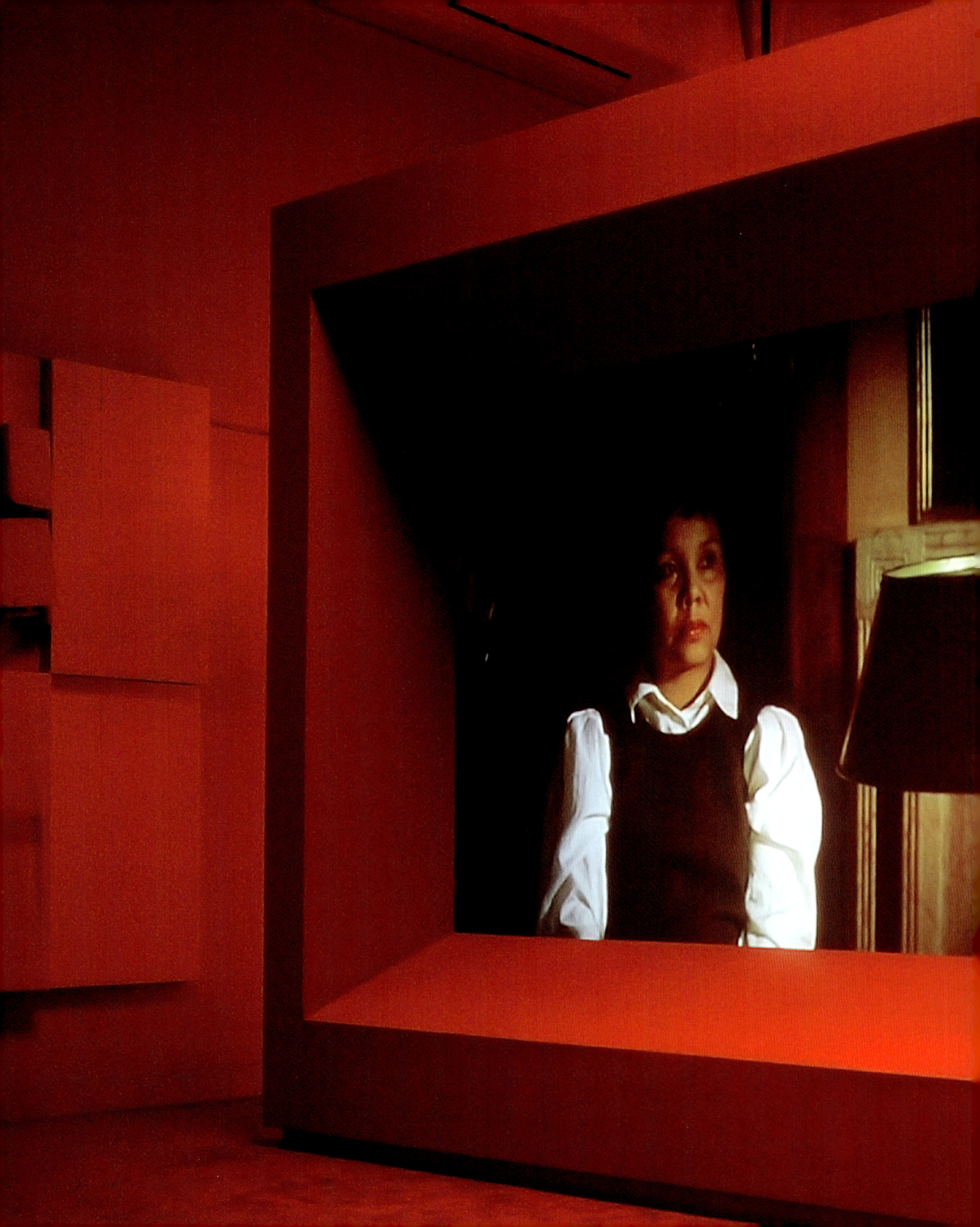

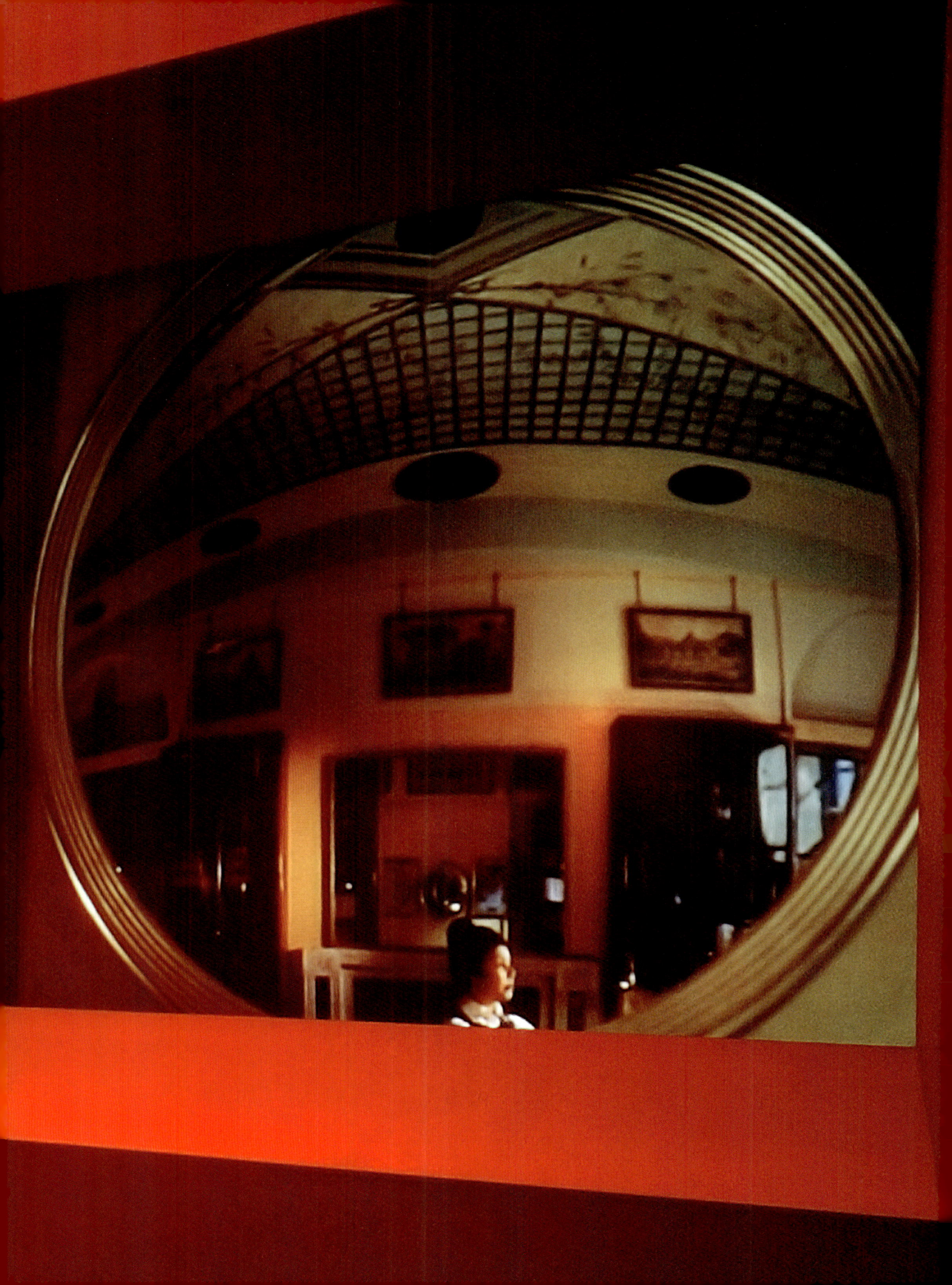

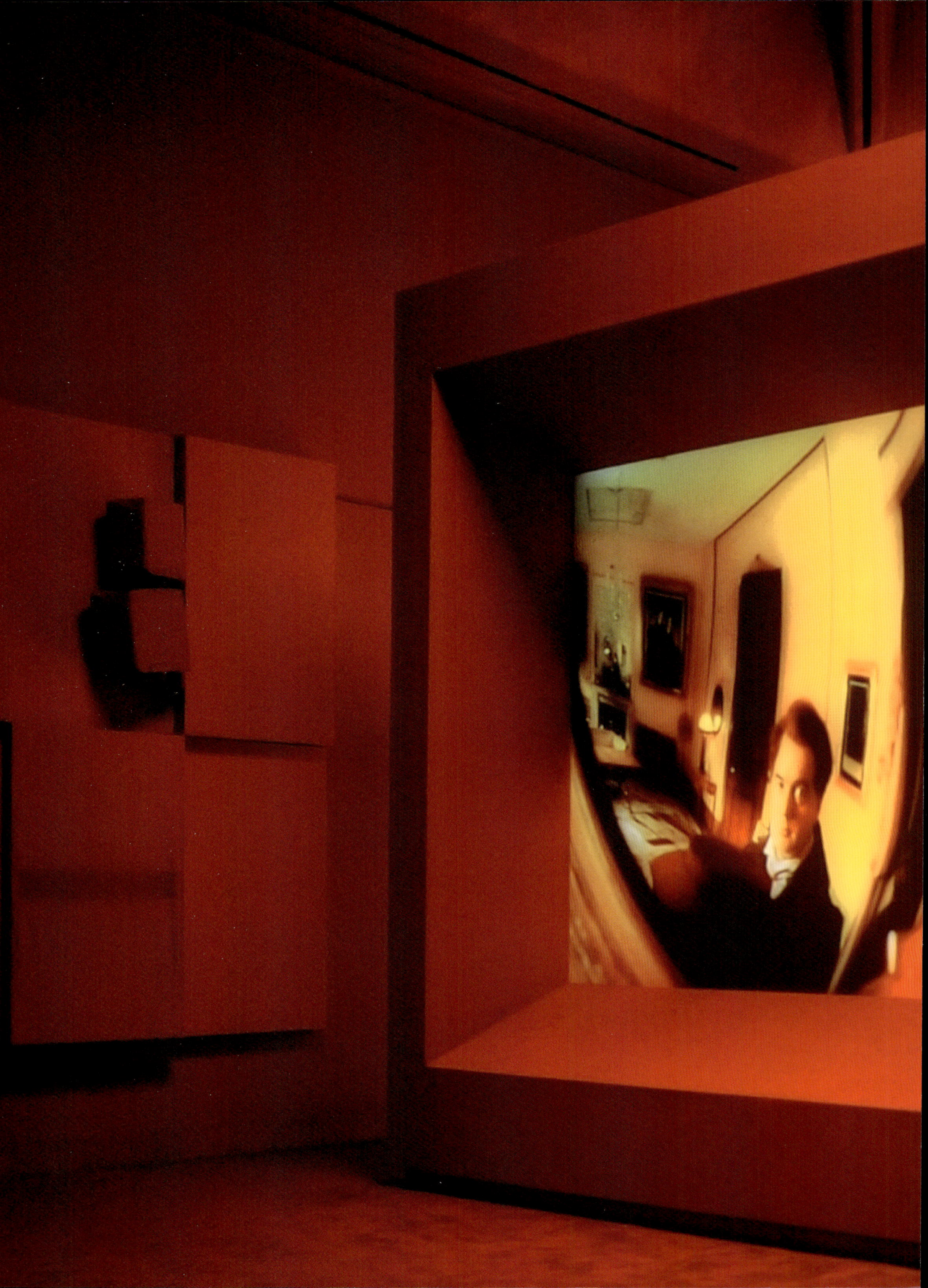

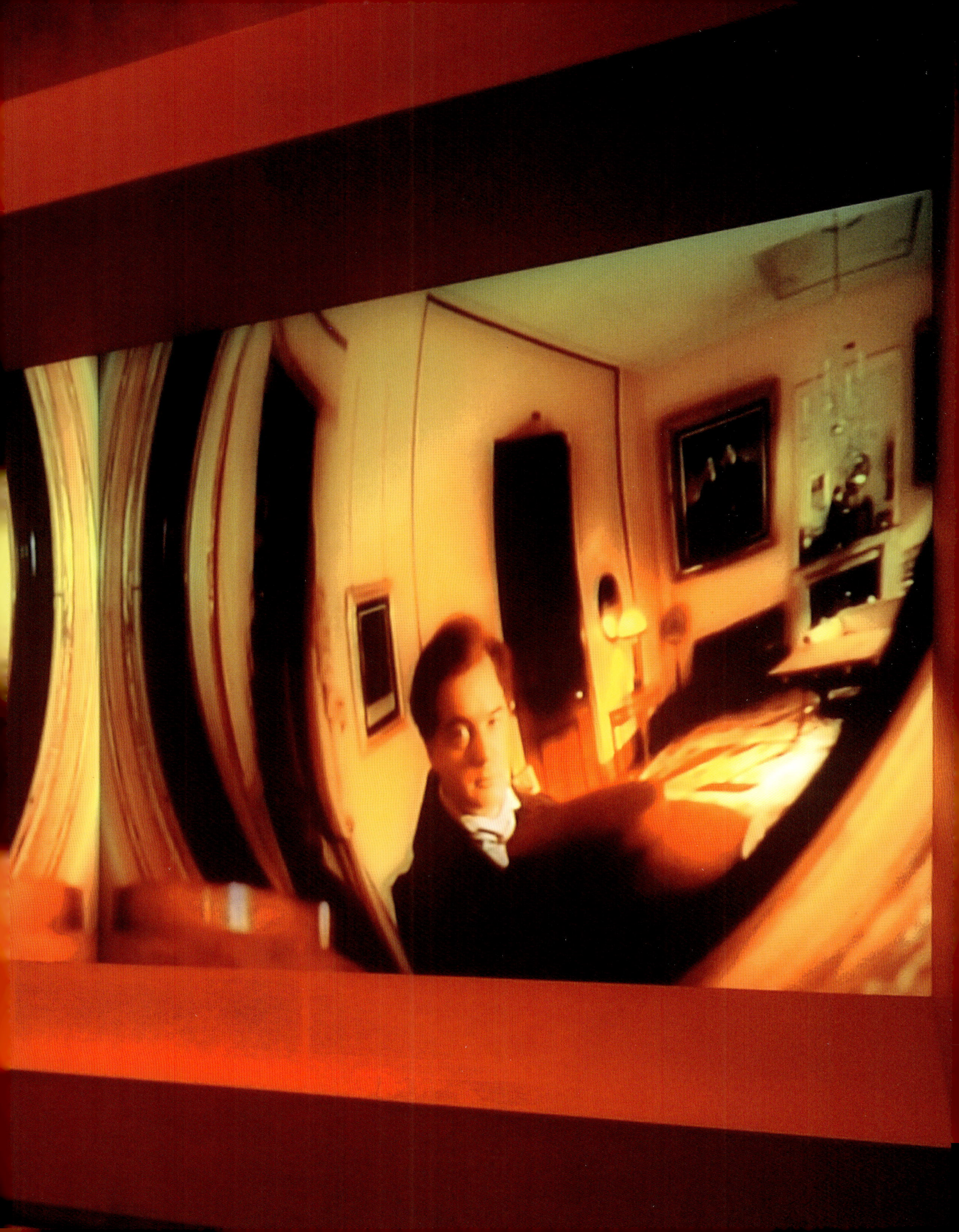

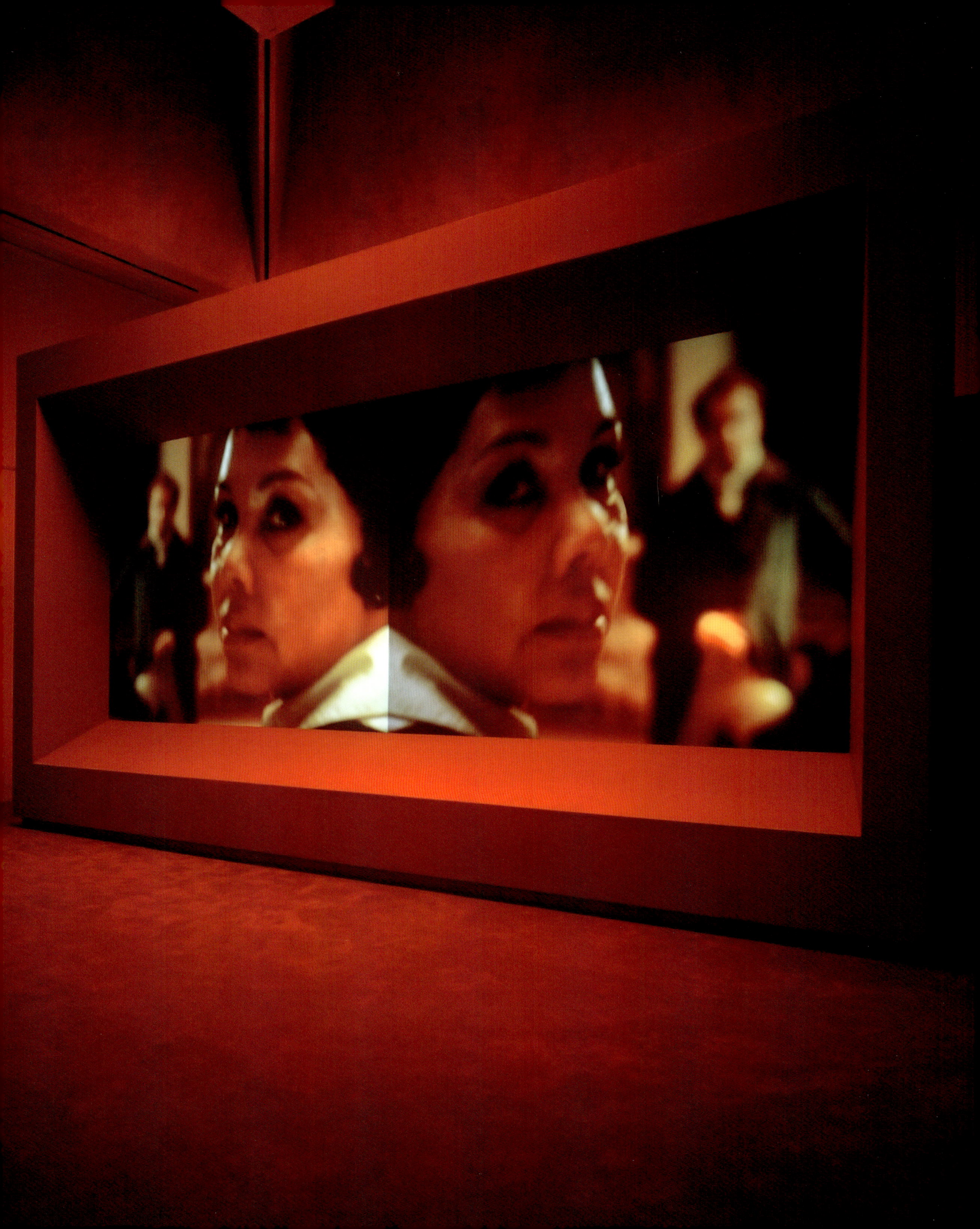

'I was trying to architect a version of the repressed'
Isaac Julien [1]

Among a row of townhouses in London's Lincoln's Inn Fields stands the Sir John Soane's Museum. It was once the home of its namesake, a neoclassical architect and lifelong collector of artworks and architectural artefacts. Enter this house-turned-museum and you enter the mind of Soane; his passions, aesthetic sensibility and worldview are told through the myriad paintings, sculptures and architectural relics that line the walls and floors. Thousands of objects, from ancient Egyptian antiquities and Roman sculpture to models of contemporary buildings, are chaotically crowded into its rooms, at times jarringly juxtaposed in the museum's interior. Built under Soane's architectural auspice in 1812, the house is a living thesis of his architectural and life philosophies.

The eccentricity of this museum, the setting for Isaac Julien's film *Vagabondia* (2000), is exposed when Julien recalls a story Soane told of a vision of his whole house in ruins that he experienced while it was being built.[2] This is a space whose own designer saw it as virtual – the perfect backdrop, then, to re-imagine history through fantasy.

In *Vagabondia*, the dreams and fantasies of a Black conservator hallucinate hidden histories behind the museum's objects and paintings. Our gaze is repositioned through the eyes of Julien's marginally constructed subject. We see the conservator in an ornate room, the ghostly spectre of Soane at a desk in the corner. While sitting, the conservator is transported to a dreaming state, moving through the halls of the museum. This shift is marked by a sonic change: the lyrical, melodious sound of classical violins and piano is replaced with percussive rhythms and an intensification of the narrator's Saint Lucian Creole. It is now dark, the public have left the building and the objects are hers to encounter and interpret.

Out of the darkness the conservator appears to emerge from a bust of Soane himself, becoming his stand-in in the film and the now architect of the space, in command of the objects she will encounter. As she moves through the museum, real life and dreams jostle for predominance as fragments of architectural models, body parts, paintings, drawings and decorative objects swell and mutate. They are doubled in Julien's two projections, a reflection of Soane's many mirrored walls, taking on hybrid forms in the space of collision where the screens meet. The fractured repetition of images, split across the two screens, displaces us from our assumed position at the centre of meaning and understanding; instead, we must attempt to rebuild a vision of the museum and its occupants from the fragments. The visual excess in this process of repetition is enhanced by Julien's use of saturated colours, superimposed images, and an oscillation between short and long shots, which together add to the ambiguity of what is real and what is imagined. House and film merge and distort in an unstable, changing landscape in which Julien disrupts binaries of author and subject, original and copy, virtual and material. Julien depicts the museum as a site constantly turning in on itself, where the lines between the inanimate and the animate blur as objects anthropomorphise under his camera's eye.

In this fantasy state the objects appear to fold in on themselves, as time and space in *Vagabondia* are collapsed. You watch Gilles Deleuze's world made real: a world of infinite folds that twist and weave through time and space. We are drawn

1. Isaac Julien, 'Converse', in *Isaac Julien: Riot*, exh. cat., The Museum of Modern Art, New York 2013, p.145.

2. Sir John Soane, 'Crude Hints towards an History of My House on L[incoln's] I[nn] Fields' (1812). A version of this text appears in *Visions of Ruin: Architectural Fantasies and Designs for Garden Follies*, exh. cat., Sir John Soane's Museum, London 1999, as referenced in Julien 2013, p.145.

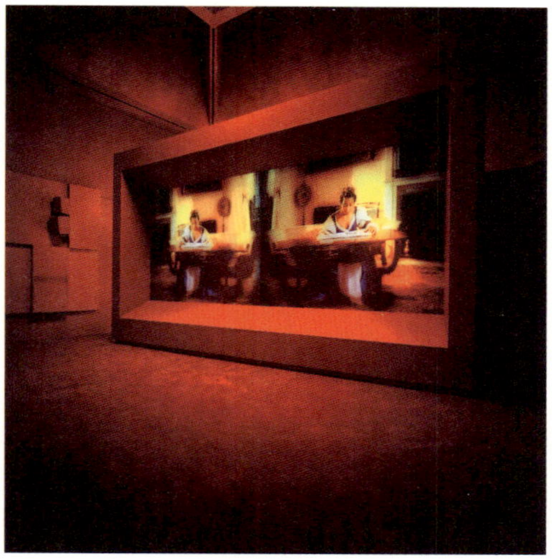

*Vagabondia* 2000, installation view, *The Turner Prize*, Tate Britain, London, 2001

into Julien's crumpled time, as visually (and knowingly) mimicked in the cascading lush red folds of a woman's dress, where events and histories become complex combinations of signs in motion, nomadic and always in the process of becoming.[3] For Deleuze, folds can be endlessly reshaped in infinite patterns where the possible and what seems mutually impossible can exist simultaneously. Therefore, established and long-repeated narratives of Soane's history become obsolete as linear time and any fixed teleological tale his objects might have told are cast off in the dreaming world of the conservator. In *Vagabondia* the museum is repeatedly made and unmade by Julien.

In common with many of Julien's works, the subject position of his protagonist is complex. As bell hooks writes in reference to the conservator's first appearance in Julien's earlier museological film, *The Attendant* (1993), she represents a space of 'cultural hybridity'.[4] Her very presence at the heart of 'white supremacist mythmaking high art is simultaneously an act of subordination and resistance'.[5] As a conservator she has an ambivalent but intimate relationship with the construction of whiteness in art, while her body is deployed to conserve and protect the objects in the museum. We see her approaching ornate paintings with white-gloved hands clutching brushes, presumably for cleaning. In life her role is to maintain and preserve the objects and the narratives they perpetuate, while in her fantasies she is set free from these constraints. Liberated in the Deleuzian folds, Julien presents a view of history that is encouraged to deviate from well-trodden paths and travel through unexpected passageways. Julien equates the fantasies of the repressed with history, calling into question the accepted power of history over the human subject. Through fantasy, he is intervening in the gaps in their historic representation.

Julien has spoken about the 1955 film *Les maîtres fous* by Jean Rouch as an inspiration for *Vagabondia*. Rouch's film centres on a ceremony performed for the camera by the Hauka, a religious sect in West Africa. In the ceremony the Hauka become 'possessed' by their white colonisers and, in a 'trance', mimic their behaviour. The film was very controversial because of the uncanny mimicry of colonial authorities, but gave Julien inspiration about how movement might allow the conservator and his other protagonist, the vagabond, to physically interact with and transgress Soane's spaces and objects.

In the ambiguous space of fantasy, the conservator sees the vagabond in the museum from her position in the raised gallery of the Picture Room. He is an elegant young Black man, staggering, stumbling and dancing in a room of the house that Soane designed especially for the series of paintings *A Rake's Progress* c.1734 by William Hogarth. In collaboration with Javier de Frutos, Julien designed a choreography to give life to the figure of the vagabond who appears in Hogarth's paintings – a figure historically eclipsed from canonical writing about the work. Here, the vagabond careens off the walls of the museum, his body jolting and spasming, almost as if it too is folding back into itself. He summons the ghosts of colonised subjects and their cultures, his movements disturbing and destabilising the stasis of the paintings and the stories they tell. The incongruity of the vagabond in the museum alludes to less fixed cultures of other places and times that are not concretely historicised in objects housed in the Western museum, and challenges long-held ideas of cultural ownership inscribed in a museum like Soane's. In the presence of the vagabond, the museum and its objects, once fixed, are now free to transform and move in unexpected ways like his own dance.

A museum functions as both set and repository for history. It is a space that accrues and archives visual culture; its objects author histories that are repeated and circulated throughout time to become the narratives of our collective culture. In Julien's hands the stasis of the museum becomes unstuck: he sets history in motion as he blurs, and often breaks, the boundaries of time and space. He transgresses canonical narratives and (re-)imagines the lives of people and objects often left in the corners of history, forgotten or ignored in our collective cultural

3. See Gilles Deleuze, *The Fold: Leibniz and the Baroque*, trans. Tom Conley, London 2006.

4. bell hooks, 'Thinking through class: Paying attention to *The Attendant*', in *Reel to Real: Race, Sex and Class at the Movies*, London and New York 1996, p.92.

5. Ibid.

memory. In Julien's work, the fixity of the museum is rejected in favour of what Kobena Mercer describes as 'a practice of critique that exhibits a careful rather than confrontational relation to the other who is discovered in spaces of cultural memory'.[6] Here, Mercer identifies Julien's sensitive (re-)imagination of the museological realm, where fantasy and dreams become vital tools in rewriting history, an ongoing project that began with *The Attendant* and *Three* 1999 and subsequently continued in *Baltimore* 2003.

In his films, Julien sees the museum as a site of temporal and spatial transgression. He is the architect of new narratives of repressed histories that restage those told in (and on) the walls of the museum. In *his* museums as sets for his films, Julien critically questions 'who sees what and what it is we're actually seeing'.[7] In other words, he centres the fantasies of his Black protagonists in museum spaces to reveal untold lives that transgress and (re-)imagine the histories told through the objects in these spaces. In subjecting history to postmodern and avant-garde scrutiny, Julien reveals its ultimate instability. His museum fantasies are a punctum to our collective consciousness.[8]

In *Vagabondia* we watch as the conservator repeatedly returns to her seat in the ornate room where the figure of Soane reads at his desk. In this constantly looping return to the realm of the 'real', Julien demonstrates the temporary nature of fantasy and dreams, reminding us that these are limited or limiting in their capacity to liberate the subject fully.

6. Kobena Mercer, 'Avid Iconographies', in Kobena Mercer and Chris Darke, *Isaac Julien*, London 2001, p.9.

7. Julien 2013, p.145.

8. Roland Barthes, *Camera Lucida: Reflections on Photography*, trans. Richard Howard, London 1982. In this text, Barthes presents the idea of the 'punctum' as the quality of the image to create meaning without invoking any recognisable symbolic system; meaning born out of a unique response of the individual viewer of the image. He describes the effect of the 'punctum' as 'pricks' or 'wounds' or 'bruises' to a particular viewer's subjectivity. This sits in opposition to the 'studium', which Barthes saw as the often repeated historical, social or cultural meanings that are drawn from an image through semiotic analysis.

Nina Kellgren: The premiere of *Looking for Langston* at the 1989 Berlin Film Festival was Isaac's first major screening and a really interesting introduction to the way he thinks about collaboration. Many of us who had worked on the production were there, as well as some of the performers. Isaac called us all up on stage at the end and introduced every single person, one by one. That's how Isaac is – he totally values collaboration and is really comfortable with acknowledging it. It doesn't matter how late it is or how much he's got on his mind, he always does it. Isaac keeps his team and has long-term collaborators, which means we work knowing about each other. It's tremendously rewarding as a conversation over time – it means I know how Adam Finch is likely to cut the footage and I know what to expect from Derek Brown, the wonderful designer on both *Looking for Langston* and *Once Again*.

Bradford Young: Nina and I first met at Camerimage, a gathering of cinematographers at a festival in Poland. I was on this incredible inter-generational women-led panel with image-makers from all over the world and I felt really honoured to be there. Nina was also on the panel, and I was struck by how intuitive and generous and sensitive and beautiful and strong her words were. She mentioned working with artists who were part of the London Film Collective scene, and that blew me away because those were the filmmakers who informed my practice as a filmmaker and made me want to stay in film school: the whole Film Collective environment, but specifically Sankofa and Black Audio, the two collectives – Ceddo as well, because I had a really intimate relationship with Menelik Shabazz. The films that Nina made as a part of those collective environments were inspiring and continue to be inspiring for the kind of film community that we're building here in Baltimore. So when Nina emailed me about the project and I saw 'Isaac Julien' in the email I kind of like closed the email! 'What's going on?' I've always loved Isaac's work. *Young Soul Rebels* was really the first work I ever saw – I saw that when I was nineteen years old – but I didn't have the language to define his work until later in my life. Now I understand it's about image-making, storytelling with still images. When you work with artists like Isaac Julien, you know that the image-makers are also given lots of space to authorise the storytelling. It's collaborative work – the cinematographer, the image-maker, the costume designer, we all have something to say and there's room for us to say it.

NK: What's so wonderful about cinematography is that you function on so many levels at the same time. It's intellectual, it's physical, it's intuitive, it's visual. I can't think of a better place to be creative. And when working with artists, there's another level of involvement to that process. What you just said, Bradford, about having plenty of space to authorise – that's key when working with artists. On a traditional narrative feature, you are sent a script from your agent because the director and producer have seen your work and like it, but it's pretty locked off at that point. Isaac never starts like that. The project is in development all the time, which keeps you on your toes: creatively, things can change very quickly, which can be challenging, but also incredibly rewarding. And while Isaac knows what he's trying to do with a piece, and can be very clear about what he likes and doesn't like, he's also finding the path. When we were shooting in London, we had a location cancel on us at the very last minute. At the time, Isaac happened to be at St Pancras, where we shot *Looking for Langston*, and in that space he thought, 'This works! We can shoot back here instead.' There was serendipity. So we got the phone call, and then it was turning the juggernaut round, since Isaac uses all the departments you have in a feature film: makeup, wardrobe, design, sound. But we could do that, whereas to pass that decision through a committee of producers at that stage would be tricky.

BY: That's what's interesting about the art context. For better or for worse, there's just so much more mitigation and less sovereignty in the film context. When I work in the film world I have to say to myself, 'I'm just a worker.' And in film, all the worker bees have to be so perfect – you have to really get the honey right! But when I started collaborating with artists I found that in the art world the process is arguably more important than the actual result. You're able to fail and trip over yourself a bit more. Working with Isaac really was an affirmation of that. The thing I really love, working with artists, is the fumbles. You fumble, and people really gather to pick you up. They don't just watch you fall and look at you on the ground and say, 'Oh. You're not supposed to fall. That's not the reason why we brought you here.' Instead it's like, 'Actually, the fumble is where we discover something interesting – let's all get on the ground.'

What I love about working in an art context, and specifically with Isaac, is that every moment is connected, but every moment is its own thing. So it matters that

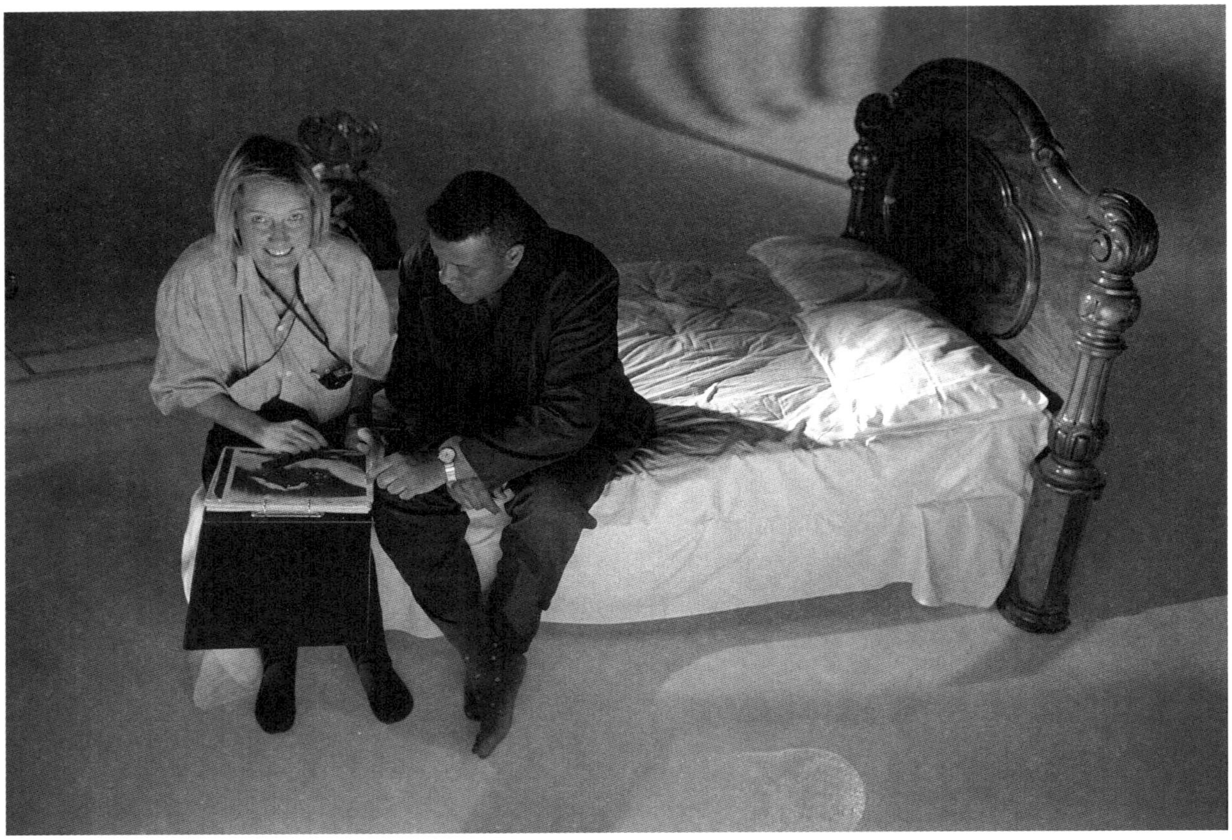

Nina Kellgren and Isaac Julien on the set of *Looking for Langston*

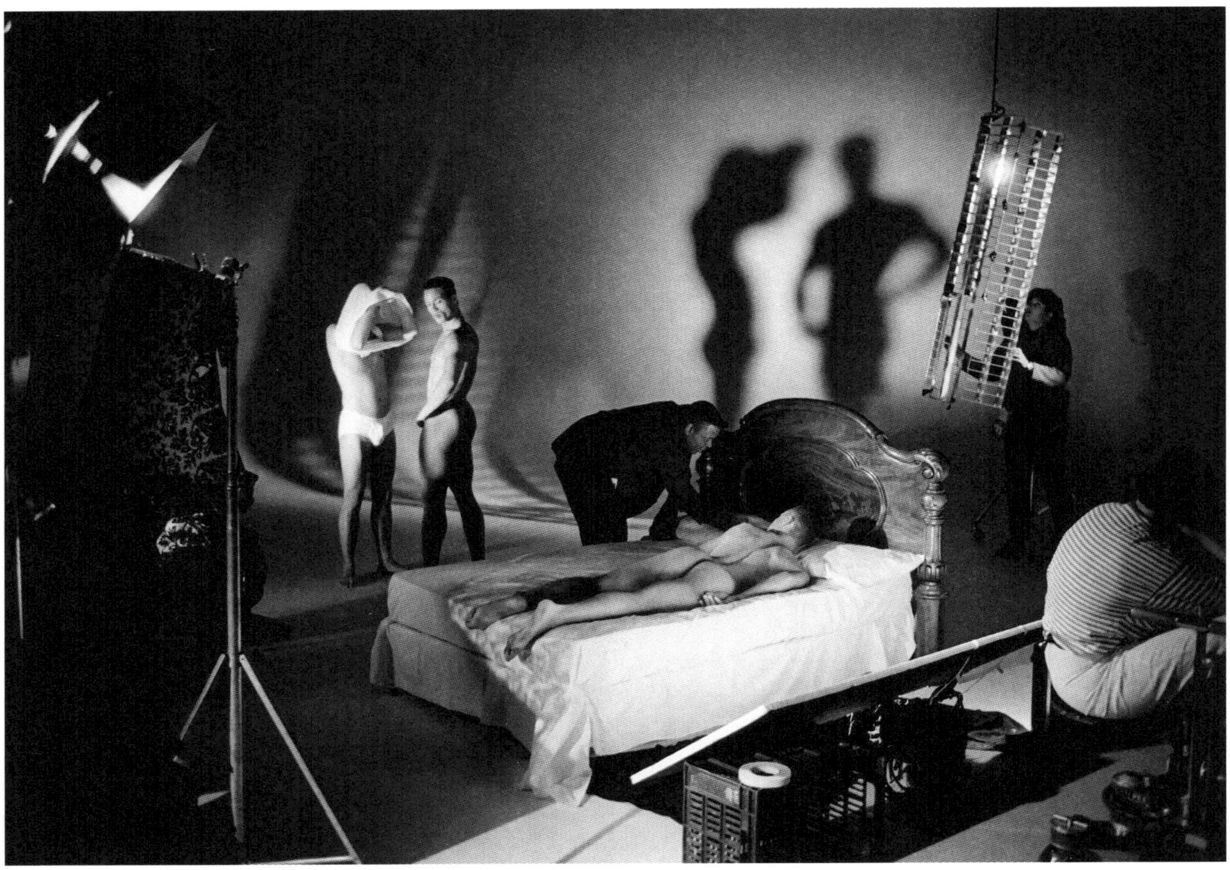

*Mise en scène No.1 (Looking for Langston Vintage Series)* 1989/2016

you're able to freely associate with the story itself, but also with the space provided.

NK: We decided to shoot *Once Again* in black and white. There's a huge beauty in black and white. You've immediately got an abstraction from the real, which already pushes it into a poetic space. There's a purity to it, and a beautiful coherence.

BY: I trained on film, but there were very few opportunities to shoot in black and white. It's what I love the most and feel most comfortable with. I wanted to be reminded of *Looking for Langston*, but also seeing what they had already done in the UK, it reminded me instantly, 'This is a moment where light matters.' I realised I needed to be aware of tonality to not only add a certain richness and depth to the image, but also for story.

Even though film is physical, in its original form, its indigenous state, it's already an abstraction of reality. In that sense *Once Again* is to me a very diasporic, pan-African film. It already goes into this abstraction necessary for pan-Africanism and diaspora, which is that is our bodies have received so much push and pull that we oftentimes have to transcend the physical and engage with spirit. That's really important. I say that more now, in my older age: I say seventy per cent of our engagement as pan-Africanists, as people conscious of diaspora, is that we have to always engage with spirit. I know Alain Locke's work well from being a student at Howard where he taught, and when you talk about Locke you also talk about an early rendering of pan-Africanism. I also think about a certain kind of social harmonic that at one level is very easy to articulate: you see it in the work of George Padmore, you see it in the work of Locke and of Kwame Nkrumah. In film you see it in the work of Ousmane Sembène, Shirikiana Aina, Safi Faye or Haile Gerima. Those are like physical articulations of this odyssey that are abstract in form but physical in the sense that our eyes are able to pan and move with things and read and digest things in a particular way.

*Once Again* really pans back to *Looking for Langston* in many ways, not just because both are rendered in black and white, but because they're both thinking about stolen objects or lost objects, and reclaiming objects that are imbued with the same spirit. My conclusion is that a lot of our contentious relationship with the universe and the societies in which we've been dispersed is because the objects that were made or infused with spirit work which could have kept us safe were taken from us. Now we're reconsidering how they should be repatriated and where they should be placed.

NK: This piece was so much about ideas about statues, about looking, about what happens when you destroy a culture and say it has no value – all those multi-layered arguments that Isaac's involved with in the piece. There was a beautiful quote from Toni Morrison about 'weather' in the treatment/script.In early conversations we had many discussions about the weather: we knew that weather was going to be a metaphor for a lot of the issues that Bradford has spoken about very eloquently. The image of Alain Locke with the snow falling on him, for instance, we shot in London.

BY: That's something that is also tangibly connected with diaspora. I often think about what it may have been like for the first enslaved Africans to come to the New World, about how if you'd never seen snow or earthquakes or hurricanes or any of this before, how treacherous that may have been to experience. So when I see the image of Locke with the snow, it's like there's some other thing in that. I often think of diaspora as, yes, the political product diaspora, but diaspora itself for me is also political. It's direct action, but also about movement, just movement itself.

NK: That's something that runs through a lot of Isaac's pieces, from *True North* and *Fantôme Afrique* to *Western Union: Small Boats* – diaspora and the movement of peoples across the world. When we're shooting those things, we're frequently using the landscape as metaphor. In *True North*, for example, the wind turns the snow into frozen waves, so there's this idea of whiteness and frozen movement. Or *Western Union: Small Boats*, shot in 2007, about 'illegal' immigration but still very, very topical – there was a lot of talk in the press about 'Fortress Europe' and being 'swamped' by migrants and 'floods', you know, that kind of language. We were shooting on a massive staircase in a palace in Sicily, with crowds of people coming in, and that wasn't working. I wanted to bring water down the staircase, but they weren't happy about that! And so we used the dancers instead, and then Isaac ran the final footage backwards to give the fluidity of these bodies either falling or coming back. That idea evolved, you wouldn't have thought of it without having a visual development process. That's the poetic level that Isaac gets to.

BY: This project for me was a bit of a baton-passing. I remember the first call I had with Nina and Isaac, which affirmed for me how important the image-maker was in the process. I loved listening to them talk! Nina would say something very specific about something they did, and Isaac was basically saying 'Carry on.' She was carrying the visual idea of the story in such a profound, direct, in-the-foreground way, and some of that I brought to the museum to think about how we photographed the statues. One conversation that I remember was about a conflict between the point of view of the character and the object as the character. We tried one thing where we circled the statues like it was from Locke's perspective, but that

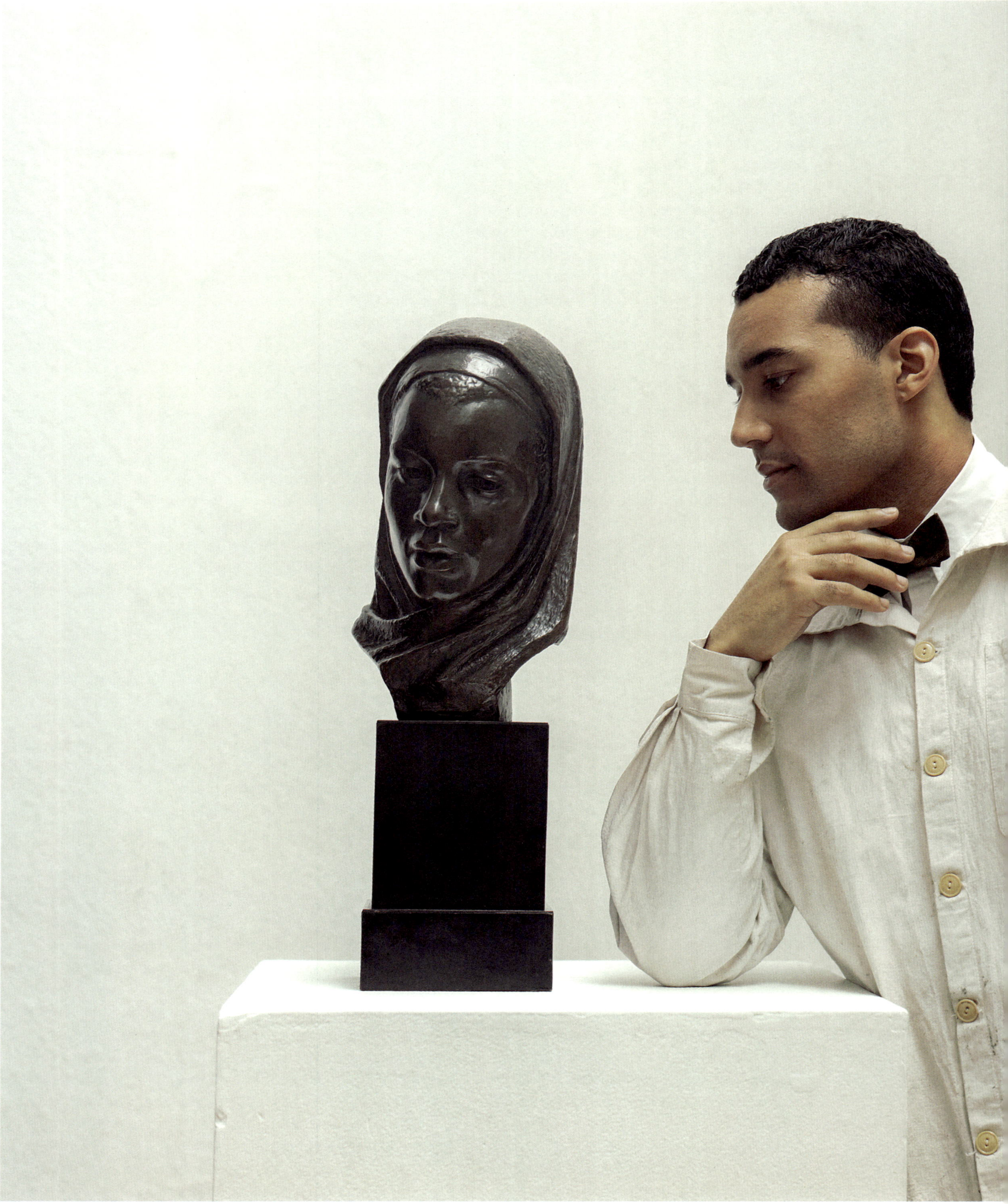

*New Negro Aesthetic (Black Madonna)* 2022

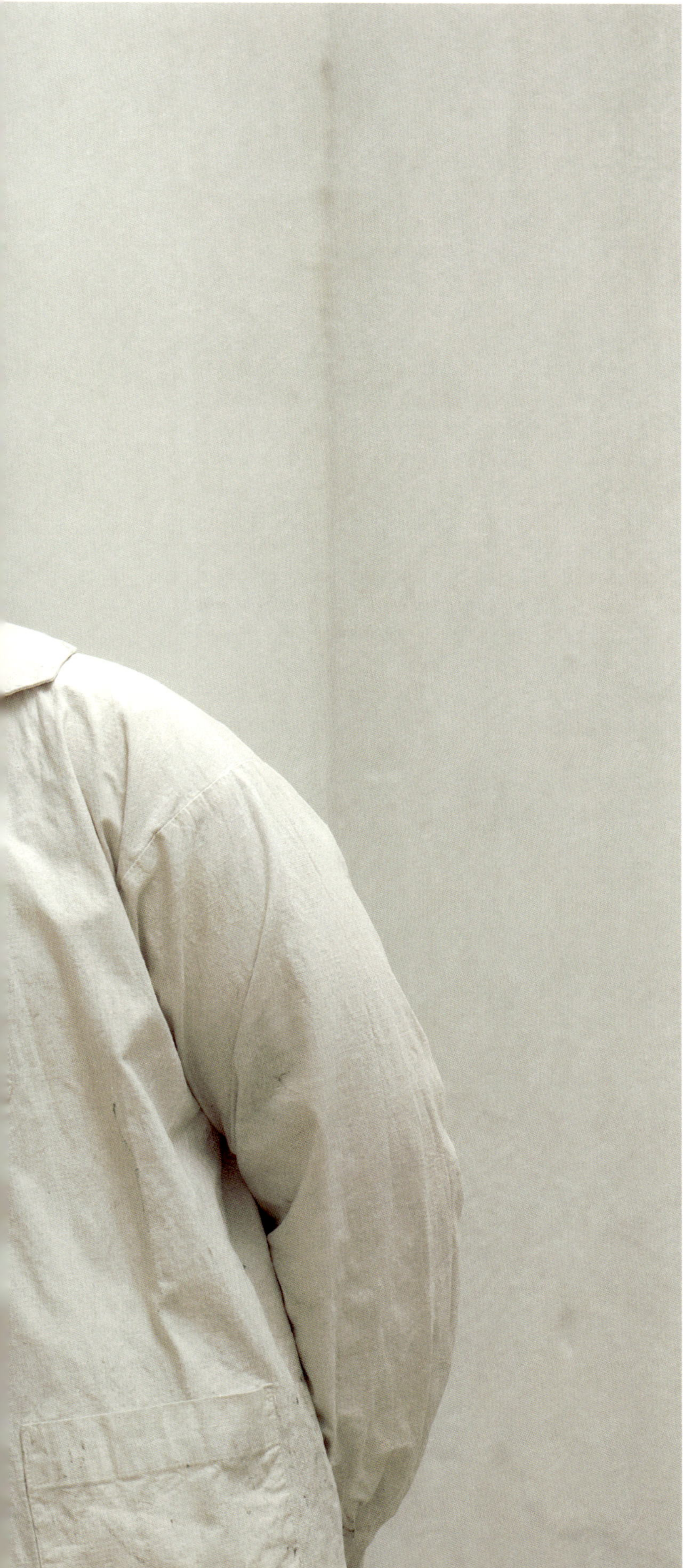

felt kind of disembodied, like there wasn't a connection between the object itself and the viewer. I said to Isaac: 'I think Alain Locke is equally an object as the objects themselves.'

NK: It's really interesting that you said that, because actually the more we shot in the UK, the more I thought 'Everybody in this is a statue.' Every character. We shot in the Pitt Rivers Museum, which is great to shoot in. Obviously, technically, it's a nightmare, because it's a hall of mirrors – but the visual value is the layering and the reflections, and the people appearing inside the cases as much as being outside and looking at the cases. It offers a rich and fabulous visual language.

There is a way of lighting and working with black and white, which is about separation and tonality. Black and white is very sculptural, inherently. You model with light and absolutely choose how you craft the face, how you present that face. With lighting there's an ideal situation where you have full control and then there are locations where you are working with a mix of lighting and what is already present and in place. At the Pitt Rivers, I had the lighting department actually following the actors around with handheld battery-operated LED panels and crafting it on the run, because that's what worked in that space.

In Bradford's work on *Once Again* there are really beautiful Steadicam shots that pick up on the pace, flow and mesmerising quality that we established in the UK. There are a lot of long shots, what we call developing shots, and when you experience the five-screen piece you physically feel the flow. That's something that I thought quite a lot about, because you really need to pay attention to the text: there's lots to hear and process. Watching an image that is flowing in that way allows your brain to hear in another way.

BY: I'd worked in multichannel before, on my own and on other artists' projects, and I knew that because we're working in a quilt, the viewer experience is so much more curated from their perspective. They can focus on one screen, not all at the same time, so each one can have its own visual identity. I really loved that. I really was having fun.

NK: I think one of my favourite shots in the piece is of Sharlene Whyte, playing the curator, opening a cabinet. It's so wonderful working with great actors, isn't it, Bradford? They give you so much. In the script it's something like 'It's as if she is going through the seven stages of grief in quick succession' – that's quite a hard call for an actor, but you can absolutely craft the shots and the lighting on the face to support that intention and performance. All our actors were remarkable to work with.

I was really fortunate to work with Sankofa early on in my career, because as well as getting the chance to shoot such interesting content I also learned a lot about how to light Black skin. And it was early days for that on film. When you think about how few opportunities there were in 1989, for Black actors on television, how few parts there used to be. So it was a special place to be, working with Sankofa in terms of developing that skill.

BY: I think that's really important. There's this current conversation about how people light Black skin – it's a conundrum, and people are really wrestling with it, trying to figure it out. In these technologies that seem to be working against us, people oftentimes find a sweet spot that creates culture, carrying on a certain kind of tradition in how it's done. I'll say personally, if somebody like Nina had not photographed the previous portion of *Once Again*, I might not have agreed to it. The reason I agreed to it was because I feel like what Nina said: part of her practice has been a constant engagement with Black bodies and lighting them. I was at Howard for eight years, only photographing Black bodies, partially because that's what I wanted to do and that's where I felt comfortable, but also because there were not opportunities for me in the industry to photograph other kinds of bodies. So, based on that constant engagement, I got better at it! And I think the work is a testament to the collaboration between what would seem to be two contentious cultural elements, a white UK photographic reality and a Black American photographic reality – the centre of it is this worldly person of a certain kind of migration. Isaac really lead the charge in that particular kind of Windrush, Caribbean diaspora to the UK context.

That's what makes it beautiful when we work together, even though we're all apart spatially. Some of those binaries, those politicised barriers, turn out to be false. In art, we find space to communicate those things and are still able to break bread with one another. And I just love the idea that maybe Nina would not have been afforded the same level of exposure if she had not been working with Sankofa, and really embraced and loved in the collective environment. That speaks to how even something that's Black-centred is egalitarian and loving. That's what the work is for me and why it's such an honour to be part of it. And it's what I hope for my children – that they understand the complications of it all, but that really what it comes down to is sitting with people long enough that you can understand what they want, what their dreams are, and then you can really help them put that on a screen for us to share.

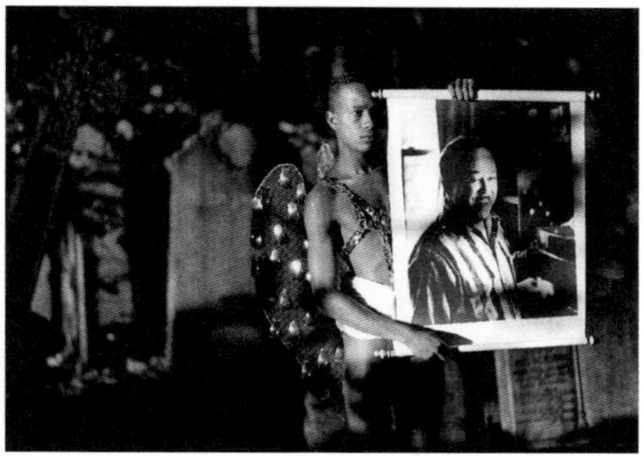

*The Last Angel of History (Looking for Langston Vintage Series)* 1989/2016

## Prelude

I have been thinking and writing about *Looking for Langston* (1989) for a long time now. Recently, however, I have become preoccupied with the end of the film on account of its staging of an encounter with emptiness, an encounter that is, moreover, a visual metaphor for the film as a whole. After all, the film refuses to 'find' Langston Hughes, and marks his queerness through a kind of archive of absence. The empty dance hall at the end of the film offers the viewer a visual cipher with which to decode the rest of the enigmatic flow of images.

At the end of Isaac Julien's beautiful meditation on the life and desires of Langston Hughes, a mixed group of Black and white gay men are dancing in a warehouse. As the music speeds up and the dancing becomes wild, shots of a white male mob (including uniformed officers) gathering outside cut in and out of the ecstatic scene. Julien's cross-cutting sequence brings inside and outside closer and closer together, and creates a fearful anticipation of a violent confrontation. The spectator fears for the gay men who have gathered together at a memorial to dance in the face of death and to love in the midst of crisis. But at the climax of this montage, the police and the white thugs enter a space that is empty and encounter only the traces of the dancers. The dancers, who have engaged in rituals of joyful mourning that exceed conventional religious practices, have now left the space for an elsewhere that we do not see and on behalf of a practice of evacuation that eludes history.

So, I return to this scene – a cipher in terms of a message that communicates through concealment, but also in the sense of an absence – to track Julien's visual lexicon of emptiness, disappearance, shadow play and fugitivity. The scene is haunting and unexpected; it withholds the confrontation that threatened to destroy the dancing community and it saves the Black gay men from history itself. If history in this film is 'the smiler with the knife', a white supremacist shaping of world and meaning that is bloody and brutal but comes disguised as benevolence, then history must be avoided at all costs. In its stead, Julien offers cinematic space, poetry, anarchival encounters and dance. These aesthetic practices allow queer bodies of colour to spin away from expression, sense, definition, message, telling, knowing and sequence, and creates the opportunity to refuse the orderly narratives favoured by mainstream cinema, chronological history and identity politics.

The practitioners of queer and Black leisure who disappear at the film's end seek to unmake the space of encounter by withdrawing. As the police look around for the 'deviants' they came to discipline, they see only smoke and mirrors, but the dancers have not simply disappeared. Representing an undercommons of sorts, they live on in a place and time that we cannot yet see – one situated, as José Muñoz put it, in a 'forward-dawning futurity', a time to come when the utopian dreams of queerness will no longer be necessary.[1]

## 1. Melancholia

For José Muñoz, *Looking for Langston* was an immensely important text precisely because it resisted biography and instead prioritised 'looking' over finding, absence over presence, and listening over speaking. Muñoz himself, a key player in the reception of *Looking*, becomes now part of the scene of mourning that the film stages; we mourn *his* loss as we watch the film that he called a 'mythotext' and that he described in terms of a deeply etched melancholia.[2] For Muñoz, the melancholia

1. José Ésteban Muñoz, *Cruising Utopia: The Then and There of Queer Futurity*, New York 2009, p.1.

2. José Ésteban Muñoz, 'Photographies of Mourning: Melancholia and Ambivalence in Van Der Zee, Mapplethorpe and *Looking for Langston*', in Harry Stecopoulos and Michael Uebel (eds.), *Race and the Subject of Masculinities*, Durham, NC 1997, pp.337–58.

that permeates *Looking for Langston* was not an indulgence, but serves rather as 'a mechanism that helps us to ... take our dead with us to the various battles we must wage in their names'.[3] At the end of the 1980s, the names of the dead – particularly the dead among the AIDS generation of Black gay men – were legion. And the film may be looking for Langston Hughes but it is also placing him within a long lineage of Black queers lost to illness, violence, disregard, incarceration, poverty, destitution.

The opening sequence, a funeral seemingly for Langston Hughes but featuring a eulogy for James Baldwin offered by Toni Morrison, reveals not Hughes (the film's subject) or Baldwin (to whom the film is dedicated) in the coffin, but Isaac Julien himself. Julien's body is literally 'in the wake', to use Christina Sharpe's term, positioned not as the masterful director but as the heir to a radical Black queer tradition of poetic rage, loss, love and disappearance.[4]

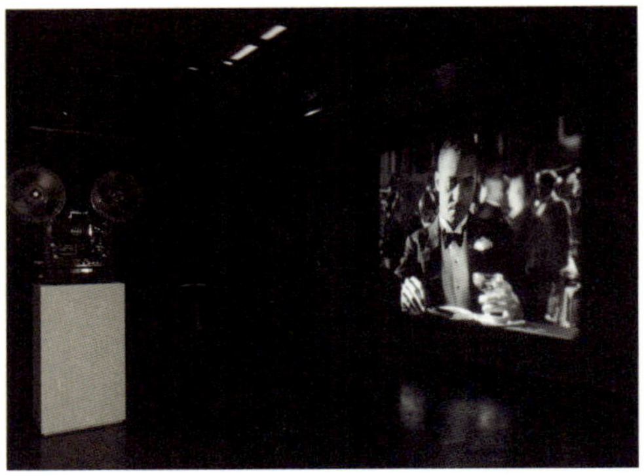

*Looking for Langston* 1989, installation view, Isaac Julien Studio, London, 2016

As we return to *Looking for Langston* and watch it again, thirty years after the original release, in an era marked once again by death, contagion, loss and rapacious leadership, we might draw close to the confrontations it stages with history, the preoccupation with emptiness that is part of its melancholic legacy, and the visual archive it offers that brims with fugitive energy and lingers on poetry rather than hard evidence.

2. History

The model of history that Julien offered in 1989 was radical for the way it made dis-appearance central to its lexicon. Yes, the film named and placed Langston Hughes both inside and outside queer history, but it also withheld the kind of biographical information that queer audiences of the time might have expected. This withholding in relation to a historical mandate to tell is a perfect example of what Saidiya Hartman, in the essay 'Venus in Two Acts', calls 'narrative restraint', and it gives rise to a visual language marked by reverie, mirrors, shadows, emptiness.[5] But it also refuses sequence, allowing eras to collapse into each other and modes of representation – photography, reflection, poetry – to collide. And so, one historical period (the Harlem Renaissance) collapses into another, the AIDS crisis, and today, the AIDS crisis collapses into the global pandemic that has again sorted humanity with ruthless efficiency into the saved and the drowned. Muñoz, in his essay on Julien's film, notes the way Julien uses montage to bring the sounds and images of one era into dialogue with another; he calls this collapse 'antiphonal' and part of a Black 'call and response' mode within which different generations of Black gay men call out to each other across history and through poetry.[6]

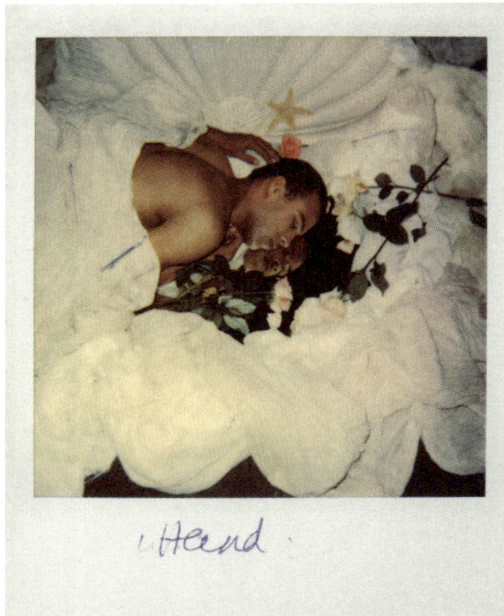

On-set polaroid, *Looking for Langston* 1989

We can find the visual coding of temporal collapse in the film in the form of cross-cutting strategies through which Julien opens holes in official histories and then pulls bodies and desires through them and into strange spaces – some urban, some pastoral, some featuring arrangements of sculpted flesh, others fragmenting the body into fetishistic pieces. But, using Mapplethorpe's photographic archive of Black flesh to ward off the fantasies of Black phallic power, Julien avoids full frontal spectacle, so that even a scene of a man watching porn is non-explicit. Bodies lost to history move through space and find each other in meadows, parks, in mirror images of Black narcissistic hope. Gay men follow each other, stalk each other, look for each other. 'We lurk in shadows', says Essex Hemphill in one of the outdoor sequences of the film. 'We are the hunger of shadows.'

3. Shadows

The sumptuous black and white imagery of *Looking for Langston* makes the shadow into a player in the film – in scenes of the graveyard, the disco, the street cruiser and the porno theatre. Not just the casting of light or dark, the shadow is history itself, stalking the real, finding the darkness. *Looking for Langston* embraces shadows and offers the night as a mysterious space of wild activity and queer dreaming:

3. Muñoz 1997, p.356.

4. Christina Sharpe, *In the Wake: On Blackness and Being*, Durham, NC 2016.

5. Saidiya Hartman, 'Venus in Two Acts', *Small Axe*, vol.12, no.2, June 2008, pp.1–14.

6. Muñoz 1997, p.342.

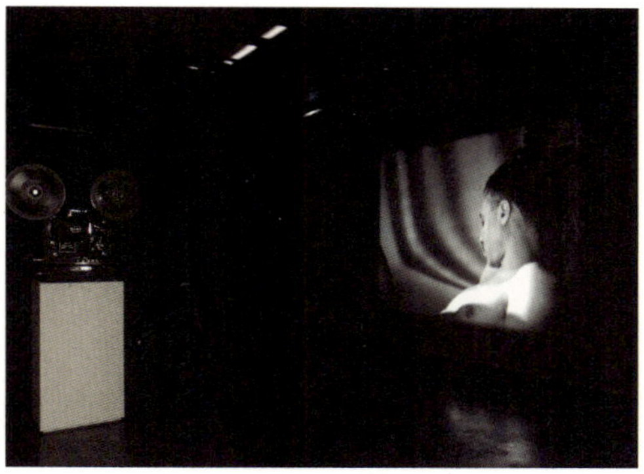

*Looking for Langston* 1989, installation view, Isaac Julien Studio, London, 2016

instead of claiming Hughes, the film pays tribute to the night worlds conjured and occupied by Hughes. Shane Vogel has offered beautiful and detailed readings of 'the queer poetics of Harlem nightlife' in Hughes's work via the language of the nocturnal, and has also respected Hughes's carefully cultivated 'sexual ambiguity'. Instead of documenting gay life, Vogel proposes, in poems such as 'Café: 3 a.m.' Hughes created, explored and celebrated 'closing time' and 'after hours' spaces to provide counter-histories of illegal spaces and the illegible Black bodies that gather there.[7] This is the Hughes that Julien finds too: a poet who embraces the night, who records a poetic anarchive of desire, who leaves signs and traces of his queer life in clubs and in the shadows of night, but who eschews the category in favour of wild illegibility.

Julien respects the fragment. He does not de-code Hughes, he does not look for and find Hughes; he does not require Hughes to appear within the logic of a clear and specific identity. Instead, Julien joins Hughes's legacy to those of Baldwin, Bruce Nugent, Countee Cullen, Bessie Smith and Essex Hemphill and proposes that we read the shadow, the fragment, the phrase, the single star - 'take just one star' - without seeking to place it back within an unbroken landscape.

4. Night

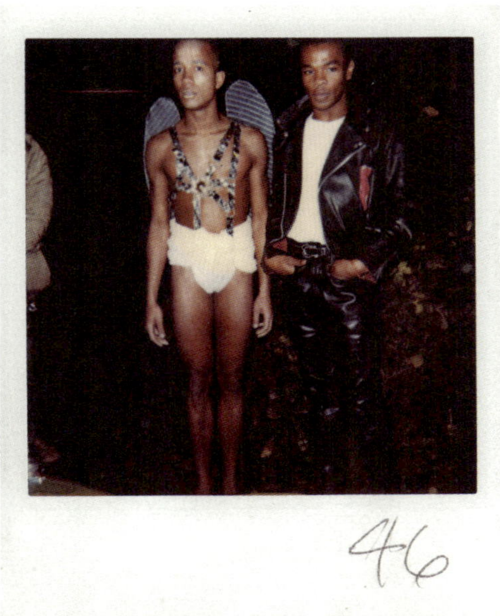


On-set polaroid, *Looking for Langston* 1989

At the film's end, these elements - looking, history, shadows, fragments - come together as fallen angels watch over the dancing queers, and as the representatives of law and order gather outside, obliterating shade, bringing the light, promising violent correction. Julien's camera cuts back and forth, glass shatters, bodies whirl, voices tumble over each other, faces find their reflection in so many mirrors, and the mob ascends to disrupt the unruly, illegal party. But as the police and their posse enter the room, they find no bodies, only the disembodied voice of Langston Hughes on the record player. We end, then, with voice, the poet's lyric, with what Fred Moten and Stefano Harney term 'the open song of the ones who are supposed to be silent'.[8] This is not a tragic ending, or an evasion; it is not the sealing off or even the opening up of history, this end, and the final scene that follows, in which Langston Hughes announces that the 'sun's arising', pulls Black gay bodies out of the way of the white gaze and its violent will to know. It leaves the audience with Hughes's own words, his own enigmatic proclamation that night time has ended, the day has begun, 'sun's arising', and that he 'could be blue, but I've been blue all night long'. This line does not mean that Hughes has escaped the blues, but only that the blues, like Hughes himself, like Julien's film, belong to the night.

7. See Shane Vogel, 'Closing Time: Langston Hughes and the Poetics of Harlem Nightlife', *Criticism*, vol.48, no.3, Summer 2006, pp.397–425.

8. Fred Moten and Stefano Harney, *The Undercommons: Fugitive Planning and Black Study*, New York and Wivenhoe 2013, p.51.

It's maddening: that muddled place of near confusion when you reach for a memory at the edge of your consciousness, only for it to slide away a moment later. That's what you were trying to work through, several years ago, having made your way through a sprawling photography exhibition at Somerset House, darting between buildings, the rain coming down in sheets, puddles like mirrors on the ground, ducking into a space set slightly away from the main building, where, finally, you found the solace you're always seeking, the solace which certain works provide: the opportunity to be still, to consider, to be moved, to be grounded. To be.

The space itself is blacked out, the only light coming from the black and white film projected across one of the walls. You quickly realise you're joining somewhere in the middle of the film, but the images are quiet, inviting; the moment you've arrived, as if by some magic, the narrator has paused, wrangling with the weight of the words he must say, what perhaps has previously gone unsaid. And in this brief pause, in place of words, you watched how the body might speak. Two men shared the soft graze of a glance across the room of dancing partygoers; later, undressed from their black tie attire, they reclined beside one another, and you imagined, in the moment they touched on screen, cool skin against warmth, the slight breathlessness of yearning, the way desire makes time slow and slur and speed up, or stop altogether. Images began to reappear and disappear, refrain and break. Pictures of men you recognise – who later you'll identify as James Baldwin and Langston Hughes – are held up, as if what you're watching is eulogy, elegy. A house track boomed out from the speakers in the space, as the sonic landscape becomes demanding, assembling its own jagged ambience. You felt your own heart like a fist against the wall of your chest; on screen, a group of armed men race up a set of stairs, aiming towards the party you've been watching, with violent intentions, only to find the partygoers are elsewhere, safe. You felt like you were in a memory of a different time, but this in itself is the work of memory: images steeped in nostalgia, the disobedience of chronology, trembling soundscapes, half-remembered sentences taking on new meaning. You felt that muddle, that maddening confusion: *I've seen this before, but I couldn't say where.* It's only later, when the muddle clears slightly, that this response will shift: *I've felt this before, but I couldn't say where.*

*

Years later, a large-scale solo exhibition of Isaac Julien's work takes place at Tate Britain. You will see those beautiful black and white images. The piece, *Looking for Langston*, is an elegiac consideration of the life of Langston Hughes, combining archival footage of Harlem in the 1920s with a staged London nightclub of the 1980s. As they did many years ago, the images throb with a yearning, a desire, a need for closeness, a want for *space*. All of the films deal with this notion, a want for space, for Blackness, for queerness; you can feel this notion in every frame, a reflection of Julien's own internal camera, the intimacies of his mind.

Across the course of the exhibition, there are further notions, further thoughts and questions: *Who Killed Colin Roach?* asks how we deal with collective tragedy, how these griefs reverberate through our lives. *Territories* takes that notion of space even further in considering the role of archiving, not merely as an act of collation for later viewing, but an act of seeing, of rendering legible the spaces and occasions in which Black people house their freedom. *Vagabondia* and *Western Union: Small*

*Boats* invite questions around capital and labour – How was the world built? How do we function in a system not built with us in mind? – while *Once Again ... (Statues Never Die)* deals with art and expression, and the sense of infinitude artistic dreaming might provide.

Throughout, you'll be struck by the emotional complexity of the films, the sense of love with which these images have been made. And what is love, really? You believe you're seeing what it might mean to Julien, among these images and sounds: the thin line between anger and sadness, and the way grief holds these things together. The need to imagine and enact a future in the now, one which looks and feels better than the present. The care with which the artist has reassembled a Black collective memory, woven from the music of our everyday lives. As you come back round to *Looking for Langston*, that same notion from years ago once more: *I've felt this before, but I couldn't say where.* And then, as the film progresses, a moment of clarity: of course, you've felt this before. Of course, you're feeling it now. With the work of Isaac Julien, across the rendering of these various moments and emotions, this isn't just the work of memory, no; what you're seeing, what you're feeling, is an act of love.

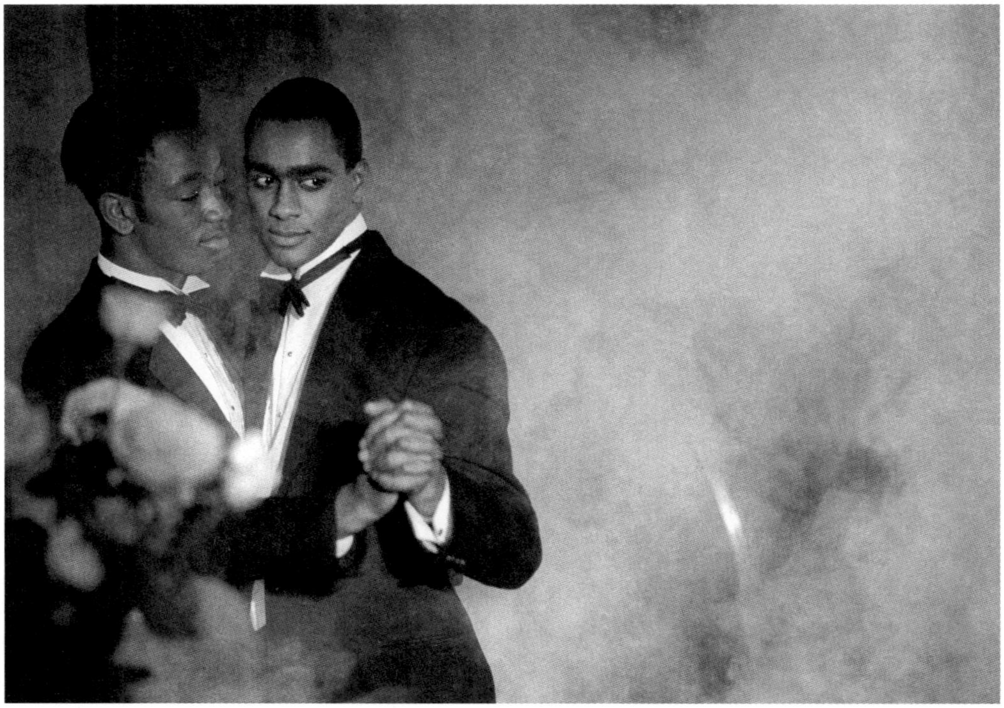



*Pas de Deux No.2 (Looking for Langston Vintage Series)* 1989/2016

# LOOKING FOR LANGSTON

# 1989

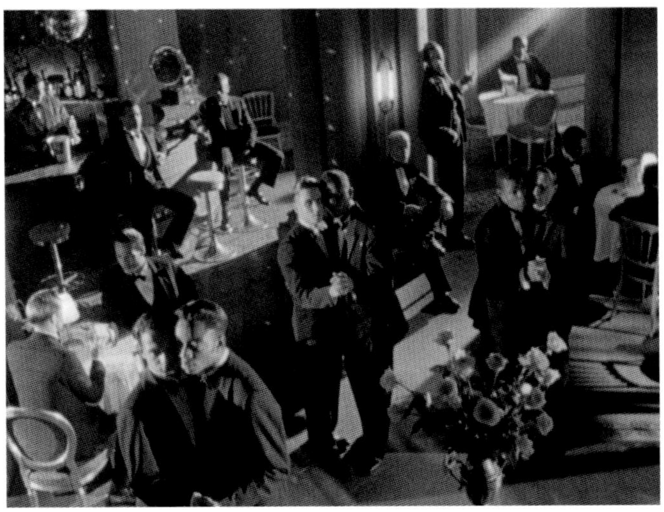

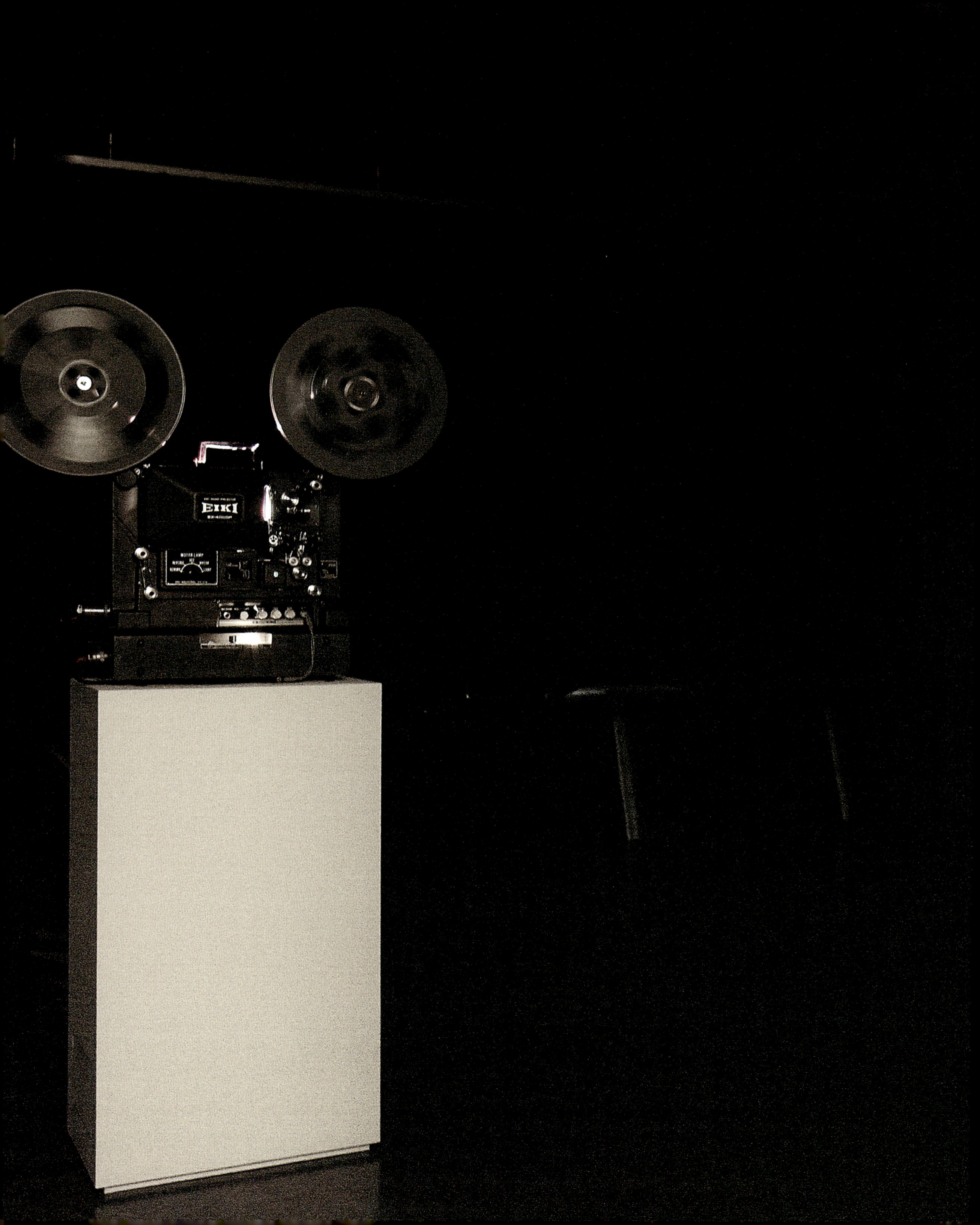
EIKI

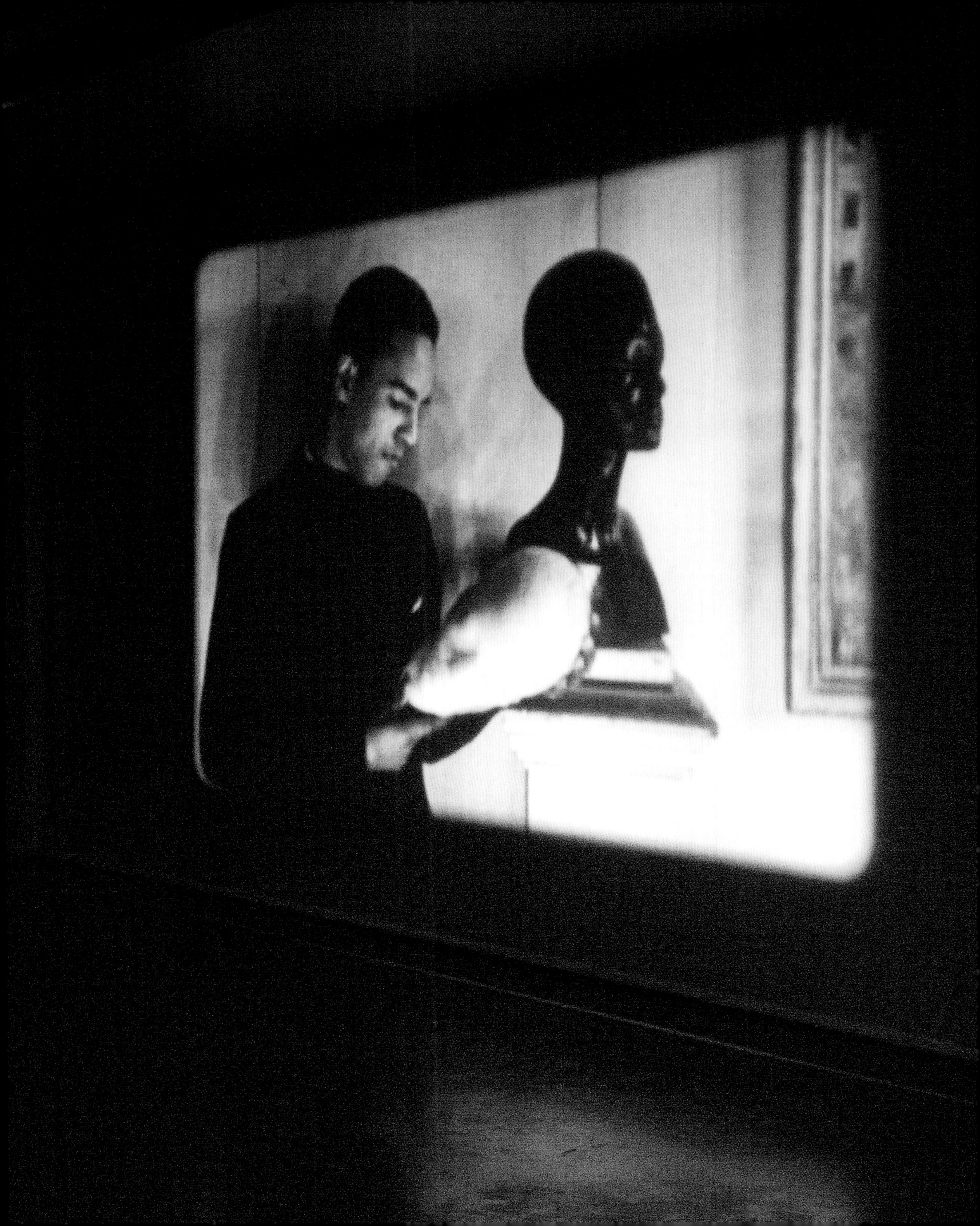

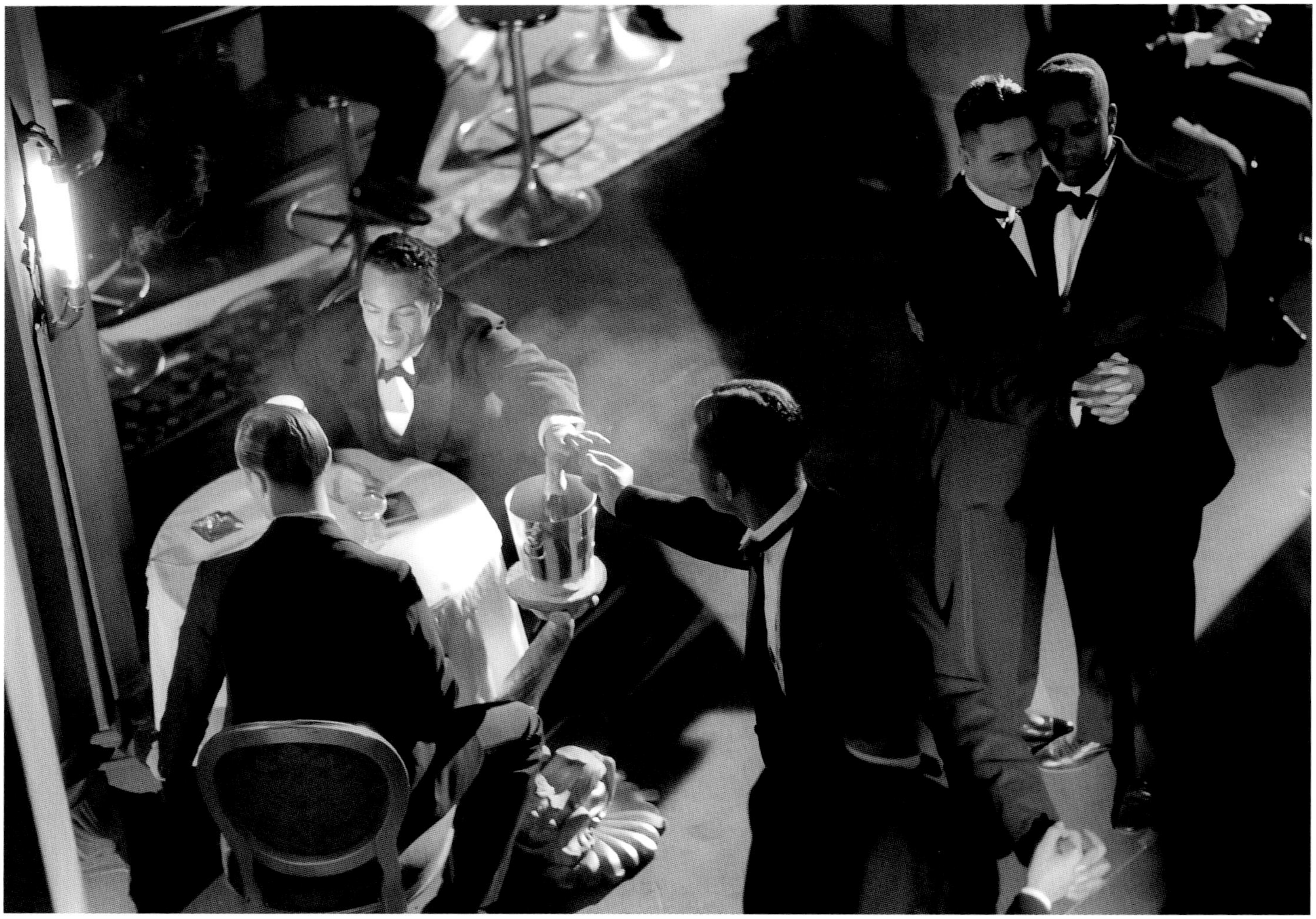

*Stars (Looking for Langston Vintage Series)* 1989/2017

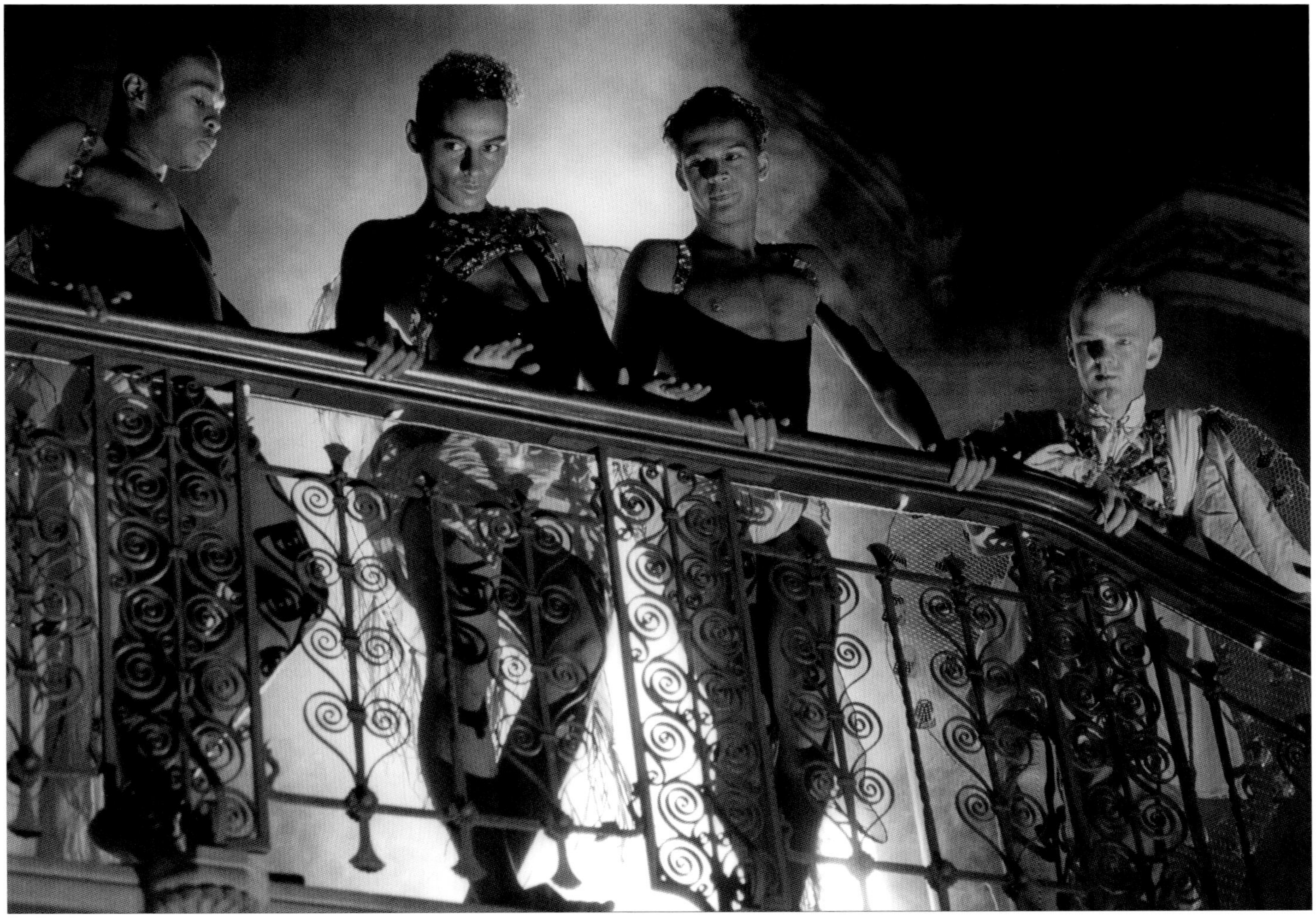

 *Film-Noir Angels (Looking for Langston Vintage Series)* 1989/2016

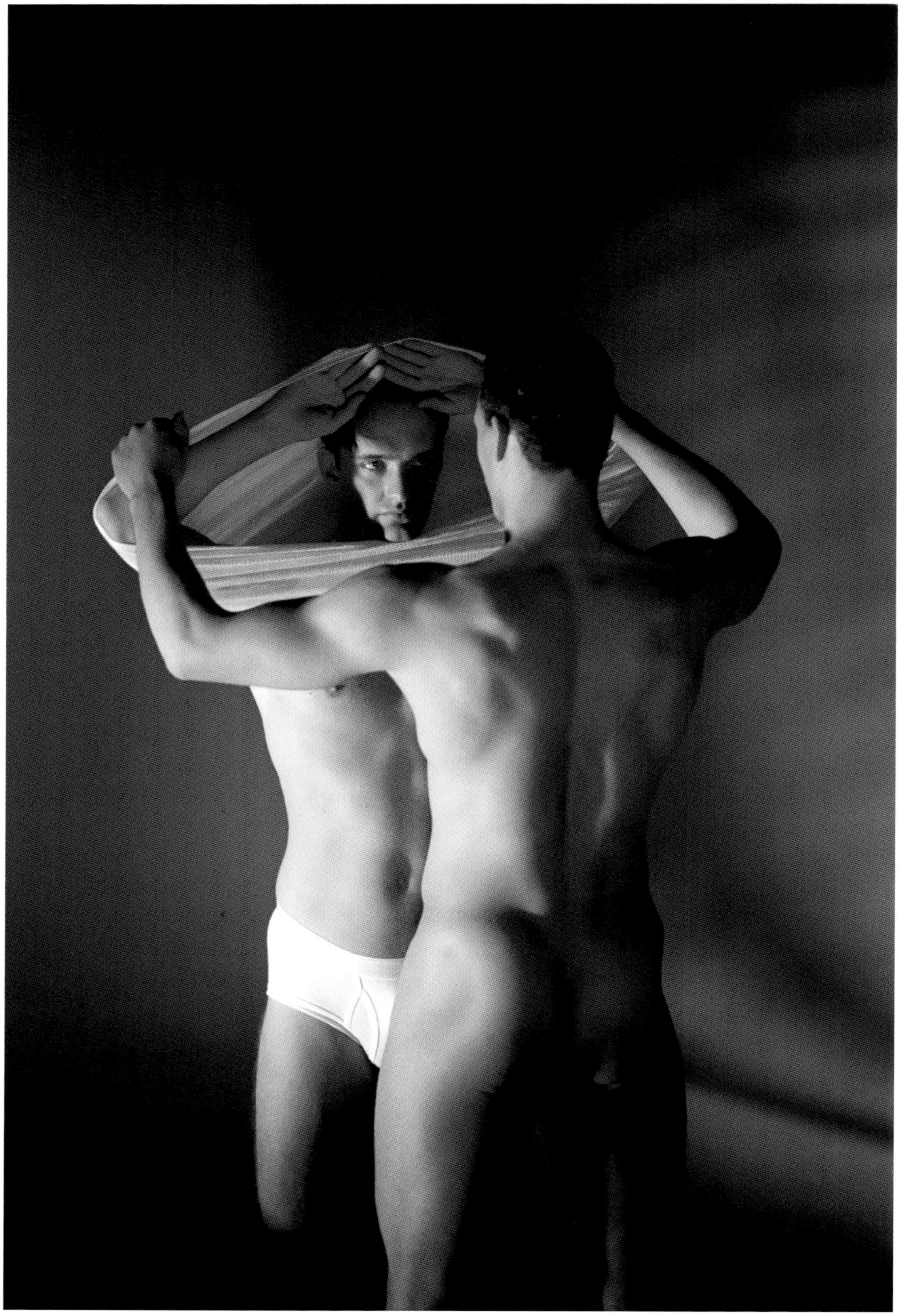

*After George Platt Lynes, Nudes 1942 (Looking for Langston Vintage Series) 1989/2016*

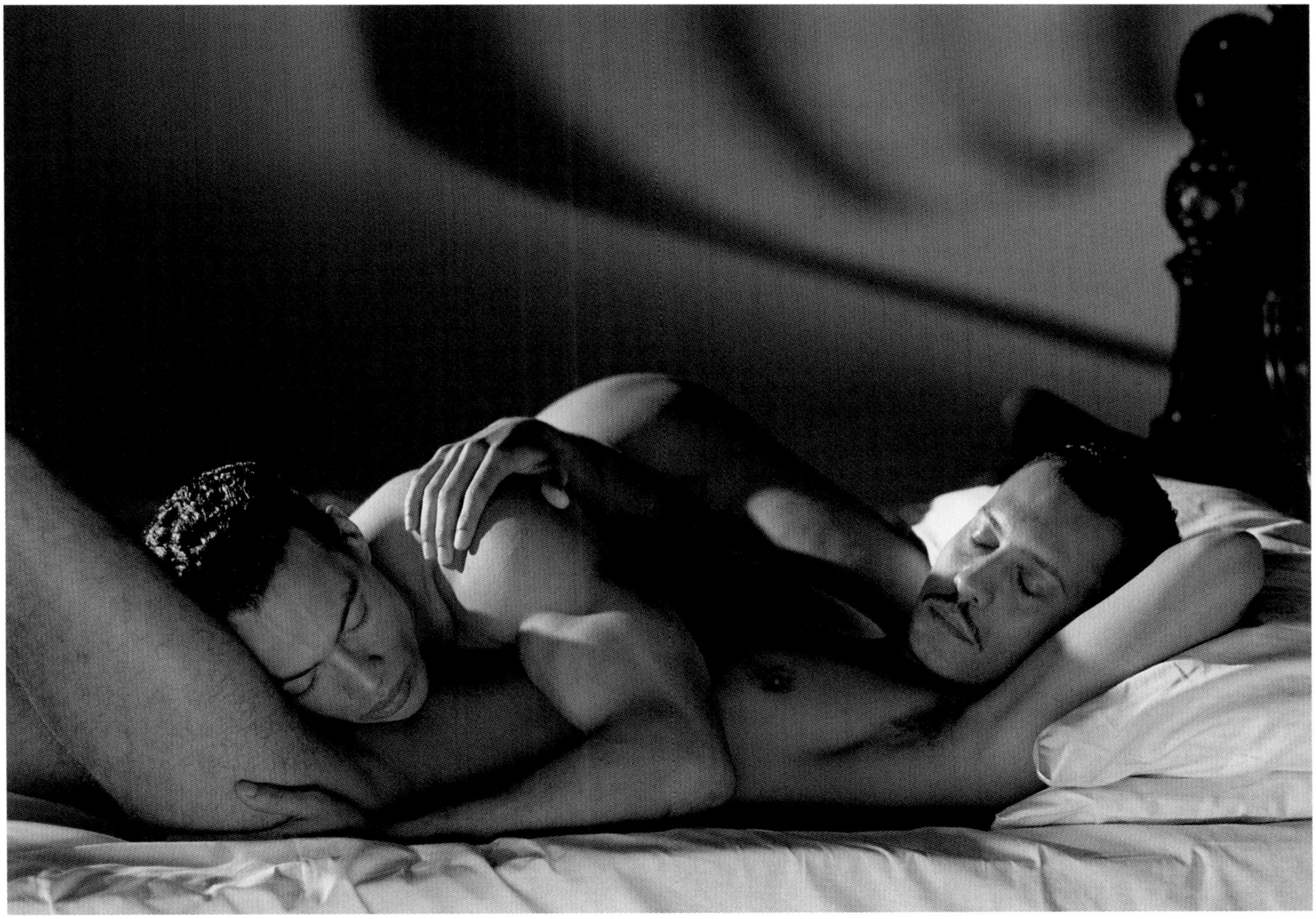

 *After George Platt Lynes, Nudes 1942 (Looking for Langston Vintage Series) 1989/2016*

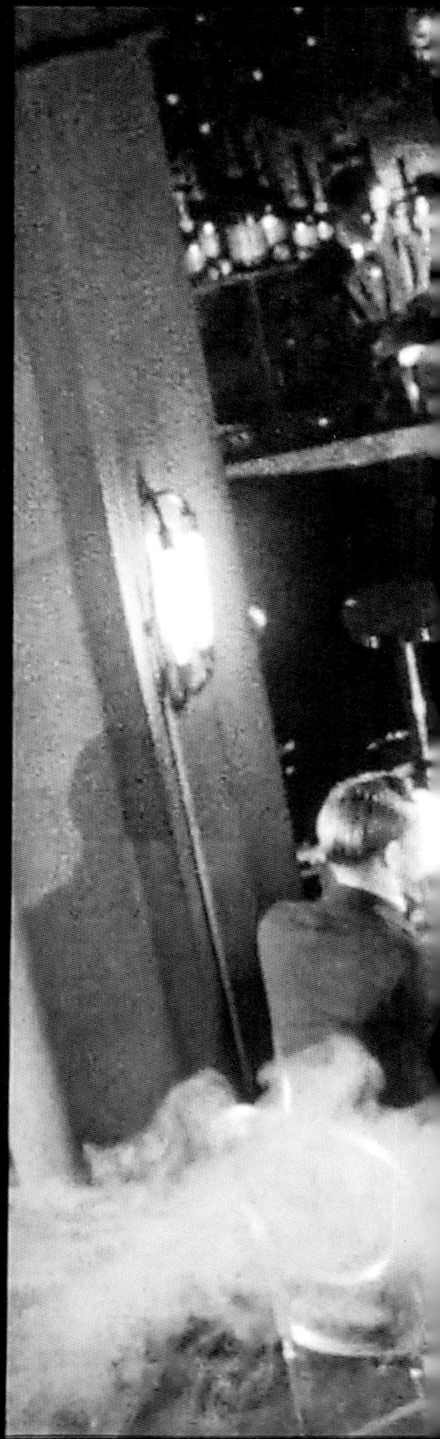

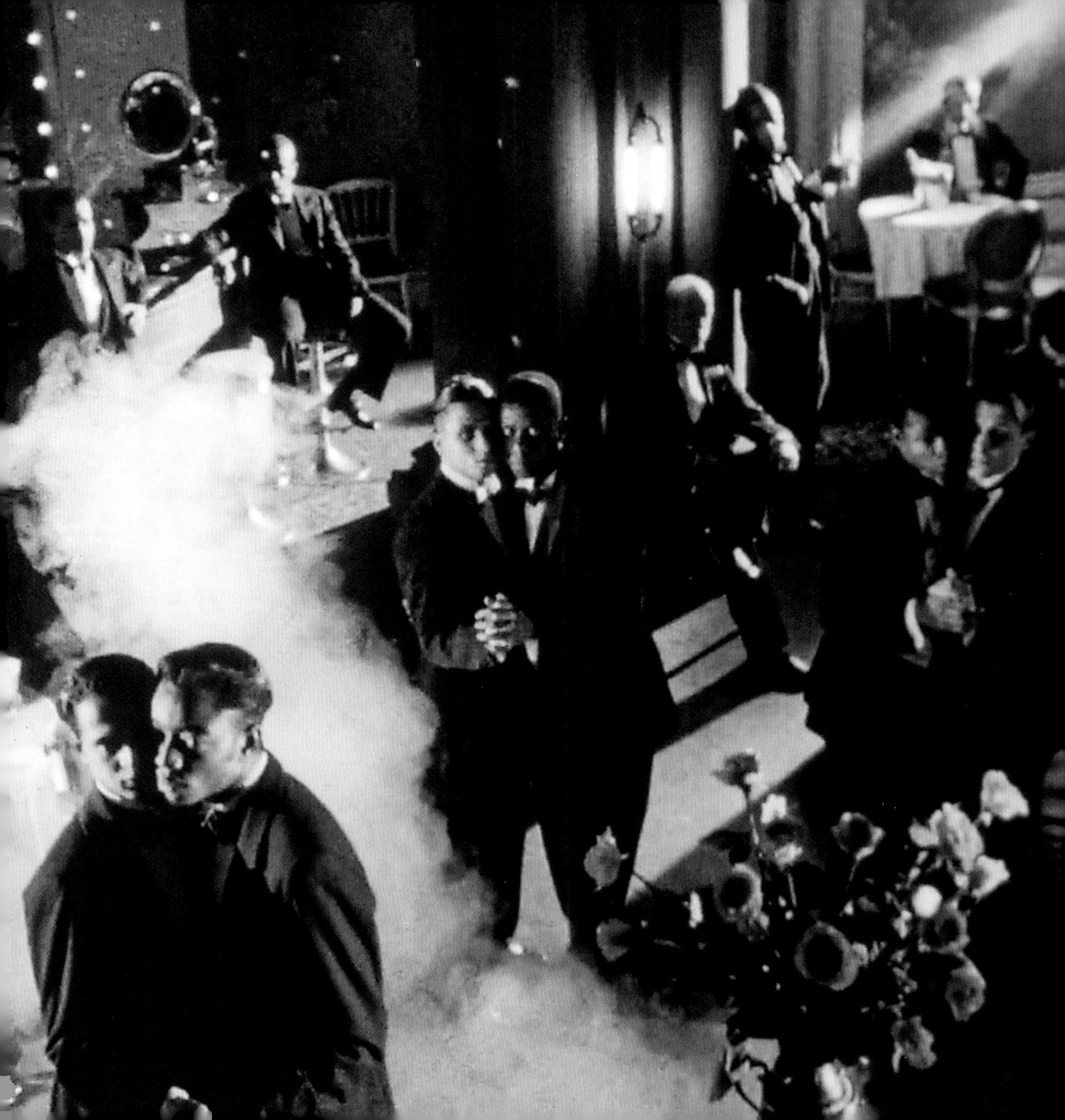

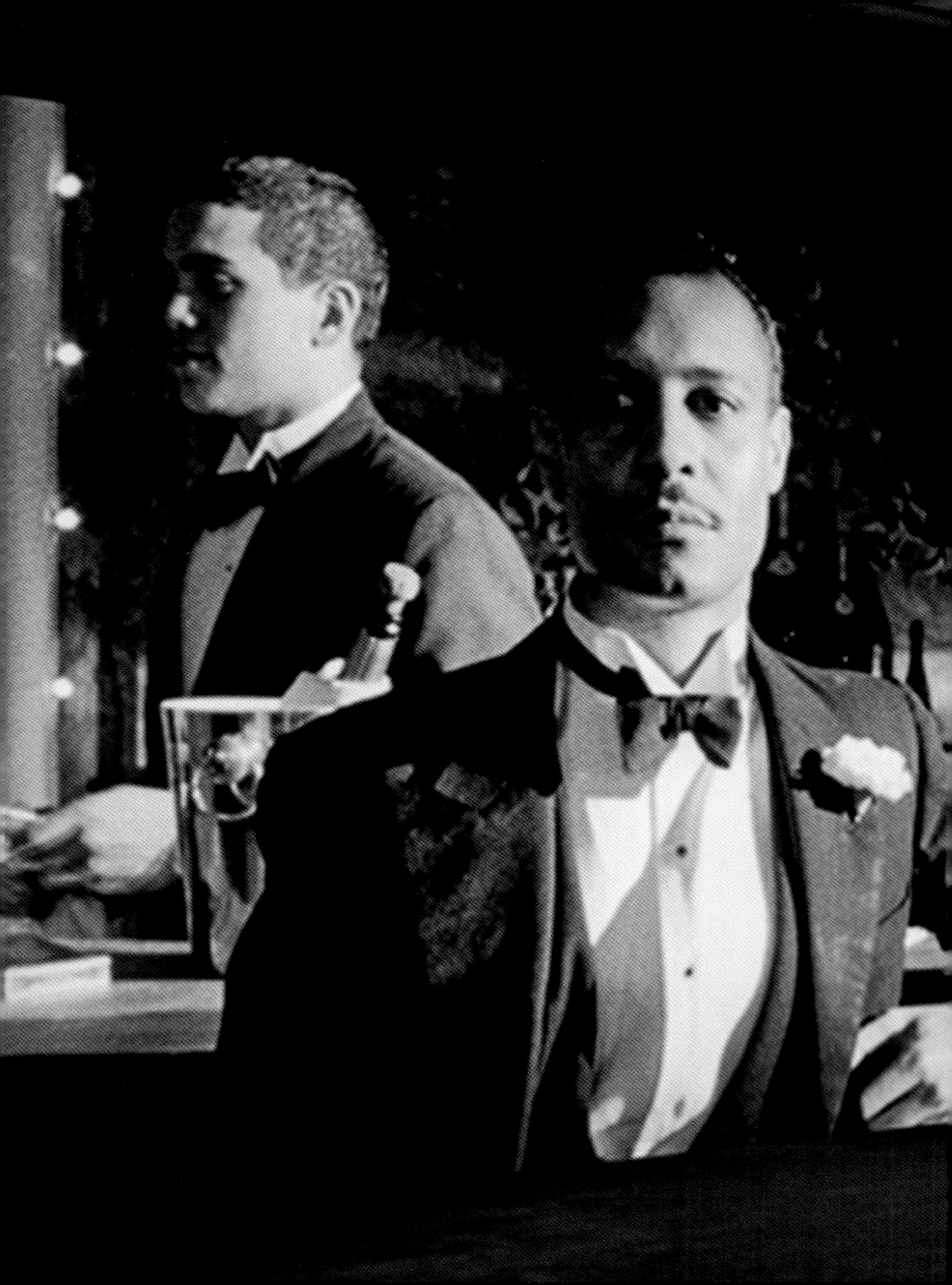

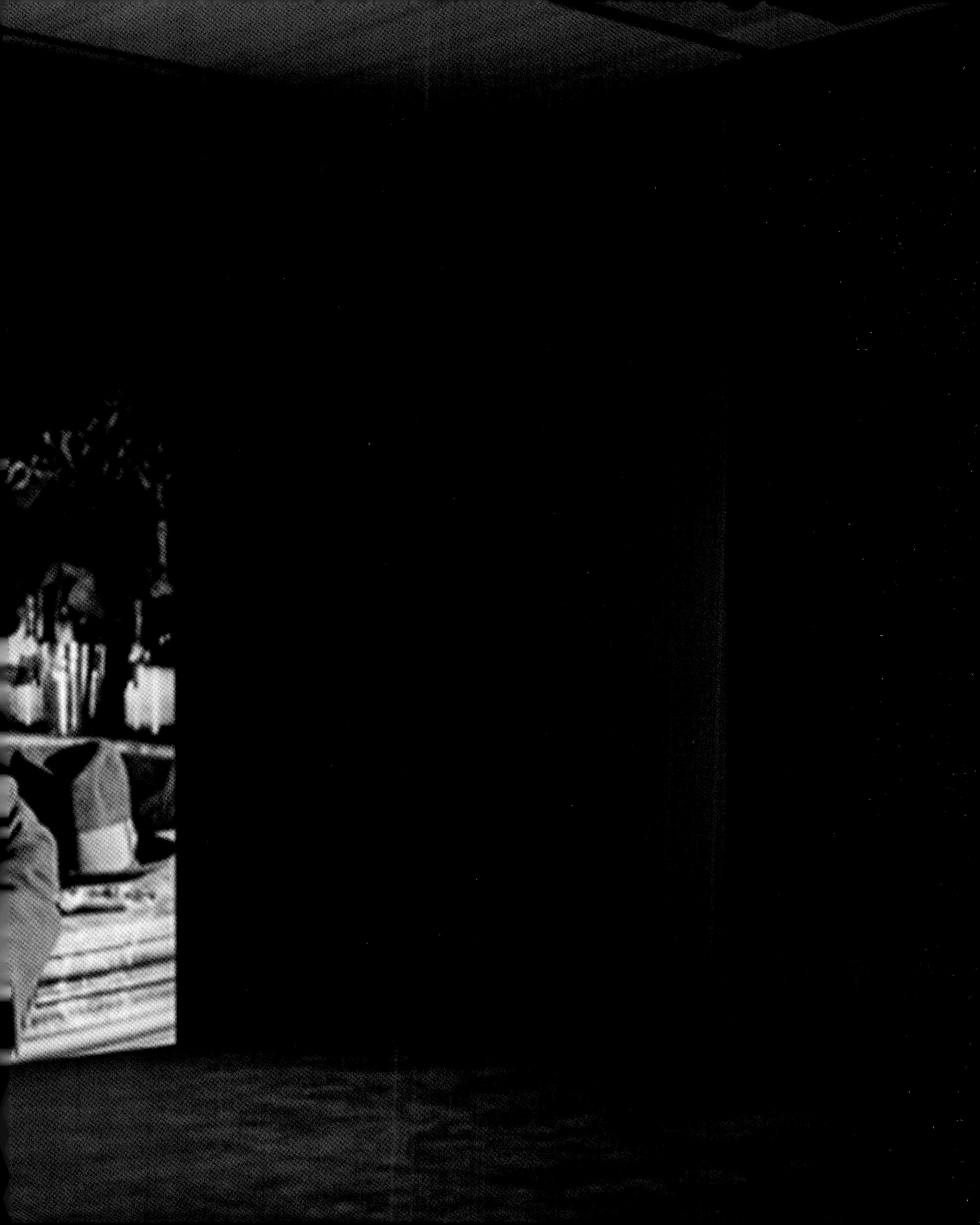

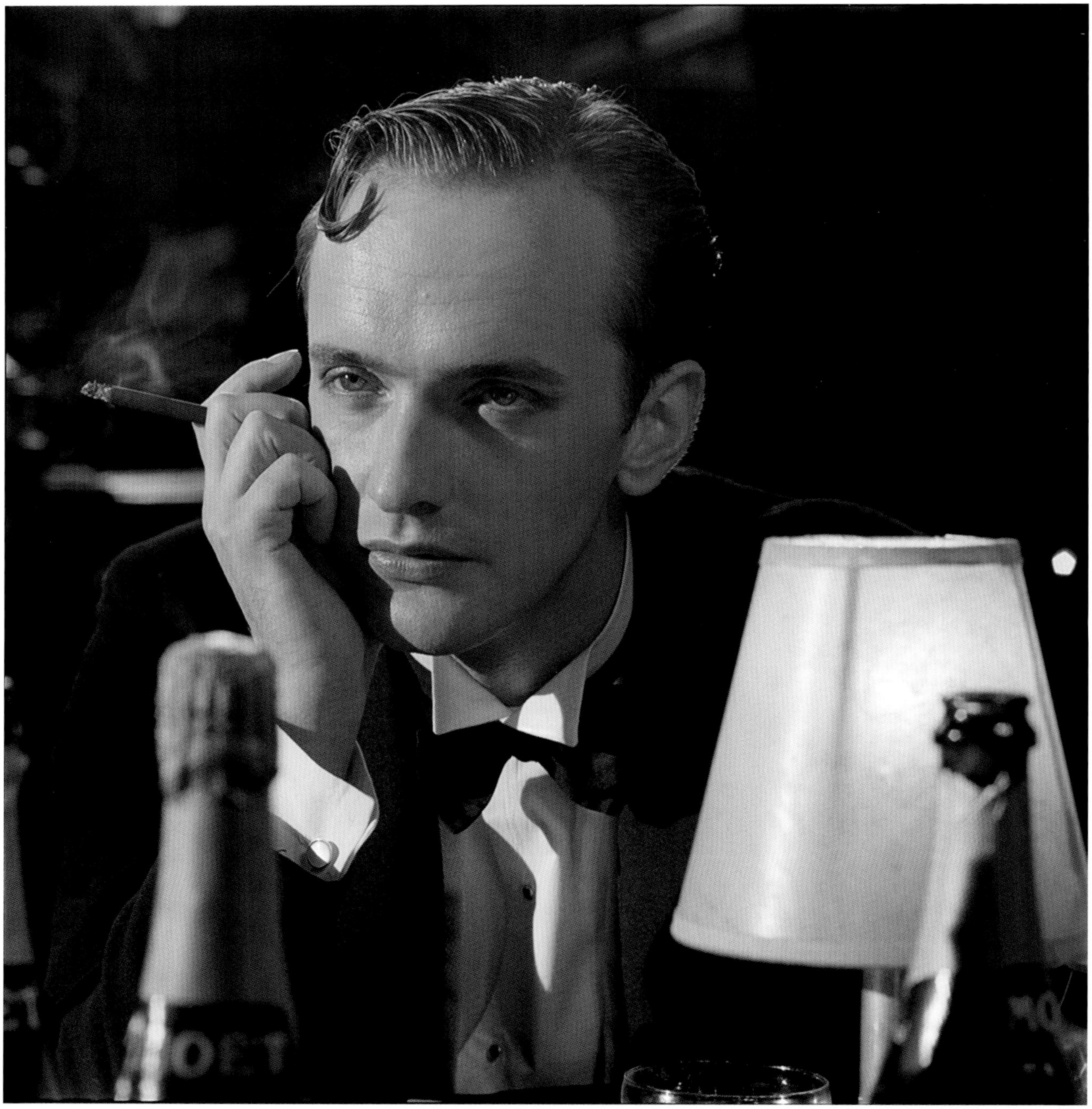


*Study for Carl van Vechten (Looking for Langston Vintage Series)* 1989/2016

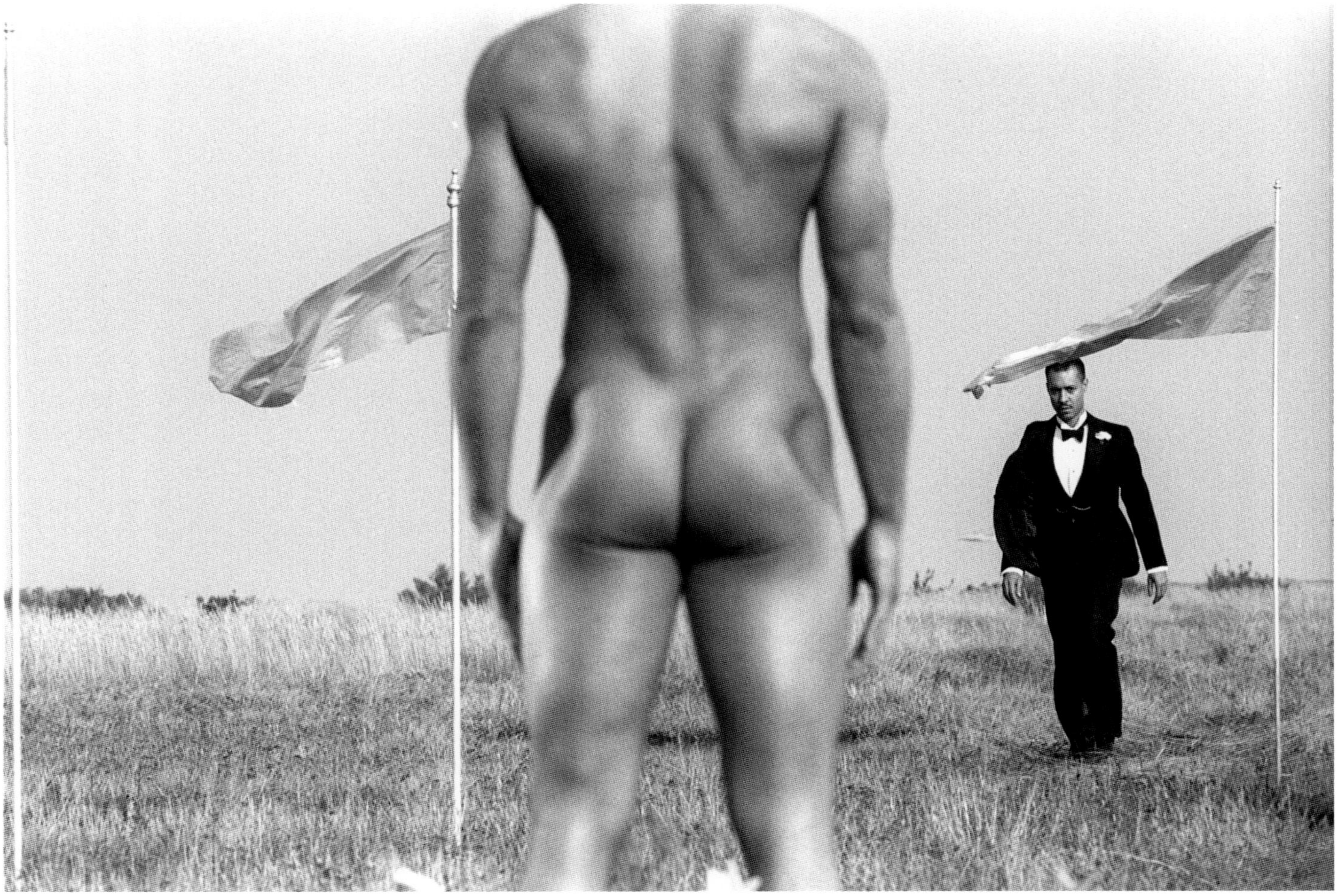

 *Masquerade No.4 (Looking for Langston Vintage Series)* 1989/2016

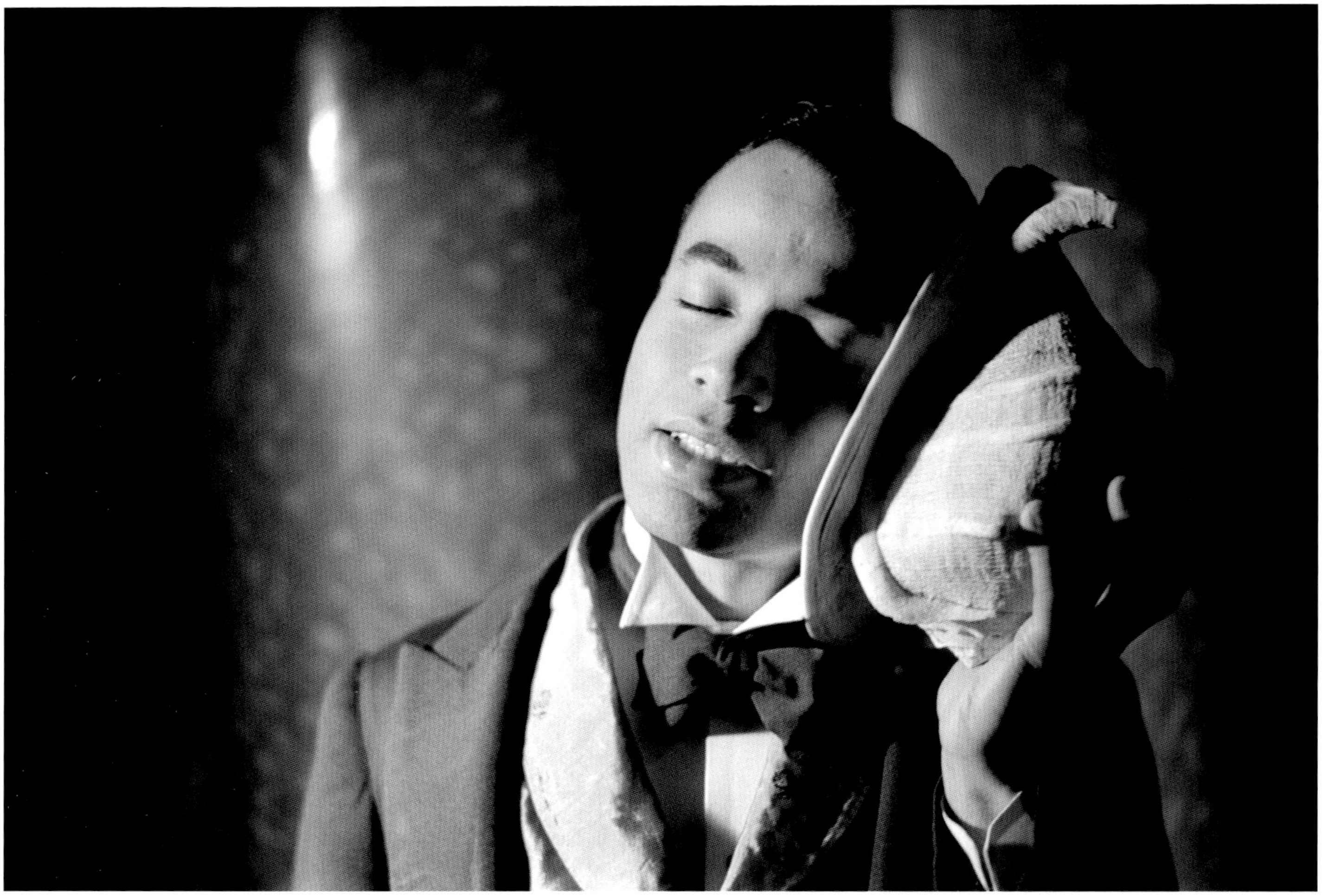

*Le Rêve No.1 (Looking for Langston Vintage Series)* 1989/2016

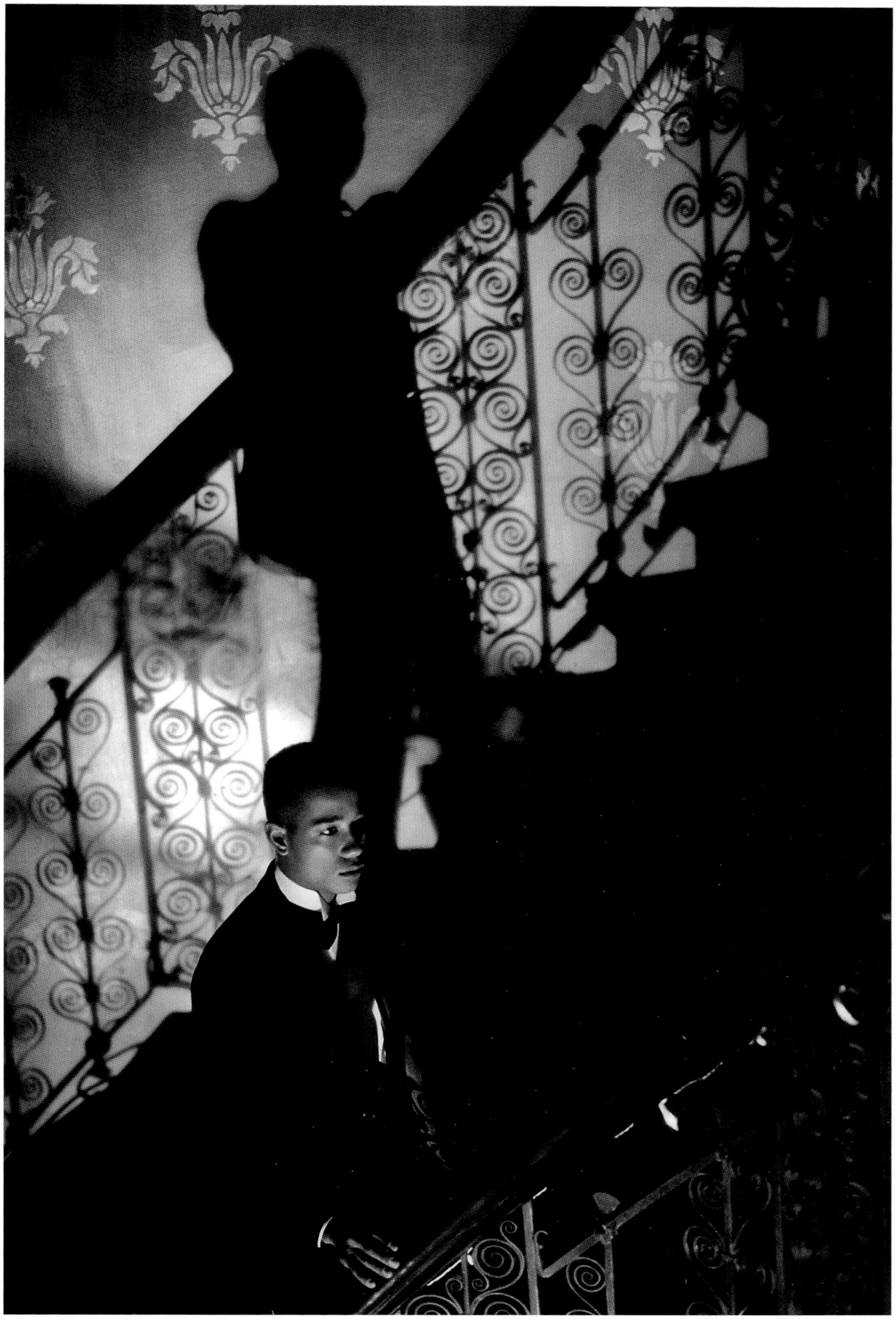

 *Film-Noir Staircase (Looking for Langston Vintage Series)* 1989

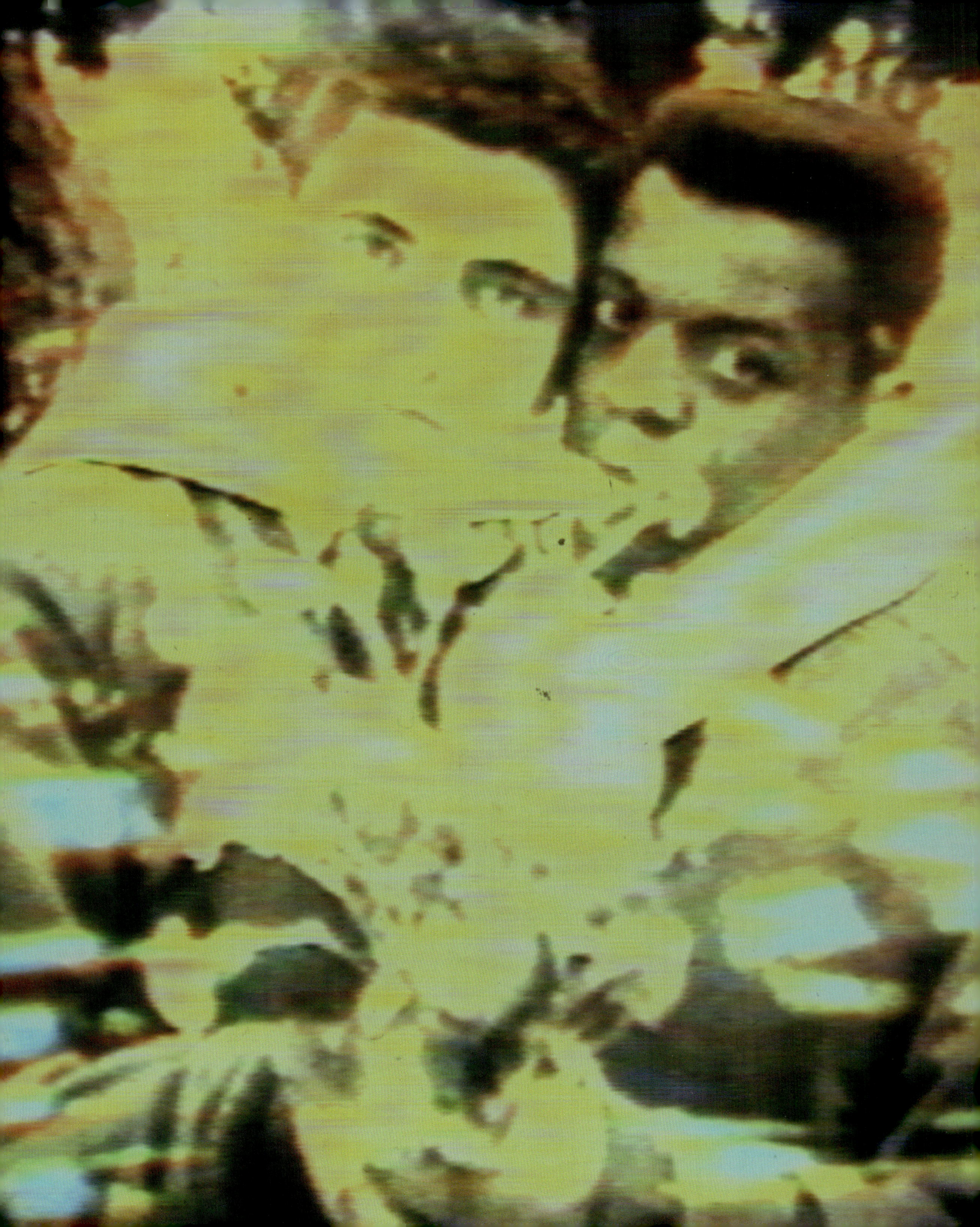

# THIS IS NOT AN AIDS ADVERTISEMENT

1987

▶ 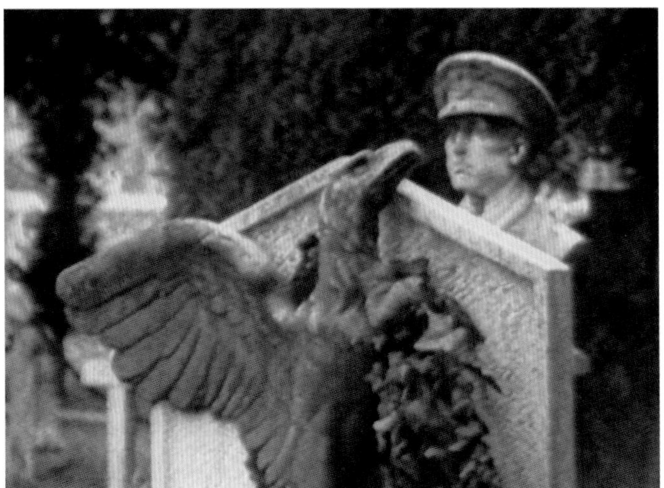

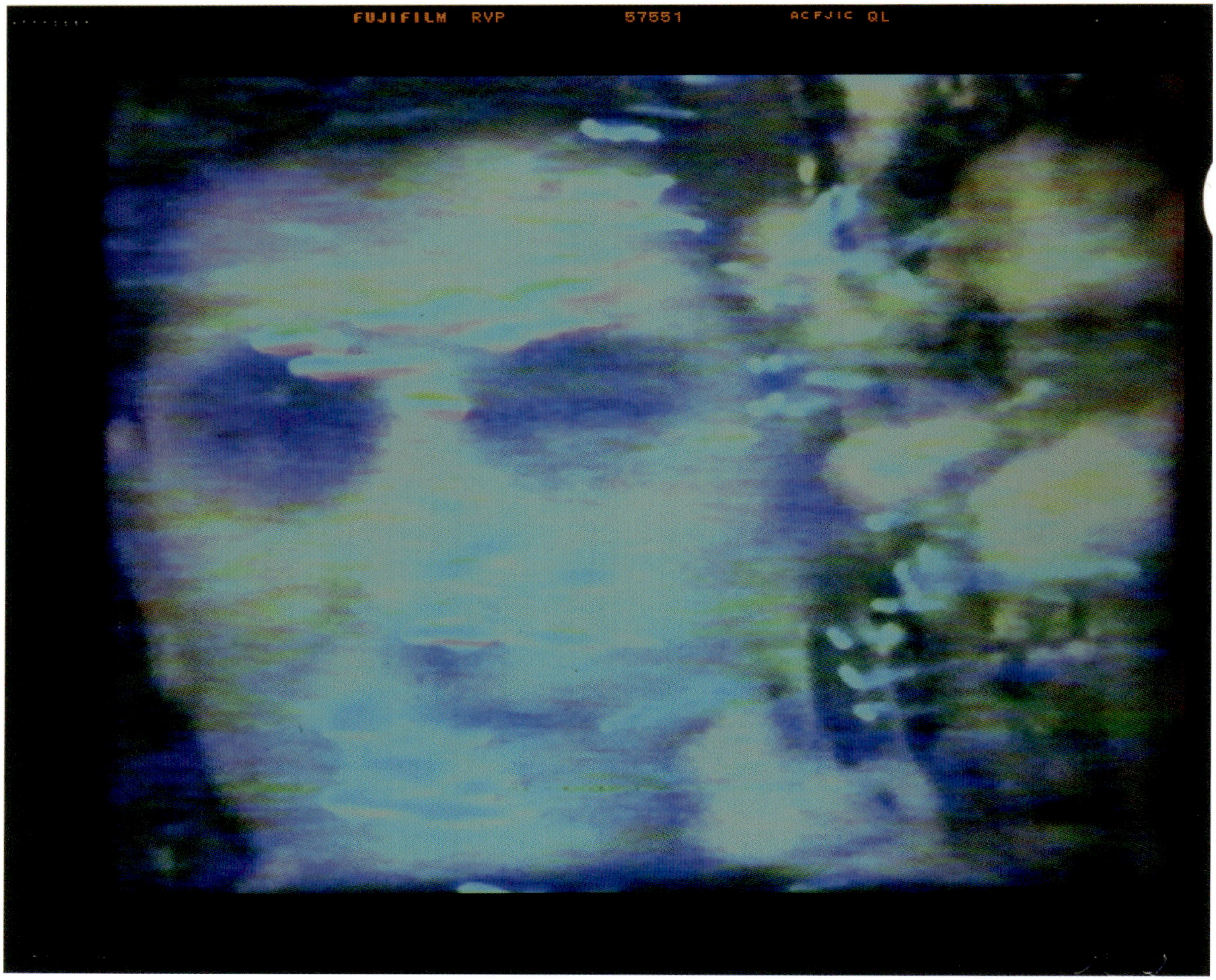


Still from *This Is Not An AIDS Advertisement* 1987

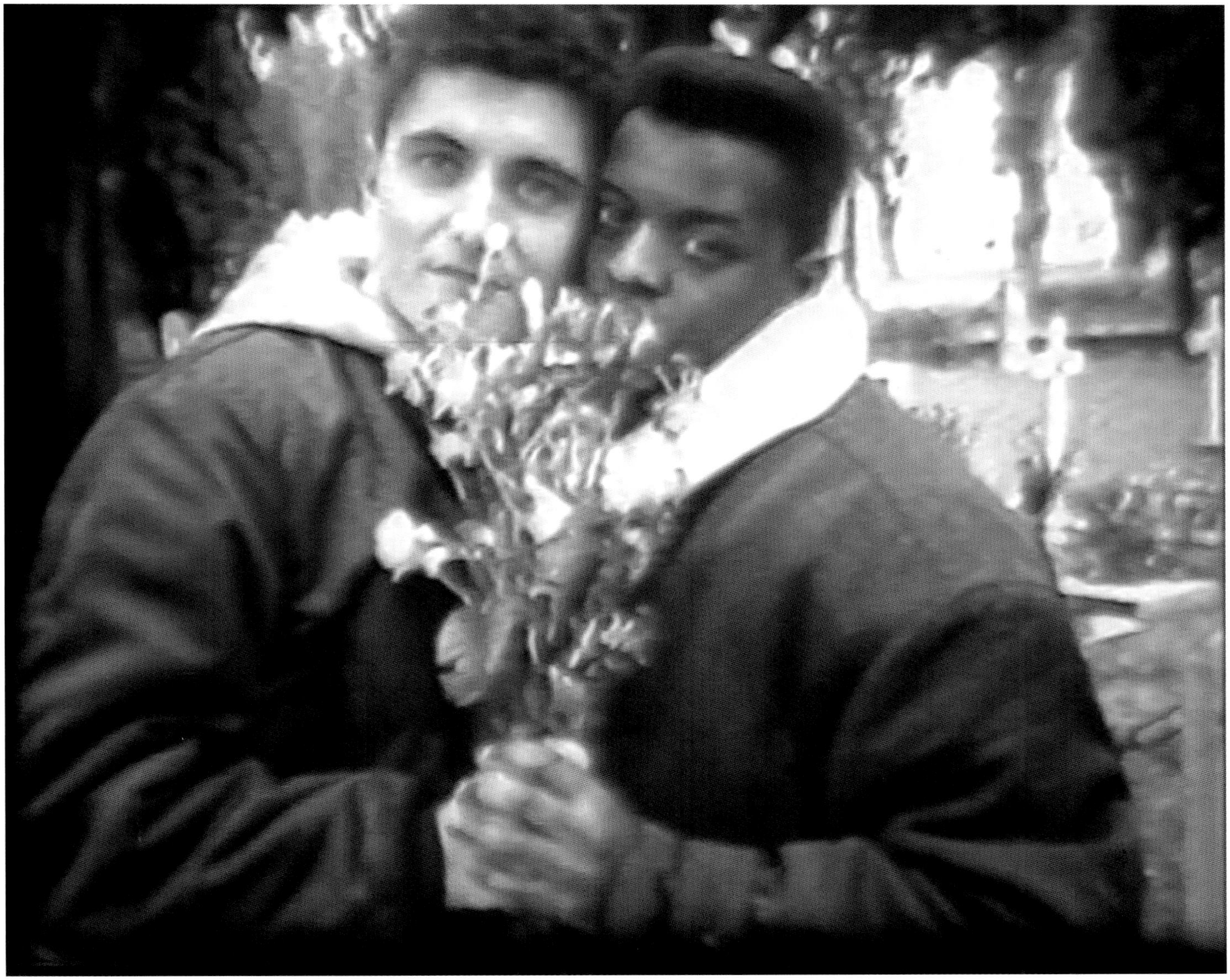

 Still from *This Is Not An AIDS Advertisement* 1987

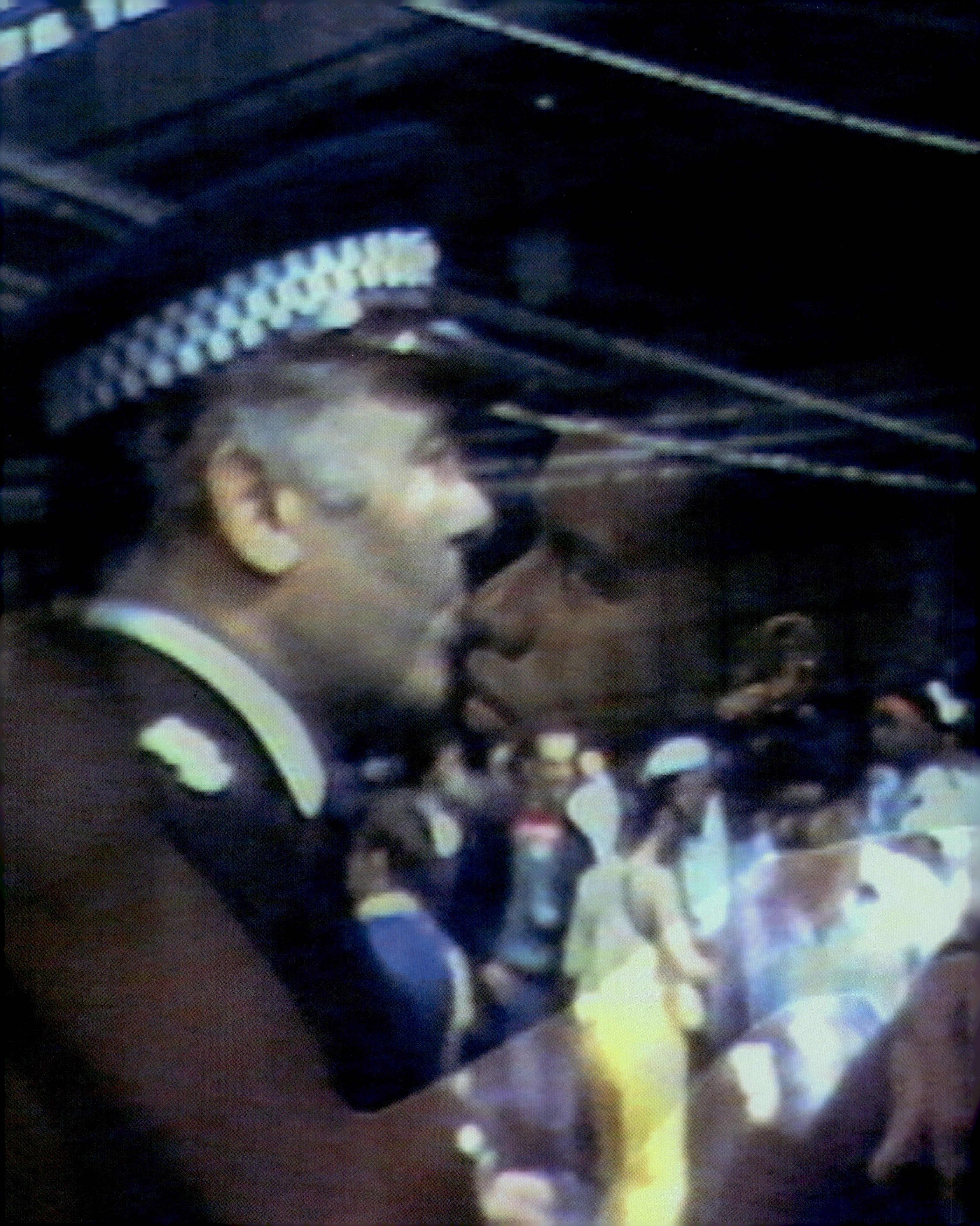

# TERRITORIES

1984

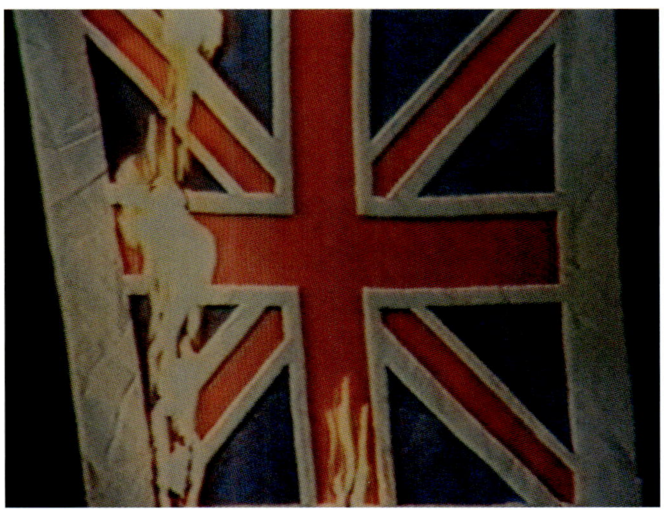

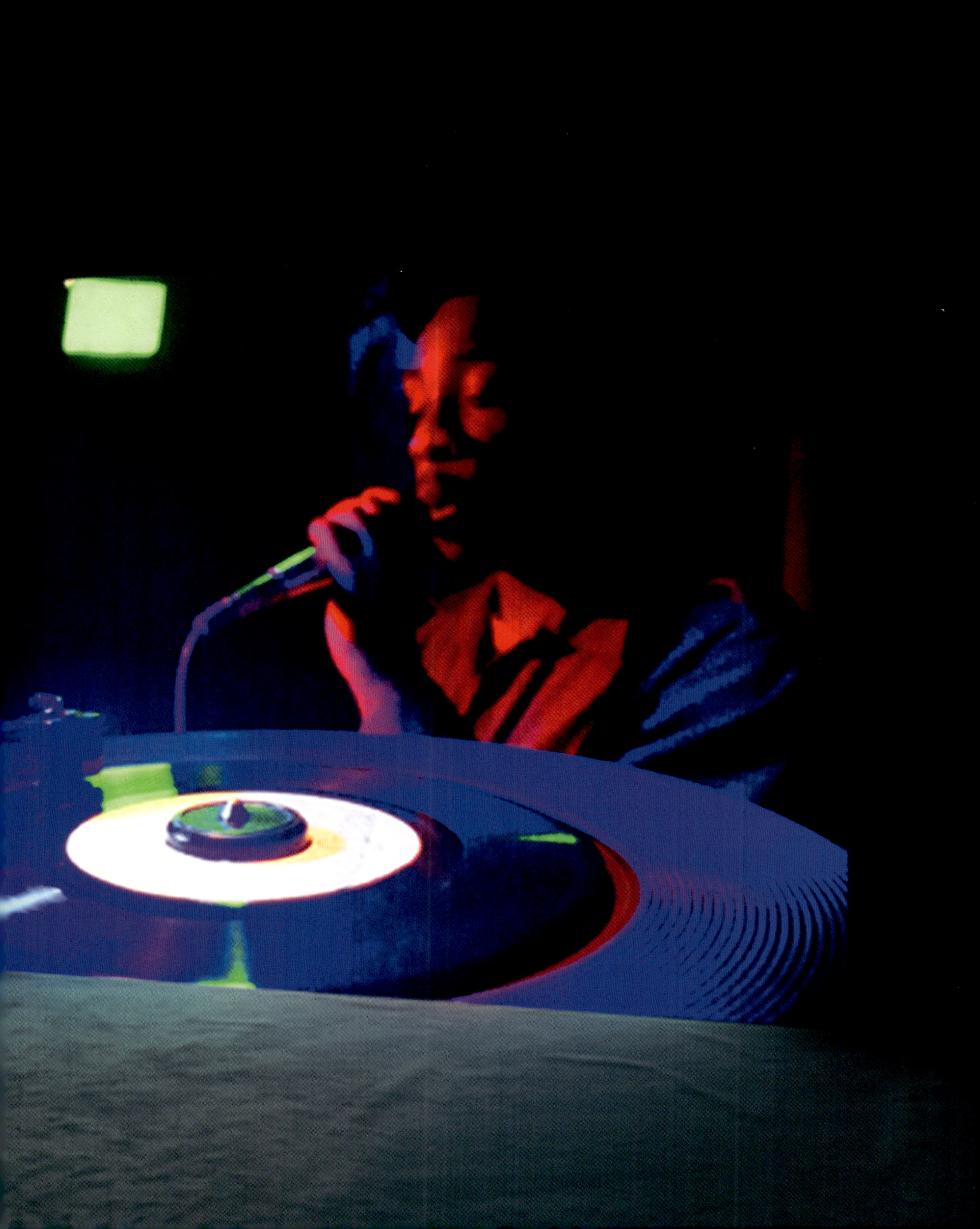

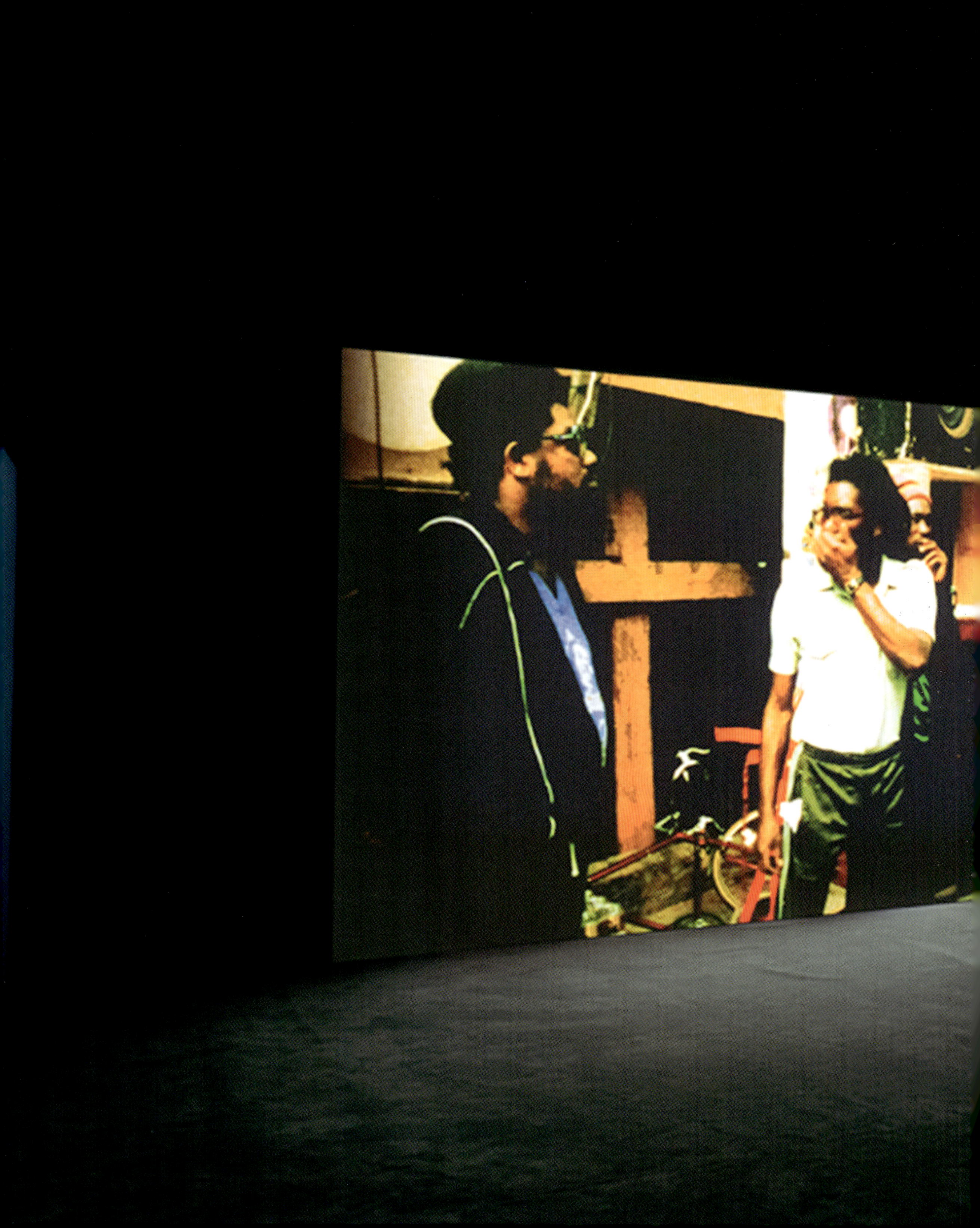

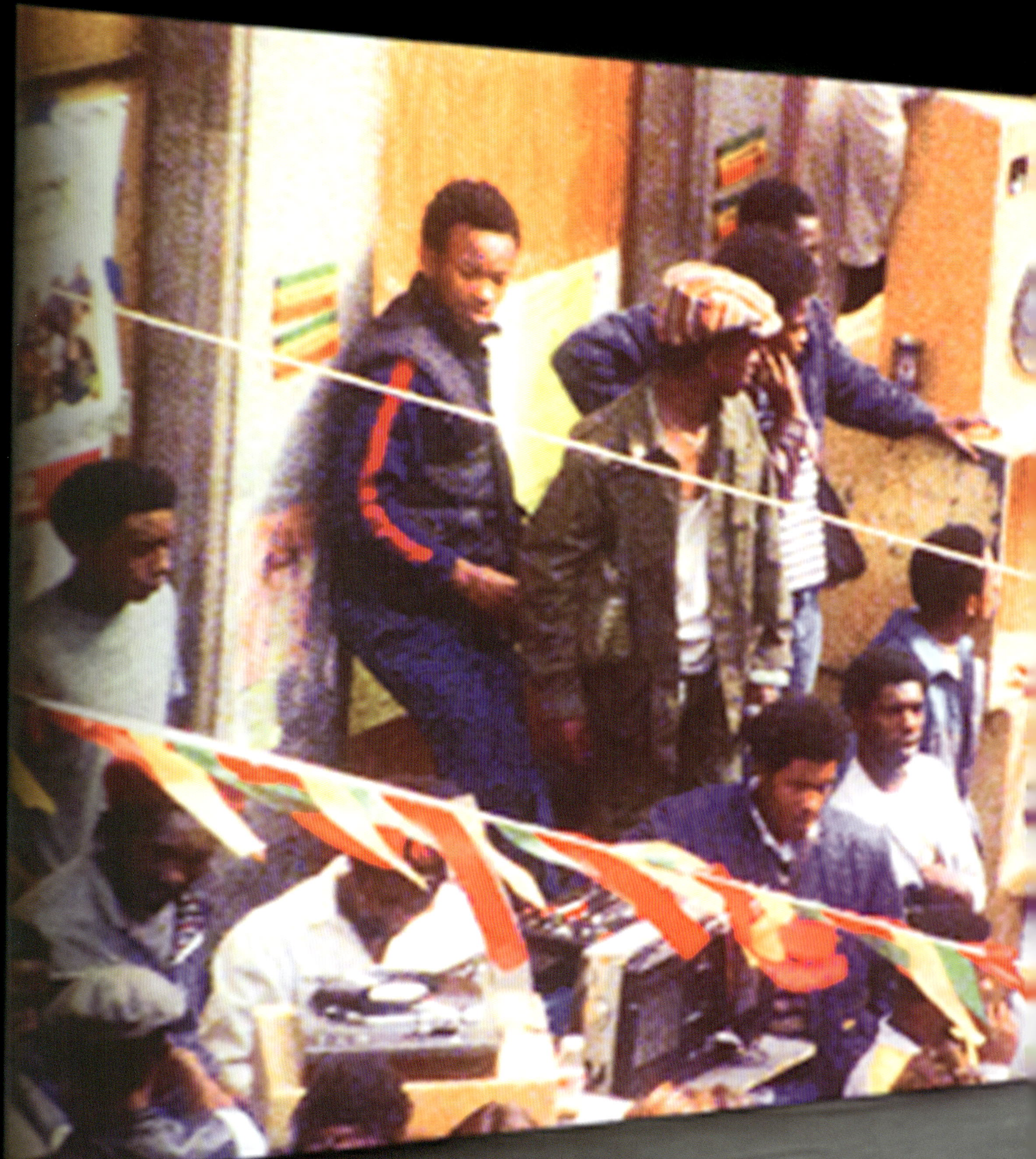

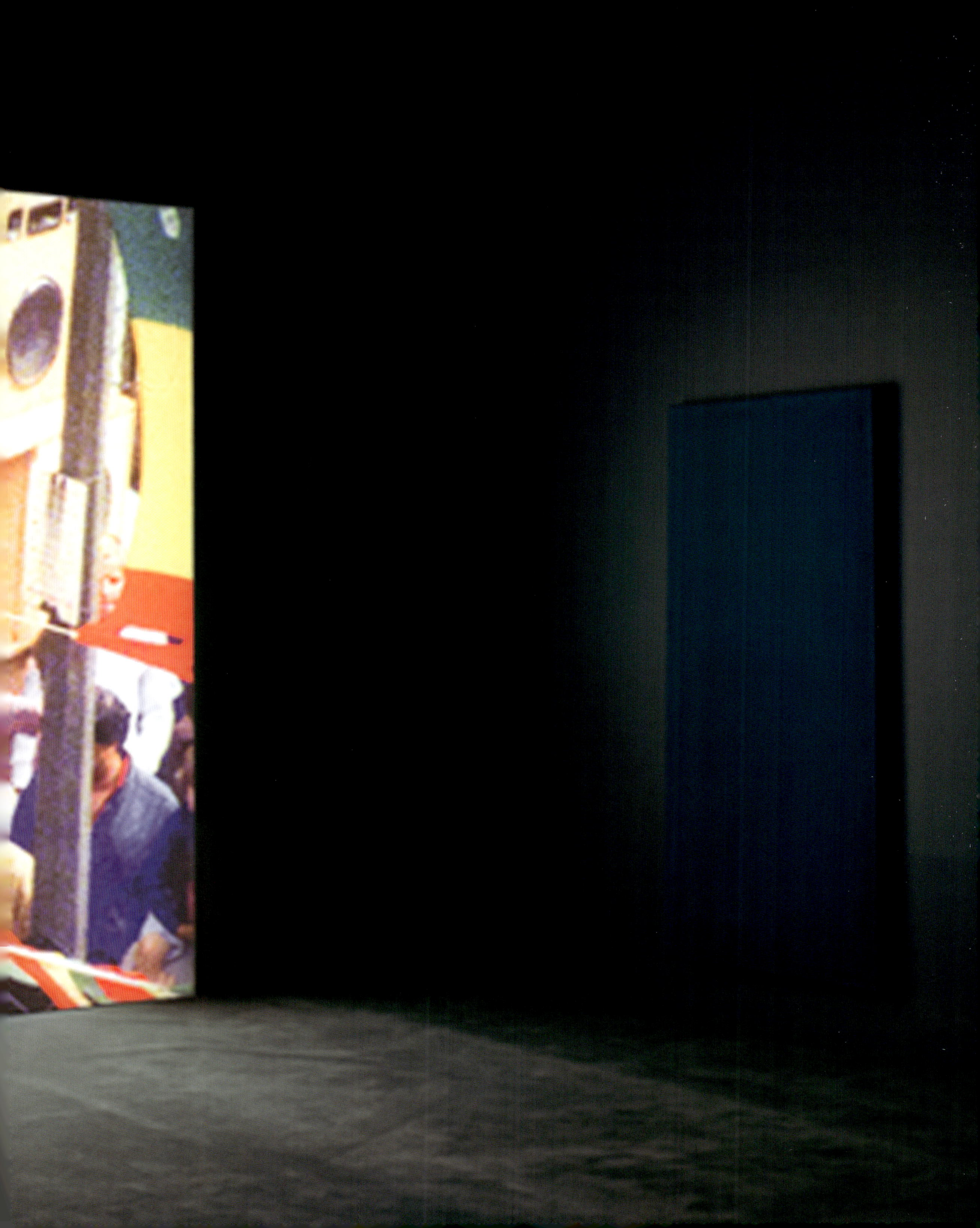

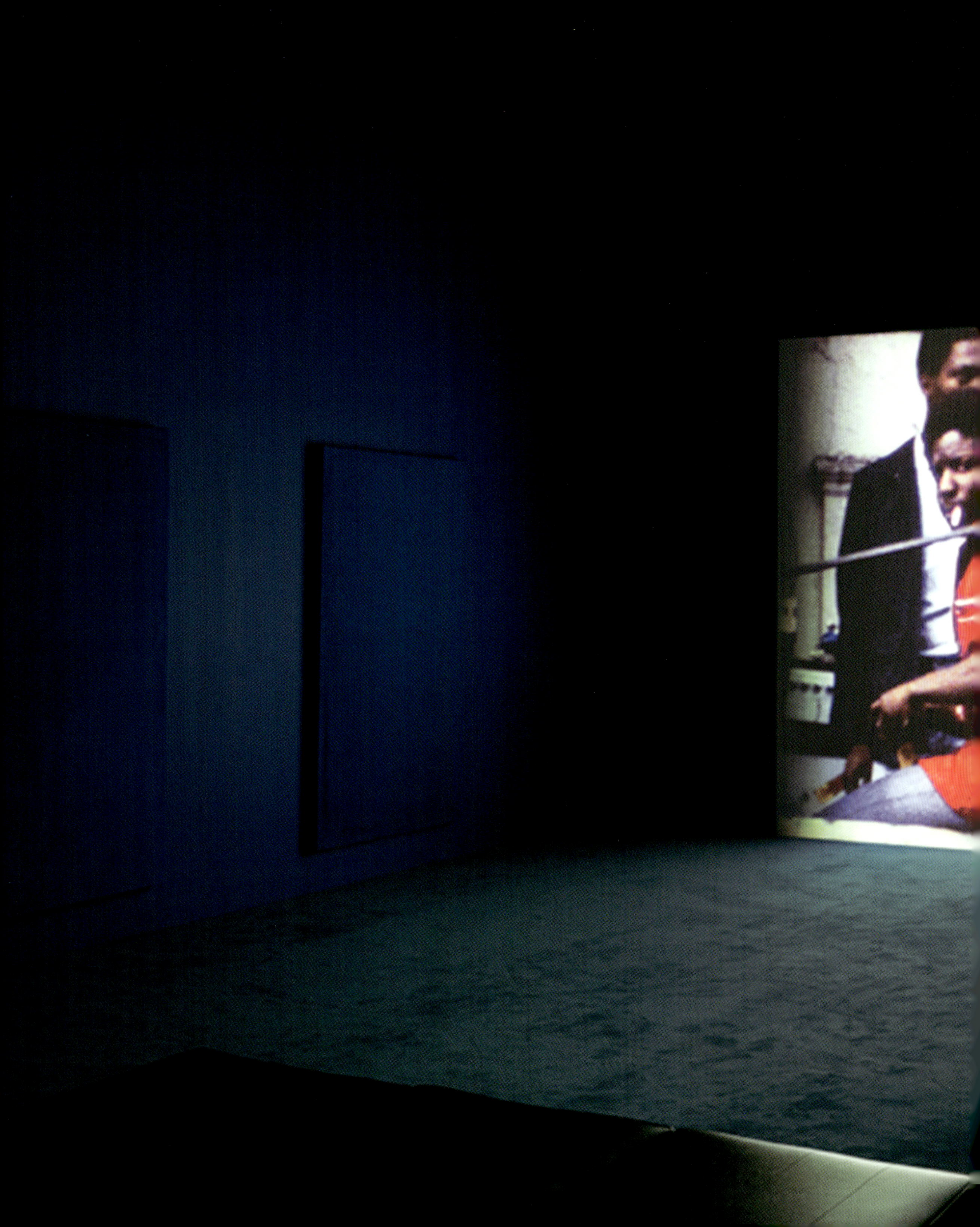

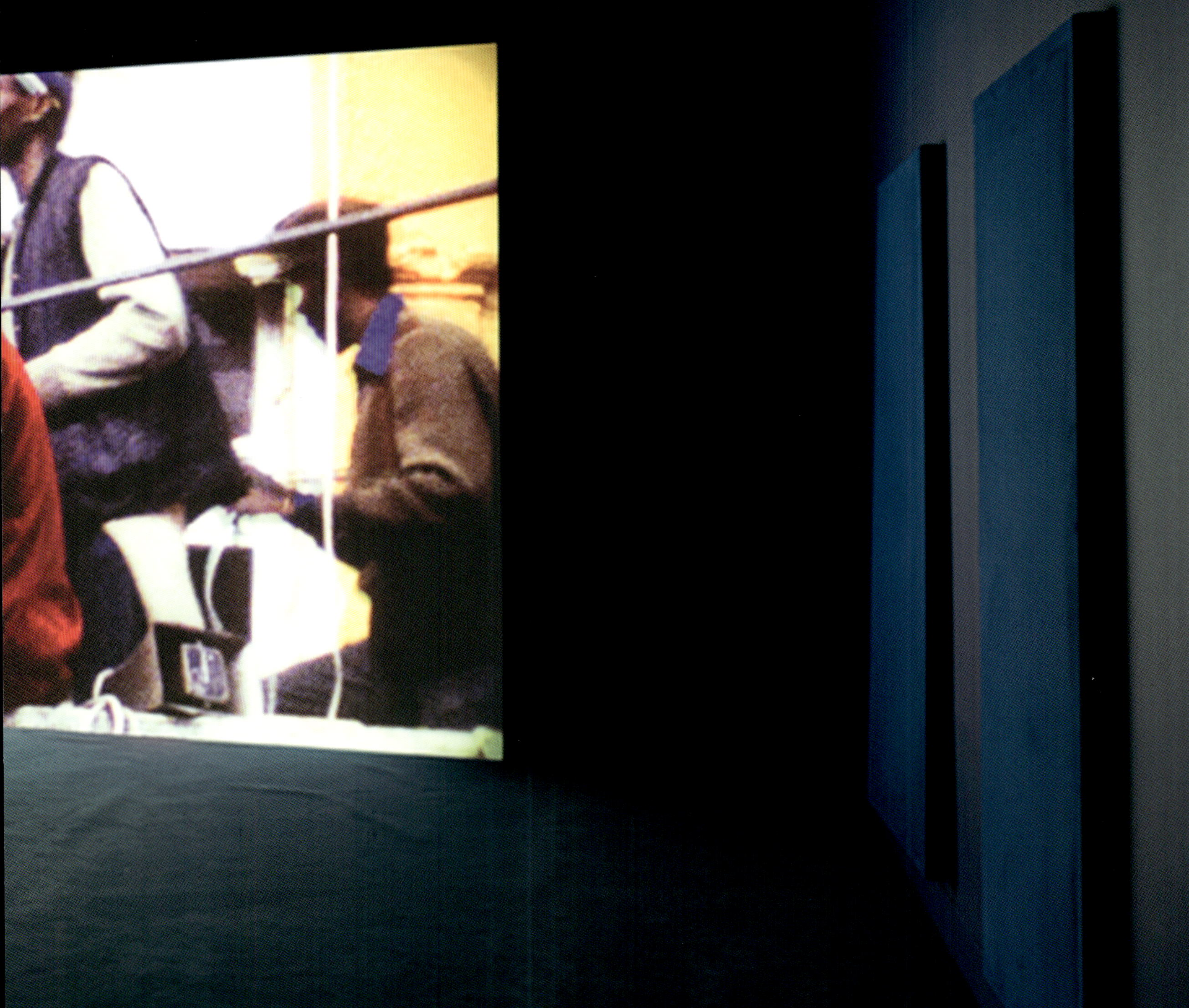

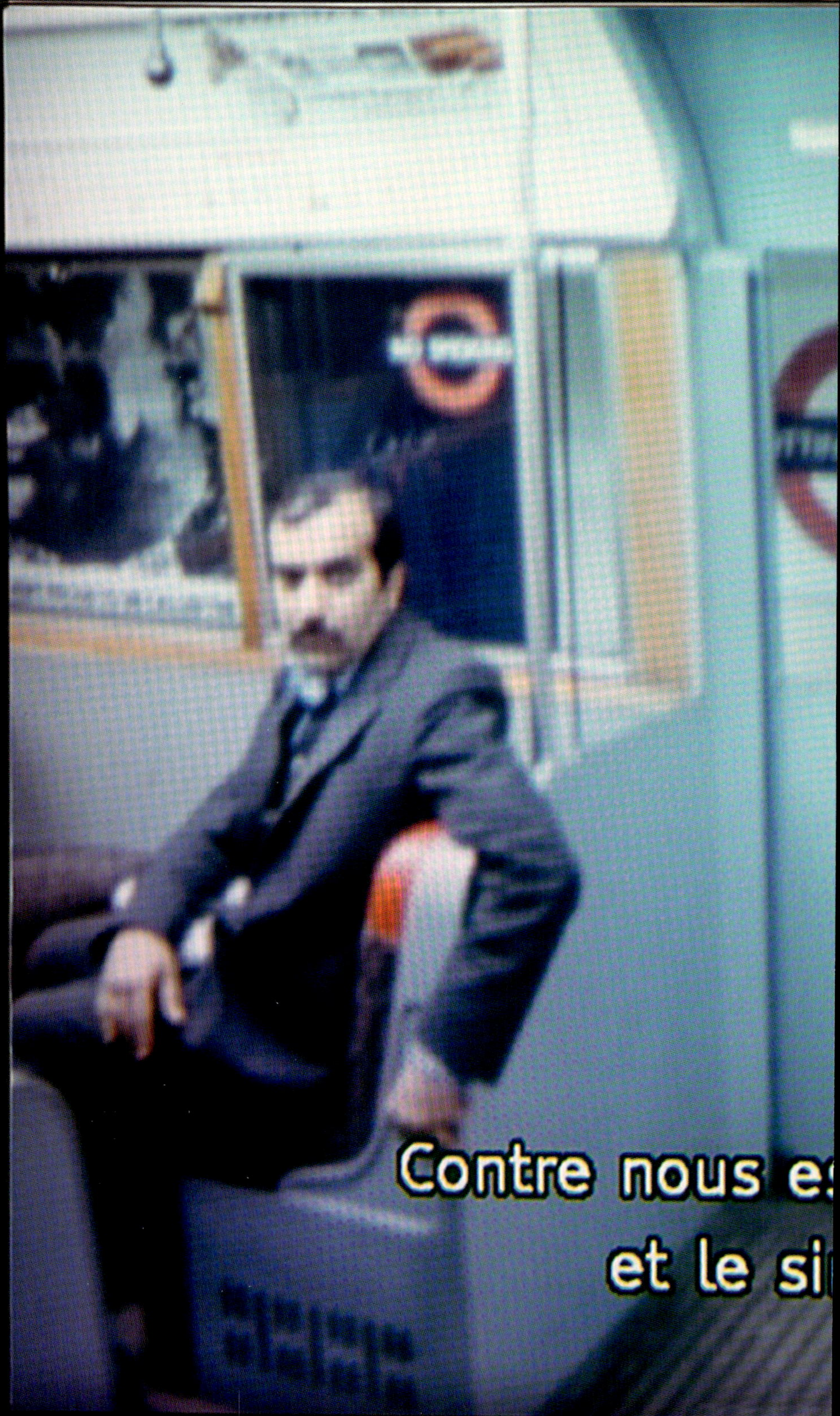
Contre nous es
et le si

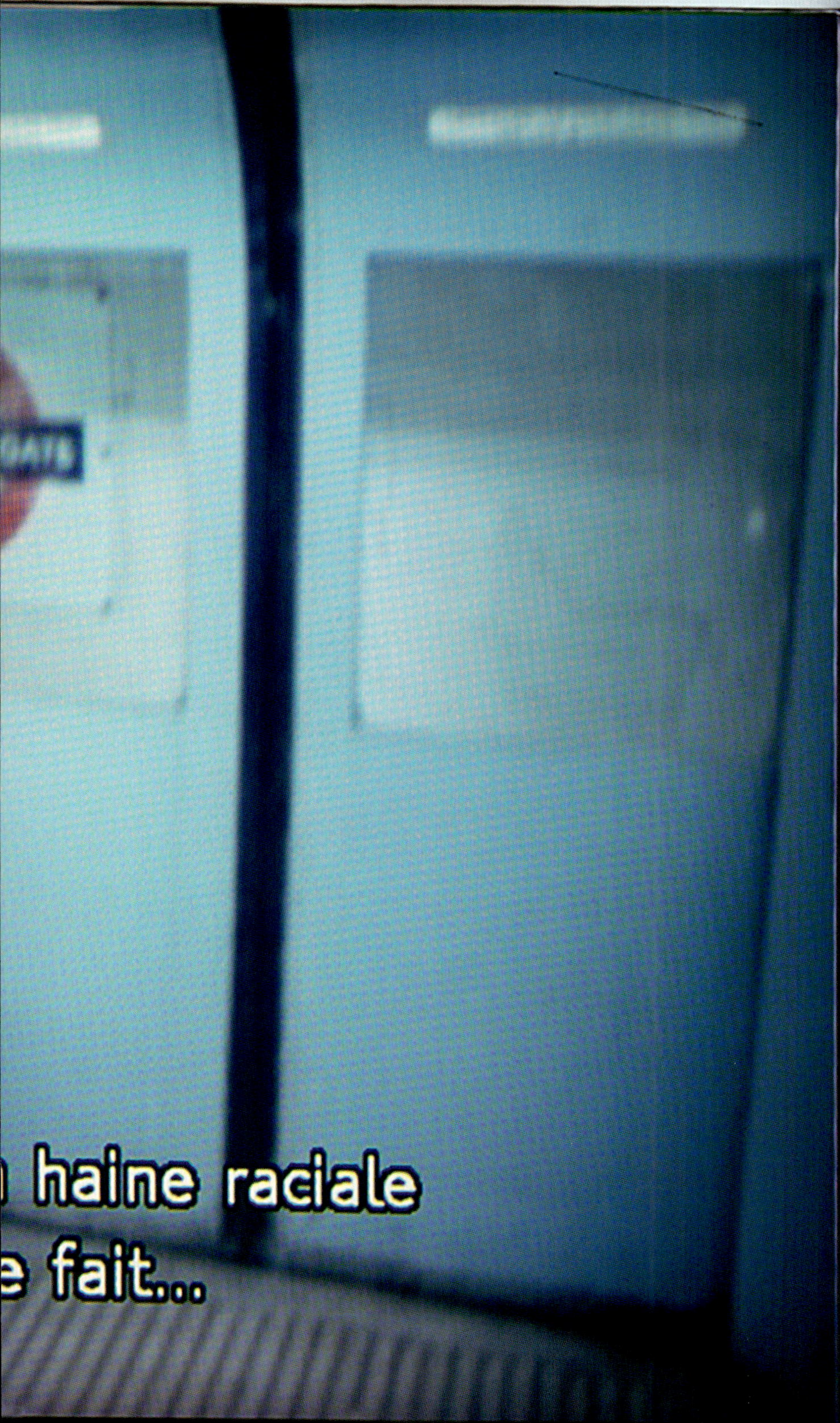
haine raciale
fait...

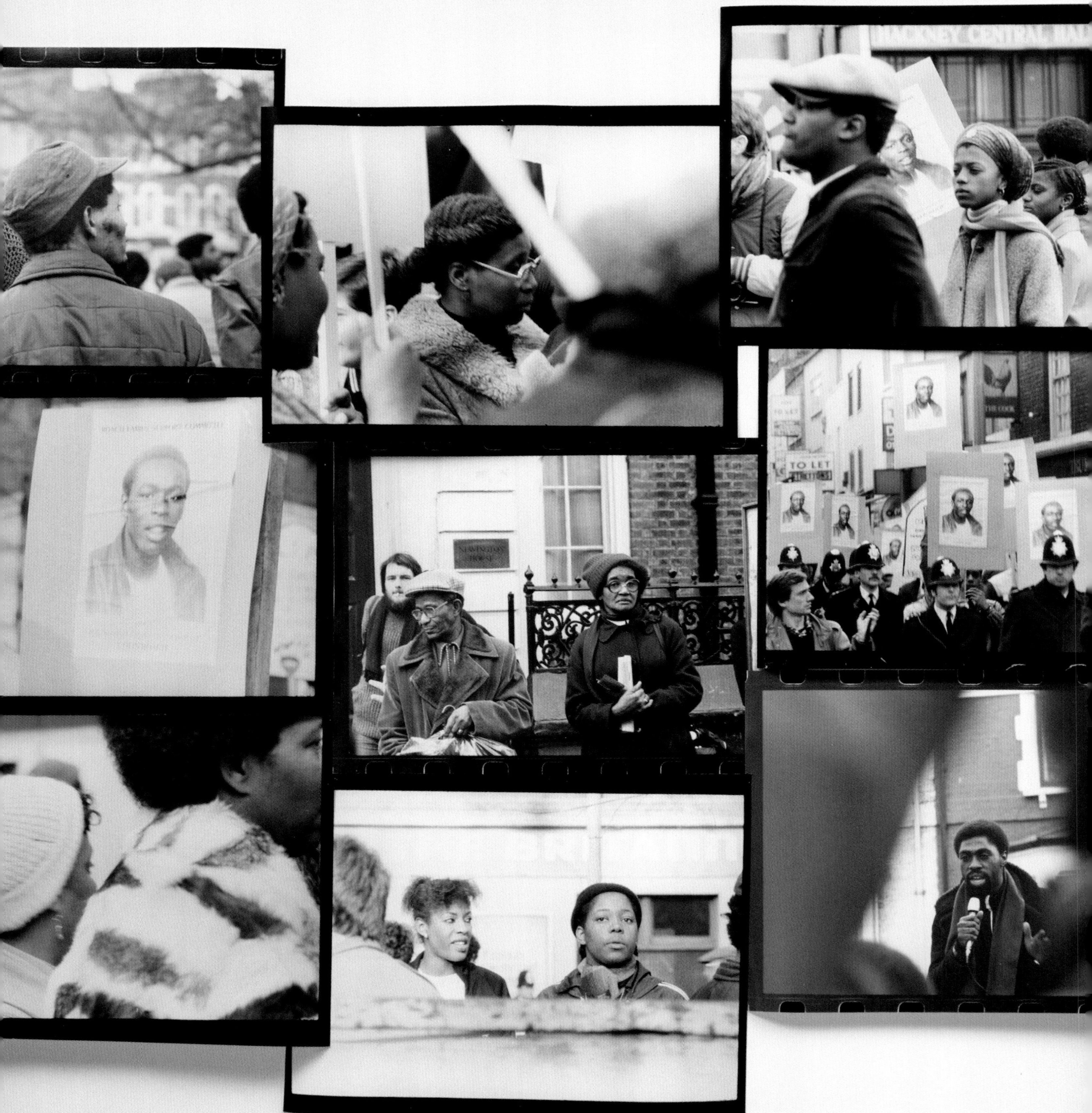
TO LET

# WHO KILLED COLIN ROACH?

1983

▶ 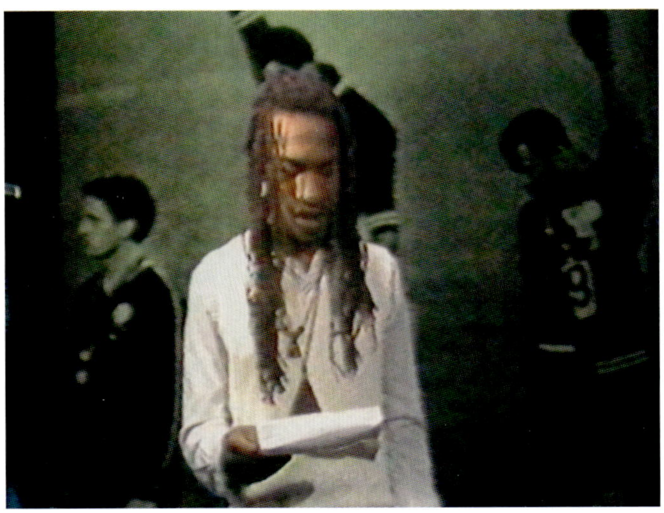

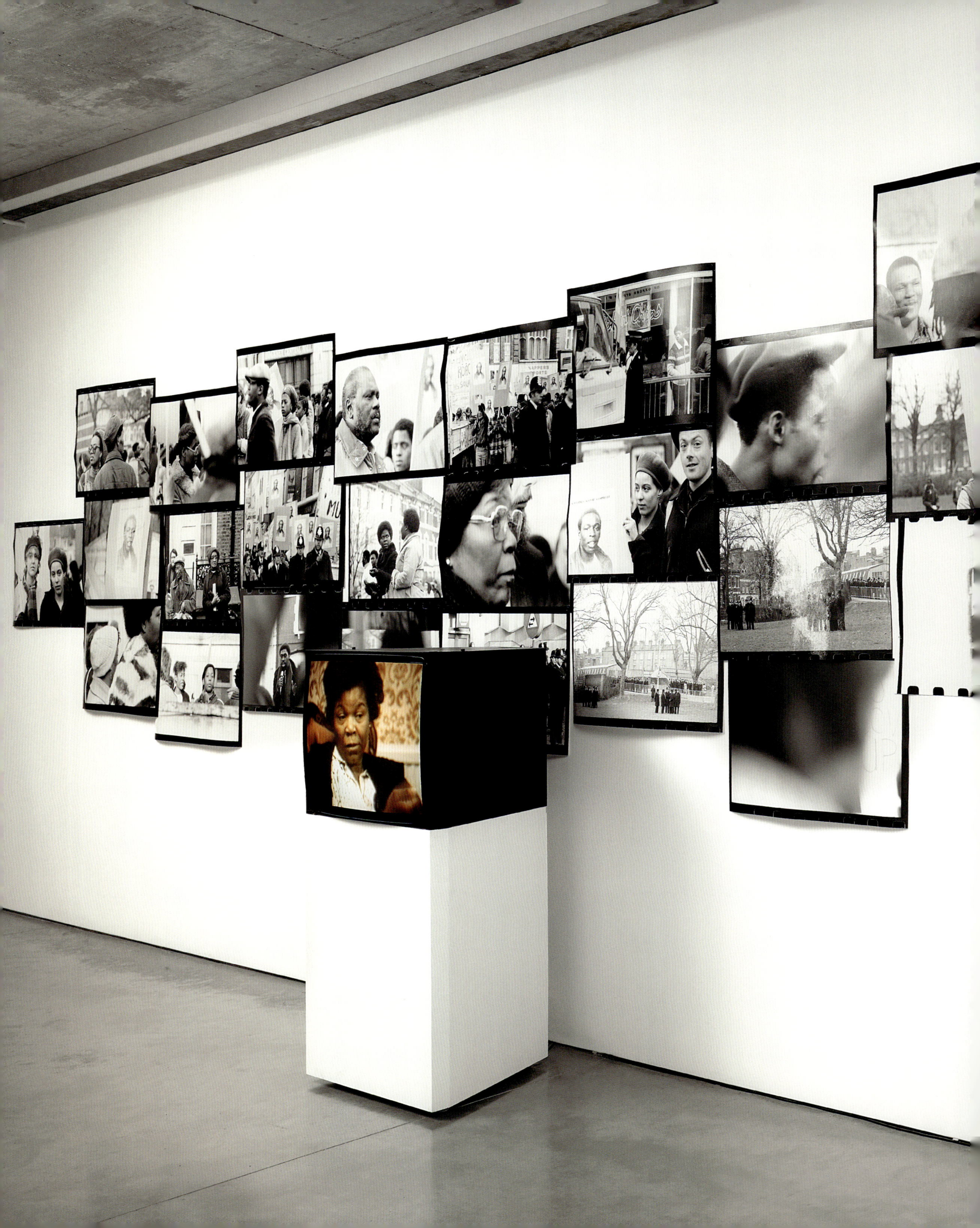

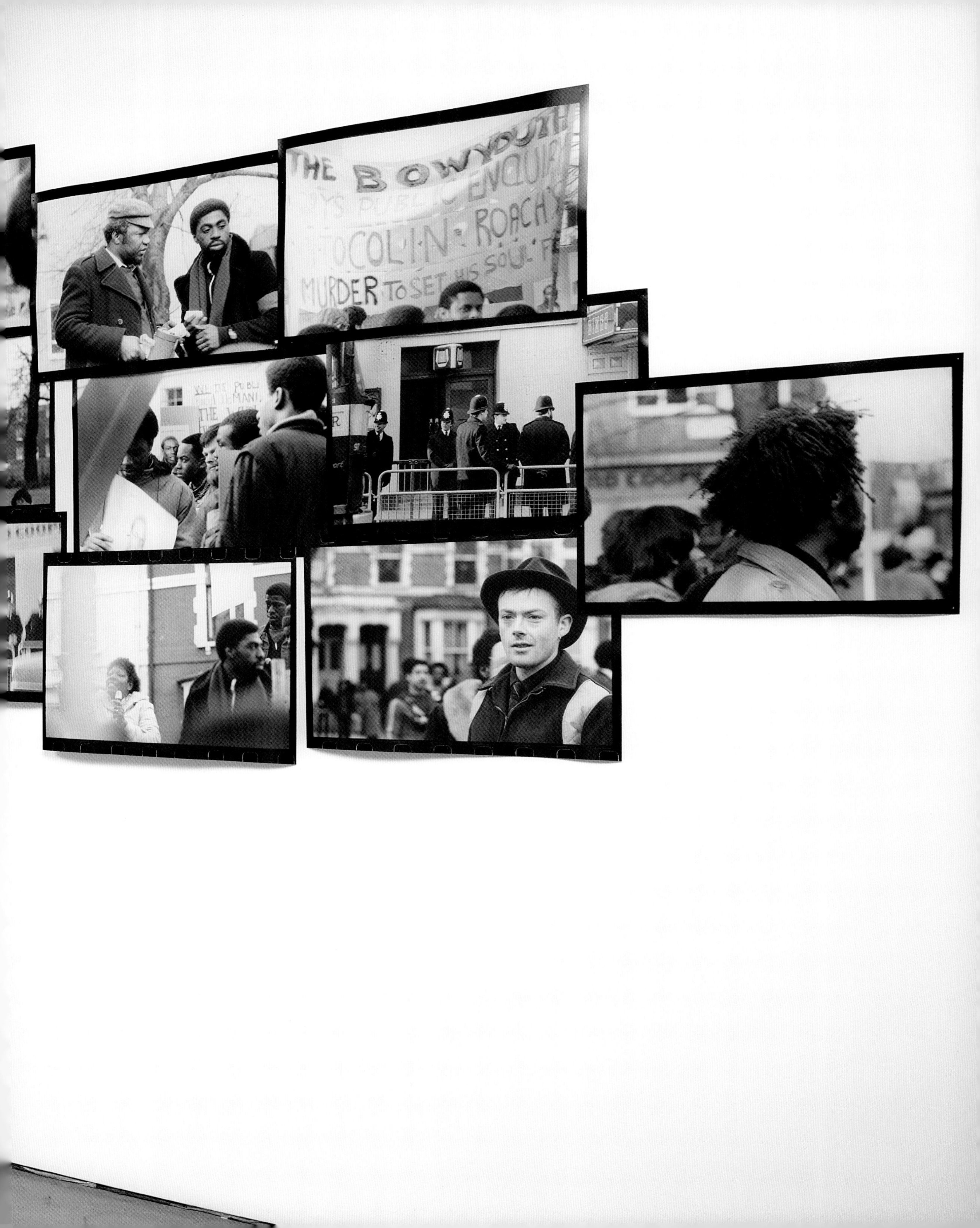
THE BOWYOUTH
COL·I·N·ROACH
MURDER TO SET HIS SOUL

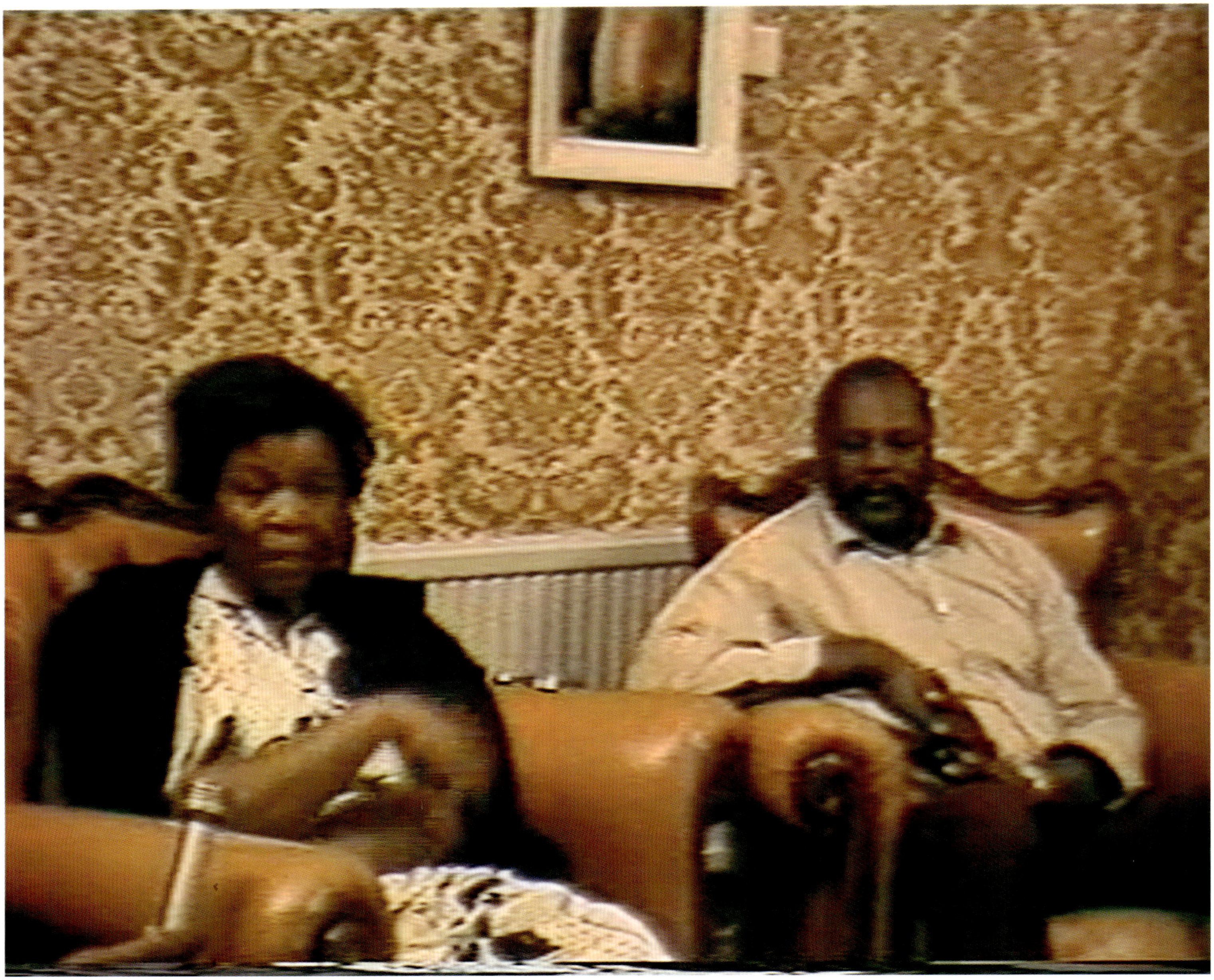

Still from *Who Killed Colin Roach?* 1983, with Colin Roach's parents

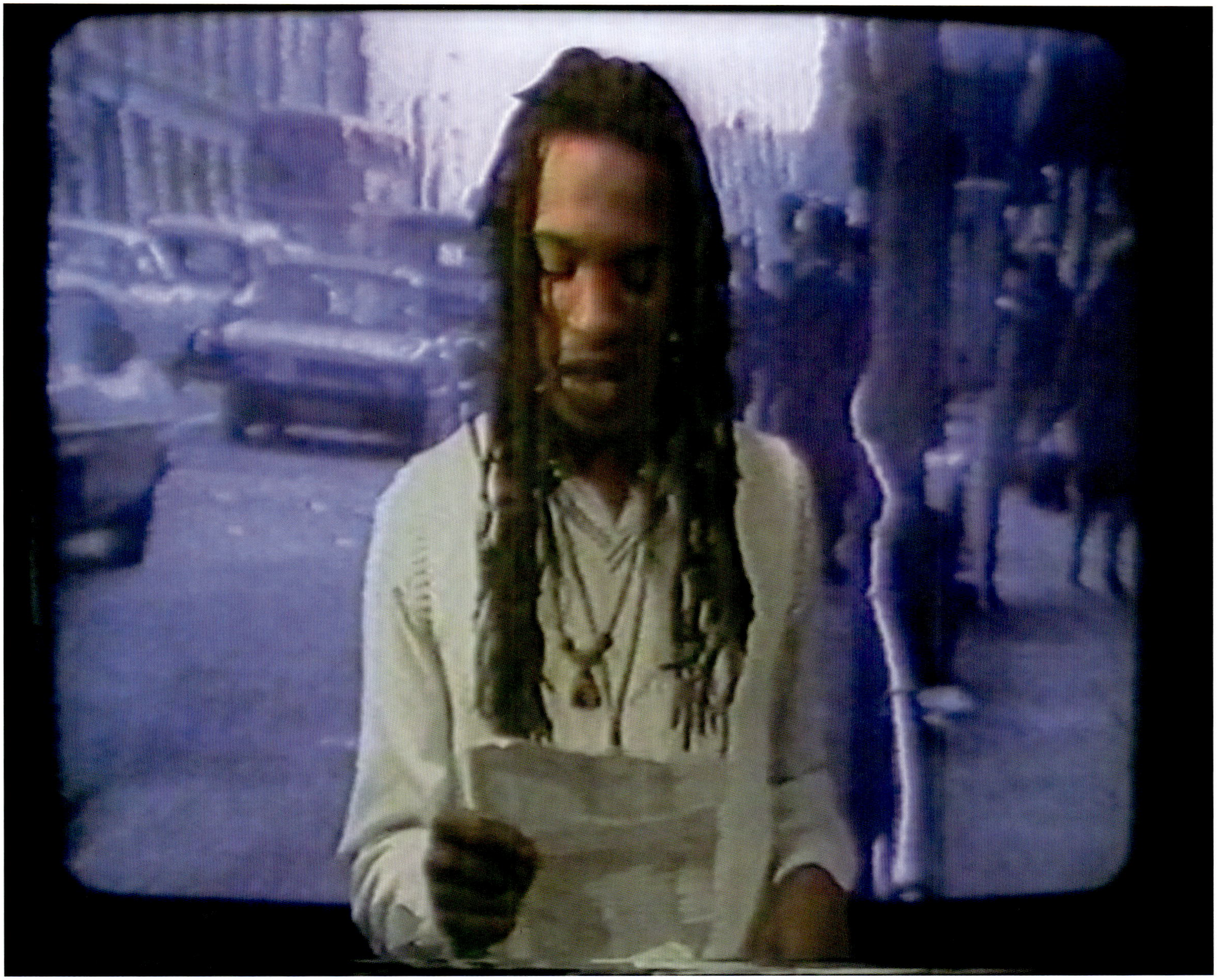

 Still from *Who Killed Colin Roach?* 1983, with Benjamin Zephaniah

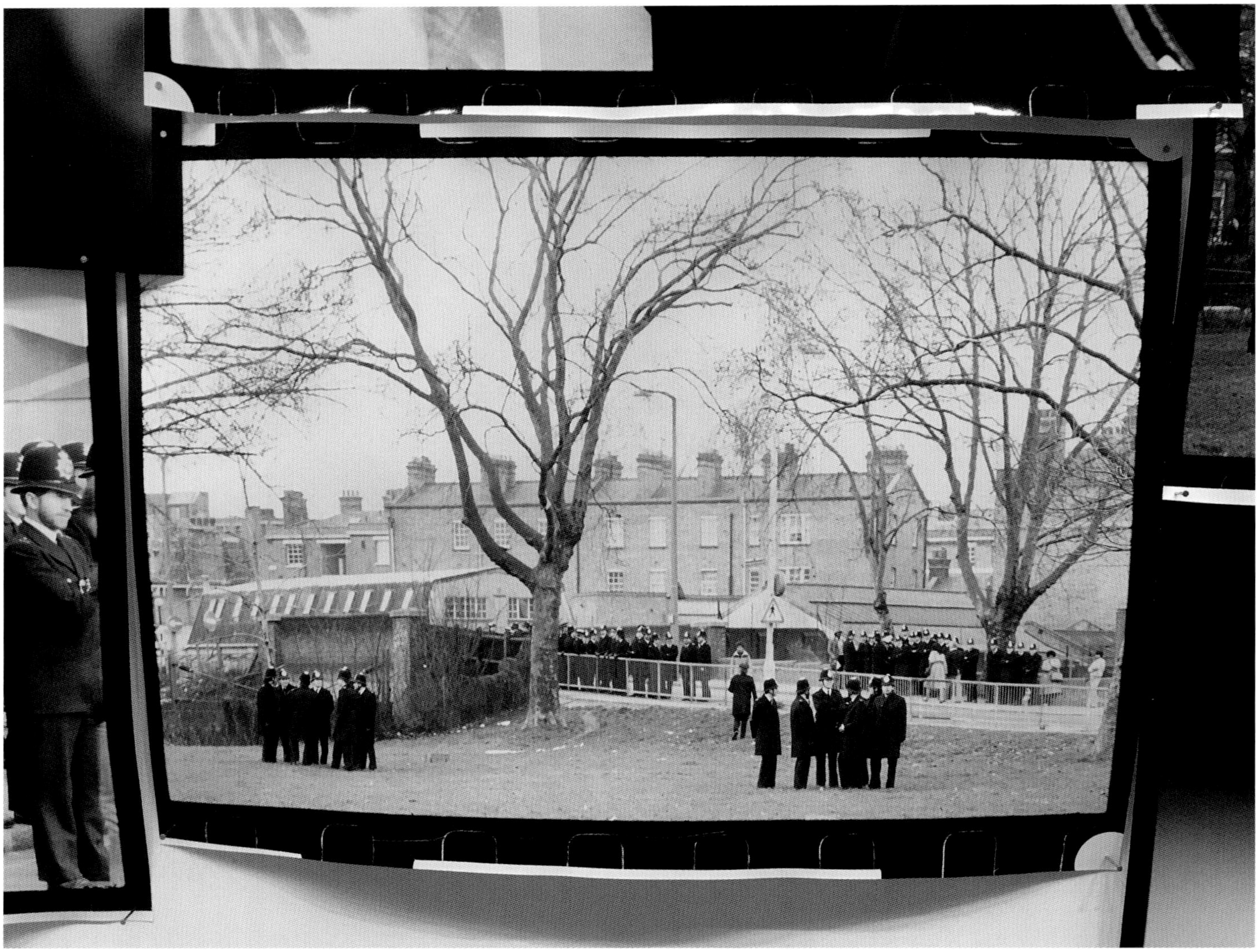

Detail from *Who Killed Colin Roach?* 1983
Photographic assemblage of 32 black and white Ilford Classic FB silver gelatin prints, 45 x 64 each

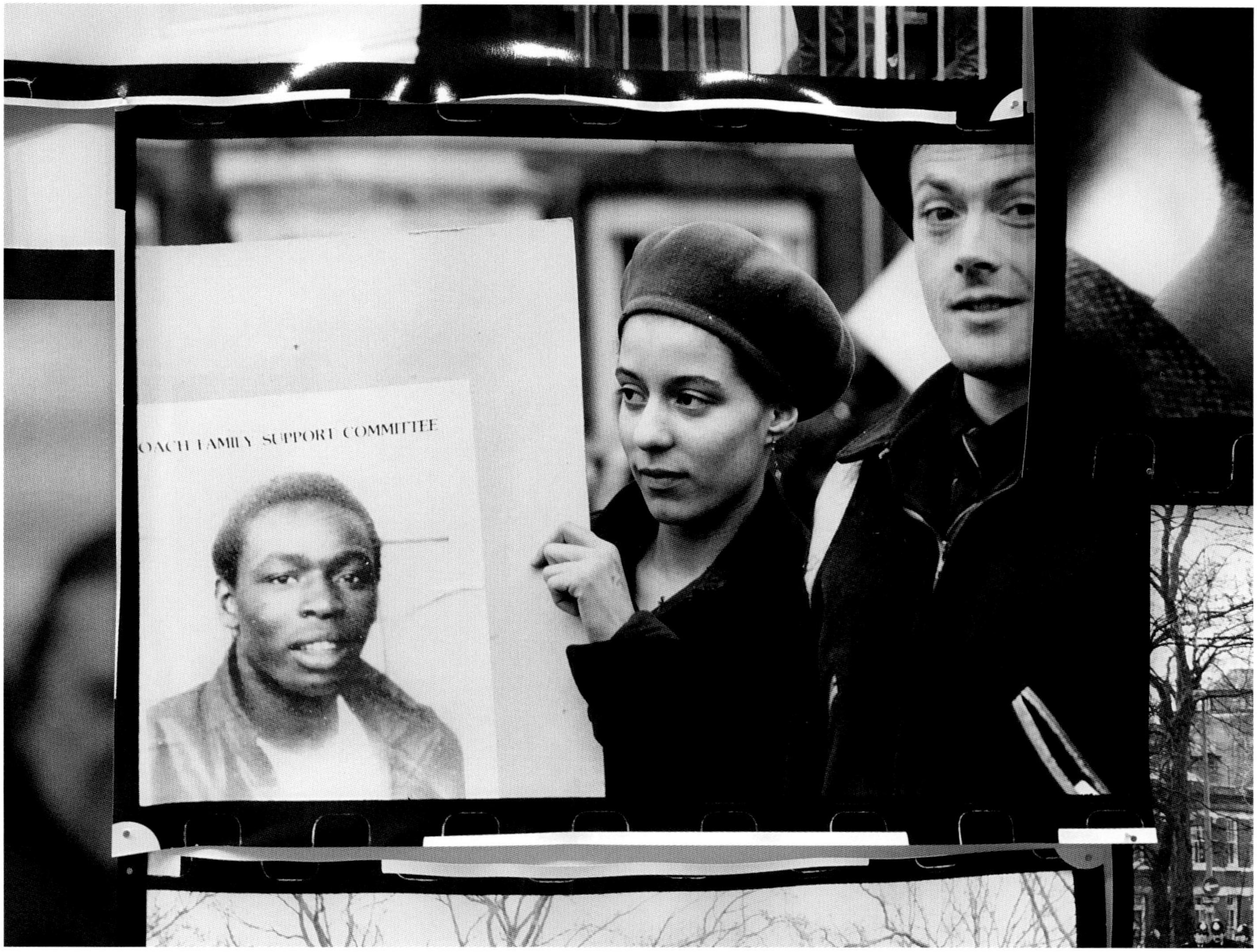


 Detail from *Who Killed Colin Roach?* photographic assemblage, 1983

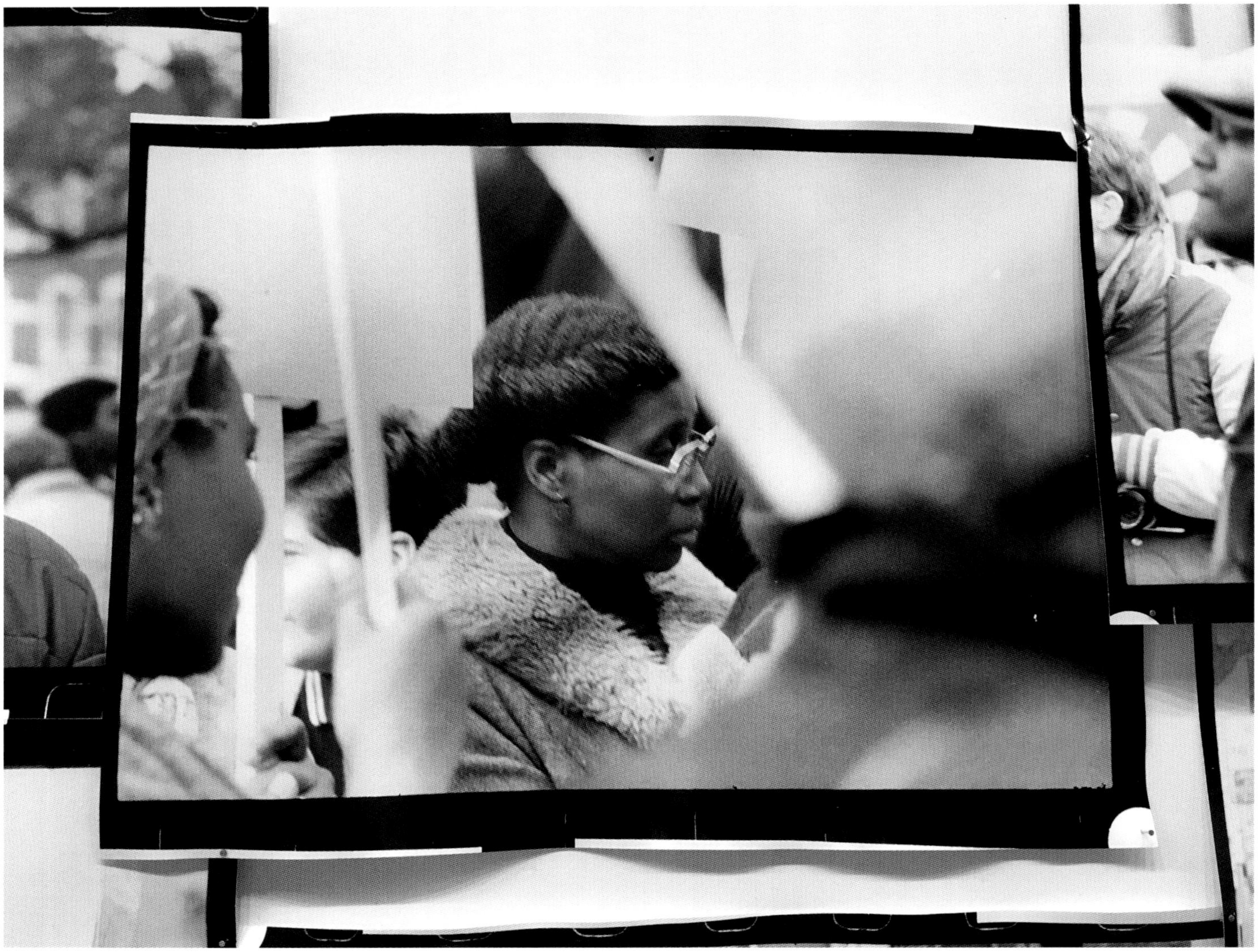

Detail from *Who Killed Colin Roach?* photographic assemblage, 1983

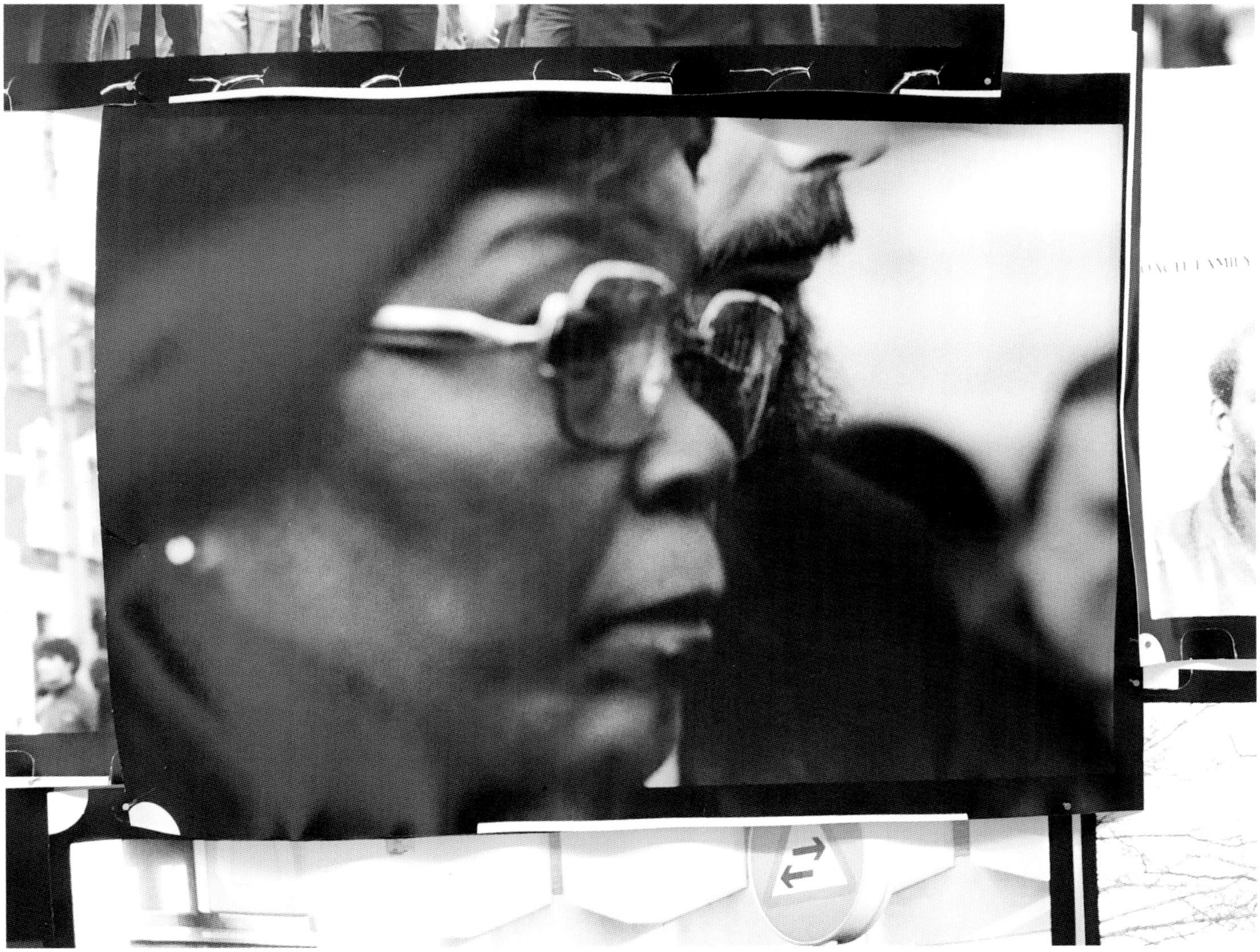

 Detail from *Who Killed Colin Roach?* photographic assemblage, 1983

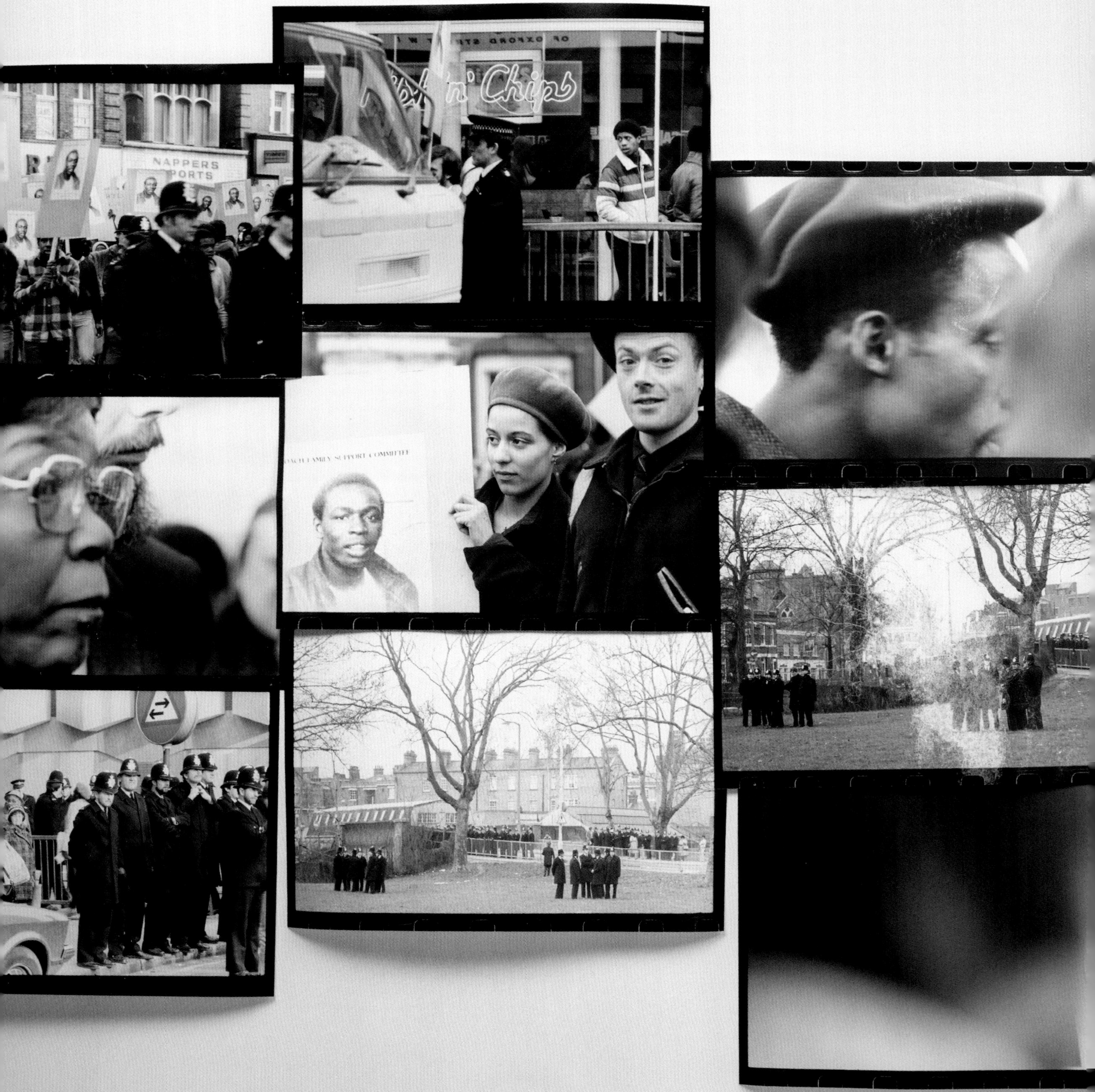
NAPPERS
n' Chips
FAMILY SUPPORT COMMITTEE

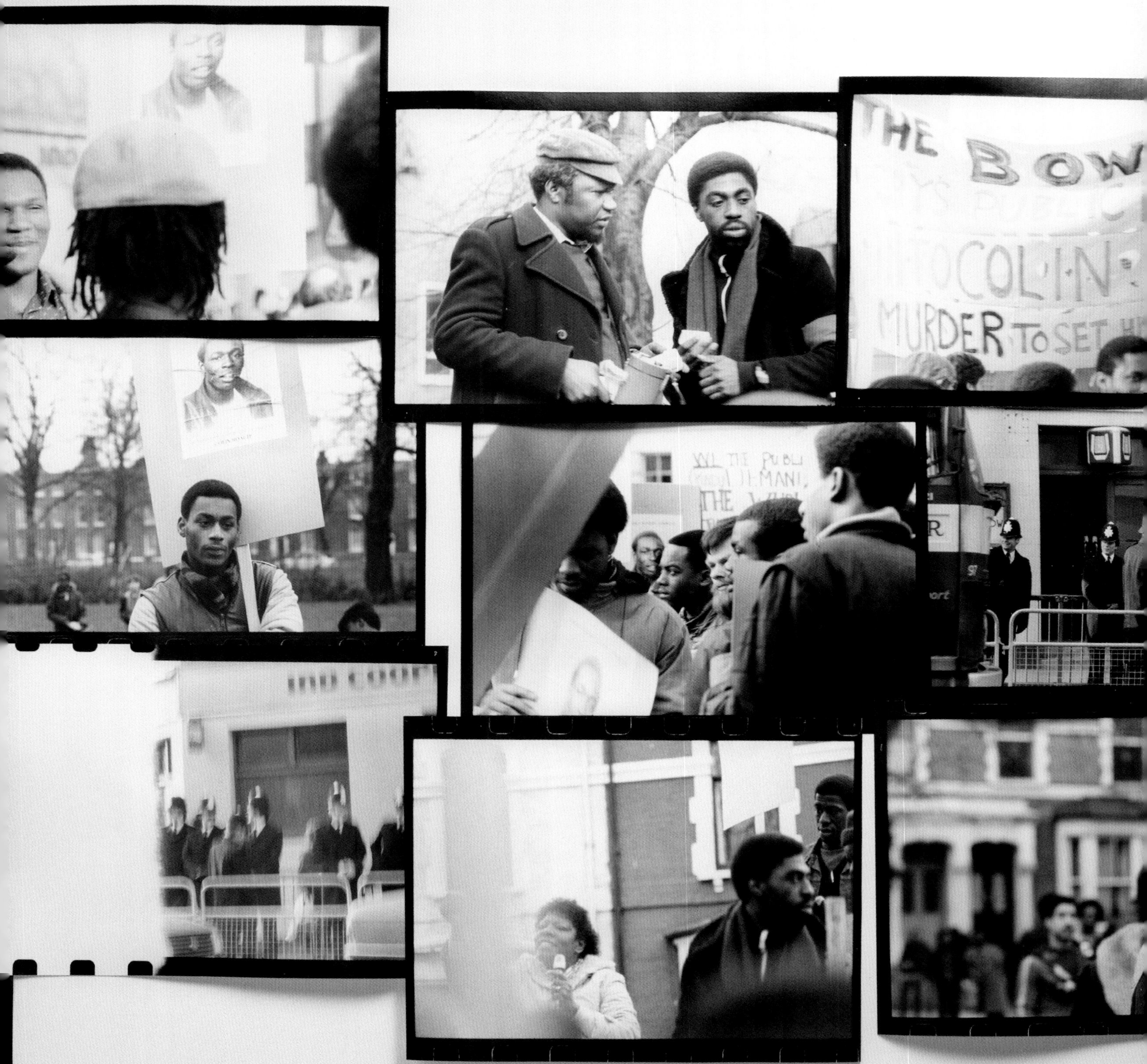
COL·I·N
MURDER TO SET

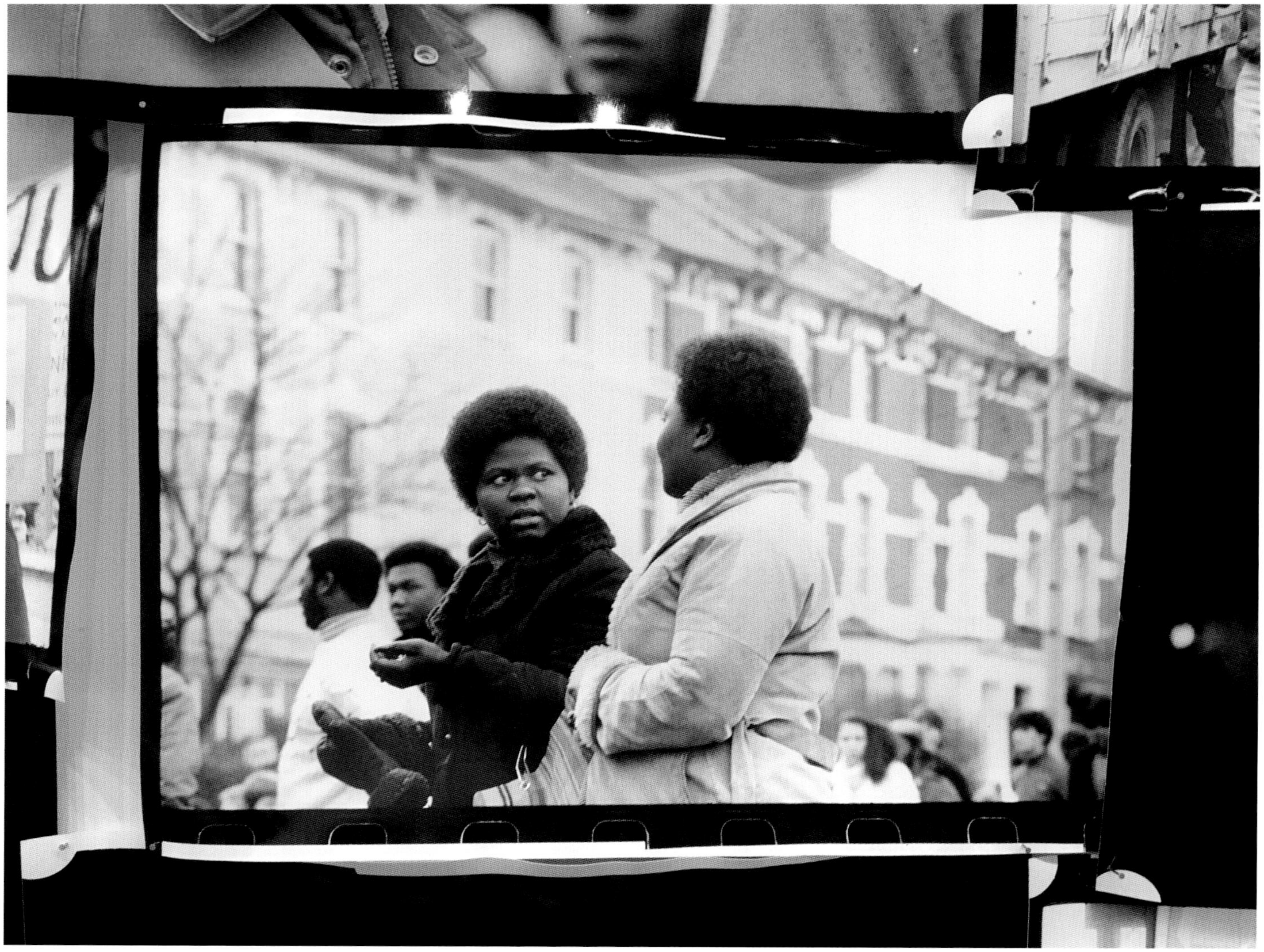

Detail from *Who Killed Colin Roach?* photographic assemblage, 1983

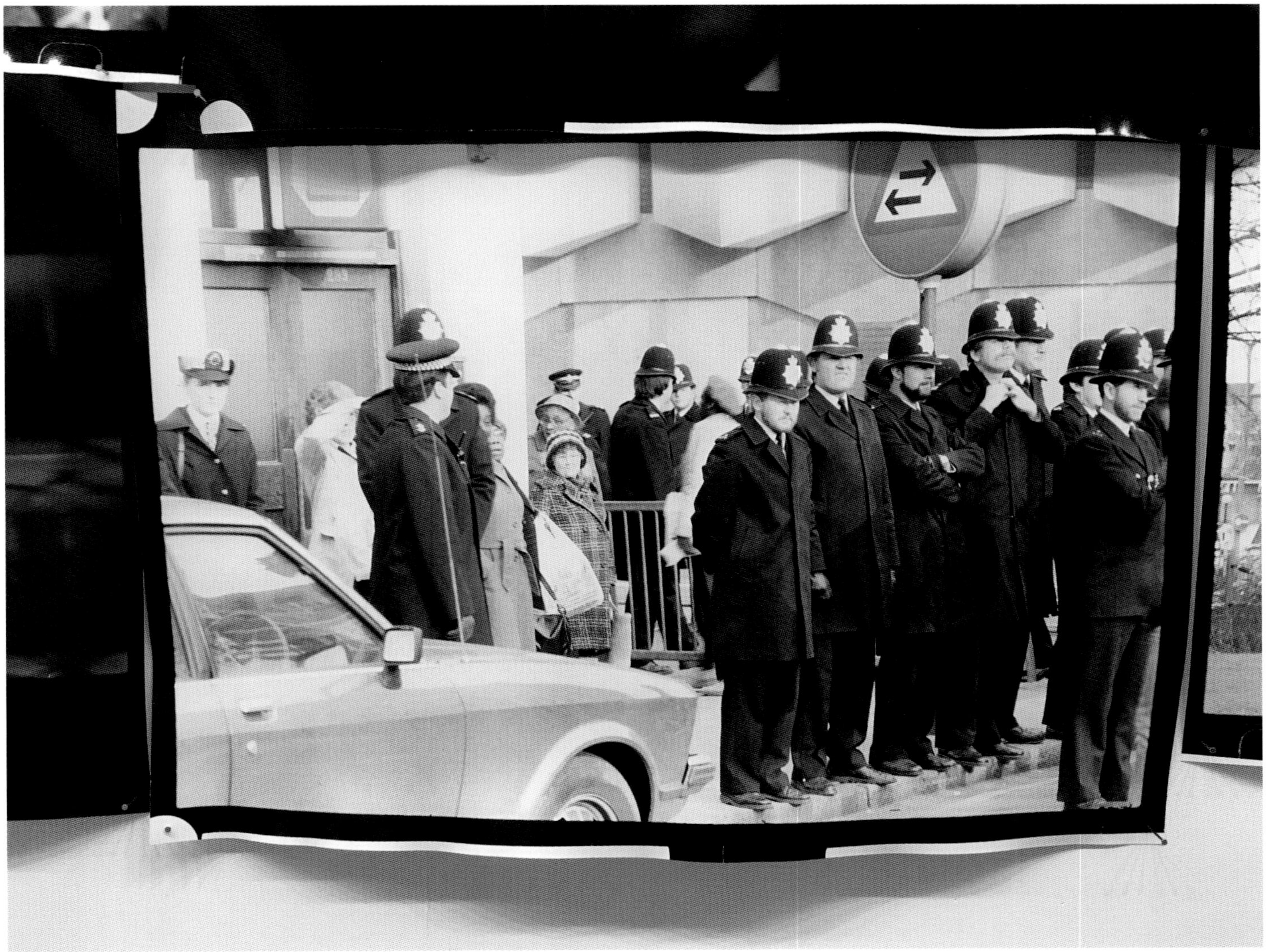

 Detail from *Who Killed Colin Roach?* photographic assemblage, 1983

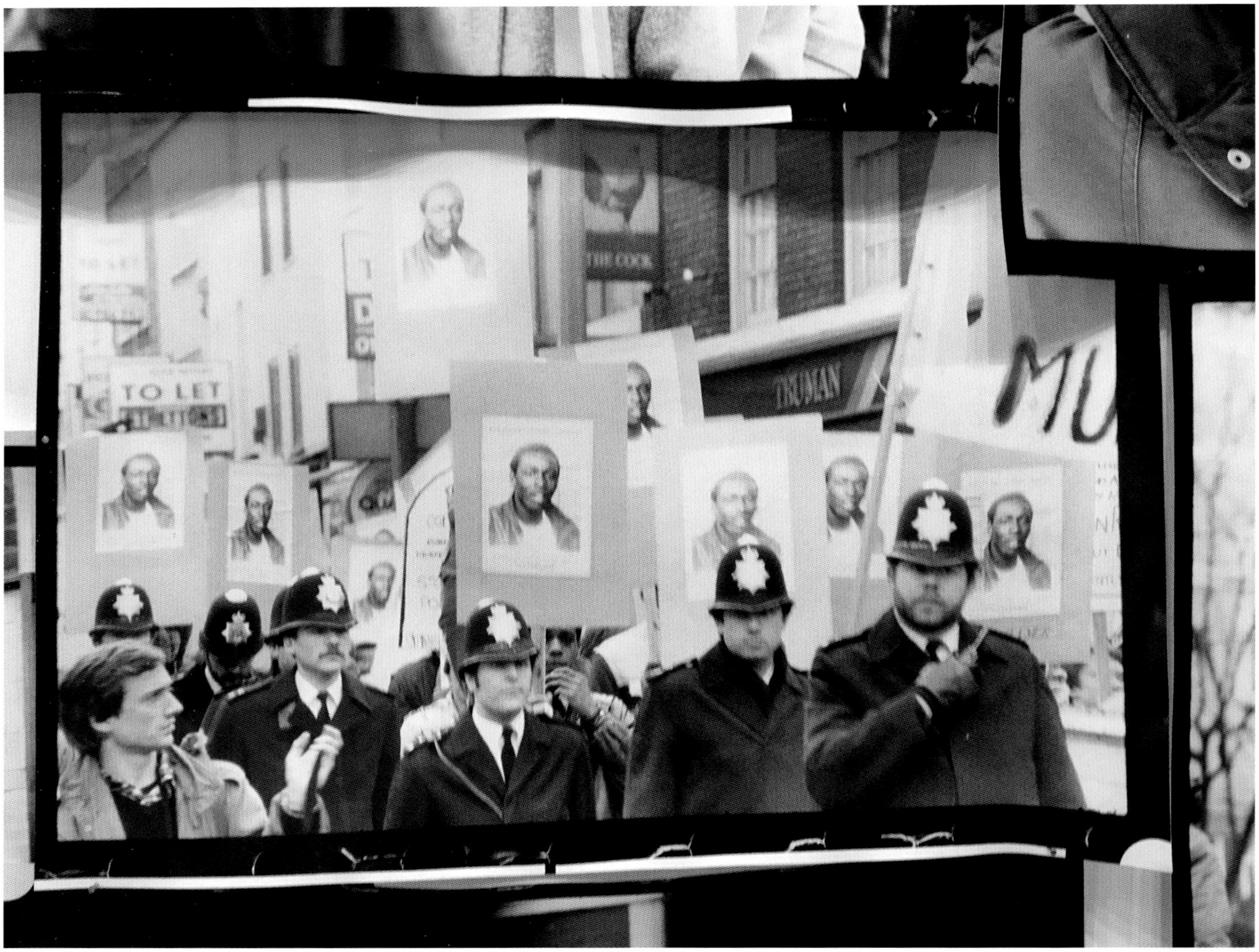


Detail from *Who Killed Colin Roach?* photographic assemblage, 1983

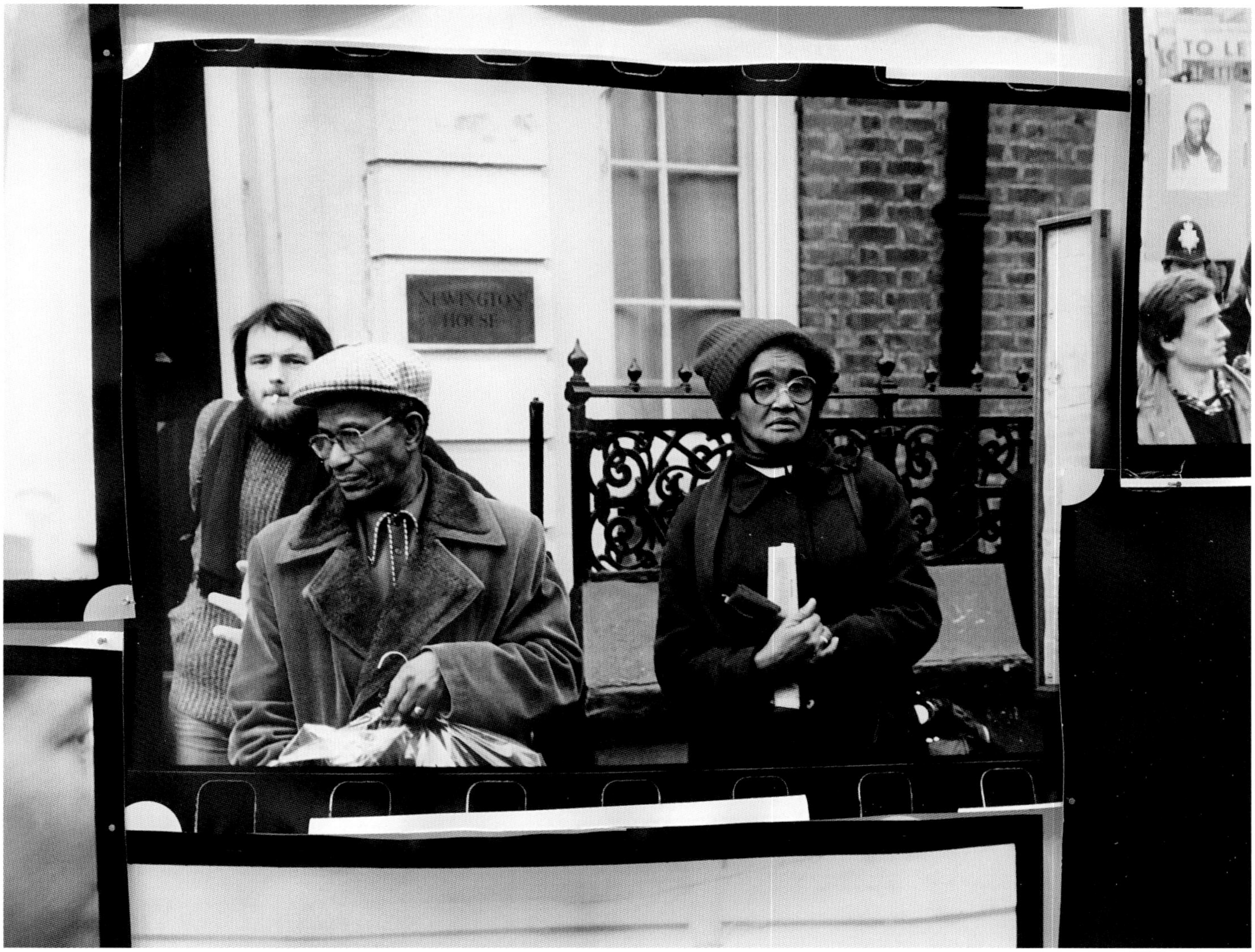


 Detail from *Who Killed Colin Roach?* photographic assemblage, 1983

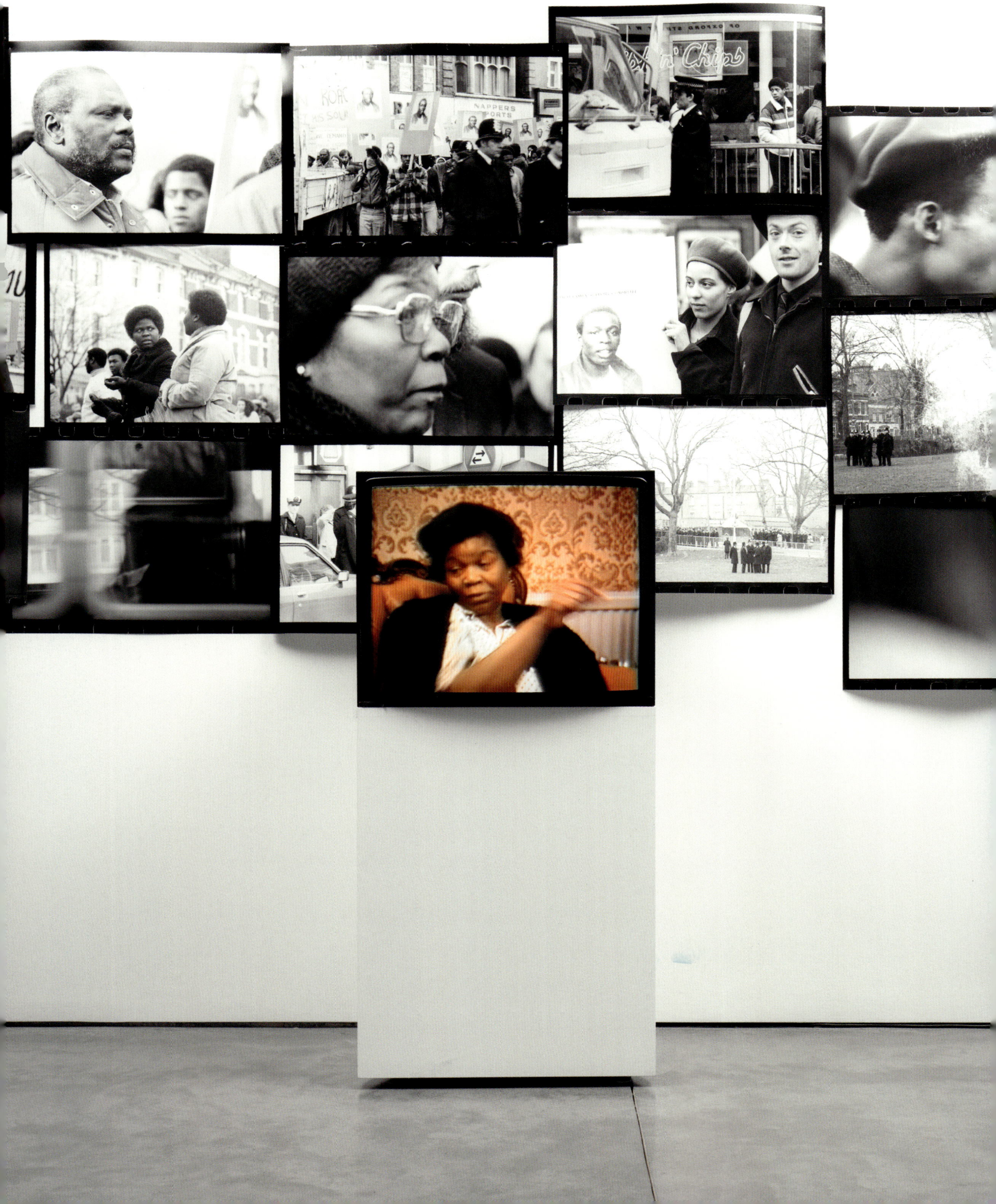
NAPPERS

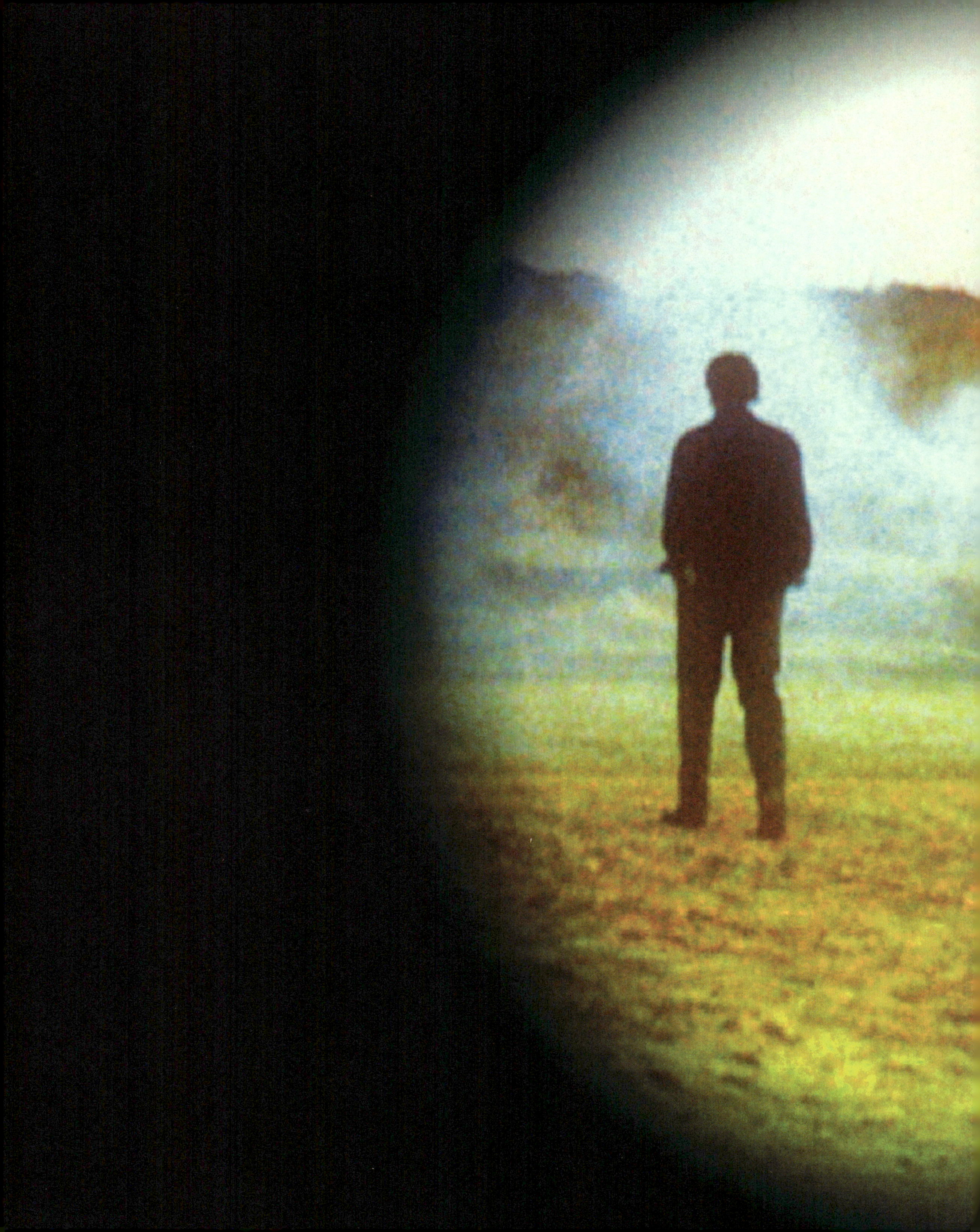

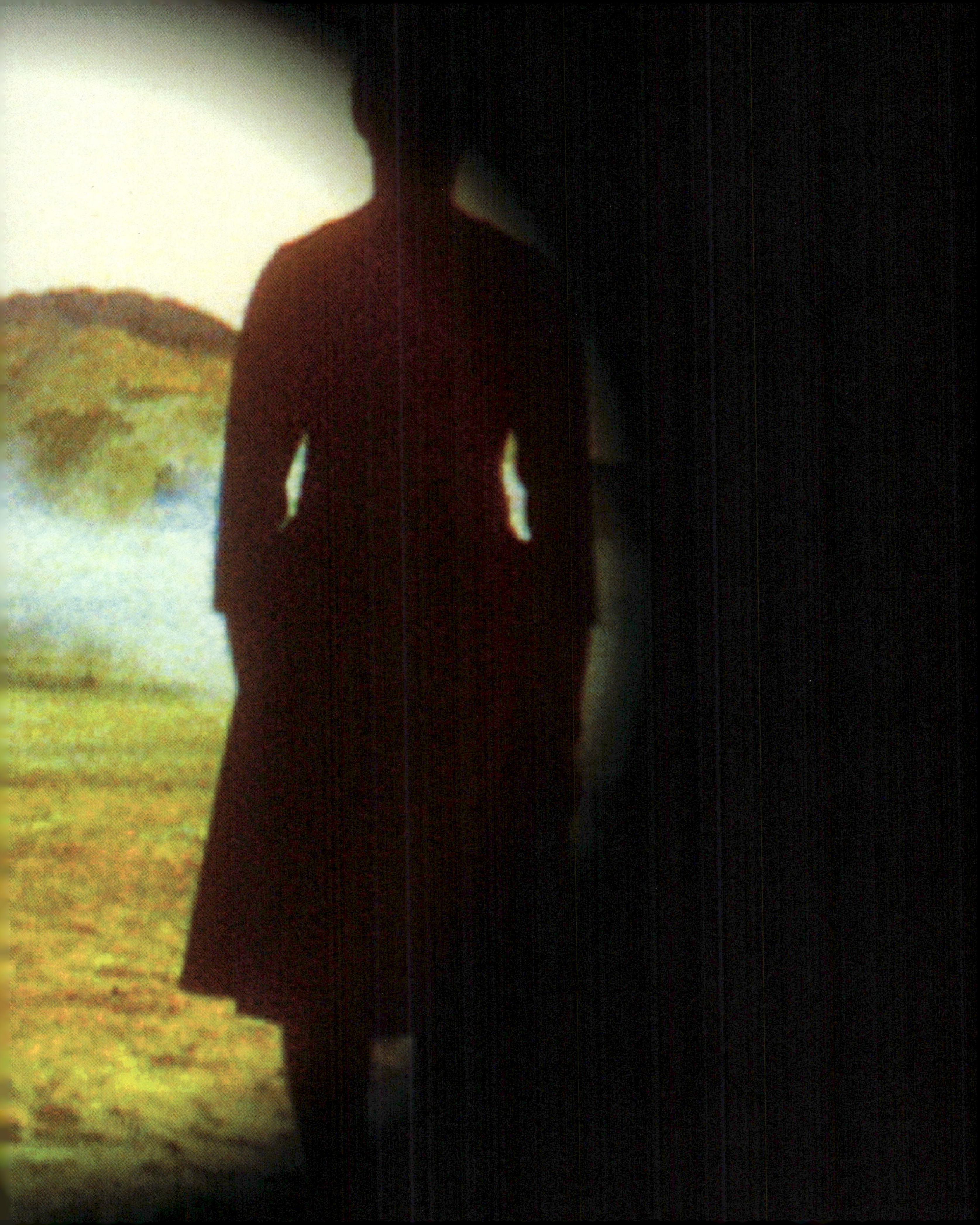

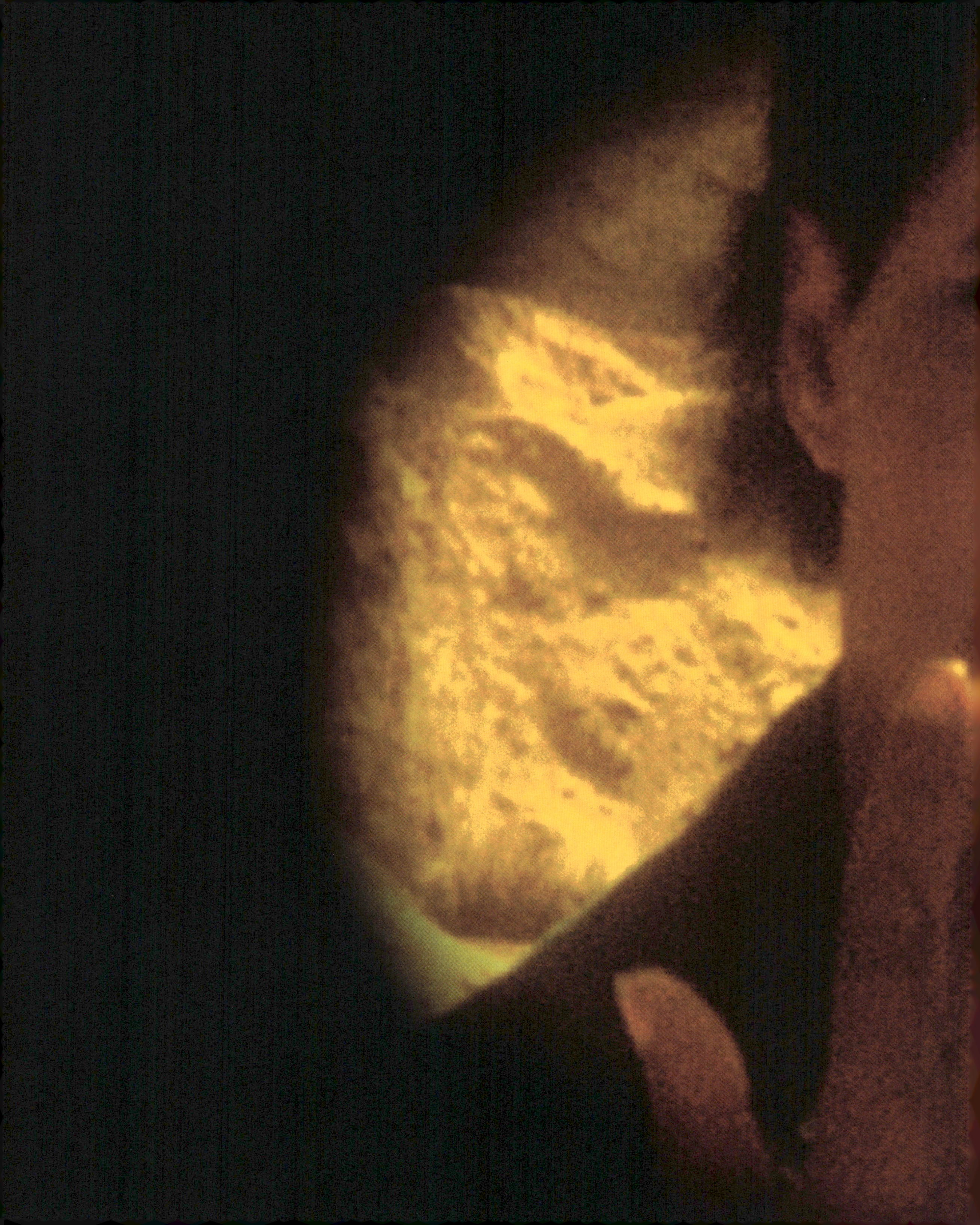

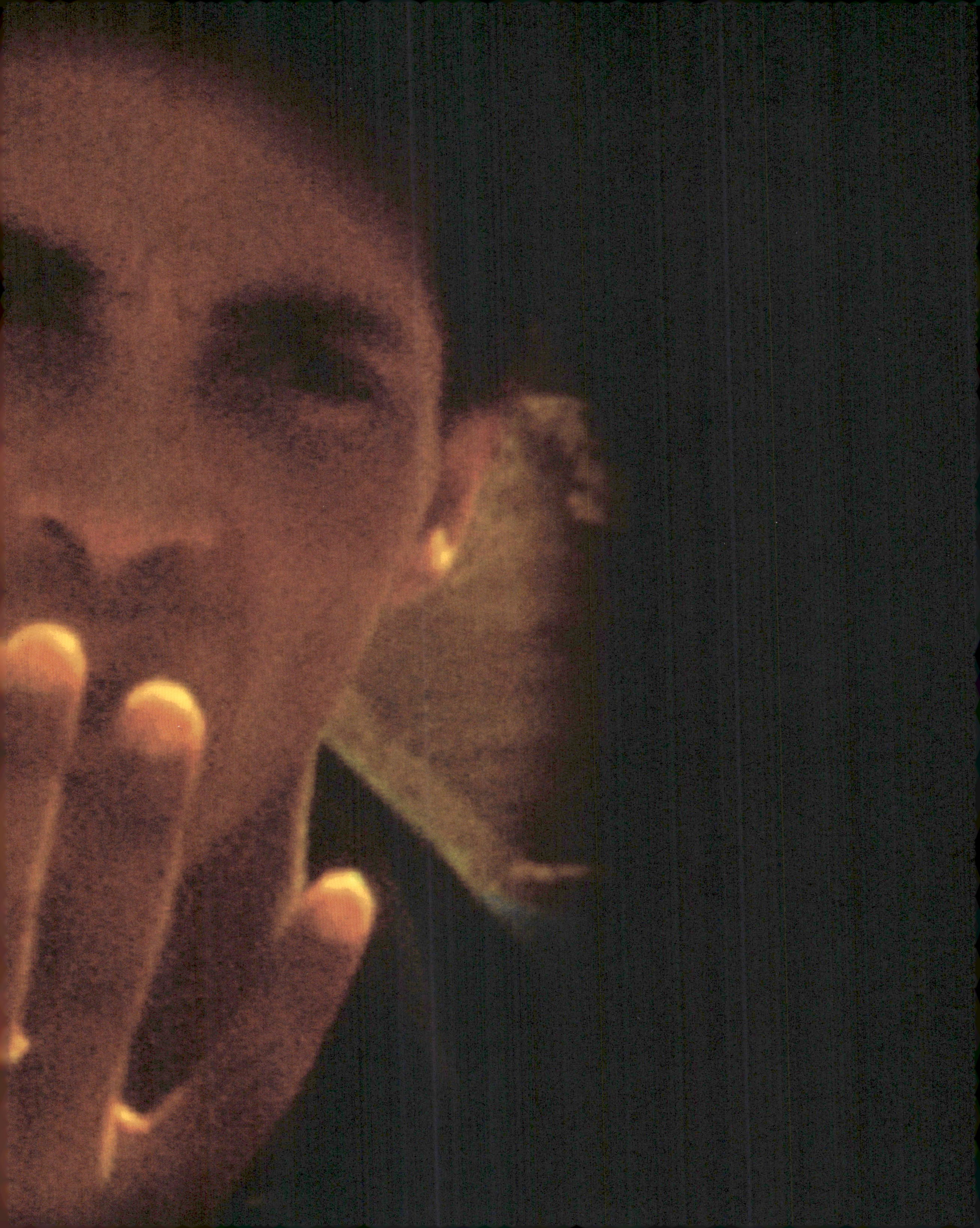

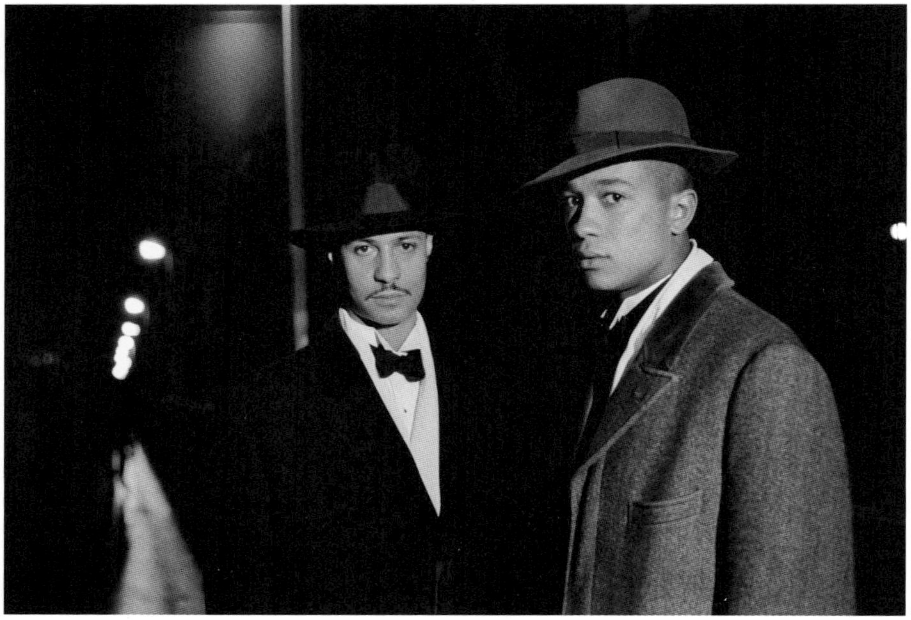

*I Love My Friend (Looking for Langston Vintage Series)* 1989/2016

To write the afterword for this book, to reflect on an artist whose practice has for almost forty years been shaping how we look back as an act of looking forward, feels both a pleasure and a momentous task. How to be brief and distilled about a practice that is so plural and expansive: in the words of Paul Gilroy, 'a unified and polyphonic cultural performance'?[1] It is also the challenge that all of Isaac's work asks us to meet, for his films are both multivalent and restless and also stilling – sometimes almost taking one's breath away with their beauty.[2] They are dense with allusion, political resonance, nuance and a gorgeous slipperiness of meaning and affect. His film works, as they have evolved over his career, are a lesson in the sensual discipline of having to look carefully and slowly and with pleasure. It constitutes a lightly worn but deeply held queer politics of looking.

Isaac is an artist who has long been at the vanguard, ahead of the times he is in and actively carving out and shaping a larger space for thinking, feeling and looking. The space for desire he created in *Looking for Langston* (1989) – recognisably Harlem Renaissance history, but also not; perhaps a King's Cross club, but not; recognisably British queer pop culture, but not – created a new political imaginary for Black British art: a place looked after by angels and also stormed by the police. The film was rooted in its time and place, at the height of the HIV and AIDS crisis and the repressive cultural politics of the Thatcher era, yet its resistance to binary or absolutist thinking makes perhaps even more necessary viewing in our own time.

His is not so much a politics of opposition, though rebellion and revolution is present from the beginning with *Who Killed Colin Roach?* 1983 through to the great oratory at the heart of *Lessons of the Hour* (2019). But it is never binary, and Isaac evinces a politics of active possibility, of permission and nuance, suggestive in its working and subtle in its influence. This seems important in our current quick-to-judge times, where polarised thinking and cultures cancelled and denounced are too often the tenor of our public debate.

1. Paul Gilroy, 'Cruciality and the Frog's Perspective: An Agenda of Difficulties for the Black Arts Movement in Britain' in *Small Acts: Thoughts on the Politics of Black Culture*, London 1993, p.105.

2. I use Isaac's first name throughout as he is an artist who I have studied and known for nearly four decades and the convention of surname address would feel inappropriate.

Isaac's work has always located itself in a slightly impossible place in our visual field, in our bodies and our public spaces. This is how I understand the multiplication of screens in his work, creating a sculpture of multiple viewpoints. It creates, too, an inescapability of looking every way we turn, which both wrong- *and* right-foots us, in that it refuses to allow our gaze to settle too much, creating ambiguity but also space between and within the images. Likewise, his use of the still image and still points within the moving field connects him to a lush lineage of alternative image-makers while also giving points of pause, for the eye and the breath, in his films. Through this, Isaac also connects the eye and the body, as the points of stillness in his work allow us to encounter our own body again in relation to the bodies on screen. Like Alex, the protagonist of *Looking for Langston*, we are often wandering and wondering through the image landscape of a wished-for yet fugitive world. This slowing down, or sometimes stilling, of the image frame draws attention to the act of looking as desire and also as bodily engagement.

If the multiplying screens of Isaac's practice proliferate viewpoints, then his turn to choreography and the dancer's body in works such as *Vagabondia* 2000 and *Lina Bo Bardi - A Marvellous Entanglement* 2019 connect eye to body to multiple screens. When we look with Isaac we also move with his bodies and through our own: the bodies of the dancers and our own physical orientation to the screen and the unfolding image sequence are highly embodied, and in an unusually visceral way. When the space of the film is also the space of the museum, as it is in *Vagabondia*, we find ourselves in a multi-layered exploration of how culture moves and places us, how the archive reveals and withholds, how the space that Isaac creates in and of the museum can be a space of resistance even as it has also been a space that excludes.

Then we move to consider Isaac's preoccupation with the practice of architecture, most memorably in *Lina Bo Bardi*, as the site and subject and form of the work. As filmic sculpture, this work marks him as the most subtle negotiator of the flawed modernist projects of the twentieth century and perhaps the greatest exponent of a counter-modernism of Black British, African American and Afro-Brazilian aesthetic experiment. We should also recognise Isaac's attention to those architectural spaces *par excellence* of popular resistance to dominant culture - the night club, dance-hall and cabaret that have long given respite and permission to the creative practices of queer folk. His creation of a sound space for desire and resistance resonates through and across his work, allied to an exacting technological precision about the fullness of sound his work requires. The aural amplitude of Isaac's work makes the space of viewing bigger. It also makes his acutely beautiful and often complex sequences deeply emotionally accessible - 'Can You Feel It?' as the soundtrack near the end of *Looking for Langston* asks us. In this, it is 'complicating but also popularising', as Isaac has it, debates about Black art and identity politics.[3]

So what are the lessons for now, his *Lessons of the Hour*? This brilliant ten-screen installation gives us Frederick Douglass's life and history, with actors performing some of his most memorable speeches and moments. This rich, resistive narrative is embedded in Douglass's brutal context, as we hear and feel the sound of the whip while we progress through the constellation of images. It gives us more image-loading and sonic encounter than we might think we could bear as we move around the installation, but the fluidity and slippage across screens, our sense that the worst is just at the edge of the field of vision, means it consciously and elegantly evades brutalising again. As a voice in the film tells us, 'the point of view from which a thing is viewed is of some importance' - a memorable understatement about Isaac's richly dissident take on history and culture. His aesthetic and political refusal to take a singular or fixed or easy view on the multidimensional and transnational encounters he evokes marks him as one of the most valuable of guides in an unfixed world.

3. 'Climbing the Racial Mountain: A Conversation with Isaac Julien', in Gilroy 1993, p.169.

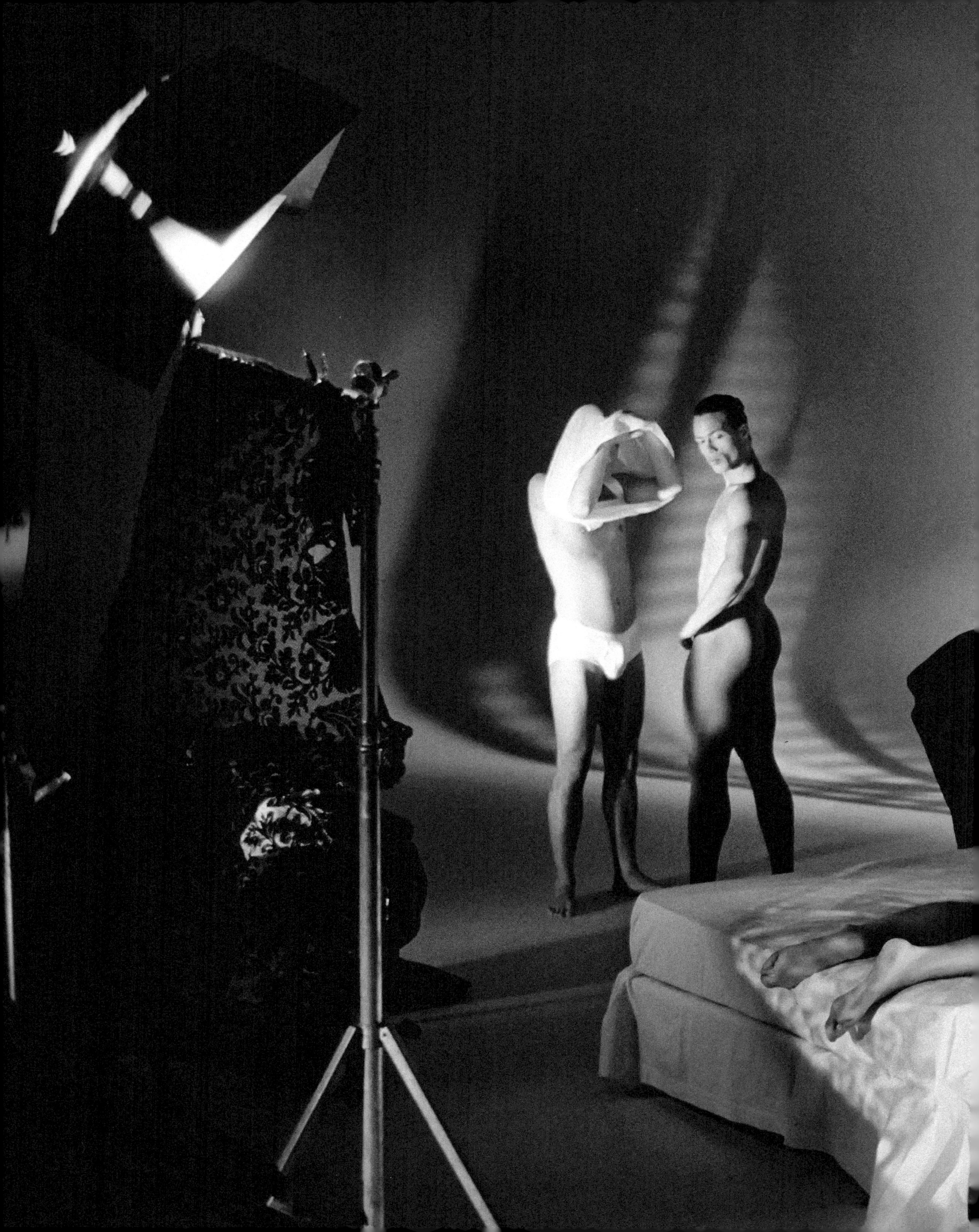

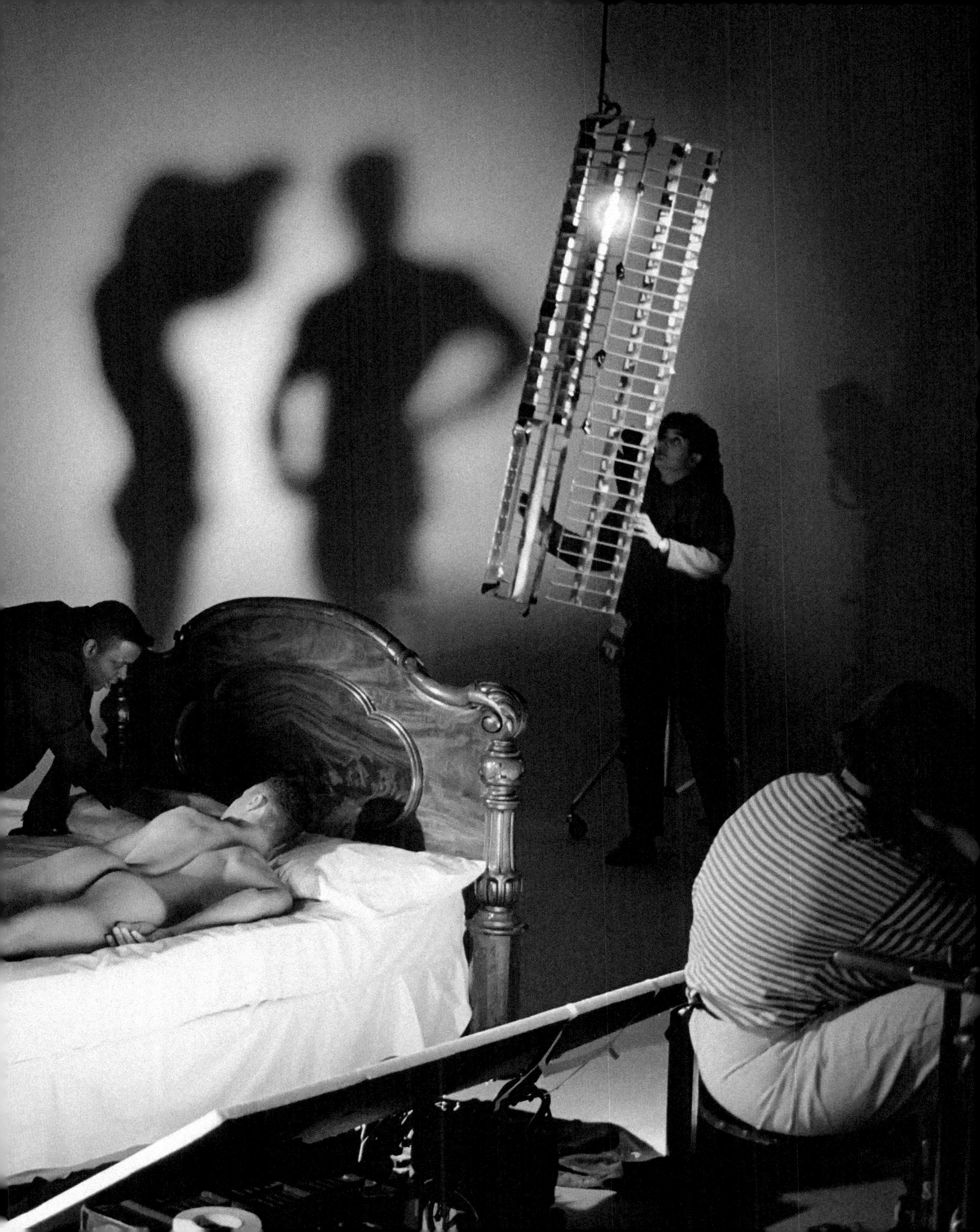

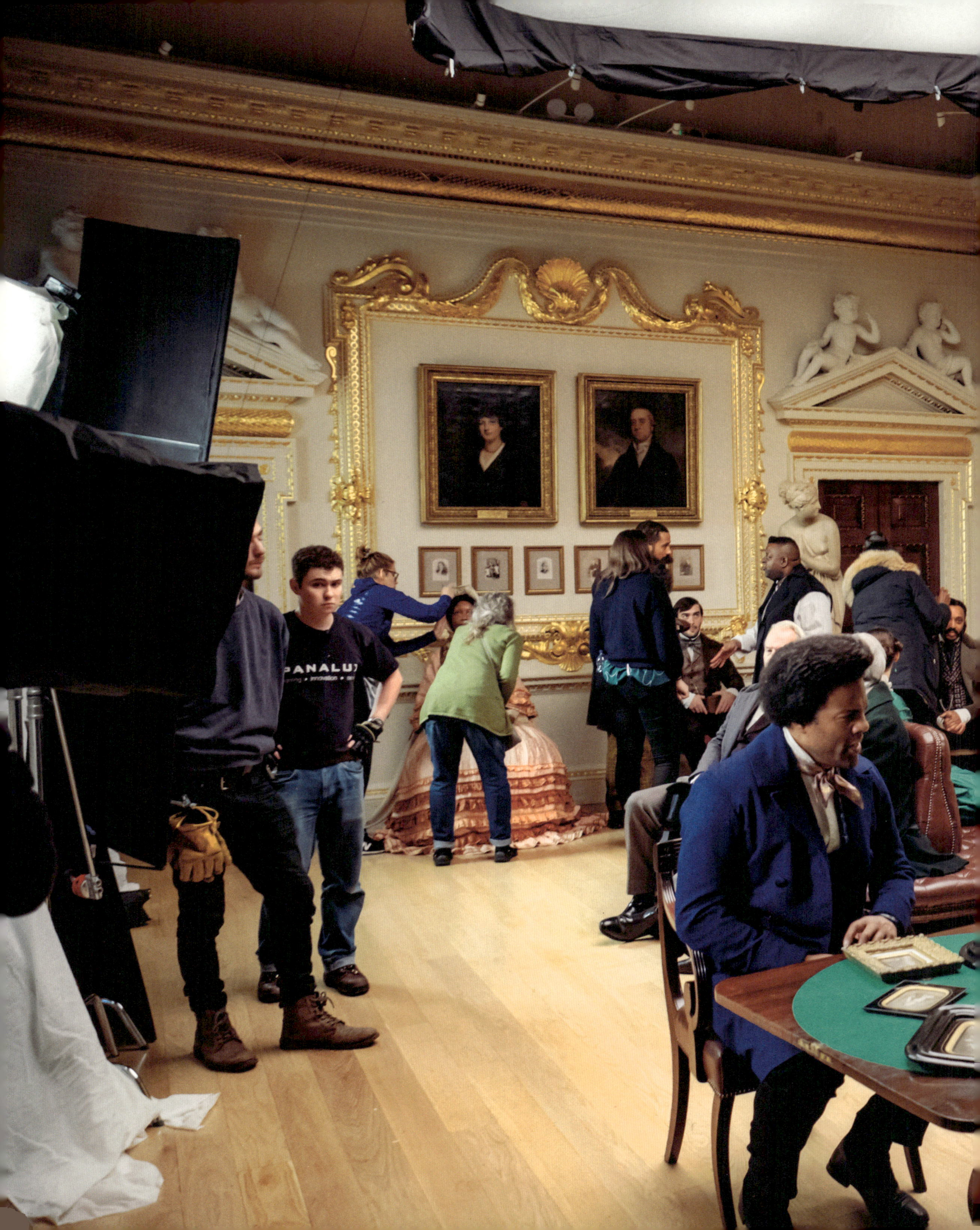
PANALUX

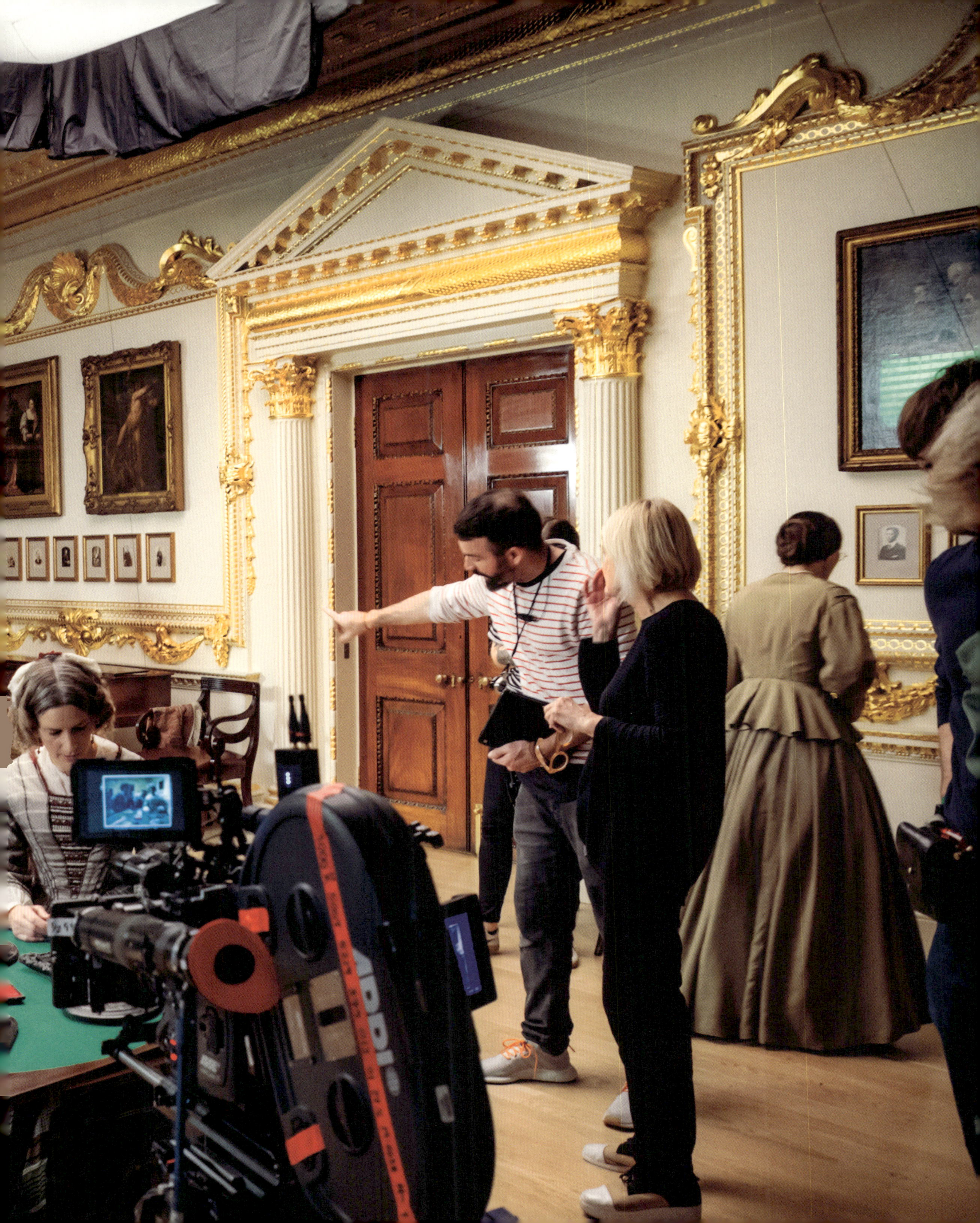

# Biographical Note

Sir Isaac Julien, RA (b.1960) is a critically acclaimed British artist and filmmaker. In 2018, Julien joined the faculty at the University of California Santa Cruz, where he is Distinguished Professor of the Arts and leads the Moving Image Lab together with Arts Professor Mark Nash.

Current and recent international solo exhibitions include *Isaac Julien*, Tate Britain, London 2023; *Lina Bo Bardi: A Marvellous Entanglement*, Philadelphia Museum of Art, 2023; *Isaac Julien: Lessons of the Hour - Frederick Douglass*, Virginia Museum of Fine Arts, 2022-3; *Once Again...(Statues Never Die)*, Barnes Foundation, Philadelphia, 2022; *Lina Bo Bardi: A Marvellous Entanglement*, Bechtler Museum of Modern Art, Charlotte, North Carolina, 2022; *Lessons of the Hour*, McEvoy Foundation for the Arts, San Francisco, 2020-1; *Lina Bo Bardi: A Marvellous Entanglement*, MAXXI, Rome, 2020-1; *Western Union: Small Boats*, Neuberger Museum of Art, New York, 2020; *Looking for Langston*, Tate Britain, London, 2019; *Playtime*, LACMA, Los Angeles, 2019.

Julien is the recipient of the 2016-17 James R. Brudner '83 Memorial Prize, the Royal Academy of Arts Charles Wollaston Award 2017, and a Goslar Kaiserring Award in 2022. He was made a CBE in the Queen's Birthday Honours 2017, and granted a knighthood as part of Queen Elizabeth II's Platinum Jubilee Birthday Honours List in 2022.

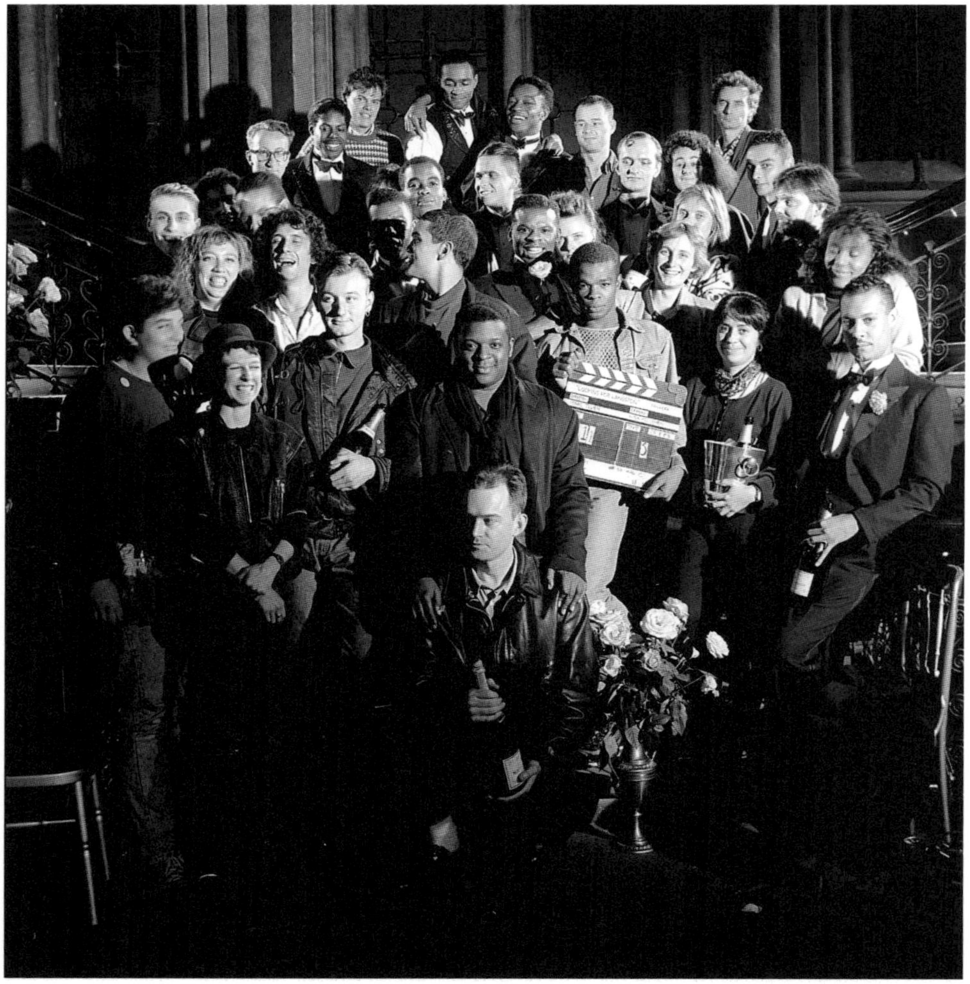

*Assemblage (Looking for Langston Vintage Series)* 1989/2016

## Solo Exhibitions

2024
*Isaac Julien: What Freedom Is To Me*, The Bonnefanten Museum, Maastricht

2023
*Isaac Julien: What Freedom Is To Me*, K21 Dusseldorf
*Isaac Julien: What Freedom Is To Me*, Tate Britain, London
*Isaac Julien: PLAYTIME*, PalaisPopulaire, Berlin
*Isaac Julien: Lina Bo Bardi: A Marvellous Entanglement*, Philadelphia Museum of Art, Philadelphia, PA

2022
*Isaac Julien: Lessons of the Hour*, Virginia Museum of Fine Art, Richmond, VA
*Isaac Julien*, Goslarer Kaiserring Award Exhibition, Goslar, Germany
*Isaac Julien: Once Again ... (Statues Never Die)*, Barnes Foundation, Philadelphia, PA
*Looking for Langston: I Dream a World*, Galeria Fonte, Inhotim, Brazil
*Isaac Julien: True North*, Ruby City, San Antonio, TX
*Isaac Julien: Ten Thousand Waves; Lessons of the Hour*, John Curtin Gallery, Perth, Australia
*Isaac Julien: Ten Thousand Waves; Lina Bo Bardi: A Marvellous Entanglement*, Samstag Museum of Art, Adelaide
*Isaac Julien: Lina Bo Bardi: A Marvellous Entanglement*, Roslyn Oxley9 Gallery, Sydney

2021
*Isaac Julien: Lessons of the Hour*, Smith College Museum of Art, Northampton, MA
*Isaac Julien: Lina Bo Bardi: A Marvellous Entanglement*, Madrid City Hall, Madrid
*Isaac Julien: Lessons of the Hour*, Scottish National Gallery of Modern Art (Modern One), Edinburgh
*Isaac Julien: Lessons of the Hour*, Galerie Ron Mandos, Amsterdam
*Isaac Julien: Vagabondia*, Institute of Contemporary Art, Miami, FL
*Isaac Julien: Lina Bo Bardi: A Marvellous Entanglement*, Bechtler Museum of Modern Art, Charlotte, NC

2020
*Isaac Julien: Western Union: Small Boats*, Neuberger Museum, New York
*Isaac Julien: America*, Jessica Silverman Gallery, San Francisco
*Isaac Julien: Lina Bo Bardi: A Marvellous Entanglement*, MAXXI – National Museum of 21st Century Art, Rome
*Isaac Julien: Lessons of the Hour*, McEvoy Foundation for the Arts, San Francisco

2019
*Isaac Julien: Lessons of the Hour*, SCAD Museum of Art, Savannah, GA
*Isaac Julien: PLAYTIME*, The Linda Pace Foundation Gallery/Ruby City, San Antonio, Texas, USA
*Isaac Julien: Lina Bo Bardi: A Marvellous Entanglement*, Victoria Miro, London, UK
*Looking for Langston*, Tate Britain, London
*Isaac Julien: PLAYTIME*, Resnick Pavilion, LACMA, Los Angeles
*Isaac Julien: The Leopard (Western Union: Small Boats)*, Block Museum of Art, Northwestern University, Chicago
*Isaac Julien: Looking for Langston*, The Linda Pace Foundation Gallery/Ruby City, San Antonio, TX
*Lessons of the Hour*, Memorial Art Gallery, University of Rochester, Rochester, NY
*Lessons of the Hour*, Metro Pictures Gallery, New York
*Stones against Diamonds*, Paco Das Artes, São Paulo
*Lina Bo Bardi: A Marvellous Entanglement*, Victoria Miro, London
*Isaac Julien: Baltimore*, Baltimore Museum of Art, Baltimore, MD

2018
*Isaac Julien*, York Art Gallery, York, UK
*Western Union: Small Boats*, ARoS Aarhus Kunstmuseum, Denmark
*To the End of the Earth*, Galerie Forsblom, Stockholm
*Ten Thousand Waves*, The Whitworth, Manchester
*Ten Thousand Waves Photographs*, Galerie Forsblom, Helsinki
*Isaac Julien: 'Film Noir-Angels' Looking for Langston*, Roslyn Oxley9, Sydney; Columbus Museum of Art, Columbus, OH
*PLAYTIME*, Amerborgh, Amsterdam
*Paradise Omeros*, Galerie Ron Mandos, Amsterdam

2017
*"I dream a world" Looking for Langston*, Victoria Miro, London
*PLAYTIME*, Platform-L Contemporary Art Center, Seoul
*Other Destinies*, Royal Ontario Museum, Toronto
*The Leopard*, International Centre for Photography, Palermo, Italy
*PLAYTIME*, Fort Mason Centre for Arts & Culture, San Francisco

2016
*Looking for Langston*, Galerie Ron Mandos, Amsterdam (2016–17)
*Refuge*, Roslyn Oxley9 Gallery, Sydney
*Stones Against Diamonds*, Baldwin Gallery, Aspen, CO

*Vintage*, Jessica Silverman Gallery, San Francisco
*PLAYTIME & KAPITAL*, MUAC (Museo Universitario Arte Contemporáneo), Mexico City
*Ten Thousand Waves*, MAC Niterói, Rio de Janeiro

2015
*Stones Against Diamonds*, Roslyn Oxley9 Gallery, Sydney
*Isaac Julien: Riot*, De Pont Museum, Tilburg, Netherlands
*Playtime* (three-screen version), Galeria Helga de Alvear, Madrid, Spain
*Stones Against Diamonds* (Rolls-Royce Motor Cars commission), Palazzo Malipiero-Barnabo, Venice; Kirche Elisabethen Church, Basel; Goodwood, West Sussex, UK; National YoungArts Foundation Jewel Box, Miami, FL

2014
*Western Union: Small Boats (The Leopard)*, Urban Video Project Everson, Syracuse, NY
*Ten Thousand Waves*, Fotografiska, Stockholm, Sweden
*Playtime: Photographic Works*, Galeria Helga de Alvear, Madrid; Roslyn Oxley9 Gallery, Sydney; Victoria Miro Gallery, London; Galeria Nara Roesler, São Paulo; Galerie Ron Mandos, Amsterdam

2013
*Better Life (Ten Thousand Waves)*, Museum De Pont Project Space, Tilburg, Netherlands
*Ten Thousand Waves*, The Museum of Modern Art, New York
*Playtime*, Metro Pictures Gallery, New York
*The Long Road to Mazatlán*, Art Institute of Chicago, Chicago
*Western Union: Small Boats*, Museum Brandhorst, Munich (in partnership with Kino der Kunst Festival)

2012
*Scopic Landscapes* (curated by Mark Nash), Galeria Nara Roesler, São Paulo
*Geopoetics*, SESC Pompeia, São Paulo
*Better Life (Ten Thousand Waves)*, Roslyn Oxley9 Gallery, Sydney, Australia; Galerie Ron Mandos, Amsterdam
*Currents 34: Isaac Julien*, Milwaukee Art Museum, Milwaukee, WI
*Ten Thousand Waves*, Museum of Contemporary San Diego, San Diego, CA
*Ten Thousand Waves* (three-screen version), Linda Pace Foundation, San Antonio, TX
*Ten Thousand Waves: Photographs by Isaac Julien*, Valentine Willie Fine Art, Singapore
*The Leopard*, Dirimart Garibaldi, Istanbul
*Icons of Art: Isaac Julien*, Rolls Royce, Mayfair, London

2011
*Ten Thousand Waves*, ICA Boston, Massachusetts, USA (2011-12); Brandhorst Museum, Munich; Galería Helga de Alvear, Madrid; Metro Pictures, New York

2010
*Ten Thousand Waves, Paradise Omeros, Vagabondia*, Bass Museum, Miami, FL
*Ten Thousand Waves* (photographs), Victoria Miro Gallery, London
*Ten Thousand Waves*, Kunsthalle Helsinki, Helsinki; ShanghART Gallery, H-Space, Shanghai; Roslyn Oxley9 Gallery, Sydney, Australia
*True North* (three-screen version), Akron Art Museum, Akron, OH

2009
*Western Union: Small Boats*, Museum Brandhorst Collection, Munich; The Centre for Contemporary Art, Ujazdowski Castle, Warsaw, Poland
*Te Tonga Tuturu/True South (Apparatus)*, Two Rooms Gallery, Auckland, New Zealand

2008
*Western Union: Small Boats*, Museu Nacional de Arte Contemporânea - Museu do Chiado, Lisbon; Galeria Helga de Alvear, Madrid
*Fantôme Afrique*, University Art Museum, University of California Santa Barbara, Santa Barbara CA
*Brutal Beauty: Derek Jarman* (curator), Serpentine Gallery, London

2007
*Western Union: Small Boats*, Metro Pictures, New York
*Currents 99: Isaac Julien* (*True North* photographs), St Louis Art Museum, St Louis, MO
*True North*, Roslyn Oxley9 Gallery, Sydney

2006
*Fantôme Afrique*, The Lab at Belmar, Lakewood, CO
*True North, Fantôme Afrique*, Kestnergesellshaft, Hanover
*True North, Fantôme Afrique*, Brändströme & Stene, Stockholm
*Looking for Langston* (film and photographs with Sunil Gupta), Metro Pictures, New York

2005
*True North*, Museum of Contemporary Art, Miami, FL
*True North, Fantôme Afrique*, Victoria Miro Gallery, London
*The Long Road to Mazatlán, Paradise Omeros, Baltimore*, Irish Museum of Modern Art, Dublin
True North (photographs), MAK Center, Los Angeles
*Fantôme Créole, Baltimore*, Centre Pompidou, Paris
*Paradise Omeros*, Moderna Museet, Stockholm
*Paradise Omeros, Baltimore, The Long Road to Mazatlan, Radioactive, Deslocamentos*, VIVO Open Air, São Paulo

2004
*Isaac Julien* (*Paradise Omeros, Vagabondia, Radioactive*), GL Strand Kunstforeningen, Copenhagen
*True North* (*Baltimore, Paradise Omeros*), Musée d'art contemporain de Montréal, Montréal
*Black Atlantic* (*True North, Paradise Omeros*), House of World Cultures, Berlin
*Baltimore*, The Contemporary, Baltimore, MD
*Baltimore* and *Baltimore Series*, Galeria Helga de Alvear, Madrid
*Paradise Omeros* (with accompanying photo works), *Three, Frantz Fanon: Black Skin, White Mask*, Museum Boijmans Van Beuningen, Rotterdam
*Baltimore* (with accompanying photo works), TENT Centrum Beeldende Kunst, Rotterdam
*Baltimore* (single screen version), Eyebeam, New York

2003
*Baltimore* and *Paradise Omeros*, Art Pace, San Antonio, TX; Victoria Miro Gallery, London
*Baltimore*, Metro Pictures, New York
*Trussed*, Sketch, London
*Baltimore*, The Aspen Art Museum, Aspen, CO
Yvon Lambert, Paris
Bohen Foundation, New York
FACT: Film Art & Creative Technology, Liverpool, UK

2001
The Fabric Workshop, Philadelphia, PA
MIT List Visual Arts Center (*Vagabondia, Long Road to Mazatlán*), Cambridge, MA

2000
*Vagabondia*, The Studio Museum in Harlem, New York
*The Long Road to Mazatlán*, Museum of Contemporary Art, Chicago
*The Film Art of Isaac Julien*, Bard Center for Curatorial Studies, New York, and touring: Museum of Contemporary Art Sydney, Sydney; Bildmuseet Umeå, Umeå, Sweden; Henie Onstad Museum, Høvikodden, Norway; Yerba Buena Center, San Francisco
Cinerama Corner House Museum, Manchester, and touring: South London Gallery, London
*After Mazatlán*, Victoria Miro Gallery, London
*The Long Road to Mazatlán*, Grand Arts, Kansas City, KS

1999
*Long Road to Mazatlán*, Art Pace, San Antonio, TX
*Three*, Victoria Miro Gallery, London
*Fanon SA*, The Arena, Oxford Brookes University, Oxford

## Awards

2022
Knight of the British Empire (KBE) for services to the Arts (Queen's Platinum Jubilee Birthday Honours List)
Goslarer Kaiserring Award, Goslar, Germany

2017
The Royal Academy of Arts Charles Wollaston Award
Commander of the Order of the British Empire (CBE) for services to the Arts (Queen's Birthday Honours List)

2016
James R. Brudner '83 Memorial Prize, Yale University
Panorama TEDDY 30 for *Looking for Langston*, Berlinale 66th Berlin International

2014
Golden Gate Persistence of Vision Award, San Francisco International Film Festival

2011
Off Festival Award PHotoESPAÑA for *Ten Thousand Waves* at Galería Helga de Alvear, Madrid

2008
Special Teddy for *Derek*, Berlin International Film Festival, Berlin
Documentary Prize for *Derek*, 34th Seattle International Film Festival, Seattle
Best Documentary for *Derek*, Milan International Lesbian and Gay Film Festival, Milan
Honorary Fellow, University of Arts, London, UK

2005
Aurora Award, Aurora Picture Show, Houston, TX

2003
Master of Arts (Honorary Degree), Surrey Institute of Art and Design, London
Grand Jury Award, KunstFilmBiennale, Cologne
Prize for Outstanding Career in Cinematography, Benalmádena, 6th Festival International de Cortometraje y Cine Alternativo de Benalmádena (ficcab), Spain

2002
Frameline Lifetime Achievement Award, San Francisco
Bohen Foundation Commission, New York
Artist in Residence, Eyebeam's Moving Image Commission program, New York
Ford Foundation Commission, New York

2001
The McDermott Award, MIT, Cambridge, MA

1999
International Artist in Residence, Art Pace, San Antonio, TX

1998
Jerome Foundation Award, USA
Andy Warhol Foundation Award, USA

1997
Pratt and Whitney Canada Grand Prize for *Frantz Fanon: Black Skin, White Mask*, 15th International Festival of Films on Art, Montréal

1996
Wexner Museum Fine Arts International Artist Award, Columbus, OH

1995
Rockefeller Humanities Fellowship Award, New York University, Centre for Media, Culture and History

1991
John McKnight International Artist Award, Minneapolis, MN
Semaine de la Critique Prize for *Young Soul Rebels*, Cannes Film Festival

1990
*Looking for Langston*
Jury Prize, 9th Festival Cinema and Homosexualities, Brussels
Co-winner, 2eme Festival Image Caraibes, Martinique
Winner, Best Film (Docu-drama category), National Black Programming Consortium Columbus, OH

1989
*Looking for Langston*
Winner, Teddy Award for Best Short Film at the 1989 Berlin International Film Festival
Special Mention, Don Quixote Award, International Film Festival, Barcelona
Winner, Axel Award, Gay and Lesbian Film Festival, Copenhagen

## Selected Academic Posts & Trusteeships

Distinguished Professor of the Arts, University of California, Santa Cruz, CA (2018-)
Trustee of Art Fund UK board (2017-21)
Regents Professor at University of California Berkeley, CA (April 2016)
Trustee of Zeitz MOCAA, Cape Town (2015-)
Trustee of Parasol Unit, London (2015-20)
Chair, Professor of Global Art, University of the Arts, London (2014-16)
Professor of Media Art at Staatliche Hochschule für Gestaltung, Karlsruhe, Germany (2008-16)
Trustee of Art Pace Foundation, San Antonio, TX (1999-2017)
Faculty member at the Whitney Museum of American Art's Independent Study Program, New York (2006-13)
Trustee of Serpentine Gallery, London (1999-2009)
Visiting Mellon Professor of English, University of Pittsburgh, Pennsylvania, PA (2006-7)
Research Fellow at Goldsmiths' College, University of London (1998-2003)
Visiting lecturer at Harvard University's Schools of Afro-American and Visual Environmental Studies, Cambridge, MA (1998-2002)

## Biennials

2023
Sharjah Biennial 15: *Thinking Historically in the Present*, Sharjah Art Foundation, United Arab Emirates: *Once Again...(Statues Never Die)*

2022
De Renava - Biennale d'Art Contemporain, International Biennale of Contemporary Art of Bonifacio, France: *Western Union: Small Boats*
FotoFocus Biennial: *World Record: Lessons of the Hour* (photography)

2021
The Guangzhou Image Triennial 2021, Guangdong Museum of Art, Guangzhou, China: *True North* (photographs)

2016
FotoFest 2016 Biennial: 16th International Biennial of Photography and Mixed Media Arts, Houston, TX: *Western Union: Small Boats*

2015
*All the World's Futures*, 56th International Exhibition of Contemporary Art - La Biennale di Venezia, Venice

2013
La Triennale, Palais de Tokyo, Paris

2012
Johannesburg Biennale, Stevenson Gallery, Cape Town: *Fanon SA 1997* and *Fantôme Créole* (photography)

2011
4th Moscow Biennale of Contemporary Art, Moscow, Russia
Gothenburg International Biennial for Contemporary Art, *Pandemonium: Art in a Time of 'Creativity Fever'*

2010
8th Shanghai Biennale, Shanghai
17th Biennale of Sydney, Sydney

2009
Arts in Marrakesh (AiM) International Biennale, Morocco

2008
7th Gwangju Biennale, Gwangju, South Korea: *Western Union: Small Boats*

2004
Whitney Biennial, Whitney Museum of American Art, New York
Berlin Biennale 04, Germany: *Baltimore* (triple screen version)
DAK'ART 6ème Biennale de l'Art Africain Contemporain 2004: *Nanook Cinema*, curated by Hans Ulrich Obrist, Senegal: *Frantz Fanon: Black Skin, White Mask*, *Baltimore* (single screen)
Busan Biennale, Busan, South Korea

2003
*Utopia Station Poster Project*, 50th Venice Biennale and Haus der Kunst, Münich

2002
Documenta 11_Platform5: Ausstellung/Exhibition, Binding Building, Kassel

1997
2nd Johannesburg Biennale, Johannesburg, South Africa

## Public Collections

Albright-Knox Art Gallery, Buffalo, NY
Art Institute of Chicago, Chicago
Bard College, Centre for Curatorial Studies Museum, New York
Bonnefanten Museum, Maastricht
Centre Pompidou, Paris
Colección Helga de Alvear, Madrid
De La Cruz Collection, Miami, FL
De Pont Museum Collection, Tilburg, Netherlands
Deutsche Bank Art Collection, Frankfurt
Goetz Collection, Munich
Government Art Collection, London, UK
Guggenheim Museum, New York, USA
Hirshhorn Museum and Sculpture Garden, Smithsonian, Washington, DC
Hood Museum of Art, Dartmouth College, Hanover, NH
Irish Museum of Modern Art, Dublin, Ireland
Julia Stoschek Collection, Düsseldorf
Linda Pace Foundation Collection, San Antonio, TX
Louis Vuitton Foundation, Paris
LUMA Foundation, Arles, France
Margulies Collection, Miami, FL
MAXXI - National Museum of 21st Century Art, Rome
Milwaukee Art Museum, Milwaukee, WI
Moderna Museet, Stockholm
MUSAC (Castile and León Museum of Contemporary Art), León, Spain
Museum für Moderne Kunst, Frankfurt
Museum of Contemporary Art Kiasma, Helsinki
Museum of Modern Art, New York
Museum Brandhorst, Munich
National Museum of Art, Architecture and Design, Oslo
Tate Modern, London
Tate Britain, London
Towner Art Gallery, Eastbourne and The Whitworth, Manchester (Moving Image Art Fund)
Wemhöner Collection, Herford, Germany
The Wonderful Fund Collection, UK
The Zeitz Foundation Collection, Germany and Kenya

## Film Installations

2022
*Once Again...(Statues Never Die)*, five-screen installation, 4K transferred to digital, black and white, 9.2 surround sound, 31 min 34 sec

2019
*Lessons of the Hour*, ten-screen installation, 35 mm and 4K transferred to digital, colour, 7.1 surround sound, 28 min 46 sec
*Lessons of the Hour*, five-screen installation, 35 mm and 4K transferred to digital, colour, 5.1 surround sound, 28 min 46 sec
*Lina Bo Bardi: A Marvellous Entanglement*, nine-screen installation, 4K transferred to digital, colour, 9.1 surround sound, 39 min 8 sec
*Lina Bo Bardi: A Marvellous Entanglement*, three-screen installation, 4K transferred to digital, colour, 5.1 surround sound, 39 min 8 sec

2015
*Stones Against Diamonds*, ten portrait monitors, high-definition video, stereo sound, 58 min 28 sec
*Stones Against Diamonds*, five portrait monitors, high-definition video, stereo sound, 58 min 28 sec

2014
*PLAYTIME*, seven-screen installation, ultra-high-definition video, 7.1 surround sound, 66 min 57 sec
*PLAYTIME*, three-screen installation, ultra-high-definition video, 5.1 surround sound, 64 min 12 sec

2013
*KAPITAL*, double-monitor installation, high definition, stereo sound, 31 min 16 sec

2010
*Ten Thousand Waves*, nine-screen installation, 35 mm transferred to digital, colour, 9.2 surround sound, 49 min 41 sec
*Ten Thousand Waves*, three-screen installation, transferred to digital, colour, 9.2 surround sound, 49 min 41 sec

2008
*Derek: Dungeness*, two-screen projection, digital video, colour, 5.1 surround sound, 8 min

2007
*Western Union: Small Boats*, five-screen installation, 16 mm transferred to digital, colour, 5.1 surround sound, 18 min 22 sec
*Western Union: Small Boats*, three-screen installation, 16 mm transferred to digital, colour, 5.1 surround sound, 18 min 22 sec

2005
*Fantôme Afrique*, three-screen installation, 16 mm transferred to digital, colour, 5.1 surround sound, 17 min
*Fantôme Créole*, four-screen projection, 16 mm transferred to digital, colour, 5.1 surround sound, 23 min 27 sec

2004
*True North*, three-screen projection, 16 mm transferred to digital, colour, 5.1 surround sound, 14 min 20 sec

2003
*Baltimore*, three-screen projection, 16 mm transferred to digital, colour, 5.1 surround sound, 11 min 56 sec

2002
*Paradise Omeros*, three-screen installation, 16 mm transferred to digital, colour, 5.1 surround sound, 20 min 29 sec

2000
*Vagabondia*, two-screen installation, rear projection, 16 mm transferred to digital, colour, stereo sound, 7 min

1999
*Long Road to Mazatlan*, three-screen installation, rear projection, 16 mm transferred to digital, colour, sound, 20 min
*The Conservator's Dream*, three-screen installation, 16 mm video transfer, colour, sound, 6 min
*Three*, single-screen projection, 16 mm, colour, sound, 20 min

1997
*Fanon SA*, two-screen projection, 16 mm transferred to digital, colour, sound, 12 min (triple looped sequence)

1996
*Trussed*, two-screen projection, 16 mm transferred to digital, black and white, sound, 10 min

1995
*Cartooned Life*, series of seven photographs, linotronic print, plus film *That Rush!*

## Filmography

2019
*Lessons of the Hour* (single screen), 35 mm and 4K colour, 5.1 surround sound, 25 min 45 sec

2013
*PLAYTIME* (single screen), edge blended double projection, ultra high-definition video, 5.1 surround sound, 66 min 27 sec

2010
*Better Life* (single screen version of *Ten Thousand Waves*), 35 mm, 5.1 surround sound, 55 min

2008
*Derek*, digital video, colour, sound, 78 min

2007
*Western Union: Small Boats* (single screen), 16 mm, colour, 5.1 surround sound, 18 min 22 sec

2005
*Fantôme Afrique* (single screen), 16 mm, colour, sound, 17 min 9 sec

2004
*Encore II (Radioactive)*, 16 mm, Super 8/ Digital Betacam, 3 min
*True North* (single screen), 16 mm, colour, 5.1 surround sound, 14 min 20 sec

2003
*Baltimore* (single screen), 16 mm transfer, colour, sound, 12 min 43 sec

2002
*BaadAsssss Cinema*, DVD, 56 min
*Paradise Omeros* (single screen), 16 mm, colour, sound, 18 min 51 sec

2000
*Vagabondia*, 16 mm, colour, sound, 7 min

1999
*Long Road to Mazatlán* (single screen), 16 mm, colour, sound, 20 min
*The Conservator's Dream*, 16 mm, colour, sound, 4 min
*Three*, 35 mm, colour, sound, 14 min

1996
*Frantz Fanon: Black Skin White Mask*, 35 mm, colour, stereo sound, 70 min

1995
*That Rush!*, 16 mm, colour, sound, 7 min

1994
*The Darker Side of Black*, 16 mm, colour, sound, 59 min

1993
*The Attendant*, 35 mm, colour, sound, 10 min

1991
*Young Soul Rebels*, 35 mm, colour, sound, 105 min

1989
*Looking For Langston*, 16 mm, black and white, sound, 46 min 29 sec

1987
*This Is Not An AIDS Advertisement*, 8mm transferred to digital, colour, sound, 10 min 26 sec

1986
*The Passion of Remembrance*, 16 mm, colour, sound, 95 min

1984
*Territories*, 16 mm, colour, sound, 25 min 45 sec

1983
*Who Killed Colin Roach?*, colour, sound, 34 min

2022
Isaac Julien, Cora Gilroy-Ware and Vladimir Seput, *Lessons of the Hour: Frederick Douglass*, London and Rochester, NY
Boris Groys, 'Vers un nouvel universalisme', in Christine Macel (ed.), *L'art à l'ère de la globalisation*, Paris

2019
Darby English and Charlotte Barat (eds.), *Among Others: Blackness at MoMA*, New York
Connie H. Choi, *Black Refractions: Highlights from the Studio Museum in Harlem*, New York
Martina Droth, Nathan Flis and Michael Hatt (eds.), *Britain in the World: Highlights from the Yale Center for British Art. In Honor of Amy Meyers*, New Haven
Ruth Erickson and Eva Respini (eds.), *When Home Won't Let You Stay: Migration through Contemporary Art*, exh. cat., Institute of Contemporary Art, Boston

2018
Karen Marta (ed.), *The Athens Dialogues: Interviews by Hans Ulrich Obrist*, London
Melissa Harris and Michael Famighetti (eds.), *Aperture Conversations: 1985 to the Present*, New York
Isaac Julien, *Isaac Julien: Western Union: Small Boats*, exh. cat., ARoS Kunstmuseum, Aarhus
Philipp Bollmann, *Sichtspiele: Films and Video Art from the Wemhöner Collection*, Berlin

2017
*Isaac Julien: Looking for Langston*, exh. cat., Victoria Miro, London & Isaac Julien Studio
Aebhric Coleman, *Isaac Julien: PLAYTIME & KAPITAL*, Barcelona
Philipp Gufler, *I wanna give you devotion*, Munich
*Diaspora Pavilion: Exhibition Materials*, London

2013
*Isaac Julien: RIOT*, exh. cat., The Museum of Modern Art, New York

2012
*Isaac Julien: Geopoetics*, exh. cat., SESC Pompeia, São Paulo
*This Will Have Been*, exh. cat., The Institute of Contemporary Art, Boston

2011
*Isaac Julien: Expeditions*, exh. cat., Milwaukee Art Museum, Milwaukee, WI

2010
Isaac Julien (ed.), Ten *Thousand Waves*, London

2009
Isaac Julien (ed.), *Western Union: Small Boats*, London

2008
Isaac Julien (ed.), *Derek Jarman: Brutal Beauty*, London

2006
*Isaac Julien: True North - Fantôme Afrique*, exh. cat., Kestnergesellschaft, Hanover
*Making History: Art and Documentary in Britain from 1929 to Now*, exh. cat., Tate Liverpool, Liverpool

2005
*Temps de Vídeo, 1965-2005: Coll ecció Nouveaux Médias del Centre Pompidou*, exh. cat., Fundación "la Caixa", Barcelona
*True North*, exh. cat., Museum of Contemporary Art, Miami, FL
*Isaac Julien*, exh. cat., Centre Georges Pompidou, Paris
Isaac Julien, exh. cat., Irish Museum of Modern Art, Dublin
*Isaac Julien: Deslocamentos*, exh. cat., VIVO Open Air, São Paulo

2004
*Isaac Julien*, exh. cat., GL Strand Kunstforeningen, Copenhagen
*3'*, Schirn Kunsthalle Frankfurt, Germany
*True North*, exh. cat., Musée d'art contemporain de Montréal, Montréal
*Black Atlantic*, exh. cat., House of World Cultures, Berlin
*Experiments with Truth*, exh. cat., The Fabric Workshop and Museum, Philadelphia, PA
*Komplex Berlin = Complex Berlin: Berlin Biennale 04*, Cologne
*Stranger Than Fiction*, exh. cat., Leeds City Art Gallery, Leeds

2003
*Love/Hate*, exh. cat., Ursula Blickle Stiftung, Vienna
*Rirkrit Tiravanija: Secession*, exh. cat., Secession, Vienna
*Utopia Station Poster Project, 50th Venice Biennale*, Munich
*Art, Lies and Videotape: Exposing Performance*, exh. cat., Tate Liverpool, Liverpool
*Créolité and Creolization*, exh. cat., Documenta11_Platform3, Kassel

2002
*The Gap Show*, exh. cat., Museum am Ostwall, Dortmund
*Screen Memories*, exh. cat., Art Tower Mito, Mito, Japan

*Unpacking Europe: Towards a Critical Reading*, exh. cat., Boijmans Van Beuningen, Rotterdam, in collaboration with Haus der Kulturen der Welt, Berlin

2001
Kobena Mercer, *Minigraph3: Isaac Julien*, London
*Turner Prize*, exh. cat., Tate Gallery, London
*ARS 01: Unfolding Perspectives*, exh. cat., Kiasma, Helsinki/The Finnish National Gallery
*The Short Century*, exh. cat., Museum Villa Stuck, Münich

2000
*The Film Art of Isaac Julien*, exh. cat., Bard Center for Curatorial Studies, New York

1999
*Rhapsodies in Black*, exh. cat., Museum of Fine Arts, Houston, TX

1998
*Frantz Fanon: Peau noir, masque blanc. Scénrio du film*, Paris

## Exhibited Works

*This list is organised chronologically.*
*All works are courtesy of the artist.*

Film and video

*Who Killed Colin Roach?* 1983
U-matic transferred to digital,
colour, stereo sound
34 min 42 sec

*Territories* 1984
16mm film transferred to digital, projection,
colour, stereo sound 24 min 6 sec

*Lost Boundaries* 1986
Super 8 film transferred to digital,
colour, silent 4 min 14 sec

*This Is Not An AIDS Advertisement* 1987
8mm transferred to digital,
colour, stereo sound
10 min 26 sec

*Looking for Langston* 1989
16mm film transferred to digital, projection,
black and white, stereo sound 44 min 26 sec

*Vagabondia* 2000
Two-screen installation, 16mm
film transferred to digital, colour,
stereo sound 10 min 21 sec

*Western Union: Small Boats* 2007
Three-screen installation, 16mm
film transferred to digital, colour, 5.1
surround sound 18 min 22 sec

*Ten Thousand Waves* 2010
Three-screen installation, 35mm
film transferred to digital, colour, 9.2
surround sound 49 min 41 sec

*Lessons Of The Hour* 2019
Ten-screen installation, 35 mm and
4K transferred to digital, colour, 7.1
surround sound 28 min 46 sec

*Lino Bo Bardi - A Marvellous
Entanglement* 2019
Three-screen installation, 4K
transferred to digital, colour, 9.1
surround sound 39 min 8 sec

*Once Again ... (Statues Never Die)* 2022
Five-screen installation, 4K transferred
to digital, black and white, 9.2
surround sound 31 min 34 sec

Photographs

*Measurements are given in centimetres,
height before width and depth.*

*Pas de Deux No.2
(Looking for Langston Vintage
Series)* 1989/2016
Kodak Premier print, Diasec
mounted on aluminum
180 × 260

*Western Union Series No.1 /
(Cast No Shadow)* 2007
Duratrans image in lightbox
120 × 120

*Maiden of Silence (Ten Thousand Waves)* 2010
Endura Ultra photograph
180 × 240 × 7.5

*The Lady of the Lake (Lessons
of the Hour)* 2019
Framed gloss inkjet photograph
mounted on aluminum
160 × 213 × 29

*Tecnologia pré-histórica / Prehistoric Technologv
(Lina Bo Bardi - A Marvellous
Entanglement)* 2019
Endura Ultra photograph facemounted
180 × 240 × 75

*Diasporic Dream-Space: The Lover* 2022
Black and white Inkjet print on
Ilford Gold Fibre Gloss
265 × 180

*What Freedom is to me (Homage)* 2022
Black and white Inkjet print on
Ilford Gold Fibre Gloss
265 × 180

# Image Credits

*All images are courtesy Isaac Julien*
*unless stated otherwise.*
*References are to page numbers.*

Installation views

*Once Again ... (Statues Never Die)*, Barnes Foundation 2022 18–25, 28–31
*Lessons of the Hour*, McEvoy Foundation for the Arts, San Francisco 42–3
*Lessons of the Hour*, Memorial Art Gallery of the University of Rochester, 2019 44–7
*Lessons of the Hour*, Metro Pictures, New York, 2019 50–1
*Lessons of the Hour*, Memorial Art Gallery of the University of Rochester, 2019 54–5
*Lina Bo Bardi - A Marvellous Entanglement* 2019, Victoria Miro, London, 2019 56, 58–61, 66–7, 70–1
*Lina Bo Bardi - A Marvellous Entanglement* 2019, MAXXI, Italy, 2020 64–5, 72
*Ten Thousand Waves* 2010, Eye Filmmuseum, Amsterdam, 2012 90–1
*Ten Thousand Waves*, Hayward Gallery, from the exhibition *Move: Choreographing You*, 2010 92–3
*Ten Thousand Waves* 2010, The Whitworth, The University of Manchester, 2018 96–7
*Ten Thousand Waves* 2010, Museum of Modern Art, New York, 2012 98–9
*Western Union: Small Boats* 2007, Metro Pictures, New York, 2007 102–5
*Western Union: Small Boats* 2007, Ruby City, San Antonio 106–7, 110–11
*Western Union: Small Boats* 2007, Royal Academy of Arts, London 112–13
*Vagabondia* 2000, The Turner Prize, Tate Britain, London 2001 114, 116–20
*Looking for Langston* 1989, Isaac Julien Studio, London, 2016 138–9
*Looking for Langston* 1989, Columbus Museum of Art, 2018 140–5
*Looking for Langston* 1989, Tate Britain, 2019 146–7
*Territories* 1984, *Life Between Islands* exhibition, Tate Britain, 2021 158–65
*Territories* 1984, Palais de Tokyo, Paris Triennial, 2012 168–9
*Who Killed Colin Roach?* 1983, Isaac Julien Studio, 2023 168, 170–1, 184
*The Lost Boundaries* 1986 186–9
*Mise en scène No.1 (Looking for Langston Vintage Series)* 1989/2016 192–3
Production documentation of *Lessons of the Hour*, on set at the Royal Academy of Arts, London, with Isaac Julien and crew and cast, including Nina Kellgren, Polly Fleury, Paul Gladstone Reid MBE, Ray Fearon, James Keith, Ukweli Roach and Vanessa Myrie, 2018 194–5

Photo credits

Art Institute of Chicago. Major Acquisitions Centennial Endowment 37
Martin Charles / RIBA Collections 80 (top)
Juan Esteves 75
Thorsten Henn 92–3
Courtesy Isaac Julien and Victoria Miro, London/Venice 56, 58–61, 66–7, 70–1,
Isaac Julien 1985 12
Henrik Kam 15, 18–25, 28–31, 35, 42–3, 79, 83
Ryan Muller 174–7, 180–3
© Musacchio, Ianniello & Pasqualini 64–5, 72, 76–7
Jonathan Muzikar 87 (bottom), 98–9
Michael Pollard 96–7
Royal Academy of Arts, Photo: Marcus Leith 112–13
Tate Photography 81 (top), 114, 116–23
Tate Photography / Lucy Dawkins 158–65
Stephen White & Co. 132 (top), 133 (top), 138–9, 140–1, 168, 170–1, 178–9, 184
© Hans Wilschut 90–1

# Index

Page numbers in *italics* refer to illustrations